W

D0834588

Please remember that this is a library book,
and that it belongs only temporarily to each
person who uses it. Be considerate. Do
not write in this, or any, library book.

A Touchstone Book
Published by SIMON & SCHUSTER

NEW YORK   LONDON

TORONTO   SYDNEY

TOKYO   SINGAPORE

THE
ENDANGERED
AMERICAN
DREAM

HOW TO STOP THE UNITED STATES FROM

BECOMING A THIRD-WORLD COUNTRY

AND HOW TO WIN THE GEO-ECONOMIC

STRUGGLE FOR INDUSTRIAL SUPREMACY

EDWARD N. LUTTWAK

TOUCHSTONE
Rockefeller Center
1230 Avenue of the Americas
New York, New York 10020

First Touchstone Edition 1994

TOUCHSTONE and colophon are registered trademarks
of Simon & Schuster Inc.

DESIGNED BY BARBARA M. BACHMAN

Manufactured in the United States of America

10 9 8 7 6 5 4 3 2 1

Library of Congress Cataloging-in-Publication Data

Luttwak, Edward
The endangered American dream: how to stop the United States from
becoming a Third-World country and how to win the geo-economic
struggle for industrial supremacy/Edward N. Luttwak.
p. cm.
Includes bibliographical references and index.
1. United States—Foreign economic relations. 2. United States—
Commerce. 3. United States—Industries. 4. United States—
Economic conditions—1991– 5. Competition, International.
I. Title.
HF1455.L88 1993
338.973—dc20   93-5715
                                                          CIP

ISBN 0-671-89667-9

ACKNOWLEDGMENTS

I welcome the opportunity to thank Steven Paul Glick, once my student and now my adviser; Denise Natali, a most skillful and indefatigable researcher; and Max Tedeschi, her able assistant. All of them uncovered elusive information and made useful suggestions. For broader help given in all manner of ways, I most gratefully thank my colleagues of the Center for Strategic and International Studies of Washington, D.C. Their number precludes any invidious naming of names, or indeed imputations of agreement with my views on matters particular or general. It is truly a great boon to pursue the lonely calling in such generous company.

To my wife,

Dalya

CONTENTS

THE ENDANGERED AMERICAN DREAM

CHAPTER 1

THE NEW STRUGGLE FOR

INDUSTRIAL SUPREMACY

Follow a traveler to New York from Tokyo—though it would be much the same if he came from Zurich, Amsterdam, or Singapore. After leaving the taxi at Tokyo's downtown City Air Terminal—a perfectly ordinary Tokyo taxi and therefore shiny clean, in perfect condition, its neatly dressed driver in white gloves—our traveler will find himself aboard an equally spotless airport bus in five minutes flat, with his baggage already checked in, boarding card issued, and passport stamped by the seemingly effortless teamwork of quick, careful porters who refuse tips, airline clerks who can actually use computers at computer speed, passport officers who act as if it was their job to expedite travel, and bus crews who sell tickets, load baggage, and courteously help the encumbered while strictly keeping to departure schedules timed to the exact minute. After an hour's bus ride over the crowded expressway to the gleaming halls of Tokyo's Narita International Airport, after the long trans-Pacific flight, when our traveler finally arrives he will be confronted by sights and sounds that would not be out of place in Lagos or Bombay. He has arrived at New York's John Fitzgerald Kennedy Airport.

Instead of the spotless elegance of Narita or Frankfurt or Amsterdam or Singapore, arriving travelers at one of the several terminals that belong to near-bankrupt airlines will find themselves walking down dingy corridors in need of paint, over frayed carpets, often struggling up and down narrow stairways alongside out-of-order escalators. These are JFK's substitutes for the constantly updated facilities of First World airports. The rough, cheap remodeling of sadly outdated buildings with naked plywood and unfinished gypsum board proclaim the shortage of money to build with, of *patient* capital available for long-term investment—although there was plenty of money for "leveraged buy-outs" and other quick deals in New York during the years that JFK decayed into a Third World airport. Equally, the frayed carpets, those defective escalators, and pervasive minor dirt show that yesterday's capital is not being renewed but is rather consumed day by day—"deferred maintenance" is the most perfect sign of Third World conditions, the instantly recognizable background of South Asian, African, and Latin American street scenes, with their dilapidated buildings, broken pavements, crudely painted hoardings, and decrepit buses.

There are, of course, many well-kept airports in the United States, and some are ultramodern. But even where there is no visible sign of one Third World trait—a sheer lack of invested capital—another is very much in evidence, even in the most shiny-new of US airports: the lack of skill and, even more, of *diligence* in the labor force, the will to work well, not for a tip or under supervision, but out of respect for the work itself, and for self-respect of course. If our imaginary traveler transfers to a domestic flight, he or she might encounter airline porters already paid to place suitcases on conveyor belts who nevertheless ask for tips in brusque undertones, just as in Nairobi, or Karachi, sometimes hinting that the baggage might not arrive safely if no money changes hands. And the passenger might then be trapped in slow lines while imminent flight departures are called out, waiting to be checked in by clerks who tap on computer keyboards very slowly, one finger at a time. But actually the phenomenon will be brutally obvious as soon as he arrives in JFK's customs-hall, where baggage is contemptuously thrown off the incoming moving belts in full view of the hapless passengers. By then, however, our traveler may be too exhausted to complain: after a long flight, he might have waited for hours to get through passport control.

For that, too, is a typical Third World trait—the chronic disorganization of perfectly routine procedures. Nowadays, the US government competes with the likes of Jamaica, spending a great deal of money to advertise for tourists worldwide (Germany, Japan, and other successful exporters have no desire to keep their citizens employed as waiters, chambermaids, and bellhops). Yet the US government will not perform properly the one tourist service for which it is directly responsible: quick, efficient passport and customs inspections. From the chaotic delays that result whenever a pair of jumbo jets land within minutes of each other, one would imagine that such an event had never occurred before, that it was a stunning surprise to all concerned, not the result of long-published schedules duly approved by the airport authorities. Two-hour delays are common at JFK and other international airports during the peak travel times (and the entire summer), and some unfortunates have stood in line for four or even five hours at US airports after exhausting intercontinental flights. Not even Lagos can compete with that.

If they are headed for a Manhattan hotel, travelers can choose between a dirty and battered bus, or a dirtier, more battered, and often unsafe taxi, usually driven by an unkempt, loutish driver who resembles his counterparts in Islamabad or Kinshasa rather than in London or Tokyo, where licensing requirements are strict and dress codes are enforced. At that point, first-time visitors might still believe that both airport and taxi are glaring exceptions to the America they had always imagined—clean, modern, efficient. If so, they will immediately be disillusioned by the jolting drive over potholed highways and crumbling bridges, through miles of slums or miserable public housing defaced by graffiti, strewn with garbage.

Not as colorful as in Jakarta or Madras, and with parked cars lining the streets to proclaim a radically different version of poverty, the passing scene will still amaze those who come from the many European and even Asian cities where slums are now reduced to isolated survivals in remote parts of town. (New York tour guides report a growing demand for the thrills of the South Bronx, from European tourists quite uninterested in the borough's pleasant greenery or the zoo, but eager to see open-air drug dealing at street corners and the rows of burnt-out houses.) True enough, after this unsettling encounter with an America already in full Third World conditions, an affluent tourist might next reach the luxurious glitter of a Manhattan hotel, but even there beggars might be standing near the door, just as in New Delhi or Lima.

▪ Is It Just New York?

The reader who can happily stay clear of Kennedy and other airports like it, and who lives far from New York, Los Angeles, and other troubled cities like them, may well object that all of the above grotesquely misrepresents the America that he knows, and the United States as a whole.

True enough, American affluence persists on a huge scale, quite unknown anywhere else, in Palm Beach, Florida, and Palm Springs, California; in Hilton Head, South Carolina, and Scottsdale, Arizona; in Beverly Hills, New Canaan, and a hundred other luxurious suburbs, expensive resorts, and plush retirement estates large and small, with their perfect lawns, spacious houses, thousands of tennis courts, and half an ocean's worth of swimming pools. After all, even within the narrow circle of the richest one-half of 1% of all American households, living in principal residences last valued at $675,500 on average, and with total net worths last estimated at $11.1 million on average, there are almost half a million families. Just below them, within the lower half of the top 1% of the wealth pyramid, there are another half a million American families with net worths of $2.8 million on average. Thus, with all their members counted, these richest American households alone outnumber the total population of some smaller countries—and more than 130 United Nations member states are outnumbered by the Americans who rate as merely affluent, who belong to the 8.5 million households below the top 1%, but still within the richest 10%, with net worths last estimated at some $756,000 on average.[1]

As for American advancement, the United States has many of the world's best universities, the most accomplished research centers, certainly the best-equipped hospitals, a great many of the largest international corporations, innumerable successful businesses, by far the greatest collection of living artists, some 41,000 miles of the world's best highways, and even some very modern and well-kept airports.

And yet, as against these tokens of wealth and success, there is the evidence of a broad degradation of standards that stubbornly emerges all around us—even when we are far removed in body and mind from our own fully accomplished Third Worlds, the miserable slums euphemistically called "inner cities," where lives are nasty, brutish, and short for babies who would be better off if they were born in Costa Rica and for youths more likely to be killed by guns and knives than all diseases combined. Rich Indians in Bombay or New Delhi or Calcutta learn from youngest childhood how to step politely over the quadruple-amputee beggar groveling in their path without ever actually looking at

THE NEW STRUGGLE FOR INDUSTRIAL SUPREMACY ■ 19

him, and how not to see the starving mother-with-child, the waifs, and
the abandoned elderly who beg from them as they go into a restaurant
or bank. Blindness too can be learned. The celebrants of American
prosperity have long since learned to disregard the inner-city poor
except when they riot, loot, and kill, as most spectacularly of late in Los
Angeles, in May 1992.

It takes less blindness-training to ignore the increasing proportion of
the *working* poor in America, for in truth they are almost invisible even
though they greatly outnumber the underclass, whether black or white,
urban or rural. Tourists in countries such as Pakistan or Brazil soon
discover that however modest their jobs, the waiters, cab drivers, hotel
clerks, and shop assistants they encounter are greatly envied, because
they already possess the greatest hope and desire of the unemployed
masses: year-round, full-time employment. Nevertheless, in countries
such as Pakistan and Brazil, even year-round, full-time employment
does not actually pay enough to avoid sordid poverty, if there is a
family to support. That too is typical of a Third World economy:
because there is little capital, labor is the abundant resource and therefore very cheap—too cheap to earn a living wage.

At the last count, fully 18% of all working Americans, presumably
quite law-abiding and certainly free of the much-discussed "intersect-
ing social pathologies" of the underclass, were exactly in that predicament, for they did not earn enough to keep a family of four above the
official poverty line even when working forty hours a week, fifty weeks
a year.[2] To be sure, that is a nationwide standard ($12,195 in 1990),
both generous in some bucolic settings and downright tragic in most
larger cities where not much can remain to feed four, after rent is paid.
In any case, only one in eight of all low-paid workers actually lived in
poverty as officially defined, either because they did not in fact have a
family to support, or because their spouses, sons, or daughters also
worked. That leaves unchanged the simple arithmetic of an economy in
which human labor alone has been cheapened: in 1990, at the last
count, 18% of all Americans did not earn enough per hour ($6.10) to
pass that test with 2,000 hours of work; in 1974, only 12% earned
below that standard. Except for the youngsters among them, just starting to work, the 14.4 million low-paid workers must be added to the
Americans whose lives are sliding toward Third World conditions.

Many other Americans will soon join them, if present trends simply
continue. Corporate executives, lawyers, investment bankers, assorted

professionals, and independent businessmen have been doing very well indeed, as we shall see. But the great mass of American employees who are not supervisors or professionals, and who do not work for the government—some 75 million working Americans in all—now actually earn less per hour than they did in 1966, once false inflation increases are stripped away.[3] As rank-and-file employees in industry, retail trade, and almost all services—even the much-touted banking, insurance, and financial services, not just the "hamburger-flipping" jobs—swim against the currents of a slow-growing economy that needs them less and less, America is becoming a country of diminished lives, in which more than half of the next generation can no longer aspire to the style of life of their parents. Anyone can see the proliferation of "mobile homes" all over the country, but few pause to ask themselves how many former home owners live in them, and how many children of home owners cannot replicate the achievement of their parents.

European immigrants once came in great numbers, attracted by high American wages. At the last count, however, there were only 82,900 Europeans among more than a million immigrants, mostly from Latin America and the poorest Asian countries.[4] On the other hand, some European corporations (lately BMW) are establishing plants in the United States, not only to sell here, as the Japanese have done, but also because they are attracted by the cheap labor and the American willingness to work long hours and to accept very short vacations by European standards. Unfortunately, the loss of classic high-wage jobs to imports, and to the overseas plants of US corporations in search of yet-cheaper labor, cannot be offset by foreign-owned assembly plants with their poorly paid jobs.

We are thus becoming Europe's own Mexico—not as an inevitable consequence of "globalization," as some seem to believe,[5] but rather because of the failure to control and offset that process in the interests of the vast majority of Americans; and that failure has been of great benefit to a small minority. The reduction in trade barriers, the diminishing incidence of transport costs in ever-more elaborate products, and the global diffusion of mass production methods—the three agencies of "globalization"—could have been, and should have been, offset by added *investment,* both in people by way of education and training, and in the overall working environment: public infrastructures, plant, machinery, and technology actually applied (though we do lead the world in inventions that others apply, from video-cassette recorders to industrial robots). If more were invested to improve the working environment of American employees, and if workers' own skills were constantly upgraded, the US economy would not be competing by cheapening the value of their labor. That, after all, is how Japan and all other First World economies have been competing very effectively, steadily increasing wages as we reduce ours, because with added capital and added skills the total value of what is produced increases even more.

Contrary to widespread belief, the productivity of American labor in manufacturing across the board is still much higher than that of Japanese labor for example, last being recorded as 64% higher on average.[6] But that advantage is smaller than it used to be (it was 92% in 1975), and it need not assure high wages when the shortage of invested capital throughout the economy leaves labor as the abundant, cheap resource. Employers need not offer wage increases when productivity grows, because they have no difficulty in hiring all the workers they need without raises. Besides, even an overall wage-cost advantage that makes US goods theoretically competitive will not gain jobs in export industries if foreign markets are closed by overt or hidden trade barriers. For example, in 1988 US labor productivity was highest as compared to Japan in processed foods (286%), leather products (238%), wood products (192%), pulp and paper (152%), and auto parts (137%)—all of them included in the official 1989 US list of products whose export to Japan is impeded by trade barriers.[7] That list also included aluminum, agricultural products in general, telecommunications equipment, pharmaceuticals, medical equipment, supercomputers, satellites, construction and engineering services, insurance, high-cube containers, semiconductors, optical fibers, aerospace, and soda ash, among other things—all of them industries in which one-sided "globalization" failed to gain potential export jobs to offset the loss of jobs to imports.

But "globalization" is not an unstoppable natural phenomenon. It *can* be managed. Too often, however, it is being managed at the American end to expand benefits to corporate management, shareholders, and elite design and development employees. At the Japanese end, by contrast, it is being managed to secure production jobs for Japanese workers (an aim never overlooked in Japan) and manufacturing earnings for corporations—as well as to transfer the gains of future technological progress in manufacturing from the United States to Japan.

In June 1992, for example, the management of Apple Computer Inc. was reported to be jubilant over its rapidly increasing sales in Japan, achieved in part by "strategic" alliances with major Japanese corporations. From less than 1% of Japan's rich personal computer market in 1988, Apple had gained 6% by 1992 and was aiming for much more. Moreover, its sales would also allow Aldus, Adobe Systems, Quark, and others to sell their Macintosh software. Apple's new alliances, however, also have another result: its smallest laptop is now manufactured by Sony; its Newton electronic organizer is manufactured by Sharp; and the new "multimedia" Macintosh that is the company's best hope for the future is to be manufactured by Toshiba.[8] Evidently Sony, Sharp, and Toshiba are more willing and able than Apple Inc. to invest in manufacturing plant and technology, and in labor training. Besides, Apple Inc. was most probably given to understand that its products would continue to be kept out of the Japanese market in one way or another—unless they were made in Japan.

But the great majority of non-elite Americans and their families have very different prospects from the managers, shareholders, and highly skilled employees of Apple Inc. If Mexico's prosperity continues to grow, the declining incomes of non-elite Americans might reach an untoward parity with the incomes of their Mexican counterparts, within the lifetime of today's teenagers. Yet that bleak prospect is ignored by the celebrants of American prosperity—as well they may, because incomes at the very top of the economic pyramid have been increasing very nicely.

The managerial and political elite that has steadfastly opened the US market, while failing to insist on a parallel opening of the markets of the leading exporting countries of Asia, has taken its full share of the added consumer satisfactions that imports allow while it has not shared at all in the loss of high-paying industrial jobs to imports. And of course these Americans receive large foreign earnings from the high-skill management, legal, technical, and entertainment services they provide, as well as the largest part of the export earnings of the more sophisticated goods in which the United States does best.

Americans like to think of themselves as a generous, warmhearted but also very practical people, quite naturally resistant to ideological fascinations. Before its downfall, Marxism–Leninism won the intense loyalty of millions all over the world, from poets and philosophers to seemingly tough-minded trade unionists. But in America only a handful of eccentrics ever fell into the trap.

Yet there is one ideology that grips the American mind—the ideology of free trade. Elite Americans are no longer seriously churchgoing but their unquestioning faith in the ideology of free trade is intact. Just as Marxism–Leninism offered the promise of prosperity for all, in exchange for giving all power to an all-wise party leadership, free-trade ideology too offers a large and attractive promise and demands something in exchange: the greatest possible prosperity for each and all in the entire world economy, if only no effort is made to protect anyone with tariffs or any other artificial barriers to free trade. And just as Marxism–Leninism was based on the theory that if capitalists were eliminated their wealth would remain and grow even more rapidly, free-trade ideology is based on the theory of "comparative advantage": if England is more efficient than Portugal in producing textiles, and Portugal is more efficient than England in producing wine, both countries are better off if England produces all the textiles they both need, and Portugal produces all the wine, each then importing its unmet need from the other.[9]

That is the theory taught in every economics class and printed in every textbook. It is logical to a fault. Why should the Portuguese strain to produce, say, three yards of woolen cloth when, with the same effort, they could take advantage of their favorable climate to produce, say, four barrels of good port wine, then ship just one to pay for the import of, say, five yards of better British cloth? As a snapshot the theory is beyond dispute. Yet it is fatally defective, because it ignores economic and technological development; in fact it ignores the future altogether.

For one thing, as prosperity grows and people are no longer content with one work outfit and one Sunday outfit, the demand for textiles increases by 200%, 300%, 500% over the years. By contrast, the individual demand for wine grows little if at all, leaving the Portuguese economy stagnant except for sheer population growth, while the English economy grows rapidly in this textiles-and-wine world. For another, the theory of free trade ignores the very different technological potential of each industry: over the years, textile producers can mechanize and eventually computerize their production, while wine is still pressed by the bare feet of peasants.

Most important by far is what happens to each society over time under the rules of free trade: the British textile industry and its skilled workers, foremen, designers, engineers, color chemists, and managers will need, and support, a whole variety of educational, technical, and scientific institutions and projects that can germinate future industrial progress. By contrast, Portuguese peasants, vintners, and landlords will need and support none of the above in their simpler economic lives. Moreover, Britain's textile industry demands a textile-machinery industry as well; which, in turn, gives birth to other industries, while Portugal's wine industry will still support only coopers and their barrel making.

The Portuguese in this classic example would therefore be well advised to ignore the theory and impose a stiff textile tariff to keep out British imports, thus allowing a textile industry of their own to grow and survive. Even if the British do not retaliate with a wine tariff of their own, as they may well do, the Portuguese standard of living will immediately drop. Instead of a desirable mix of good native wine and good imported cloth, the Portuguese will have to get by with small quantities of inferior cloth, inefficiently produced against the grain of Portugal's comparative advantage. But in a textile-and-wine world that is the only way for the Portuguese economy and society to develop at all. As it does, moreover, the technologies and institutions they acquire will open new avenues of industrial growth, including some in which Portugal might be less inefficient, or even quite efficient.

Japan was in Portugal's position twice within a century. First when the country was initially opened to foreign trade after the intrusion of Commodore Perry's American fleet and the 1868 revolution. And then again in 1945, when Japan's economy was in ruins, and even its surviving industry was badly outdated after many years of war production (Japan's war had started in 1936, long before Pearl Harbor). The United States was then of course the world's most efficient producer of virtually every industrial product; in some cases—including the first civilian electronics—it was the *only* producer.

Japan should therefore have been content to produce raw silk, paper lanterns, and the cute mechanical toys in which it still had a comparative advantage, while importing almost all other industrial goods. For very little could be produced efficiently given the state of Japanese industry. But instead of being paralyzed by theory, the Japanese simply ignored it, preferring the development of their economy to efficiency and an immediately better standard of living. High tariffs, tight quotas, and outright import prohibitions kept out US and other foreign goods to assure well-protected markets for Japan's feeble industries, which were also helped directly with low-interest investment loans, tax exemptions, and plain subsidies.

The Japanese people thus paid twice for industrial development, first by having to buy inferior homemade products at high prices instead of better/cheaper imports; and then because it was their taxes that paid for all the bounty given to industry. As consumers, and taxpayers, the Japanese were ill-treated. But as producers, their lives prospered and grew, with ever-wider opportunities both in rebuilt industries and in brand-new industries, as well as in the service superstructure that goes with them: banking, insurance, financial services, advertising, and more. They had to wait until the 1980s for any rapid rise in their standard of living, but the dignity of employment was assured to virtually all almost from the start, along with the increasing satisfactions of personal and national achievement.

To be sure, even free-trade theory recognizes an exception: it allows that "infant" industries (or war-ravaged industries) can be usefully protected for a short while, until they can stand on their own feet. But the politicians, academic economists, government officials, and journalists who "believe" in free trade are not really guided by the theory. They are, after all, believers in an ideology, not thinkers. Thus they fail to recognize the real significance of the tidal waves of rapid technological development that can now totally outdate products in a few years (remember "eight-track tapes"?) and entire industries in a few more (e.g., batch-production steel). That significance is simply this: nowadays a perfectly grown-up industry can become a helpless infant at any time. Aside from the world leader of the moment in any particular industry or product line, all other countries might be left only with infants in need of protection.

If help is refused in horror of the evils of "protectionism," technologically overtaken industries must die, as the US consumer electronics industry has died, instead of recovering to compete again—as they might, if their markets were protected for a while. Hence the theory is itself invalid for all practical purposes, because the one allowed exception for "infant" industries happens to apply precisely to the fastest-growing, most creative, and most promising industries. In other words, the exception is now more important than the rule.

There are other things, too, that the politicians, academic economists, government officials, and journalists who believe in free trade fail to recognize. One is that today's economic world is far removed from Main Street, USA, with its strictly private business, all equally subject to the rule of balance sheets, profit and loss accounts, and possible bankruptcy. National bureaucracies and governments not only regulate and tax but also manage state-owned companies or entire industries in some countries, and actively help private business in many more countries. They keep out foreign competition by means fair or foul, they provide market information (and sometimes the fruits of industrial espionage), they give research and development grants, they issue loan guarantees for corporations in trouble, they award extraprofitable contracts to strengthen favored "chosen instruments," they coinvest in plant and machinery, or simply hand out money. Only in freewheeling Hong Kong and Macao is the idealized state of "free enterprise" closely approached. Elsewhere, including the United States (remember the Lockheed bailout—one of many—and the Chrysler loan guarantee?), it is rather "state-assisted enterprise" that should be celebrated by euphoric after-dinner speakers.

Of course these things are known to all. But free-trade ideology, like all ideologies, has a curious effect: it has a way of creating confusion in the mind of believers between what ought to be and what is. They *know* that the world is far different from Main Street, USA, yet they do not truly accept that reality in their minds. When it comes to the specific cases, they invariably oppose protectionism of any sort for any reason at any time—as if by keeping faith with the ideology its assumptions would miraculously become true. Even when the strongest case is proven, they take refuge in the claim that trade barriers would inevitably end up protecting only sloth and inefficiency. Yet there is no reason why purely domestic competition should not suffice to keep businesses on their toes in any large economy, with different competitors in each industry. There was certainly no sign of lethargy or corporate self-indulgence in Japan, through decades of protectionism.

There is one final parallel with Marxism–Leninism: the true believers in free trade are ready to sacrifice hugely for the sake of the splendid promise of their ideal—jobs, businesses, entire industries abandoned to foreign competition. Sometimes there is no alternative, as with industries based on cheap labor (e.g., handprinted cotton goods). But as often, temporary protection is just what the (Japanese) doctor would have ordered, to allow overtaken industries to recover and flourish again. Instead, they are irrevocably abandoned, sacrificed on the altar of theoretical beliefs. Ideologues can be expected to do that of course—but in this case they account for a large proportion of all American politicians, academic experts, government officials, journalists, and opinion leaders.

■ REALITIES OF THE GLOBAL MARKET: AIRBUS INDUSTRIE

As it happens, the world's airliner industry provides the most extreme example of the divergence between the truths-in-theory of the ideology, and sordid reality. To begin with, the *only* significant foreign competitor for the two remaining American producers of jet airlines, Boeing and McDonnell-Douglas (MacDac), is the European consortium Airbus Industrie.[10] Ostensibly a commercial company like any other, Airbus is in fact heavily subsidized and financially guaranteed by the governments of France, Germany, Britain, and Spain. Each has its own favored aerospace company—its "chosen instrument"—and they form the Airbus consortium among them: France's Aerospatiale and Deutsche Aerospace have a 37.9% share each, British Aerospace has 20%, and Spain's CASA has 4.2%. These companies are neither small nor weak. In combination, including their military divisions, they employed some 550,200 people in 1990, as opposed to 161,700 for Boeing and 121,190 for McDonnell-Douglas, and in that year their total sales amounted to $84.8 billion, almost twice as much as McDonnell-Douglas and Boeing combined. But what makes Airbus Industrie so formidable is the government support it receives.

It now costs billions of dollars to design and engineer in detail a new airliner—money that Boeing and MacDac must borrow up front, and pay interest on every day during the several years that pass from the start of design to the first sale of a completed aircraft. That, obviously, is a very heavy burden, especially with the high long-term US interest rates caused by the American refusal to save, and the heavy government borrowing needed to cover huge federal deficits. But Airbus Industrie is virtually exempt from such financial agonies: its first airliner, the A300, was launched in May 1969 with $800 million in government subsidies; the A310 that followed was developed from July 1978 with a $1 billion subsidy; next the A320 was started in March 1984 with $2.5 billion; finally the A330 and A340 were launched in June 1987 with $4.5 billion in government subsidies.

Admittedly these are not outright grants but rather loans from each government to its own "chosen instrument" aerospace company—except that no bank in the world has ever dealt so kindly with a borrower: first, the interest rate is, in effect, zero; second, Airbus Industrie need repay its loans only if it happens to have money to spare. So far, however, the consortium has continued to lose money, even though by 1990 it had delivered more than 700 aircraft to 102 different airlines all over the world. No normal commercial enterprise, not even the very largest of international corporations most heavily shielded by banking support and interlocked shareholdings, could have survived the cumulative losses of Airbus Industrie over the years. There is certainly no prospect that the four sponsoring governments will be repaid: their total subsidies were last calculated at $26 billion.[11] But profit and loss accounts are for "little people," in the memorable phrase, a category that includes McDonnell-Douglas and even Boeing in this case.

When some European economic experts complained about the huge cost of Airbus to the French, German, British, and Spanish taxpayers, their impertinence was firmly dismissed by Erich Riedl, Germany's aerospace coordinator: "We don't care about criticism from small-minded pencil-pushers."[12]

Facing a competitor that can sell below cost year after year, decade after decade, *and* continue to expand, Boeing and McDonnell-Douglas have naturally lost many potential sales simply because they were underpriced. An Airbus Industrie executive put it plainly: "If Airbus has to give away airplanes, we'll do it."[13] At least so far, no airliners have actually been given away—but quite a few have certainly been loaned away. Determined to challenge the American airliner industry in its own home market, in 1978 the consortium achieved a major breakthrough by successfully selling twenty-three of its A300 airliners to Eastern Air Lines—a huge order from what was then very much a leading US airline, won against fierce competition from Boeing and McDonnell-Douglas. But they never had a chance.

To win the order, Airbus Industrie did not limit itself to offering low prices. It also leased four of the twenty-three aircraft to Eastern for $1 a year—not bad for a 248-seat jet airliner. That very size, as it happens, was a problem that almost stopped the deal. For the A300 was simply too big and too costly to operate for Eastern, which really needed a 170-seat aircraft for its key Florida routes. Boeing's 727 was just right, but Airbus won anyway, simply by paying an operating subsidy to Eastern: ". . . the seller agrees to compensate the buyer for the difference in operating costs between the desired one hundred and seventy seat capacity aircraft [and the A300]" read the contract.[14] That subsidy-gift was truly an extraordinary concession by Airbus Industrie: its money would flow into Eastern's coffers every year for the twenty-odd years of the operating life of an airliner. Cutthroat competition is the rule in airliner sales, but nothing like it had ever been seen before. It would be seen again, however.

The outcome of the Eastern affair was a series of ineffectual complaints from Boeing ("We can compete with Airbus on technical merits, but we cannot compete with the national treasuries of France and Germany"[15]) and from individual members of Congress making their little speeches without any intention of actually taking any action. True to the standard American belief that free trade should be free even when it is not, the Carter administration did not intervene, citing a variety of counterarguments: the strategic need for alliance solidarity within the West, the general insignificance of Airbus Industrie (which then had little more than 5% of the world market), the burden of many unsold aircraft ("whitetails") on its hands—and, of course, the consortium's denials that it had been unfair in any way.

Those denials might even have been persuasive were it not for the riotous noises coming out of Eastern. Frank Borman, its ex-astronaut chief executive, a man of sober restraint, had been prosaic to a fault—even dull—when traveling to the moon, but in the wake of the Airbus contract even he could not contain his enthusiasm: "If you don't kiss the French flag every time you see it, at least salute it. . . . Airbus . . . subsidized this airline by more than $100 million."[16]

At the time, it was widely believed that the Eastern deal was a unique market-opening gambit, and that Airbus Industrie would act more soberly in the future now that it had achieved its aim of penetrating the US market. But in 1984, when the consortium had grown to the point of winning 16% of worldwide sales—three times as much as it had in 1978—there was a second chance to penetrate the US market, and Airbus did it again, once more winning an order by drastic underpricing. This time, too, the client was a troubled airline: Pan Am, once the greatest of them all and still of vast fame all over the world, but already very weak financially, and destined for the bankruptcy that would finally come in 1991.

Airbus Industrie sold Pan Am twenty-eight airliners (twelve A310s and sixteen A320s) with options for forty-seven more—a huge order obtained by equally huge concessions. First there was the usual free lease, this time of twelve older A300s (the consortium then had twenty-four "whitetails" on its hands) pending delivery of the new A310s and A320s. Prices were of course very low, certainly much below cost. And then there was a loan guarantee. Because of its colossal past reputation, Pam Am was still regarded as a premier airline. But bankers knew the truth and would not lend it any money except at high-risk rates, of the sort that gamblers might pay but impossibly costly for an airline. Airbus Industrie overcame the problem without a hitch: it guaranteed the loans needed for its own sale. That allowed Pan Am to borrow cheaply—not on its own dubious credit but on credit of the governments of France, Germany, and Britain.

Outside the American market, the consortium did not have to resort to such complicated maneuvers to win deals: low prices and low-interest loans were usually quite enough. Needless to say, Airbus Industrie can always offer lower interest loans than its US competitors, because it can count on subsidized finance from its government sponsors. Airliners are expensive and mostly bought on credit, so this advantage alone is decisive in many cases. Moreover, only US companies are barred by law from paying bribes to airline purchasing officials—a law that is effective, if only because of the fear of inevitable leaks from within the company.

The Reagan administration reacted with extraordinary force to the Pan Am affair—it actually complained. Its special trade "strike force" dared to declare the Airbus subsidies an "unfair trade practice." Finally, in 1986, the US Trade Representative, Clayton Yeutter, uttered fighting words: "It's time we sat down and discussed just how the Airbus consortium is functioning."[17]

Negotiations duly began with the governments of France, Germany, and Britain, which of course are still continuing at a leisurely pace now with the European Community, while Airbus Industrie's share of the world market has passed 25%—one-quarter of all sales—not bad for a consortium that has yet to earn one cent of profit. In the meantime, there were solemn promises of good behavior, but in 1989 the German government gave $2.3 billion of "exchange rate" subsidies to Daimler-Benz, which was then taking over the German role in the consortium through its Deutsche Aerospace subsidiary. The United States reacted most forcefully once again: it filed a complaint with GATT, the General Agreement on Tariffs and Trade, denouncing an "illegal export subsidy." Negotiations are continuing on that also.

Against this highly provocative US reaction—negotiations were actually *started* a mere eight years after the Eastern sale—an Airbus counterreaction was inevitable. This time it came not from a tactless German but from a suave and most measured Briton, Richard Evans, then chief executive officer of British Aerospace: "Airbus is going to attack the Americans, including Boeing, until they bleed and scream."[18] In the meantime, Airbus Industrie has never ceased to complain that it is the target of unfair American propaganda.

Its spokesmen claim the US government funding of aviation research by NASA, the National Aeronautics and Space Administration, is the equivalent of a subsidy—even though NASA's research results are openly published for the use of all, Airbus included. A seemingly stronger claim is that the Pentagon's funding of research and development for military aviation also yields technological know-how that Boeing and McDonnell-Douglas can use in their civilian aircraft. That was undoubtedly true until the 1960s, when bombers and tankers were still subsonic aircraft of conventional design, and were bought by the hundreds. There is certainly a definite resemblance between Boeing's KC-135 tanker and its 707 airliner, both mass-produced from the late 1950s. But ever since then, only supersonic and "stealth" bombers have been developed with US Air Force funds, aircraft totally different in every way from civilian airliners. Moreover, because they are produced only in small numbers, their high-cost, virtually hand-worked technology is almost useless for cost-conscious civilian production.

The debate continues, but the truth is simple: to be able to start in the business, in competition with US airliners produced by companies that originally grew with military orders from the US government, Airbus obviously needed a great deal of help from its own sponsoring governments. It is, however, the seemingly endless continuation of its subsidies that gives Airbus Industrie its special character.

Evidently the US airline industry, Boeing and McDonnell-Douglas and all their subcontractors, inhabits a world far different from Main

Street, USA. While it has to meet payrolls on time, find its own investment capital, pay interest on every penny it borrows, and face enormous risks each time it launches a new aircraft, Airbus Industrie, like Taiwan Aerospace and the Japan Aircraft Development Corporation, is no more exposed to the vagaries of free markets than the Vatican. Yet even now the true believers have no other suggestion than to invite Boeing and McDonnell-Douglas to "compete harder"—as if any private company can compete against a rival that can, in effect, print its own money by way of interposed governments. In May 1990, after more than twenty years in business and the sale of more than 600 airliners, the president of Airbus Industrie expressed the *hope* that its losses might end by 1995![19] Whatever it is, Airbus is certainly not a commercial phenomenon, against which commercial companies can compete with normal commercial methods.

■ US CITIZENS: CONSUMERS OR PRODUCERS?

Actually the advocates of free trade do have an answer to the Airbus Industrie problem, and all similar problems. They smile at the foolish generosity of the French, German, British, and Spanish governments in subsidizing the consortium. They welcome the gifts made to Eastern and Pan Am, and they would welcome additional below-cost sales to United, American, and Delta as well, the more the better. They invite us to stop complaining, and instead sit back to enjoy the subsidies, which in effect subsidize our own consumption, at the expense of European taxpayers. Obviously they believe that the Europeans are stupid to fund the Airbus extravagance, and that Americans would be stupid to reject its gifts.

That is certainly a perfectly logical answer in the immediate present, but it overlooks the ultimate result. In the twenty years from 1971 to 1991, Airbus Industrie increased its share of worldwide airliner market from near zero to 26%. In the process, the American airline industry lost that much in production and sales, mostly overseas sales of course. The lost 26% of airliner sales could have reduced the US trade imbalance (only the chemical industry exports more) and increased the profits of Boeing, McDonnell-Douglas, and all their subcontractors. Those profits, in turn, could have provided more capital for research, development, plant, and equipment. Moreover, Airbus Industrie is still expanding. Its managing director, Jean Pierson, has published the consortium's ambitious goal: "If we make no mistakes, we should achieve a 40% share of the market in the next fifteen years."[20]

If that comes to pass, McDonnell-Douglas is unlikely to survive in the airline business, and Boeing, too, would be much weakened. In any case, tens of thousands of well-paid American industrial workers, scientists, technicians, designers, engineers, managers, and salespeople would lose their jobs in the industry. Further jobs would be lost in great numbers in the many different industries that supply materials, components, and machinery. All the lost jobs would mean as many lives disrupted and most probably diminished; and nationally, there would be a further slide toward a prevalence of low-paid, low-skill service jobs in US economy—not "flipping hamburgers" perhaps, but certainly some ex–airliner builders would end up cleaning and maintaining Airbuses.

Welcoming the subsidies thus safeguards the interests of US citizens as consumers but ignores their very different interests as producers. There is no need or justification for pulling out a handy (Japanese) calculator to evaluate the costs and benefits on each side of the ledger. The extra consumption provided to a high-consumption society by European subsidies cannot begin to be compared to the dignity that comes from worthy employment and the deep satisfactions of working in an exacting industry. That is what the governments that sponsor Airbus are buying with their subsidies: desirable jobs for tens of thousands of European workers, satisfying careers for aircraft designers and engineers, and challenging managerial positions. As against all that, affluent European taxpayers need give up only a fraction of their income, a thin slice of their abundant consumption. Is that a stupid choice?

There is also a further step in the future—the moment when all gifts must be repaid. For one thing, even if it is subsidized, the kind of imported consumption that displaces home production can only last as long as there are still forest acres, famous buildings, golf courses, technologies, companies, and entire industries to sell off—to the extent that the dollars sent abroad are not invested in Treasury bonds or other debts that must in turn be paid off. Moreover, unless stopped by US government action far more determined than seen so far, Airbus Industrie really will be able to make Boeing "bleed and scream." When the consortium has its own jumbo-sized 747 competitor ready (it is now being engineered), Boeing will lose its monopoly of those largest airliners, the key to its ability so far to match Airbus prices for smaller aircraft. If it cannot continue to make a large profit on the 747s to offset the unprofitability of its other sales, Boeing would start to decline quite rapidly, eventually going out of business altogether. At that point, there would be no more competition, and no more subsidized sales for US airlines or anyone else, unless of course by then the Japanese have entered the game—with their own subsidies.

Airbus Industrie is by no means a unique case. On the contrary, virtually every promising industrial sector has its own version of Airbus Industrie in one country or in several, whether for computers and data processing software, biotechnology, advanced materials (superconductive, amorphous, or ceramic), satellite launchers, telecommunications, and more. If there is no subsidy for a chosen corporation or consortium as in the Airbus case, then there is a state-funded "national technology program" that serves the same purpose for an entire industry.

▪ **GEO-ECONOMICS**

The broader meaning of this new phenomenon is plain enough. Unlike the handouts given to failing industries, or the payments that powerful farm lobbies can extract from American, European, and Japanese taxpayers, the support of technologically advanced companies or entire industries is an *instrument of state power*. Thus it is not more and not less than the continuation of the ancient rivalry of the nations by new industrial means. Just as in the past when young men were put in uniform to be marched off in pursuit of schemes of territorial conquest, today taxpayers are persuaded to subsidize schemes of industrial conquest. Instead of fighting each other, France, Germany, and Britain now collaborate to fund Airbus Industrie's offensive against Boeing and McDonnell-Douglas. Instead of measuring progress by how far the fighting front has advanced on the map, it is worldwide market shares for the targeted products that are the goal.

In the Middle East, in the Balkans, and in other such unfortunate parts of the world, old-fashioned territorial struggles continue as they did throughout history. In those backward zones of conflict, military strength remains as important as ever. And so does diplomacy in its classic form, still serving as it always did to convert the possible use of military strength into an actual source of power and influence, whether to threaten adversaries or to reassure weaker allies. But in the central arena of world affairs, where Americans, Europeans, Japanese, and other advancing peoples both collaborate and compete, the situation has changed drastically. War between them has become almost unthinkable, while external dangers of attack are either remote or localized now that the ex–Soviet Union no longer threatens and no longer arms and supports aggressive smaller allies such as Cuba, Vietnam, and Syria. Hence both military power and classic diplomacy have lost their traditional importance in the central arena of world affairs.

But the millennium of brotherly love has yet not arrived. The internal solidarity of peoples still derives from a common "national" identity that excludes other peoples. To say "American" is to speak of something that is meaningful only because there are non-Americans. In many cases, it is still a cultural identity that defines the "we" as against the "them." To be French or Italian or even Brazilian is a much more specific "we" than the multicultural American "we." In some cases, as in Japan, this exclusive identity is still widely imagined to be racial, although it is enough to see a Japanese crowd, ranging in color from pink-white to olive green to expose the fantasy. But whatever the nature or justification of national identities, world politics is still dominated by states (or the association of states that is the European Community) that are based on a "we" that excludes a larger "them." States are, of course, *territorial* entities, marked off against each other by borders, jealously claimed and still often closely guarded.[21] Even when there is no thought of military confrontation, even when they cooperate everyday in dozens of international organizations and many other ways, the very nature of states is relentlessly adversarial.

But states and governments are not merely adversarial by nature, and they do not merely reflect, as a mirror might, the underlying national identity. Consciously or not, their everyday actions and declarations meant to protect, promote, or advance "national interests," also tend to stimulate, encourage, accommodate, harness, and exploit adversarial popular sentiments that define a "we" against a hostile "them." In the backwaters of world politics, where territorial conflicts continue, wars or threats of war provide an ample outlet for hostile sentiments. But when it comes to the central arena of world politics where Americans, Europeans, and Japanese collaborate and contend, if is chiefly by economic means that adversarial attitudes can now be expressed.

This new version of the ancient rivalry of states, I have called "geoeconomics."[22] In it, investment capital for industry provided or guided by the state is the equivalent of firepower; product development subsidized by the state is the equivalent of weapon innovation; and market penetration supported by the state replaces military bases and garrisons on foreign soil as well as diplomatic "influence." The very same things—investment, research and development, and marketing—are also done every day by private enterprises for purely business reasons. But when the state intervenes to encourage, help, or direct those very same activities, it is no longer plain vanilla economics that is going on, but rather geo-economics.

The geo-economic arsenal also includes other weapons old and new. Tariffs can be merely taxes, imposed with no other aim than to raise revenue; likewise, quota limits and outright import prohibitions may be meant only to cope with an acute shortage of hard currency. But when the purpose of such trade barriers is to protect domestic industry and allow it to grow, it is again geo-economics that we face, its equivalent of the defended frontiers and fortified lines of war and old-style world politics.

There are also hidden trade barriers, the geo-economic equivalents of the ambush, that most powerful of tactics in war. One is the deliberate framing of health and safety regulations or any other regulations of labeling, packaging, recycling characteristics, etc., to exclude imports. Prohibitive tariffs or outright import bans can do that more straightforwardly of course, but most countries have signed the General Agreement on Tariffs and Trade (GATT), which limits the imposition of tariffs at will. Thus some countries will resort to regulatory trickery to camouflage trade barriers. In the case of Japan, for example, until the 1980s foreign cars were *individually* inspected for compliance with Japanese safety rules. The Japanese government did not satisfy itself by testing a single example of any given model as other countries do. Instead the importer was forced to pay an inspection fee for each car, and had to wait patiently until the customs officials completed their inspections, car by car, for an entire shipload. Had the US government adopted the same rule, it alone might have stopped the great flood of Japanese automobile imports.

But what most resembles the ambush are the many customs-house conspiracies that circumvent the GATT rule against arbitrary tariffs and quotas. During the early 1980s, for example, the French government decided that its domestic electronics industry could learn to compete with the Japanese in producing video-cassette recorders. But with Matsushita, Victor-JVC, Toshiba, Hitachi, and Mitsubishi, among others, already in full mass production, they were offering VCRs of ever-higher quality at falling prices. French industry clearly needed time to design its own products and tool up—a couple of years at least. The French government's solution was not lacking in humor. It issued a routine administrative decree that required all VCRs imported from overseas (i.e., Japan) to pass customs inspection at Bayeux, the very small town in Normandy that is famous for its medieval tapestry of William the Conqueror's invasion of Britain. With Bayeux the only allowed port of entry, Japanese VCRs airlifted to Paris first had to be transported there overland in bonded containers. Then the containers had to be unloaded for inspection in the usual way before the import companies could pay the duty and collect their goods.

Regrettably, however, the Bayeux customs house was very small and so badly understaffed that usually there was only one inspector on duty at any one time. Even more regrettably, the lone Bayeux inspector was a man of rather comfortable habits. He never arrived at the office before 10 A.M., he promptly left for lunch by 12:30, and being something of a gourmet even by French standards, he did rather tend to linger over his lunch. Indeed, he rarely returned to his desk before 3 P.M., then being understandably lethargic until the office closed at 5 P.M. As Japanese VCR exports to France collapsed, the Japanese government duly complained—but not too much—it could hardly run the risk of a comparison with its own practices.

For the Japanese, reliance on unwritten and undeclared customs-house obstacles to trade has been exceptionally broad. Aside from specific maneuvers meant to keep out specific imports, the normal operating procedure of Japanese customs is itself an obstacle to free trade. Every single container, every single case, every single box, and every single package—including air-express envelopes—must be individually opened for the inspectors (the US and most other countries do only spot checks, otherwise relying on the exporter's declaration). When the inspectors eventually arrive, it is part of their duties to record an image of what they see. Japan sends its cameras all over the world, but Japanese customs inspectors do not employ them. Instead they *sketch* the imported article in a freehand drawing, often achieving a pleasing artistic effect. In the process, imports can be fatally delayed. For example, it is this tribute to art that stops many foreign salesmen from having any samples to show during their visits, unless forewarned.

Delay for its own sake may only irritate, but some delays are much more purposeful, and only part of larger maneuvers. Imports of new high-technology products that threaten domestic industries can sometimes be defeated, and not merely delayed, by employing the device of compulsory "standards." In telecommunications and broadcasting, for example, frequencies are allocated by the state for each separate purpose, cycles vary, and so on. If new products arrive on the world scene that threaten local industry, the relevant state authority can stop all imports by announcing that it must first decide what standards should be laid down. Then it can secretly consult with local industry so as to deliberately set standards that will exclude imported products, or at least those made by the strongest competitors. At that point, the announcement of the new standards is held up until local industry has tooled up and is fully prepared for mass production. When that moment arrives and the market is finally opened to all with great fanfare, the locals can start to sell—while foreign exporters are just starting to reconfigure their products. These maneuvers have been used most recently on cellular telephones and high-definition TV, in the American–European–Japanese "war of HD-TV standards."

Deliberately difficult standards can keep out imports even when there is nothing new to regulate. For example, Japanese standards require that plywood be made of tropical hardwoods, not pine or other soft woods. There is no reason that should be so, because soft wood is just as good for the purpose, and of course much cheaper. But the effect has been to protect Japan's plywood industry from American and Scandinavian competitors, which have the unbeatable advantage of using a much cheaper raw material. And there has also been a side effect: the irrevocable destruction of tropical rain forests of the Philippines, Thailand, Indonesia, and Malaysia, now spreading to Burma, Cambodia, and Laos. American and European plywood, by contrast, is almost entirely made from the wood of totally reproducible pine trees, including fast-growing southern pine. Thai exports are still quite likely to be cased in plywood—plywood made in Japan from imported hardwoods, though no longer from the magnificently tall teak trees of Thailand itself, which have all been cut down long ago.

Trade barriers mostly serve to preserve the local market for local industry, but sometimes they can help the growth of export industries as well. Countries that have scarce natural resources can impose export taxes on raw materials but not on worked products, to encourage the growth of local processing. Most African countries, for example, no longer allow the export of raw logs, but only of wood already cut into planks and studs. Many in the United States have urged a similar rule, without effect so far; hence American national forests are still being cut down for the sake of lumberjack "jobs," it is said, even though many more sawmill jobs could be had if the export of raw logs were stopped. Saudi Arabia and other oil producers achieve the same effect by selling crude oil at high prices, while offering refined products and more especially petrochemicals at low prices.

IS GEO-ECONOMICS NEW?

Some would dismiss the preceding remarks from start to finish as nothing more than new verbiage for old themes. It is certainly true that rulers and states have always pursued economic goals and have never lacked for economic quarrels with other rulers and states. Sometimes special tolls and duties, trade prohibitions, or outright blockades were sufficient, but sometimes marketplace rivalries were finally settled with blood and iron. Twenty-two hundred years ago, Rome and Carthage fought over Mediterranean trade, as well as for security against each other and for glory—and commercial wars were hardly a novelty even then, not by thousands of years. In the centuries that followed the fall of Carthage, many more wars would be fought for commerce and for valuable resources, although only fanatical Marxist–Leninists seriously try to explain the cause of every war as purely economic.

In the past, however, the outdoing of others in commerce and industry was often overshadowed by more pressing priorities of war and diplomacy, chiefly the quest for security—a sufficient reason for many wars—but also the pursuit of glory or internal political advantage by single rulers or ruling groups, by ambitious individuals, or by entire castes. Then commerce and its needs were utterly subordinated, as profitable trade links were cut by warring armies, and as wars were fought alongside trading rivals against trading partners. Thus in 1914, France, in alliance with Britain, its chief rival in the colonial trades, went to war against its chief trading partner, Germany. Certainly if security needs dictated an alliance against a common enemy while, by contrast, there was a head-to-head competition in commerce or industry with that very ally, the preservation of the alliance had absolute priority, for its aim was survival, not merely prosperity.

That, indeed, is how all the commercial quarrels between the United States and Western Europe—over frozen chickens, microchips, beef, and others—and between the United States and Japan—over everything from textiles in the 1960s to supercomputers in the 1990s—were so easily contained during the decades of the Cold War. As soon as a trade dispute became noisy enough to attract the attention of the political leaders on both sides, it was promptly suppressed, often by paying off the loudest complainers. What could not be risked was the damage that unchecked trade quarrels could do to political relations, which would in turn threaten alliance solidarity before a menacing Soviet Union.

Now, however, as the importance of military threats and military alliances continues to wane for the countries in the peaceful central arena of world affairs, economic priorities are no longer suppressed but can instead emerge and become dominant. Trade quarrels may still be contained by the fear of their purely economic consequences, but not by political interventions that have powerful strategic reasons. And if the internal cohesion of nations and countries must still be preserved by a unifying external threat, that threat must now be economic, or rather geo-economic.

Exactly this recasting of public attitudes is already manifest in the (economic) fears that many other Europeans express before the industrial might of undivided Germany, and even more in American attitudes toward Japan. Gorbachev's redirection of Soviet foreign policy had barely started in the mid-1980s when Japan began to be promoted into the role of America's Chief Enemy, judging by the ample evidence of opinion polls, media stories, books, articles, even advertisements, and countless congressional pronouncements. It was as if a country long united internally by a common fear of the military strength of Soviet Union had moved as one to find a geo-economic substitute in Japan, so as to preserve its unity. From the late 1950s, it was the shock of the Soviet launch of the Sputnik satellite and the apparent Soviet lead in ballistic missiles that persuaded the American people and government to pour money into higher education and science in order to win the military-technological race. Thus fear provided the motive for a common effort, and some sacrifice. Today, educational reformers all across America cite the Japanese lead in public education to solicit support and money for their schemes. Enemies real or imagined can be useful.

Are the world's most advanced countries therefore regressing to a new age of mercantilism? And is *geo-economics* nothing more than an unnecessary new word for that ancient practice? There are parallels, of course, for in both cases rulers or states induce countries to act against each other in commerce and industry, instead of merely trading with each other for the good and sufficient private reasons of the traders themselves. But the goal of mercantilism was to acquire ships and gold—not a foolish aim for kings in need of fleets and of gold coin to pay their troops. With gold, regiments could be raised to win wars; without it defeat was inevitable. Gold was thus military strength at only one remove, unlike agricultural or commercial wealth that was hard to tax, if it could be taxed at all before the age of file cabinets and computers. Hence mercantilism was purposeful even if harmful: by seeking to export and not import, the trade of all was ultimately damaged, but in the meantime taxable gold would accumulate within the ruler's reach. Mercantilism was an economic activity but its purposes were strictly political.

Because in geo-economics the ultimate purpose is itself social and economic, i.e., to maximize high-grade employment in advanced industries and sophisticated services, all is different within it: the means, from research and development to export finance; the immediate goals of technological and market superiority; and the consequences, internal and external. Internally, any gains do not strengthen a king but rather improve employment. Externally, even the vigorous pursuit of geo-economics need not lead to "beggar-my-neighbor" policies of import bans and high tariffs or indeed any tariffs at all, though they might be export incentives. Certainly it is not a quest for gold, or for wealth itself in any form, that drives the new form of international rivalry.

Above all, mercantilism was always overshadowed by war. In its age, when commercial quarrels became sufficiently inflamed to degenerate into political quarrels, they in turn could lead to war, and often did. In other words, mercantilism was a subordinated form of state action, easily displaced by war. Whatever was done in the strictly economic sphere was therefore governed by the ever-present possibility that the loser in the mercantilist (or simply commercial) struggle would try to recoup his losses under the very different rules of war. Spain might decree that all trade to and from its American colonies could only travel in Spanish ships and through Spanish ports, but British and Dutch armed merchantmen could still convey profitable cargoes to disloyal colonists in defiance of Spanish sloops, and with war declared privateers could seize the rich cargoes bound for Spain. Likewise, the Dutch sent their frigates into the Thames to reply to the mercantilist legislation of the British Parliament that prohibited their coastwise English trade, just as much earlier the Portuguese had sunk Arab ships with which they could not compete in the India trade.

Geo-economics, by contrast, is a game that can be played only by countries that have already ruled out war among themselves. Import-restricted supercomputers cannot be forcibly delivered by airborne assault to the banks or universities that might buy them, nor can competition in the world automobile market be pursued by sinking roll-on car ferries on the high seas. Armed force has thus lost the role it once had in the age of mercantilism—as an admissible, almost routine adjunct to economic rivalry. Instead in the new geo-economic era now emerging, not only the causes but also the instruments of rivalry must be strictly economic. If commercial quarrels do lead to political clashes, as they are now much more likely to do with the waning of alliance imperatives, those political clashes will have to be fought out with the weapons of commerce: the more or less disguised restriction of imports, the more or less concealed subsidization of exports, the funding of competitive technology projects, the support of selected forms of education, the provision of competitive infrastructures, and so on.

Not all states are equally capable of implementing geo-economic policies, and not all states are equally inclined to try. For all sorts of reasons, historical and institutional, ideological or political, some states will be more active than others in the new form of international rivalry, with some even refusing to act at all, just as states as varied as Burma and Switzerland desired only neutrality in the age of war. But in most advanced countries nothing has been determined as yet. Instead, the desirable extent of geo-economic activity has itself become a focal point of political debate and partisan controversy. In the United States, Democrats and Republicans are in dispute over "industrial policy"—that being the jargon phrase for furthering the growth of promising industries. In France, the same governing elites that long pursued vast military and diplomatic ambitions are now easily shifting their attention to the pursuit of equally vast geo-economic ambitions—Airbus is just one of their endeavors. In most other European countries, by contrast, the public debate is unfolding between the US and French extremes, while even in Japan there is now controversy over the wisdom of an unlimited geo-economic activism.

CHAPTER 2

OUR JAPAN PROBLEM

American society is unique in that it is based on ideas and not on a national culture or ethnic solidarity, as are almost all other societies. An idea-based society has only two modes: internal strife over ideas (reaching the point of civil war—and the US Civil War was the bloodiest of all wars till then), or a marvelous cohesion in the presence of a threatening external enemy. The Soviet Union performed that function very well for more than forty years, finally resigning exhausted in August 1991. Saddam Hussein volunteered Iraq for the post but was much too weak to keep at it for very long. In that enemyless condition, the United States could have been riven by its controversies, over abortion, sexual harassment, affirmative action, etc.

But fundamentally Americans strive for unity, no matter how much they enjoy their controversies. It is therefore a basic instinct of American society to search for an external Enemy that can assure its cohesion—and Japan is the only possible candidate. True, Japan has no rival ideology, except for its "developmental capitalism" which hardly attacks core American values, while ideological enemies are much better for America's deeply ideological society. But necessity is the mother of invention, and any careful student of the American media has been able to see how Japan has gradually been turned into the new Chief Enemy, headline by headline ("Japan conquers 30% of the US auto market"—not Toyota, Nissan, etc., but *Japan*).

The standard preliminary is also well under way. After the Second

World War, the gradual emergence of the Cold War was accompanied by an intensifying witch-hunt aimed at American Communists (some of whom were indeed Soviet agents), which culminated in the years of McCarthyism. This time it is those Americans who lobby and speak for Japan that are being exposed as agents of influence. The purpose is the same: to prepare for external conflict by weeding out the disloyal within.

Of course, the animosity is equally bitter on both sides. For while the Japanese have continued to disregard American economic interests, responding to all complaints with clever tactical maneuvers rather than an intelligent strategy of long-term cooperation, the US government has ignored the political interests of the Japanese, their perfectly under-standable desire to be treated as one of the world's greatest nations, entitled to that measure of recognition, including a seat on the UN Security Council alongside yesterday's Great Powers, Britain and France. Instead, Japan has been treated as a ward and source of ready cash by the US government, rather than as a valid global partner worthy of respect. Naturally the Japanese have responded with expressions of contempt for America and Americans. As long as the twin deficits, the trade balance and the "respect balance," persist, only a gloomy forecast can be realistic.

▪ THE "TRADE-FRICTION" STAGE

For many years now, American–Japanese relations have been in an "average" condition: worse than the year before, but better than the year after. The tensions that started in a small way in the 1960s—an economic era ago for Japan, when cheap textiles still loomed large in its exports—marked the start of the long "trade-friction" stage in US–Japan relations.

Friction is an engineering term. It describes the very minor rubbing, chafing, or superficial grinding (one can *hear* it in the Japanese word for it, *masatsu*) that may occur in a machine otherwise well designed, whose parts do fundamentally fit together. Usually a steady supply of lubricating oil is quite sufficient to overcome friction and keep the machine running smoothly. Thus the very use of the phrase by Japanese apologists, and the Americans who echo their views, was meant to suggest that all was well in the overall economic relationship, except for minor irritants and avoidable misunderstandings.

It was an explanation that suited many people for a long time. From the successive presidents down, US officials were happy to accept the friction theory because it fitted in with their overriding geopolitical priorities in waging the Cold War: Japan was an ally first, a trade competitor only second. Early on and certainly until the later 1950s, their first priority was to enrich the Japanese, for fear that they would otherwise be attracted to communism. By the time it became clear that the Japanese Communist party was not much of a threat, Japan had become a valued ally, whose airfields, ports, and industrial capacity had already played a significant role in the Korean War. With American prosperity still exuberant, the loss of some minor market shares to Japanese exporters seemed a small price to pay for the rising economic strength of an increasingly important ally in the great struggle with the Soviet Union.

Still, some "frictions" inflicted more rubbing, chafing, and grinding than others. In a famous case, President Richard Nixon thought that Japan's Prime Minister Eisaku Sato[1] had promised to impose "voluntary" restraints on the export of synthetic textiles to the United States at their November 19–20, 1969, White House meetings, during which Nixon for his part agreed to return Okinawa and the rest of the Ryukyu islands to Japanese control by 1972. For Sato, it was a personal political victory of great magnitude. The reversion of the Ryukyus—occupied by the United States since 1945—had already been ordained by prior US–Japanese understandings. But thanks to Nixon, Sato would get the credit, and moreover Nixon allowed him a major new concession: the exclusion of nuclear weapons for the remaining US bases in Okinawa.

For Nixon, limits on Japanese synthetic textile exports to the United States were also important, for they would enable him to keep a campaign promise. Not all such promises cause sleepless nights before their exact fulfillment, but that particular promise was different. It had been made to Senator Strom Thurmond, then still a very rare bird as a southern Republican, and a key figure in Nixon's entire "southern strategy," designed to keep the Democrats out of the White House for good by seizing their southern strongholds (ironically, but appropriately, Nixon's true successor, President Carter, was not only a Democrat but a southern Democrat).

It was therefore with mounting anger that Nixon learned over the next several months that no limits on Japanese synthetic textile exports were forthcoming. One possibility was that Sato had employed the fluidity of the Japanese language to sound as if he were making a promise, while actually only promising to try, in a style calculated to suggest that his best efforts might not be good enough (*Nan to ka yarimasho*, "I'll do something somehow," or *Zensho shimasu*, "I'll take care of it," according to Japanese press speculations).[2] Another possibility was that Sato had in fact made a definite promise, in order to obtain what he wanted from Nixon, while intending all along not to keep his promise. And indeed, as a former chief of the Ministry of International Trade and Industry (MITI), he was unlikely to sanction any limits on the ever-ascending progress of Japanese exports. The final possibility was that Sato had been sincere in his promise, but without effect, because MITI officials would not allow a mere politician to disrupt their plans for the growth of Japan's textile industry, even if he was a former MITI minister and the sitting prime minister to boot.

The third explanation must have sounded most improbable to Richard Nixon, given his own imperious command over officials high and low. Yet it is the most likely. MITI had sent its own investigative delegation to the United States in September 1969, two months before Sato's visit. A very judicious body, though perhaps not utterly objective in every possible way, MITI's on-site inspection team consisted of the chief of its Textile Bureau, the chiefs of the bureau's First Market, Fibers and Spinning, and Textile Export sections, and junior officials.[3] All in all, it was an investigative team with more than a passing interest in Japan's textile exports.

With extraordinary detective skills that would have put Sherlock Holmes to shame, they unraveled all the complexities of the American spinning and weaving industry in a mere four days (September 15–19). Their finding was that contrary to the superficial impression caused by unemployment and plant closings, the American textile industry was thriving and that it was suffering no damage—none whatever—from imports. Oddly enough, the American side in the negotiations that followed the Nixon–Sato meeting did not give up its demands in order to celebrate the newly discovered prosperity of the textile industry. As for the Japanese side, it followed the guidance of MITI's uncompromising Textile Bureau and would offer only one year of restraint strictly out of politeness.

One result was the publicly declared breakdown of the talks on June 24, 1970.[4] Another was Nixon's steadfast refusal to treat Japan as an ally in the months and years that followed; Sato had embarrassed him with his southern constituency, and he would see to it that Sato would be embarrassed in turn. In the greatest of the Nixon *shokus*, on June 15, 1971, Secretary of State William P. Rogers gave Japan's ambassador to Washington, Ushiba Nobuhiko, less than thirty minutes of advance notice of Nixon's sensational announcement that he would soon visit Beijing at Mao Tse-tung's invitation. Because Japan had long refrained from opening diplomatic relations with Beijing in deference to American wishes, it might seem that its prime minister should have been given a decent interval of advance warning. But Nixon was content to leave Sato looking like a fool.

As the years passed, there were mounting complaints from an ever-wider spectrum of American corporations and unions that faced increasingly effective Japanese competition at home while being unable to sell in Japan, but US policy fundamentally did not change. By the early 1980s, Japanese exports were displacing the output of entire American industries, from automobiles to forklift trucks, and virtually all types of consumer electronics, while, by contrast, Japan imported mostly raw materials and farm products from the United States, timber in raw logs, soybeans, tobacco, cotton, cattle hides, feed grains, etc.— and not even enough of them to avoid mounting trade deficits: $10.4 billion in 1980, $15.8 billion in 1981, $16.9 billion in 1982, $21.0 billion in 1983.[5]

On the other hand, those were among the peak years of the entire Cold War, with nuclear anxieties acute again, US–Soviet arms-control talks totally cut off for the first time since 1969, Soviet armed forces at war in Afghanistan, secret struggles of subversion and black propaganda in full swing all over the world, Soviet-sponsored terrorism in the Middle East and Europe, and Soviet arms deliveries into Nicaragua and even little Grenada.

As the geopolitical struggle approached its final climax, the Reagan administration was far more interested in Japan's role as an ally on the American side than in its role as a formidable adversary of American industry. In any case, textbook free-trade doctrine—an article of faith for most Reaganites—decisively condemned the protectionist alternative. Import barriers would hurt the Japan ally materially and antagonize Japanese opinion, but they would only weaken American industry, they believed, by encouraging managerial sloth and trade-union greed. That not only Japan but also Korea and Taiwan were doing exceedingly well with their own very thorough versions of protectionism did not

impress US officials who knew far more about diplomacy than international trade. They were fond of pointing out that when supposedly
voluntary limits were set on the number of Japanese cars exported to
the United States, forcing up their prices, General Motors, Ford, and
Chrysler did not try to expand their sales by undercutting the Japanese,
but instead chose to increase their prices as well.[6]

The notion that when an industry is granted tariff protection by the
public, so to speak, it can also be told what to do in the public interest
(the Japanese approach) was of course never considered—it would
have violated the holy principles of free enterprise. But chiefly and
above all, the upkeep of the US–Japanese alliance in what could at any
time become a life-and-death struggle was altogether more important
in the eyes of the US government than mere commercial considerations. No member of Congress could afford to manifest such aristocratic disdain when confronted by the bitter complaints of constituents
hurt by Japanese imports or unable to export to Japan or both of those
things, but most shared the geopolitical priorities of the policymakers,
and also their deep ideological belief in the doctrine of free trade.

There was also some genuine intellectual confusion. In America,
laws and regulations are literally meant, and what is not forbidden is
allowed. In particular, every import restriction is published in very
detailed regulations, and what is not restricted is freely allowed into the
US market. Japan, by contrast, is a country that works by unwritten,
unstated rules in a web of implicit understandings that define what is
allowed—and what is not allowed is forbidden—including imports not
specifically wanted. Thus when American businessmen complained
that they simply could not sell in Japan, congressional and administration officials alike would look up the Japanese tariff book, see a low
tariff or no tariff at all, look up the list of quotas or prohibitions only
to find very few, and would then turn around to accuse American
would-be exporters of not trying hard enough, of not adopting their
products to Japanese tastes, of not speaking the language, etc. That was
of course the Japanese explanation, which notably failed to explain why
the Koreans could not export much to Japan either, even though they
were certainly trying hard enough, did speak the language, and their
cheaper consumer goods were selling very well all over the world—
except in Japan.

Ignorant of how things really work in Japan, US officials and even
private "Japan experts" would repeat the standard Japanese advice that

to overcome the many difficulties of penetrating the Japanese market, it was best for American exporters to enter into joint ventures with one of the nine major Japanese trading companies, the *Sogo Shosha* (C. Itoh, Sumitomo, Marubeni, Mitsui, Mitsubishi, Nissho Iwai, Tomen, Nichimen, and Kanematsu-Gosho), leaving all the marketing to them. Those Americans who echoed the Japanese line on this matter also perhaps did not realize that each of the *Sogo Shosha* already has it own Japanese industrial partner in almost every field, so that many US–Japanese joint ventures ended up with the underlying US expertise passed along to the hidden Japanese partner.

The US corporation that sells only to a Japanese marketing partner is not really *in* the Japanese market, and cannot keep up with its trends to exploit new openings—thus sometimes leaving them to the hidden competitor in the joint-venture bed. But more generally, joint ventures have usually been a way of keeping outsiders safely out of Japan, even while allowing their technology or even their products and services to come in. As for the non–high tech American presence so evident all over Japan, which the innocent still now mistake for evidence of US market penetration, the 7-Elevens, Kentucky Fried Chicken outlets, McDonald's, etc., are all 100% Japanese-owned operations, up to and including the Tokyo head office, and pay only the usual modest royalties to the US name companies.

Many of those who were telling US exporters to try harder, especially during the early "trade-friction" stage, honestly did not know that Japanese manufacturers of baseball bats, skis, infant clothing, and processed foods were effectively protected by "safety" standards deliberately written to exclude imports; that automobiles, medical equipment, and telecommunications gear were kept out by the simple expedient of individual, item-by-item, customs inspections, in place of the broad by-the-model certifications accepted all over the world; that communications satellites, cigarettes, and supercomputers were fully or partly excluded by unwritten government procurement practices (Japan has a state monopoly on tobacco), in spite of a specific promise to stop them given in the 1979 "Tokyo Round"; that imports of soda ash, chemical fertilizers, plywood, integrated circuits, silicon wafers, and auto parts were effectively strangled by tacit agreements between the members of Japan's corporate families (*keiretsu*-s); that textiles and gasoline were kept out by informal government "advice" to potential importers; and that kidney dialysis machines and shipping containers, among other things, were kept out by arbitrary health insurance and size-and-weight regulations.[7]

It is entirely characteristic, by the way, that even the compiler of the list concluded in 1990 (!) "Now is not the time to abandon free-trade principles . . . [in dealing with Japan]."[8] Such is the power of ideology over the otherwise rational mind. Instead of being devoted to the protection of the sacred principles of free trade, the Japanese are devoted to the protection of real-life industries, the jobs of their employees, and the stability of communities that imports would especially threaten: Satsuma orange growers, Kobe beef raisers, rice farmers throughout Japan, and many localities specialized in some industry or craft.

Japanese trade policy even protects the interests of the despised Eta minorities, now politely renamed *burakumin*, "village people." Some 3 million in number, they are physically indistinguishable from other Japanese but are nevertheless outcasts because their ancestors were butchers (against Buddhist principles), leather workers, or grave diggers. Other Japanese will not marry them (hundreds of private detectives specialize in uncovering the invisible taint), and no established corporation would hire them, but the Japanese government imposes a low quota on leather-good imports to protect their traditional trade. It would never occur to the US government to protect the interests of American blacks or Native American craftsmen in its trade negotiations, but nothing is more natural for the Japanese. They, after all, never forget that the economy exists to serve society, and not the other way around.

As far as the Japanese government and Japanese big business were concerned, the friction theory was obviously attractive. With it, the persistent trade imbalances and the many restrictions on US exports and also on financial, professional, and service activities in Japan could continue unimpeded. All that was needed was a generous supply of lubricating oil to overcome the friction and keep the machine going, by way of some export restraint in the number (but not the quality) of cars, ample promises that Japanese imports of American goods would soon increase, a great deal of propaganda to explain the Japanese predicament (large population, little usable land, no raw materials) through an entire network of Japanese-subsidized American "Japan experts" and academic institutions, and an increasing expenditure on lobbying.

Many famous Washington lawyers, assorted ex-politicians, ex-officials, and institutional entrepreneurs of one sort or another were also enthusiastic promoters of the friction theory—for they were eager to sell the necessary oil to the Japanese government and big business. In a standardized routine, they would first warn Japanese prospects of acute frictions to come, and would then offer their services for a fee, often successfully. Of course, if a Japanese former senior government official were to emulate his American counterparts, setting up in business as a Tokyo lobbyist for US interests, nobody of importance would ever talk to him again.

■ THE "STRUCTURAL" STAGE

All good things must come to an end. By the mid-1980s Japan was exporting far more advanced products, and the American public had finally learned that the trade balance was not some technical matter of concern only to specialists, for it had a strong impact on each side's industrial progress and on employment and income—sometimes their own employment, their own income. And Americans had also learned that the US–Japan trade balance did not favor one side and then the other with the ebbs and flows of currencies and commerce, as in US–European trade, but was permanently kept in deficit by Japanese policies, habits, and business practices. After long being satisfied with Japanese promises of more imports to come, the US government finally decided that only deep structural changes could open the Japanese market, and that decision inaugurated a new stage in American–Japanese relations.

For by then, clamorous evidence that the doctrinal free-trade "machine" was not working in the case of Japan was discrediting the friction theory. Economists in general and Japanese apologists in particular had long insisted that the US–Japan trade deficit was entirely due to "macroeconomic" factors, i.e., federal deficits and the overvalued US dollar, not Japanese import barriers overt or disguised. They argued, quite persuasively it seemed, that by distributing more dollars into the American economy than were collected in taxes, the large post-1981 federal deficits were creating extra demand that was not offset by extra personal savings. Because foreigners were willing to ship goods to the United States in exchange for dollars, the result was to increase the trade deficit instead of causing inflation, as in countries such as Brazil or Argentina, whose currency is not accepted as a payment in itself.[9] Further, they ceaselessly pointed out that the dollar was in any case greatly overvalued (it had increased 40% against major currencies since 1981), thus greatly hampering US exports not only to Japan but to all countries. Armed with this superior logic, the luminaries dismissed the claims of the ignorant protectionist mob and refused to occupy themselves with obscure details of Japanese trade practices—their elegant theories proved that they were quite irrelevant anyway. United States exports were too expensive because the dollar itself was overvalued, and that was that.

It followed that when the dollar was hugely devalued in 1985, making foreign goods much more expensive for dollar buyers, while American goods in turn became much cheaper for foreign buyers, US exports to Japan should have increased dramatically, while Japanese imports should have collapsed, thus closing the trade gap. And in fact the 1985 devaluation duly worked its promised magic in the case of US trade with the European Community, rapidly converting a large deficit into a handsome surplus by 1990. But even though the dollar went down from its 1985 average of 238 yen to 168.52 in 1986 and then 144 in 1987, there was a continued *increase* in Japan's surplus in its merchandise trade with the United States, from $43.5 billion in 1985 to a peak of $56.9 billion in 1987, and then still $52.6 billion in 1988, $49.7 billion in 1989, and $41.7 billion in 1990, in spite of the recession that started in that year, and then up again in 1991 and even more in 1992.[10]

Thus the economists and Japan apologists had been proven doubly wrong. First, although the federal deficit was larger than ever, the US trade deficit with the European Community quickly diminished after the 1985 devaluation from a peak of $22.3 billion in 1986, to $21.9 billion in 1987, $11.6 billion in 1988, $0.99 billion in 1989, becoming a surplus of $4.9 billion in 1990, with further surpluses since then. Thus the strict logic of this bit of "macroeconomics" has turned out to be irrelevant in the case of US–European trade. Second, the devaluation did increase US exports to Japan—but only slightly more than Japanese exports to the United States: between 1985 and 1990, US exports to Japan enjoyed a "logical" increase of $25.8 billion; but Japanese exports to the United States increased by a "counterlogical" $24.0 billion, including $8.9 billion since 1986. All this did not mean that federal deficits and low savings are not important; they are. Nor did it mean that exports and imports are not governed by exchange rates; they are. But the great discovery of 1985 to 1990 was that there is economic logic and then there is culture, and that in Japan's case culture can defeat the logic.

It was then that the second, "structural," stage in US–Japanese economic tensions began, with the emergence of a radically different theory. It held that the machine was not well designed after all, and that its parts—specifically certain Japanese parts—did not fit together, but rather blocked the workings of the free-trade machine. Hence lubricating oil was no longer considered sufficient, and the offending parts would have to be cut off.

Official acceptance of the theory starting in 1984–1985, i.e., even before the great devaluation, resulted in industry-specific "Market-Oriented Sectors Selective" talks over forest products, medical equipment and pharmaceuticals, electronic products and software, and telecommunications equipment and services.[11] But with progress very slow and of uncertain real effect, the US government next proposed the altogether broader "Structural Impediments Initiative," under which many Japanese practices were classified as barriers to free trade, to demand their abolition. A long series of negotiations ensued.

Some of the listed impediments are both official and overt, such as the complete prohibition of rice imports, which is so rigorously enforced that when a few bags of US rice were included in a 1991 international food fair, Japanese Ministry of Agriculture officials ordered their removal, threatening to arrest the American exhibitors (four policemen did come to ensure that no offending US rice remained on show[12]). Other impediments arise from behind-the scenes bureaucratic decisions that grant or refuse licenses, permits, and access to banks, insurance companies, brokerages, and lawyers from the United States. Others still are inherent in the customary organization of the Japanese economy. Most important are the *keiretsu* links that cause most Japanese corporations to buy from other members of the same corporate family, thus excluding imports as well as other Japanese suppliers. But there are many other traditional practices that also have the effect of keeping out outsiders, which range from unwritten rules that limit door-to-door sales to some goods and not others (magazines yes, books no) to the secret sharing-out of public works among favored contractors who in turn pay vast amounts to key politicians. Some impediments, finally, are both legal and customary. For example, Japan's huge number of tiny shops (1.5 million at the last count) and a whole hierarchy of wholesalers and subdistributors are kept in business both by a specific "Large-Scale Retail Store Law" that restricts department stores and supermarkets mainly to city centers, and also by the Japanese preference for buying fresh food every day.

Eventually, more or less for rhetorical purposes and to poke mild fun at the American approach, the Japanese government came up with its own list of impediments, including the huge and persistent US federal deficits, the short-term mentality of American businesspeople, low educational standards in the US labor force, and so on. The American side solemnly promised to look into each question.

Because the doctrine itself remained unchallenged, logically it was Japan itself that had to be "wrong." At its simplest, the Structural Impediments Initiative (SII) was therefore intended to redesign the Japanese economy so that it would finally fit the doctrine. But of course it was still the geopolitical context that was decisive: as long as the Cold War was still very intense, the imperative of alliance solidarity would reliably suppress all commercial quarrels, truly reducing them to mere "frictions." But when Gorbachev began to dismantle Soviet military power after 1986, the strategic inhibition that prevented the deterioration of commercial quarrels into political fights was weakened step by step. Clearly *something* had to be done, and SII was the outcome.

Again, the remedy suited many people. For well-meaning diplomats on both sides, SII provides a marvelously ample agenda for years of negotiations, with pleasant residence in Tokyo's ultraperfectionist Okura Hotel (where late-night room service orders last arrived in three and a half minutes flat for cold servings) for visiting American officials, and in Washington's lavish Four Seasons Hotel for their Japanese counterparts. For American officials no longer content with mere hopes and unfulfilled promises that sometimes date back to 1966, SII offers the prospect of satisfyingly concrete action on specifics, that famous "getting down to the nitty-gritty" that remarkably ungritty officials are forever invoking.

For Japanese big business, on the other hand, SII is a minor irritant and a huge help: now "American pressure" can be invoked to overcome legal and customary restrictions that have long hampered big-business ambitions. Before SII, the large corporations interested in expanding their supermarkets and other large retail outlets did not seriously lobby against the Large-Scale Retail Store Law, because they did not want to antagonize other Japanese, i.e., the millions of small shopkeepers, sub-distributors, wholesalers, and their families. With SII, by contrast, the Americans could be blamed, while Japanese big business would reap the benefits of repeal.

Likewise, big business has no use for Japan's rice farmers, and would gladly see the end of them, in order to remove that particular irritant in Japan's dealings with rice-exporting countries, two of which are especially important for the Japanese: the United States and Thailand. But again, big business cannot risk offending the politically powerful rice farmers and is therefore very happy to have the US government attack them instead. Not for nothing is jujitsu one of the national arts, aimed at defeating an enemy with his own strength—except that in this case two enemies can be defeated by each other. Actually, when one listens to the big-business advocates of opening Japan's rice market, one has the impression that they had already calculated that it would be much more profitable to build "Old Japan" Disneylands in place of rice-farming villages, complete with holographic images of rice farmers at work in folk costumes, and excellent recordings of their traditional songs.

Actually the new big-business consensus that rice farmers and small shopkeepers should be sacrificed is not only cynical but also quite irresponsible, because once again American expectations would be raised only to be disappointed. As big-business experts know better than anyone, even if all the rice paddies of Japan were paved over to provide parking lots for supermarkets and large-scale stores, the US–Japan trade gap would hardly shrink because the United States is not much of an exporter of consumer goods.

It is highly significant in itself that the abrupt switch from the min-imizing friction theory to the enormously intrusive "structural" theory has not provoked a fundamental reappraisal of US–Japan relations by the two governments, or even by the usual experts at large. It reveals a cultural distance that is amazing in the age of rapid travel and instant telecommunications. After all, the first theory implied that all was well except for minor problems at the edges, while the second implies that the most drastic changes are required in Japanese society—changes that would dislocate the lives of tens of millions of people, and attack the very base of Japanese culture.

For what the Americans and Japanese promoters of SII define as mere "impediments" are actually surviving islands of tradition and tranquillity in a thoroughly confused society now undergoing frenetic change. True, less than 4.5 million Japanese are full-time rice farmers, but along with the millions who farm part-time, they are the ones who preserve the characteristic village-and-paddy scenery of Japan, and also many aspects of its traditional culture, with its crafts, heartily enjoyed festivals, and beloved folk songs. The importance of this rural culture in the moral economy of the Japanese—even urban Japanese, indeed especially urban Japanese—is far greater than the impact of high rice prices on steadily expanding family budgets.

There is nothing exotic about this preference for culture over efficiency. Certainly without rice protectionism, only the Japan of ugly, formless, and overcrowded cement conurbations, anodyne suburbs, modern mass-tourism resorts, and, of course, golf courses would remain, alongside an abandoned countryside. Japan is a rich country; it can afford to protect its rice farmers just as the French, Germans, and other Europeans protect their own small farmers—and the cost is well worth it to preserve the authenticity of rural life. But Europeans avoid the inanity of pleading the need for "food security," as the Japanese have done. From the European point of view, the vineyards of Provence, the mountain dairy farms of Bavaria, and the olive trees of Tuscany need no excuse. In highly advanced countries where less than 5% of the population works the land, the subsidized upkeep of agriculture resembles more and more the upkeep of national parks, and with equal justification.

Likewise, the million and a half mostly tiny shops and the tens of thousands of small-scale wholesalers and distributors are not only "impediments" to imports (because of the system of manufacturers' tied credits that few exporters can match) but also employ some 7 million Japanese, many of them too old for any other employment. If supermarkets and department stores were allowed to spread freely as in the United States, these old people would be condemned to the idle, empty lives of poor pensioners. With that, the already grim urban landscape would be further degraded by the disappearance of the cheerful little shops that enliven otherwise dreary streets and serve as informal social venues. It is not at all certain, moreover, that US exports would increase even if all the little shops were eliminated. After all, Japanese big business is far better placed to claim shelf place in the new supermarkets and department stores—owned, of course, by its own retail affiliates.

If the ultimate purpose of US–Japanese diplomacy and therefore of SII is to ensure the amity of the two peoples, it must be spectacularly counterproductive. So far, the negative impact of the trade imbalance has all been felt on the American side, with jobs lost or threatened, entire communities as well as industries forced into decline or actually extinguished, and the unease caused by the Japanese ownership of so many US banks, media companies, industrial corporations, transplant factories, office buildings, forest lands, golf courses, and even the Seattle Mariners baseball team. Now SII gives good reasons for many millions of Japanese—tens of millions adding relatives and sympathizers—to dislike the United States just as so many Americans already dislike Japan.

Every society can tolerate only so much *rapid* change, and that limit is always lower when the change is imposed by foreigners. The counterdoctrinal but very Japanese remedy of "managed trade," with trade imbalances reduced by political orders, would not cause any such social dislocations, nor the resulting animosities. Yet that remained an unthinkable remedy for the US government until most recently, because it clashes with the ideology of free trade, and ignores economic efficiency. At a time when Marxism–Leninism has collapsed because its subordination of culture and society to politics was finally recognized as inhumane, the ideology of free trade remains triumphant, even though it subordinates both culture and society to economic efficiency, as if Americans and Japanese were desperately poor and had no other choice.

■ TWO SOCIETIES IN CONFLICT

That the Structural Impediments Initiative subordinates society to economy makes it a foolish policy, but foolish policies can persist for years albeit at some great ultimate cost. What guaranteed that the "structural" stage and SII could not long endure is something else: the collapse of the Soviet Union. When the "structural" stage began in the mid-1980s, the Cold War was still at its peak. The new market-opening negotiations were unpromising from the start, and the American sense of shared economic interests with Japan was rapidly fading. But Japan was still a valued ally in the face of the Soviet threat, and that alliance kept US–Japanese relations on a tolerably even keel, though overt clashes were becoming more frequent. The "trade-friction" stage had lasted more than twenty-five years, but the "structural" stage would last less than five. Inevitably, when there was no longer a dangerous Soviet Union on the scene to suppress US–Japanese commercial quarrels, they emerged in full force and would no longer be contained by new promises of structural changes to come. Until then, American rancor over one-sided trade had aroused mostly incomprehension among the Japanese, who found it difficult to understand why the US government did not simply stop whatever imports it did not want, as Japan had been doing all along.

Had Gorbachev's policy of slow change under Communist party control been allowed to continue, thereby preserving the Soviet Union and thus at least some of the "Soviet threat," the equally slow process of SII would have had a chance. True, progress in opening the Japanese market has been small indeed. But if the Cold War had lingered, the United States would still have had a Chief Enemy in Moscow to focus on, and even meager SII results could have sufficed to contain anti-Japanese sentiments.

As it was, however, the total collapse of the Soviet Union left the United States without a Chief Enemy in working order. Japan's first misfortune is that it is now the only possible candidate for the role of America's Chief Enemy. Its second misfortune is that behind a conventional Western-style parliamentary-democracy facade, Japan does not have a government that can actually *make* decisions on any large matter, such as how to avoid a collision with the United States. It can only present decisions reached by a broad consensus that may never emerge, or at least not in useful time. Indeed, by Western standards, Japan scarcely has a government at all.[13] In the first instance, that political incapacity reflects the exceptional independence of the career bureaucrats who run the key ministries and agencies—their very real power to impose the "office view" on the politicians who serve as their ministers and nominal masters. Japanese practice thus inverts democratic theory, by which elected politicians who represent the voters are supposed to act on their behalf through the obedient civil (and military) servants of the state.

All over the world civil servants have many ways of delaying and deflecting policies they dislike while promoting the policies they prefer, but Japan's bureaucrats are in a class of their own. Greatly respected by society at large because of their strict selection on pure merit, they form a self-confident and often domineering elite as compared to the corrupt and therefore low-prestige politicians who usually keep their ministerial posts for only a year or two, and who cannot bring in their own followers to oversee the career officials. Only in the United States does each new administration appoint a cast of thousands to impose its own chosen policies on the bureaucracy. But in most democratic countries ministers have at least a small "political cabinet" staffed by their own followers, while prime ministers (and the president of France) can place their own aides in dozens of government posts. In Japan, on the other hand, career officials refuse to allow their ministries and agencies to be contaminated by the presence of political appointees. That alone effectively prevents most ministers from finding out what is going on under them, let alone dictate policies in detail. Among the few exceptions are ministers who were themselves civil servants and who thus still have bureaucratic prestige and bureaucratic allies of their own.

Both politicians and bureaucrats are tied to big business, but while politicians are little more than hirelings on the payroll, bureaucrats see themselves as the teachers and guides of Japanese society, including big business, which, however, they respect as the source of Japan's prosperity, and also as their future employers. *Amakudari,* "descent from heaven," is the revealing word for the retirement of senior bureaucrats into corporate jobs, sometimes top management positions but often mere sinecures.

When it comes to issues important for Japan's economy, as US–Japan questions mostly are, the politicians who happen to be serving as ministers in the government of the day generally follow the lead of the bureaucrats they are supposed to be directing, while the bureaucrats in turn consult big business and expert opinion before reaching a decision. But because the interests of different industries and different corporations are usually diverse and frequently contradictory, and experts often disagree, the bureaucrats will not pronounce until a consensus has emerged—a process that may take years, if a new consensus emerges at all; often it does not.

Procedurally, new policies are framed (after the required consensus has emerged) by interministerial committees staffed by senior officials. In reality, informal elite circles that meet at more or less regular intervals over dinner in hotel restaurants, Geisha restaurants (*ryotei*), and Tokyo's genuinely exclusive clubs are more consequential, because they are engaged in the actual business of consensus making.

Often centered on a group of university classmates (a solidarity that lasts for life), these informal gatherings are perhaps the truest government of Japan. Though by nature elitist, they do embrace the diverse sectors to which their members belong, so that research institutions, commerce, finance, and industry may all be represented, and not just government bureaucracies, or just big business. Some have chosen to depict this phenomenon as: (1) undemocratic, (2) uniquely Japanese, and (3) sinister. Evidently Japanese practice is being compared to American or European constitutional theory.

Actually all functioning societies have elites, and all successful societies have their own venues where members of diverse elites can communicate in some privacy. Even in the all-in-public United States, the meetings of the Council of Foreign Relations and others such are supplemented by more informal and more confidential gatherings; the British still have their country-house weekends and the major London clubs; German bankers and industrialists favor shooting parties in addition to the cozy meetings of their "industrial chambers"; and the members of different Italian elites assiduously attend the large and showy conferences that fill the Italian public calendar—and not for the sake of their mostly ceremonial formal sessions. Japanese elite gatherings differ only in their small scale, which rarely exceeds the mere dozen or so that classic *ryotei* rooms can accommodate; that, if anything, ensures a more democratic multiplicity of elite in-groups, because it takes many in-groups to form the required consensus. What the Japanese system does ensure, to a far greater extent than in any other democratic country, is that the official government is largely a facade.

Over the years, US presidents have kept asking successive Japanese prime ministers to do this or that, as if they had powers of decision comparable to those of European prime ministers, who are the actual heads of their governments and leaders of their parties. In Japan, however, prime ministers are at most leaders of one faction of the majority Liberal Democratic Party,[14] and they must share power with other factions. Some prime ministers, like Yasuhiro Nakasone (1982–1987) and Toshiki Kaifu (1989–1991), are not even that, but merely "shadow warriors" (*Kage musha*), front men chosen by more powerful faction leaders who do not want the hot seat, or cannot have it because of some too fresh involvement in one of the frequent "money politics" scandals. In any case, even a prime minister who is his own man, like Kiichi Myazawa, who replaced Kaifu in 1991, cannot order his fellow cabinet ministers to follow his lead, but can only solicit their support because each has his own factional backing and is not a mere appointee, as US cabinet members are.

Moreover, neither the prime minister nor the members of his cabinet can command the bureaucracy, but can only present their policy ideas, if any, to the various ministries and then await the agonizingly slow emergence of a consensus. Mostly, politicians do not even try to formulate policies. Instead they are content to represent the views of their officials in the cabinet and before parliament—not because they lack a taste for power but because they are mostly absorbed in the factional struggles that ravage the Liberal Democratic Party, as well as in their occasional electioneering and frequent embarrassments in scandals public and private. And bureaucrats, of course, prefer continuity rather than change, especially the sort of drastic change that would be needed to avoid a collision with the United States.

Hence the Japanese society that can only advance on a straight course was almost bound to collide with the American society that was actively if unconsciously searching for an enemy. Two things are remarkable about this highly avoidable outcome. First, neither Americans nor Japanese have even considered the hugely successful European formula for economic cooperation based on intersociety deals, not efficiency. If French and Germans had tried to perform intrusive SII-like surgery on each other, their armies would now probably be facing each other across the Rhine. Instead they supported—and support—each other's "impediments" (heavy industry, agriculture) through common European institutions, thus forcing the French and the Germans into the embrace of common interests. Second, there is a supreme irony in the fact that two of the world's least materialistic peoples are divided by economic quarrels.

Many Japanese and some Americans still seem to believe that cost/benefit calculations, i.e., the desirability of Japanese goods and Japanese investment, will prevent a breakdown in US–Japanese economic relations even without decisive action to open the Japanese market. Alas, societies in collision do not behave like prudent bookkeepers, for otherwise human history would have evolved far differently with neither a Second World War nor a First, and indeed with almost no wars at all.

With Japanese politicians unable to command the bureaucrats, and the bureaucrats unwilling to oppose the desires not only of big business but of almost any Japanese economic interest however narrow, the progress of SII has been agonizingly slow, as compared to what remains to be done. The *1989 National Trade Estimate Report on Foreign Trade Barriers* of the US Trade Representative still listed unresolved "impediments" that were preventing or diminishing US exports of: cigarettes, leather goods, wood and paper products, aluminum, agricultural products in general, feedgrains, telecommunications equipment, pharmaceuticals, medical equipment, food additives, supercomputers, satellites, construction and engineering, legal services, insurance, high-cube containers, semiconductors, TRON real-time operating systems nuceli, optical fibers, aerospace, auto parts, and soda ash—because of every possible barrier ever invented to stop or impede imports, whether openly published, such as tariffs, quotas, outright prohibitions, arbitrary regulations, the Large-Scale Retail Store Law, etc.; or covert, denied, or at least unacknowledged, such as collusion between big-business corporate families, government procurement practices and preferences, and many different unwritten restrictions on marketing methods, promotion techniques, etc.

Over and above all that, already amply sufficient to fuel a trade war, the 1989 Report denounced the "pernicious administration" of the Japanese patent office, which routinely held up US applications, usually to buy time for Japanese competitors to research and develop their own way around the patent; the delay in registering trademarks, for a similar purpose; and the inadequate protection of sound-recording copyrights. By 1992, the ill-feelings caused by the disappointing outcome of the second, "structural," stage in US–Japan relations had definitely given way to a third stage of society-to-society confrontation, marked most visibly by the debacle of the December 1991 visit to Japan of President Bush. But the turning point from an imperfect amity to a barely controlled animosity had already been passed by 1989 at the latest. The episode is worth recalling at length for it illustrates how Americans and Japanese go about the business of agreeing or disagreeing with each other, and more broadly how very peculiar US–Japanese dealings truly are.

■ FSX, OR THE DOWNFALL OF GEOPOLITICS

It is fitting that a historical turning point of our most unromantic age should be linked to the cold acronym FSX, so lacking in the resonance of "The French Revolution" and others such. FSX stands for "Fighter, Support, Experimental," specifically a projected Japanese fighter for the late 1990s. What reveals the FSX controversy as a major turning point is its outright reversal of American priorities. For thirty years, the dominant concern of the US government had been that Japan should have an effective air force, no matter how its fighters were made and by whom. By the end of the controversy, only the impact of the project on the US economy was of any real interest. Before the controversy, the critical technology-transfer concern was that US civilian technology might be diverted for military purposes. By the end, it was the opposite diversion, from military to civilian purposes, that was the only real concern.

Not a country of maverick individualists, Japan famously operates by consensus. But when the cherished goal of developing an all-Japanese fighter became a definite plan, the FSX project did have a leader, Tsutsui Ryozo, then technical director of the "Air Self-Defense Force," Japan's euphemism for its air force. Tsutsui-*san*[15] lacks neither charm nor patience, but both were to be sorely tested when his once-obscure project exploded into a huge US–Japanese controversy, marked by bitter public accusation, and one of the most strident congressional debates in years.

By the time the FSX project was started in a small way in the mid-1980s, the Japanese companies that had produced most of the combat aircraft of the Second World War, Fuji, Kawasaki, and, above all, Mitsubishi,[16] had long since been revived to form the core of an aerospace industry that also includes Nissan, the car company that also makes space rocket-boosters, and the military segments of the electronics giants Fujitsu, Hitachi, Mitsubishi Electric, and Toshiba, all much better known for the civilian products that account for the vast majority of their sales. Over the years, Japan's aviation industry had built some transports, executive jets, unusual amphibian aircraft, and jet trainers/light fighters of their own design, but mostly they manufactured American-developed combat aircraft under license.[17]

At the outset of Japan's rearmament in the late 1950s, that arrangement was most satisfactory for both sides. By the 1980s, however, it satisfied neither side. From the US point of view, licensed production had once been indispensable to allow the poor Japan of the 1950s to acquire combat aircraft that it could not afford to import outright. There is rich irony in the fear of many Americans today that the

Japanese aerospace industry could become a formidable competitor, for its very existence is the result of deliberate American policies. By the time Japan surrendered in August 1945, little remained of the much-bombed aircraft factories and their reconstruction was out of the question: by order of General Douglas MacArthur, the unchallenged shogun of the US occupation, Japan was to completely abandon the manufacture of all weapons of war for all time.

But his eternal decree did not last even five years. When North Korean troops swept across the 48th parallel on Sunday, June 25, 1950, to invade South Korea, they did more than start a local war. They abruptly transformed the Cold War from a political struggle waged by diplomacy, propaganda, and secret operations into a military confrontation that threatened to explode in concurrent European and East Asian wars. With only occupation troops and the dubiously usable fission bomb in hand to resist Stalin's armies, a then demobilized United States launched its own frantic rearmament[18] and tried to muster all possible strength from allies old and new.

In Japan as in Europe, only the rebuilding of local military strength could relieve the burden on the armed forces of the United States. And unless they could be equipped with weapons produced by their own factories, allied forces could only be armed with American weapons, in scarce supply during the Korean War itself, and always costly to the US taxpayer.[19] To encourage the rapid growth of aircraft as well as all other military production, the United States supplied its allies with large quantities of machinery under various aid programs, gave away government-owned weapon blueprints, and actively encouraged US companies to be liberal in licensing their own technology, asking them to provide detailed, factory-floor production skills as well as the designs themselves.

At the same time, the United States turned to the local industries already in place, but idled by the lack of demand, to purchase whatever could be of use for the great rearmament effort. In the case of Japan, it is universally agreed that its great economic upsurge was started off by the wave of American military buying of 1950 to 1953, which revived industries both heavy and light, from shipbuilding (for landing craft) to textiles (for uniforms).

That these measures would inevitably strengthen the civilian industry of allied countries hardly distressed the American policy officials of the time. As they saw it, the more prosperous a country's economy, the greater would be its potential to contribute to the overall strength of the Western alliance. Driven by the urgency of alliance-building, and re-assured by the general belief that the United States was in any case destined to remain the world's largest net exporter of both agricultural and industrial goods, a narrowly "geopolitical" outlook became the rule in Washington, for the first time in American history except for the two world wars.[20]

In that world view, military and diplomatic goals entirely dominated foreign policy, with economic calculations considered only insofar as they defined the resource limits of rearmament. And those calculations were uncontaminated by any trace of un-American pessimism about the future of the US economy, or indeed any long-term perspective at all. True, it was hardly feckless to disregard the trade balance during the first postwar decade, when the US trade surplus was huge and US exports were only limited by the worldwide "dollar shortage," the result of the world's seemingly insatiable demand for the products of American factories and farms. But when the first trade deficits were recorded even before the end of the 1950s, priorities in Washington remained quite unchanged.[21]

Later, as Japan became a great exporting nation less and less in need of saving hard currency, the State and Defense departments continued to focus exclusively on the purely strategic aim of strengthening the Japanese armed forces without regard to where their aircraft came from, but others—including a growing number in Congress—disagreed more and more loudly. In their view, licensed manufacture was dis-placing possible exports of complete aircraft to a country greatly dis-inclined to import any civilian goods.[22]

From the viewpoint of Japanese industry, on the other hand, the licensed production of military aircraft already fully engineered in the United States was a better bargain than self-sufficiency. While it did of course restrict opportunities for local design and engineering, the trans-fer of American know-how introduced advanced metalworking meth-ods and new skills in the assembly of complex electronic and mechanical components—as well as high standards in quality control across the board.

By the 1980s, however, the Japanese no longer needed to be taught quality control, metalworking, or anything at all to do with electronics. True, the complexity of combat aircraft had continued to increase, and by then Japan was producing two of the most complex of all, the P-3C antisubmarine patrol aircraft and the F-15 heavyweight fighter, the latter turned out by the aviation department of Mitsubishi Heavy Industries, Japan's "fighter house" still widely remembered for its formidable *zero-sen* of the Second World War.

To manufacture F-15s or P-3Cs was not child's play, but it was no longer man's work either for an industry that had by then nurtured far greater ambitions. To go on cutting metal along templates that others had designed no longer satisfied Mitsubishi engineers eager to design complete combat aircraft once again. Likewise, their colleagues at Mitsubishi Electric had an advanced "phased array" radar design ripe for engineering in detail; Fuji Heavy Industries (another producer of combat aircraft till 1945) had a new technique to build airframe structures out of carbon-fiber composites instead of aluminum; Ishikawajima-Harima (Japan's leading manufacturer of licensed engines) dreamed of developing its own jet engines at last; and the electronics giants were especially frustrated by their confinement to the assembly of American-developed electronics.

Hence Mitsubishi and its potential subcontractors powerfully encouraged Tsutsui Ryozo and his colleagues when at last they set out to initiate the development of an advanced all-Japanese fighter in its totality—wings and fuselage, engine and radar, flight avionics, electronic warfare devices, and all ground equipment. An all-Japanese FSX would transform Japan's aerospace industry and more than that, for the making of all the diverse parts of a contemporary jet fighter from scratch requires an entire structure of laboratories, test facilities, materials plants, and specialized component plants, in addition to the tooling, workshops, and assembly lines that suffice to manufacture aircraft already fully engineered by others.

What then ensued, however, was not a fighter program but a highly emotional drama in three acts. First there was heated debate within Japan itself, because the aviation industry and government officials of Tsutsui's persuasion were confronted by the strong opposition of the prestigious Foreign Ministry, the *Gaimusho*. Very much aware of Japan's dependence on both American strategic protection and American markets, the diplomats feared that to insist on self-sufficiency in combat aircraft might inspire Americans to cultivate some self-sufficiency of their own, both in strategy and in commerce. With Soviet military aggrandizement then still at its historic culminating point, it was not the time to weaken the American inclination to defend Japan with its aircraft carriers, fighter wings, Marine division, and a shadowy but still invaluable nuclear guarantee. And with protectionist sentiment already rising in the United States, it was not the time to advertise a desire to close an important market to American exports.

The *Gaimusho* is far more powerful in the governance of Japan than Tsutsui's Air Self-Defense Force, but in policy fights it is often outmatched in turn by an even more powerful force: MITI, the Ministry of International Trade and Industry. The supposed guiding spirit of Japanese industry, greatly feared by business worldwide for its supposedly predatory inclinations, MITI could have played the castle in the FSX chess game, to support the Air Self-Defense Force pawn against the *Gaimusho*'s bishop.

As the most nationalist of Japanese ministries (its officials have been known to declaim old antiforeigner slogans, only half in jest),[23] remarkably persistent in favoring self-sufficiency in all things, and specifically the leading governmental promoter of Japan's technological advancement, MITI could have been expected to support Tsutsui's plan with much enthusiasm. Certainly there were close links with Tsutsui, because the otherwise very civilian MITI has much influence over the acquisition of military equipment. Capitalizing on the lifelong loyalty of bureaucrats to the ministry in which they begin (and usually end) their careers, MITI has colonized the major equipment-buying offices of Japan's military establishment by securing those positions for its own "detached" officials—who nevertheless remain MITI-men first and last.

MITI has been fundamentally interested in civilian rather than military industry of any kind, but the development of an all-Japanese FSX by Mitsubishi would make it that much easier to develop civilian aircraft in its wake. That potential "spin-off" could be expected to interest the ministry much more than the fighter itself. On the other hand, the spin-off approach is not MITI's favorite way of doing things: its officials firmly believe that the way to do something for industry is to do it, rather than to rely either on spontaneous market forces or the incidental side effects of a military project.

In any case, while MITI's Aviation and Ordnance section supported Tsutsui's plan, the higher-ranking International Trade Policy Bureau did not, again because of the American protectionist reactions it might cause. Thus the castle was reluctant to shield the pawn against the bishop in the FSX chess game of the competing bureaucracies.

The diplomats also had many allies in and out of Japan's government who disliked the FSX because they dislike any growth in the still very small military industry (which accounts for only 0.1% of the Japanese work force).[24] Many Japanese in and out of government, old and young, share a healthy phobia against all things military, because they know that Japanese institutions tend to have better engines than brakes, and they remember how the fast driving of the 1930s resulted in the fiery crash of 1945. In this case, the fear was that a more prosperous military-aviation industry that employed more people would inevitably increase the overall weight of the military interest in Japanese politics. Militarism is by no stretch of the imagination a potent force in Japan, but that remains true precisely because it has been very actively resisted. Even the decision in principle to allow not more than 2,000 Japanese troops to take part in UN "peacekeeping" missions was hugely controversial, and the Diet only passed a law to that effect in June 1992 after many safeguards were added (excluding any combat role, among other things). It is not only leftists who believe that the same qualities of discipline and loyalty that make Japanese corporations so successful can be acutely dangerous when the disciplined loyalists are armed.

The plan for an all-Japanese FSX therefore encountered much resistance within Japan itself. As so often happens in all countries, however, the narrow-deep interest of the FSX enthusiasts prevailed over the broad but diffused concerns of their opponents. Hence, by June 1987, the decision to proceed with the aircraft was all but made.[25]

With that Act Two began, this time in the United States. American diplomats and defense officials had campaigned against the FSX from the start, though only very quietly to avoid offense. In gentle little chats with their Japanese counterparts, they did not even try to propose the straight purchase of US-made fighters, as many members of Congress and Americans at large would have wanted. That, the Japan specialists believed (as is their wont), was a futile, "nonnegotiable" aim.[26] Instead they argued that Mitsubishi should codevelop the new fighter with a US aerospace company, rather than go it alone.

Because there was no possibility that the US government would fund the American half of an entirely new fighter specifically designed to meet Japanese requirements, "codevelopment" would mean in practice that the two partners would jointly upgrade an existing US fighter. The leading candidate was the F-16 Falcon, a machine already successful enough, yet ripe for drastic enhancements. Its manufacturer, General Dynamics, had long been trying to obtain US or European funding for a new Agile Falcon with larger wings for more range/payload, and even more "bells and whistles," i.e., electronic devices. By having the Japanese reengineer the F-16 with General Dynamics, the United States would not entirely lose the Japanese fighter market, Japanese industry would still be able to progress far beyond mere licensed production, the US Air Force would have a new option for its own procurement, and the US government would acquire a new aircraft for export (if Japan retained its own prohibition on all weapon exports). All in all, a codeveloped FSX might be almost as good a deal as straight exports to Japan, except for the (disregarded) loss of production jobs.

When US officials and industry executives heard from their own contacts of the imminent decision to go ahead with all-Japanese FSX, their patience and their discretion both came to an end. Leading figures in Congress were immediately informed, and their reaction was nothing short of vehement. The United States was doing so much for Japan, they cried, yet the ungrateful Japanese would not even purchase fighter aircraft in small recompense for their protection, and in exchange for their access to rich American markets.

Tempers were not improved by rumors reaching Washington that Tsutsui and his colleagues were claiming that an all-Japanese FSX would be technologically superior to any codeveloped fighter, a claim that had to be dismissed as arrogant bravado because the Japanese had not even built a prototype as yet—but which was nevertheless infuriatingly credible to the many on Capitol Hill who prefer to drive Japanese cars, watch Japanese television sets, and use Japanese office machines.

Tsutsui had not in fact been so immodest. His claim was that only a new design could meet the very specific Japanese requirement for an aircraft capable of attacking the ships of a Soviet invasion fleet with rather heavy missiles. Among other things, that called for two jet engines for greater safety over water—a preference shared by the US Navy. On the other hand, Tsutsui simply ignored the existence of a ready-made US aircraft highly suitable for that very purpose, the Navy's F/A-18, in which the A stands for attack, and which does have two engines as well as a sufficient range and payload to have met the Japanese requirement.

As it happened, the times were exceptionally inauspicious for any congressional benevolence toward an all-Japanese FSX. The tide of Japanese imports was rising ever higher to reach the inordinate annual level of $85 billion by the end of 1987.[27] Conversely, American would-be exporters to Japan were complaining more loudly than ever that their efforts were being frustrated by customs-house conspiracies. Those trade quarrels involved billions of dollars and tens of thousands of jobs, yet it was an utterly insignificant $20 million Japanese export, not to the United States but to the Soviet Union, that was then causing the greatest outrage.

A Toshiba subsidiary had conspired with the state-owned Norwegian Kongsberg weapon factory to sell highly advanced metal-milling machines to the Soviet Union. Those machines are used to smooth to the nth degree the surfaces of metal objects of complex shape, and Soviet factories could have used them to polish any number of much-needed goods. As it happens, however, they were actually employed to minimize the asperities of Soviet submarine propellors—huge metal castings weighing tons—thereby drastically reducing their tell-tale "cavitation" noise. Submarine warfare is the warfare of the blind, in which victory goes to the most silent boat with the best sonar ears. The quieter boat is not only harder to detect but can also use its own sonar with less own-noise interference.

The sale had been made in 1981, the machines were delivered in 1983 and 1985,[28] and Western navies had just started to report a sudden downfall in their ability to detect the newest Soviet submarines, when a Japanese executive less than typically loyal to his company revealed the reason. The scandal exploded in 1987, just in time to prepare the worst possible reception for an all-Japanese FSX. As the company far more active in military production and thus presumably more cognizant of what it was doing, Kongsberg was certainly more guilty than Toshiba. And it was a Japanese and not a Norwegian who spilled the beans. Yet the fury was directed at Japan, for reasons all too obvious: it is certainly not the Norwegians who highlight American economic inadequacies by defeating American primacy in one industry after another. While some members of Congress colorfully smashed Toshiba television sets on the steps of the Capitol, many more prepared to smash the FSX, by threatening all manner of retaliation in commerce and strategy alike.

Japan's diplomats in Washington did not fail to report the ugly mood of Congress: punitive trade measures unthinkable till then had suddenly become possible. Concurrently, US officials high and low transmitted their own warnings of imminent congressional mayhem to

Tokyo, mostly in very proper "more in sorrow than in anger" tones, heard not least from those very officials who had been most active in pouring gasoline on the congressional fires. Finally, the great regiment of Washington lobbyists, consultants, and political lawyers in the pay of Japanese corporations and the competing Japanese bureaucracies[29] kept their handlers fully briefed as always, this time to alert them that terrible events were about to unfold.

Their alarm had sharp personal undertones: of late, quite a few lobbyists for Japanese interests had noticed that their visits to government officials and formerly expansive congressional buddies were greeted with increasing suspicion. Lists were being compiled of Washington notables on Japanese payrolls, and soon they would feature in magazine articles largely made up of such lists. In one respected weekly, the cover was suitably decorated with a flaming red sun that almost covered a map of the United States to headline the story "Yen for Power," whose subtitle accurately announced the contents: "In think tanks, universities, corporations, and Washington law offices, Japanese money is reinforcing one side of the debate on trade, industry, and America's future—and is creating a subtle climate of corruption." Names were then duly named.[30]

Once these urgent warnings reached Tokyo, the *Gaimusho* had all the evidence it needed to prove its long-held claim that an all-Japanese FSX could undermine the entire, precious relationship with the United States. With MITI uncharacteristically passive, the *Boecho,* Japan's Defense Agency (not ministry), had to fight the *Gaimusho* on its own, and the match was most uneven. In spite of the passage of decades, Japanese military institutions must still expiate the shame of their 1945 defeat in traditional fashion, by keeping a low posture. What truly guarantees the *Boecho*'s bureaucratic inferiority, however, is a uniquely Japanese phenomenon, the recruitment pecking order. While the *Gaimusho* has always been able to recruit its aspiring young diplomats from the top-scoring graduates of the most prestigious Japanese universities, the *Boecho* is mostly staffed by the alumni of lesser institutions—and that critically affects its social prestige and bureaucratic influence.

In no other country are universities ranked so precisely, from the two formerly "imperial" state universities of Tokyo (*Todai*[31]) and Kyoto (though the private Waseda is becoming a real challenger) down through other universities, public, private, national, and city. And in only a few countries do graduation rankings matter so much beyond strictly academic circles. Above all, in no other country does the prestige of government departments and even private companies critically depend on the exact nature of the university degrees of their officials or executives. In Japan, however, respect for education amounts to a veritable secular religion, and the *Gaimusho* is the leading beneficiary immediately after the high-prestige Ministry of Finance—not least in its frequent struggles with MITI.[32]

With the *Gaimusho* taking the lead, by July 1987 Tokyo's leading informal policy groups had reached an anti-FSX consensus. At that point, with the *Boecho* easily defeated, all that was needed was to impose the consensus on the *Gaimusho*'s nominal political masters, the ministers of the Nakasone government then in office.[33] As noted, only a few ministers or even prime ministers have any real power on large questions, as the FSX certainly was, and they are mostly former civil servants who can still rely on their bureaucratic prestige and bureaucratic allies. One of these exceptions, Noboru Takeshita, was later to intervene at a crucial moment, with decisive effect.

The one valid role for political leaders in the governance of Japan is to represent powerful voting blocs (e.g., the rice farmers) and such minor business interests that the bureaucracy does not already adequately represent for some reason or other. Mitsubishi, however, was not in that category, being, on the one hand, very well represented as a top class *keiretsu*, and, on the other, rather ambivalent about the FSX. Had the entire family of Mitsubishi corporations decided to support the house aviation company with all its vast resources and immense prestige, the anti-FSX forces might have been faced with a far greater power than the *Boecho* and Tsutsui's cohort of aviation enthusiasts could ever had hoped to muster.

But even the multibillion dollar FSX revenues over ten years were little more than small change in the Mitsubishi universe, in which aside from the Mitsubishi Bank (the world's third largest bank on a deposits basis) and Mitsubishi Trust and Banking (the fourteenth), the *annual* sales of the three largest industrial companies alone, Mitsubishi Electric, Mitsubishi Motors, and Mitsubishi Heavy Industries, already then exceeded $40 billion. Because a good part of their export sales would have been endangered by American protectionist reactions, the commercial arithmetic of the House of Mitsubishi went against the FSX. Thus the hapless politicians of the Nakasone government were spared the agony of being the objects of an epic policy struggle between forces more powerful than themselves.

Act Two thus came to an end in September 1987, when Yuko Kurihara, then head of the *Boecho,* announced during a Washington visit that Japan had accepted the codevelopment formula advocated by US officials all along. Mitsubishi Heavy Industries and its subcontractors would radically upgrade the F-16 Falcon in conjunction with its original developer, General Dynamics. The latter would receive a license fee for the technology of the original aircraft, and would share with its own subcontractors in the engineering work needed to turn the F-16 into the FSX, whose cost was estimated to exceed $1 billion. Finally, the US government would have free access to the new technology developed by the American partners though paid for by Japan, and it would also be allowed to purchase any Japanese-developed technology incorporated into the FSX.

Caspar Weinberger, then secretary of defense, was jubilant, and quite certain that the victory had been won because of his own lawyerly skills in persuading the Japanese politicians he had met of late.[34] Of course he had been briefed about Japan's politics as well as the FSX; and he may even have been told of the various stages of consensus-building that were going on behind the scenes, but which occasionally surfaced in public remarks. But transcultural communication is a tricky thing. Especially in regard to Japan, Americans may learn that this or that is true, and yet finally not accept it as *the* truth, because matters are done otherwise in the United States. Like other high US officials before him, Weinberger evidently could not free himself of the delusion that his Japanese counterparts had powers of decision similar to his own, and could therefore believe that *he* had won, and not Japan's own anti-FSX forces.

Tsutsui and his fellow fighter enthusiasts in the Air Self-Defense Force, in the *Boecho* as a whole, and throughout the aviation industry were obviously most unhappy with the outcome of Act Two. But the deed was done and the time had come to begin work after so many years of talk. Before the engineers could begin their labors, however, General Dynamics and Mitsubishi Heavy Industries had to negotiate the highly complicated commercial contracts that would define the work of each side, the payments for themselves and their subcontractors, and the required technology-sharing procedures. And that negotiation in turn could not begin until the two governments had first drafted a sufficiently detailed Memorandum of Understanding—that MOU would add all the necessary fine print to the generalities of the Kurihara promises of September 1987.

It turned out that to reach agreement on the exact terms of the MOU was far from easy. On the American side, the State Department and Pentagon negotiators were uneasy about the vague definition of the development work-shares for each side, loosely stated by Kurihara at "between 35 and 45%." Moreover, in the wake of the Toshiba/Kongsberg submarine disaster, the technology-control office of the Pentagon wanted assurances that the Japanese would take great care to preserve the secrecy of the technical novelties that would go into the FSX. On the Japanese side, on the other hand, the career bureaucrats sent to negotiate the MOU discovered that Kurihara had exceeded his brief in promising free US access even to purely Japanese technology, or else that the Americans had misunderstood his polite nods as a valid promise (which, of course, only they could actually sanction). Weinberger thought that he had won the war. He had not. And it had not been a war, but only a skirmish.

Not until November 1988, in the final weeks of the Reagan administration, was the MOU finally signed by the two sides. Now at last General Dynamics and Mitsubishi could start their own bargaining over the terms that would allow the engineers to begin their years of work.

There was, however, one more hurdle to be overcome before the companies could start to negotiate: as with any other arms deal of any size, the US Senate could stop the MOU by passing a motion of disapproval within thirty days of its formal presentation. Many senators had been dangerously aroused by Act One, but it seemed unlikely that the MOU would encounter fresh trouble in that final scene of Act Two. After all, the State Department and the Pentagon had obviously taken their time to negotiate the MOU very carefully. And Reagan's last secretary of defense, Frank Carlucci—widely respected, unlike his predecessor—strongly endorsed the agreement, as did the equally respected Secretary of State George Shultz.

In any case, the 1988 general election had just ended and it was unlikely that the Senate would choose to immerse itself in the technicalities of the FSX upon reconvening—not with the far juicier confirmation hearings for the new appointees of the Bush administration coming up. And, indeed, once President Bush was inaugurated in January 1989, most Senators seemed much more interested in the life and loves of John G. Tower, the supposedly hard-drinking and womanizing intended secretary of defense, than in the carbon composites and electronic secrets of the FSX. Only twenty-one Senators declared their opposition to the MOU, a small number given the Democratic majority and all the prior excitements.[35]

Thus there was not supposed to be an Act Three at all, and, indeed, when it started, the new attack on the FSX agreement came from an entirely unexpected direction. In February 1989, while the Bush administration was still being formed, with most of its key officials not yet confirmed by Congress and many not even nominated, Robert A. Mosbacher, the new secretary of commerce, strongly objected to the MOU and flatly declared that it should be renegotiated. When the news of Mosbacher's first sally leaked out, veteran Washington observers were at first amazed, and then dismissive. The Commerce Department had always been low on the Washington totem pole, and had always before lacked the staff expertise to challenge the combined wisdom of the State Department and Pentagon over matters both foreign and military, such as the FSX.

As for Mosbacher himself, a remarkably handsome Texas oil man of great wealth, he was widely regarded as an amiable mediocrity who owed his appointment entirely to his services to the Bush campaign (he had been the finance chairman). Presidents normally reward financial helpers with reasonably glamorous ambassadorships far removed from serious policymaking, and as a sometimes sailing partner of King Juan Carlos of Spain, Mosbacher had been expected to go to Madrid. It was known that Mosbacher was a personal friend of the president and might thus be influential in some way, but he was also thought to lack the intellectual authority to take on diplomats and defense officials over a question as complicated as the FSX.

The Japanese were at first shocked by Mosbacher's intervention, but were then reassured to hear from their Washington lawyers and consultants that Mosbacher was a lightweight, and that his challenge of the MOU would quickly be silenced by Secretary of State James Baker (also the president's friend) with the full support of the Japan specialists in both the Pentagon and the State Department. That was a reassurance greatly welcomed by Nakasone's successor as Japan's prime minister, Noboru Takeshita,[36] who had an exceptional need for smooth US–Japanese relations.

When Takeshita traveled to Washington in February 1989 for a postinauguration visit with the new president, the home replay of the resulting imagery of a statesman engaged in statecraft was even more valuable politically than usual for him: his government was already ravaged by the *Recruit* "money-politics" bribery scandal that would eventually destroy it in a humiliating debacle.[37] While in Washington, Takeshita declared that it was imperative that the MOU be finally approved by Congress by March 31, the last day in Japan's fiscal year, for otherwise the first contract to Mitsubishi could not be issued until the new budget would be approved, several months later, leaving Mitsubishi engineers idle in the meanwhile. The US government's Japan specialists heartily agreed, warning all and sundry that with a general election imminent, the downfall of Takeshita might lead to a Socialist victory, which would endanger the entire alliance relationship after four decades of close US–Japanese cooperation.

Even if he was the president's friend, it thus seemed impossible that Mosbacher, the untaught Texan, would be allowed to blunder his way into a matter as sensitive as the FSX, at such an exceptionally delicate time. But that is exactly what happened—and with decisive effect. In public and in National Security Council meetings behind closed doors, Mosbacher persistently argued that the MOU was fatally flawed because its State and Pentagon negotiators had treated the FSX largely as a foreign-policy and defense issue, when in fact it was just as much an industrial issue.[38]

Adopting the language of his opponents, Mosbacher pointed out that in the presence of a much diminished military threat from Gorbachev's retreating Soviet Union, economic considerations should logically rise in priority—and the MOU as it stood did not reflect that change. Specifically, the "about" 35% to 40% work-share for General Dynamics and its American subcontractors established by the MOU was secured only for the *development* of the aircraft, and not for its production thereafter. Hence the agreement was worth only half the $1 billion originally advertised by Weinberger in the wake of the Kurihara promise. Mosbacher insisted on a guaranteed 40% share of production as well as development, which would provide $2–2.5 billion of work on the envisaged 130 FSX fighters, almost as much as the outright sale of 130 cheaper F-16s.[39]

Beyond that, Mosbacher and Under Secretary Dennis Kloske had spotted what most of the experts had missed: the question of production aside, there was a crucial difference between "about 35% to 40%"

and a flat 40%, and it was *not* a matter of assuring an extra 5% of work and money for American industry. In the building of modern fighters, the airframe, the engine, and the electronics each account for roughly one-third of the total cost. With 65% of the total project budget, the Japanese side could just about squeeze in the engine, as well as much of the electronics and some of the airframe modifications; but with 5% less, the engine would have to remain for the American side—a decisive advantage in retaining control of the entire project.

Finally, Mosbacher and his advisers surprised the experts even more by delving into the technicalities of the know-how that should and should not be transferred—hardly *small* technicalities because they might yet determine the future of the American aircraft industry, civilian as well as military. The F-16 is a "fly-by-wire" aircraft, which means much more than the replacement of hydraulic and mechanical links to the ailerons, tailplane, flaps, and other control surfaces by electrical wires. Such wires are much lighter, cheaper, and more easily safeguarded by redundancy, but wires alone would still leave the pilot with the task of aiming the aircraft's flight in this way or that by moving the control surfaces, often then having to correct the joystick commands to compensate for momentum as well as leads and lags in the aircraft's response. With "fly-by-wire," by contrast, joystick commands do not go straight to the actuators that physically move the control surfaces. Instead, they are fed to a flight-control computer, which continuously receives updates on the aircraft's movement through the air, and which can therefore convert joystick commands as required, to immediately obtain the desired response by the aircraft.

That crown jewel of American aviation technology made the F-16 vastly superior to Soviet fighters otherwise beautifully designed for air combat such as the MiG-29 and Su-27. And that same computer technology allows civilian jetliners to be flown more safely and more economically than with any manual system. The secret is not in the computer itself but at the heart of the very intricate software, the "source codes"—and that was a technology that Mosbacher was determined to keep for the United States, along with that other crown jewel, the "hot section" core of the jet engine. To be sure, the F-16/FSX needed its fly-by-wire computer to fly at all, but for that there was a simple solution: the United States would supply the computer, but only as a "black box" already programmed for use by the pilot, without supplying the source codes.

In spite of the strongest State Department and Pentagon objections, by mid-February 1989 Mosbacher won a three-week delay in the submission of the MOU to the Senate, to allow him to document his criticisms and draft remedies to be negotiated with the Japanese.[40] By early March 1989, Mosbacher had persuaded the president to make his own position the policy of the United States, and by the end of that month a first attempt at a fresh negotiation with Nishihiro Seiko, the *Boecho*'s deputy director, had failed in the face of Japanese resistance.

The Takeshita government was by then in great peril, but Mosbacher had demolished the State/Pentagon claims that the original MOU was satisfactory, and the Bush administration now held firm to Mosbacher's demands: the 40% share of production and the withholding of the source codes and engine core.[41] In what had by then become a very public quarrel—certainly the loudest US–Japanese controversy since 1945—Kichiro Tazawa, one more of the *Boecho*'s ephemeral director-generals, bitterly complained to the press that Washington was repudiating an agreement already signed, sealed, and delivered, implying that Japan would refuse to change the terms of the MOU.[42]

That reflected Tokyo bureaucratic realities. Industry and Tsutsui's band of do-it-yourself enthusiasts were so outraged by Mosbacher's additional demands that even the *Gaimusho* hesitated to press their acceptance. Diplomats generally favor acceptance in most things, but they do not favor the breaking of agreements, and now the precious consensus on a codeveloped FSX had been shattered by the United States breaking a fully negotiated agreement. In other words, the transcultural difficulty was on the Japanese side this time: having learned and relearned the truth that the US Congress really does decide on matters, many Japanese officials ultimately do not accept that truth, because their own Diet is so powerless by standards of any Western parliament, let alone the US Congress.

As the dispute became more bitter, newspapers in the United States were filled with opinion pieces pro and con, some of which were clearly written in Japan's paid service, while others did not refrain from evoking the specter of Japanese militarism.[43] As for the Japanese media, they vehemently criticized the Bush administration's reversal of Reagan's policy on the FSX, as might have been expected. But the most important result of the abundance of new information coming out on the details of the FSX deal was to expand the ranks of its critics on Capitol Hill. Among other things, many in Congress were outraged to discover that General Dynamics would receive a license fee of $1 million for each aircraft built—a sum both outrageously large, inasmuch as it would go to a private company while the F-16 had originally been developed at the taxpayers' expense, and also outrageously small, given the multibillion dollar technologies contained in the aircraft. And that was only one complaint in a flood of angry charges. A news headline of the time captured the moment: "An unbuilt military aircraft may be about to send the American–Japanese alliance into a tailspin."[44]

For that very reason, no doubt, i.e., the imminent possibility that the alliance could indeed be fatally damaged, the negotiations made rapid progress even as the public quarrel reached its climax. That was largely due to the decision of Prime Minister Takeshita to settle the issue once and for all, even if all the latest American demands had to be accepted. Weakened though he was by the *Recruit* scandal, Takeshita was an exceptionally powerful figure by the standards of Japanese politicians— certainly altogether more powerful than his predecessor, the much-publicized Yasuhiro Nakasone.

In the United States, Nakasone's influential academic contacts had persuaded the press that he was most unlike previous Japanese prime ministers—not one more colorless and feeble compromiser thrown up by the factional intrigues of the ruling party but a true leader, decisive, outspoken, charismatic, and uniquely capable of imposing his will on recalcitrant bureaucrats. The unusually tall and handsome Nakasone was certainly cut out for the role in American eyes—he *looked* like a leader. Moreover, he liked to be photographed in traditional dress, incidentally reminding Americans of the supremely decisive heroes of samurai films.

American media, not notably well informed on Japanese politics, duly made much of Nakasone. In the many articles that appeared at the time, often decorated with well-chosen photographs, the key theme was the parallel between Japan's new status as an acknowledged economic superpower and Nakasone's new status as a world-class leader. Largely because of this, President Ronald Reagan went out of his way to cultivate Nakasone as no Japanese prime minister had ever been cultivated before, and again the press made much of the "Ron–Yasu" relationship, from which great things were expected—specifically an end to the persistent inability of Japanese leaders to impose their supposedly free-trade ideas on MITI and the rest of the economic bureaucracy.

Behind Nakasone's impressive image, however, there was a sad political reality: though indeed talented and energetic, Nakasone simply lacked the power to have his way with the fellow politicians of his own cabinet, let alone the bureaucrats. Actually he had less power than some of his most "colorless" predecessors. As the leader of a very small faction of the Liberal Democratic Party, he was not his own boss but only the chosen front man (*kage musha*, "shadow warrior") of the large Tanaka faction,[45] which at the time happened to lack a suitable candidate of its own for the prime ministership. That support was so effective that Nakasone's tenure as prime minister was exceptionally long,[46] but it also tied his hands because the Tanaka faction would not let him have any real control over the Ministry of Finance, depriving him of the power of the purse. By American or European standards, that meant that he was not a head of government at all, because it is by the purse that governments govern, except in unfortunate countries where bayonets (or machine guns) enforce the ruler's will.

As compared to Nakasone, Takeshita's image and public-relations machine was feeble indeed, but his actual power was altogether greater because his own faction controlled the balance of power within the ruling party. Thus when Takeshita finally decided in April 1989 to finish with the FSX imbroglio, he was able to force the divided bureaucracy to accept his decision.

Even so, it was not entirely by compromise that the new consensus was hammered out between the competing bureaucracies. Most important, Tsutsui and his colleagues refused to accept the flight-control computer as a closed "black-box" item, declaring that new source codes would instead have to be written in Japan, even though a *two-year* delay in the program would be required (a telling indication of just how valuable that intangible technology really is). Thus, by the beginning of May 1989, the Japanese negotiated and accepted a rewritten MOU that met Mosbacher's demands almost exactly including the denial of source codes. That much-altered accord was duly presented to the Senate,[47] and swift approval was universally expected: the new MOU was a much better deal than Weinberger's original version had been.

That, however, was not the end of Act Three. It soon turned out that the successful renegotiation of the MOU had only been a first scene. The second was played out at length in the US Congress, which never suffers from a lack of theatrical talent. The matter at hand was a possible motion of disapproval for the codevelopment of the FSX, but in fact it was the totality of US–Japanese relations that became the subject of heated debate. Senator Byrd of West Virginia, the former majority leader, spoke for many, albeit in his own very personal style:

> Mr. President, go out and ask those who have lost their jobs in optic fiber [sic], cameras, computers, radios, black and white television sets, color television sets, shipbuilding, steel. Ask them how they would vote today. . . . We have to send a message to Japan that we are not going to take it lying down anymore. And we have to send a message to our own wimpy diplomats.

After that, Senator Byrd quoted a poem, at length.[48] In that same debate, Senator Riegle of Michigan offered a novel reason for rejecting the MOU. While some had argued that the MOU should be approved because it had already been substantially negotiated by the Reagan administration, for Riegle that in itself was a good reason to reject it:

> [Given that] the last President . . . is about to go over [to Japan to] receive a $2 million fee for spending a week . . . giving speeches around that country, to feel that somehow we are obligated by a deal made by that President, I think is just wrong thinking. Japan is taking out of this country right now every month somewhere between $4 and $5 billion net.[49]

Riegle then went on to recite an entire catalog of complaints: Japan's "predatory" trading practices, MITI's supposed plan to take over the world's aircraft industry, the conjectured Japanese role in the October 1987 stock market crash, "trade cheating" in general, the burden of overseas debt, and more.

The list of charges was completed by the several Senators who invoked the Toshiba affair yet again during the debate (again failing to remember it as the Kongsberg/Toshiba affair) to raise the specter of fresh FSX-connected technology leaks. Others even suggested that the new aircraft would compete with US-built fighters on the world's export market, ignoring the common opinion that Japan's self-imposed prohibition on all weapon exports is thoroughly embedded in its basic political consensus. Finally, Senator Dixon of Illinois, the floor manager of the MOU's opponents, preferred to question the very idea of codevelopment, or indeed licensed production for that matter:

I say "Buy the F-16" and for those . . . who say the deal is done,
I say [that] if they will not buy the F-16 we will not buy their
cameras, their color TVs, and their telephones.[50]

In an abrupt change of tone, Dixon then briefly indulged in sena-
torial eloquence: ". . . and the other things that are part of an honorable
exchange in commerce between two great nations." Just after that,
however, Dixon reverted to a ruder style in quoting a newspaper: "The
'S' in FSX stands for sucker."

The congressional opinion leaders among the swelling ranks of the
opponents to the renegotiated MOU, chiefly Senator Bingaman of New
Mexico and Representative Mel Levine of California, were perhaps less
colorful but also a good deal more specific. While presenting a full
panoply of security, technical, and economic arguments, they were
most insistent on the industrial argument: the codevelopment of the
FSX should be rejected because it would enhance Japan's ability to
develop *civilian* aircraft in competition with American industry.

On the face of it, the congressmen were making much out of very
little, for neither the F-16 nor the FSX would make a fit prototype for
a jet airliner, while in any case Japan's aviation industry hardly seemed
a formidable competitor for Boeing and McDonnell-Douglas. With only
a very modest home market for military aircraft, and with all military
exports prohibited, the industry lacks that foundation of guaranteed
profit margins that so greatly assists its American and European counterparts.[51] It also lacks the hidden advantage of being able to work out
solutions for difficult engineering problems on the government's time,
by incorporating such costly work in current military projects. Nor can
it benefit from the one "spin-off" that is beyond question: the ability to
cheaply engineer marketable products by minor modifications ("civil-
ianizing") of fixed-wing transports and helicopters originally developed
at the government's expense.[52] Hence it is not surprising that Japan's
aviation industry has been quite unable to produce civilian airliners in
competition with Boeing or McDonnell-Douglas, let alone the doubly
subsidized European Airbus consortium.

And yet Senator Bingaman, Representative Levine, and those who
followed their lead in both houses did have a valid argument, though
not necessarily one that they cared to express in public: Fuji, Kawasaki,
and Mitsubishi could indeed become formidable competitors of Boeing, not because of the FSX but simply because they are Japanese. That

in itself gives them access to a highly skilled and highly disciplined labor force, the product of a well-schooled and well-ordered society, in which individuals remain inclined to seek their self-fulfillment in work well done rather than in self-indulgence. To be sure, older Japanese continuously lament that the younger generation nowadays pursues the joys of Venus and Mammon rather than the Zen of perfectionist labor. And it is also true that depictions of all Japanese as humorless automatons is a racist caricature: around a minority of earnest company-men and obedient factory workers, there is a nation blessed with a great abundance of artful dodgers, assorted bohemians, millions of fitfully hardworking farmers, keepers of tiny shops and tinier bars that provide more diversion than income, demonstratively idle gangsters, and Tora-san types. (Mr. Tora, the improvident hero of a long-running series of films, benevolently feckless, warmly human, and far from hardworking, is a common Japanese type.)

Still, for all that, the Japanese industrial labor force undeniably works long hours, its productivity steadily increases (US industrywide productivity per work hour was 192% of the Japanese level in 1970, and 164% in 1988), so that labor costs for industry have hardly risen even as the wages themselves have greatly increased (exceeding US levels by 1987). Moreover, since the end of the 1950s, Japanese unions have also been famously cooperative, with strikes a rarity and the rapid acceptance of new production methods a definite norm.[53]

What is true of labor is doubly true for capital. Simply because they are Japanese, the major companies active in aerospace, like all Japanese companies of some standing, have access to abundant long-term capital, often from their own "house" banks—with Mitsubishi notably having two, the Mitsubishi Bank and Mitsubishi Trust and Banking, each of them huge.[54] United States companies of standing can also raise much capital for one, two, or three years. But it remains more difficult for them to find *patient* capital, which can be invested in long-term technology projects—such as new aircraft, for example—without having to satisfy crippling demands for quick profits from shareholders, bondholders, or equally impatient commercial banks.

So far, of course, Japanese labor and Japanese capital have been otherwise employed, but all along it was the potential ability of Mitsubishi et al. to create a world-class aircraft industry that propelled the strongest congressional opposition to the FSX agreement. And even with Mosbacher's additional safeguards, congressional fears centered on the transfer of technology, for that would provide the missing ingredient in the trio of skilled labor, capital, and know-how that would allow Japan to penetrate into the last sanctuary of American industry.

Specifically, rejecting the administration's insistence that neither the F-16 nor the FSX would make a fit prototype for a jet airliner, the congressional opponents argued that in practice it was of little use to withhold "source codes" or any other narrowly defined technology. Once hundreds of American and Japanese engineers would begin working together on both sides of the Pacific, the Japanese aviation industry would inevitably benefit from a flood of know-how of all kinds, deliberately passed on or not, military or civilian, FSX-relevant or merely easily picked up on factory floor and laboratory bench.

Those circumstances would, of course, favor a two-way flow of information, but Bingaman, Levine, and many others in Congress remained quite unpersuaded by the administration's high opinion of the value of the "back-flow" of Japanese-developed FSX technology that the United States was to receive under the MOU. With more prescience than some, Bingaman, Levine, and their colleagues anticipated that Mitsubishi and its subcontractors would resist any excess of enthusiasm in giving away for free the technology that they had developed at great cost over the years.

For all the harsh talk, the second scene of Act Three did not end with a congressional motion of disapproval. Senator Lugar of Indiana, the very able floor manager of the Republican minority, had found allies for the administration even among some of the leading Democratic senators, including the much-respected Senator Bradley of New Jersey. But the Senate did not simply accept the MOU either. Instead it demanded further restrictions that virtually courted its rejection by Japan. Although their burden was mostly to spell out in greater detail and in more definite language the Mosbacher conditions already successfully negotiated, the agreement had been undone once again.

In Japan, the congressional debate and its outcome evoked extreme bitterness. It seemed that the entire enterprise had failed, in spite of the many concessions already granted step by step over three years, and in spite of so many agonizing compromises from the starting point of an all-Japanese FSX. It was the Americans, after all, who had insisted on codevelopment, forcing Tsutsui and Mitsubishi with the rest of the industry to abandon their bright vision of an independently designed fighter of the highest quality. And now the Americans had rejected their own proposal, so reluctantly accepted in the first place by the Japanese.

For Japanese opinion at large, which could not share in the industry's compensating satisfaction of reverting to an all-Japanese FSX, there was nothing to assuage the profound resentment provoked by the long list of congressional accusations. For them as for most voices in the Japanese media, cause and effect were not in doubt: the American economy was in decline because of American self-indulgence both public and private, but instead of blaming themselves, the envious Americans were unfairly accusing Japan of all sorts of sins.

Within the *Boecho,* and even within the *Gaimusho* to some extent, many officials were induced to consider, perhaps for the very first time, a strategical self-sufficiency far more complete than even a fully Japanese FSX could ever provide. If what Congress had done accurately represented the true state of *Nichibei kankei*—Japanese–American relations—it was possible that the moment had arrived when the Japan end of the relationship should seriously plan for the end of America's long tutelage and most valuable protection. But the strongest reaction came from the institution that provides a forum for the most powerful of all forces in Japanese society, the *Keidanren,* the Federation of Economic Organizations, a.k.a. big business.

In a report produced by an *eighty*-man committee representing virtually all Japanese firms active in military production, the *Keidanren,* very significantly, called for more spending on military research and development. After noting that the latest 1989 *Boecho* budget provided only 82.8 billion yen ($595 million) for research and development, a mere 2.1% of Japan's total military spending, as compared to 12.3% of the US defense budget, 11.7% of the British, and 5.4% of the West German, the *Keidanren* report urged the government to provide the costly research facilities that private industry could not afford, notably a high-speed wind tunnel for the development of airframes, and an instrumented firing range for the testing of missiles (Japan's missiles had been tested on US ranges). Eighty-man committees normally cannot agree on anything more controversial than motherhood. But this particular *Keidanren* committee had a leader whose views might well be expected to be very definite: Masao Kanamori, chairman of Mitsubishi

Heavy Industries, the FSX prime contractor, whose own laconic comment was unexceptionable: "A one-sided flow of technology is not good."[55]

The third and final scene of Act Three unfolded in the White House at the beginning of August 1989. For what the Congress had done, the administration could undo by a presidential veto. After much counting of heads to ensure that the opponents of the MOU did not have the two-thirds majority needed to override the president, the veto was duly imposed giving the green light for the FSX as negotiated after all. The *Boecho*'s latest director-general, Taku Yamasaki, greeted the news with much relief. But it turned out that the end had not yet arrived, and the drama continued into an unexpected Act Four.

Having at long last received permission to begin their own commercial negotiations, General Dynamics and Mitsubishi quarreled almost immediately over the "back-flow" provision of the MOU. On the American side, it was vividly recalled that Congress had finally been won over by the argument that the United States would acquire some valuable Japanese technologies by codeveloping the FSX. As far as Mitsubishi was concerned, however, it was absurd to give away valuable corporate property to another corporation—and a foreign corporation to boot.[56] If some transient head of the *Boecho* of long ago (i.e., Mr. Kurihara) had made promises to that effect, it was just too bad: serious industrialists cannot be expected to underwrite every act of reckless generosity perpetrated by ignorant politicians. In the end—and that finally seemed to be the end of the road—it was not until February 1990 that the two companies settled their differences (General Dynamics will have to pay for whatever technology it chooses to buy), and the engineers could finally begin their work.[57]

▪ THE FUTURE

American–Japanese relations are now fractured not only by the chronic trade deficit but also by a "respect deficit," for just as the Japanese continue to disregard American economic interests, the US government disregards Japanese political interests. For example, during the US–Soviet and US–Russian economic aid negotiations of 1990–1993, Bush and Clinton officials barely mentioned the intense Japanese desire to recover the northern territories, the island just north of Hokkaido seized by the Soviet armed forces in 1945—even though Japan was expected to fund a large part of any aid. It matters not at all that a perfectly good argument could be made that the preservation of Russia's fragile democracy was more important than the northern territories even from a strictly Japanese point of view. What *did* matter was that the return of the northern territories was Japan's declared precondition for any large-scale aid to Moscow, and that many Japanese felt very strongly on the issue. To ignore that precondition and those popular feelings showed a total lack of respect quite inconsistent with all the fine words about Japan being America's ally, friend, and partner.

Actually the Russian aid controversy only added to the "respect deficit." When Iraq invaded Kuwait in August 1990, the Bush administration did not consult the Japanese government on the crisis, in spite of Japan's very large dependence on oil from the Persian Gulf, and then added insult to injury by loudly demanding that Japan pay $13 billion as its share of the costs—an amount calculated on the basis of unilateral Pentagon estimates. And that was only an episode, as compared to the continuing US failure to support Japan's desire for permanent membership in the UN Security Council, alongside the faded Great Powers of the past, Britain and France, as well as the United States, China, and Russia. The official US excuse was that other countries, notably India and Nigeria, were also demanding permanent seats on the Security Council. India is, of course, the world's largest democracy and is in many ways an admirable country in spite of its extreme poverty. But nobody was asking India to match Japan in paying for a significant proportion of the UN budget, or to fund the global environmental initiatives, or to provide all manner of other aid. As for Nigeria's claim, it was simply absurd. While Nigeria's population may be just larger than Japan's (the number is unknown), its status as black Africa's most important country is of little consequence on the global scene. The mere fact that US officials compared Japan with Nigeria greatly added to the "respect deficit."

Disrespect has been answered with ridicule. American protests about unfair trade evoke Japanese derision instead of the earnest consideration they deserve, and Americans are frequently viewed with scorn, tinged with fear. That posture is fully reflected in the treatment of US–Japanese questions and of the United States itself in the Japanese media. There are exceptions, among columnists and academics who write in the press,[58] but, in general, only the Japanese viewpoint on trade issues is conveyed, and it is quite exceptional to come across an article that dwells on the many contrived obstacles that all foreigners face trying to sell in Japan. On the other hand, American shortcomings are made much of. When in 1991 Yoshio Sakurauchi, former foreign minister and Speaker of the lower house in the Japanese Diet, and as such a leading politician, declared that the source of the trade problem was that "US workers are too lazy. They want high pay without working. About 30% cannot even read so managers cannot convey their orders in written form. Therefore they get a high ratio of bad parts,"[59] he was merely expressing a common view, as was Prime Minister Yasuhiro Nakasone in 1986 when he said that blacks lower US intelligence levels, and Foreign Minister Michio Watanabe in 1988, when he explained the high level of US consumer debt by saying that blacks use credit cards irresponsibly. Given the standard media line that the United States is in decay because it is a disordered, mixed-race society particularly afflicted by an excess of blacks, the May 1992 Los Angeles riots received coverage that managed to be sensationalist even though the reality was sensational enough.

As for the trade deficit, and the attempt to reduce it by the removal of "structural impediments," the situation is just as dismal. Negotiations proceed on many issues, and progress is frequently claimed, but even such progress is accompanied by the continuation of Japan's general refusal to accept for itself the open-market rules that ensure its own success as an exporter to the world. For example, after President Bush pressed the matter during his December 1991 visit to Japan, a new US–Japan agreement was announced with great fanfare in April 1992, which was to open Japan's market to foreign paper products. In the previous year, Japan had imported only 3.7% of its total demand for paper products (including 1.7% from the United States), in spite of the fact domestic paper was substantially more costly than imports would have been. Under the agreement, the Japanese government (i.e., MITI) pledged to promote foreign sales of paper products by, among other things, encouraging companies that were major paper buyers to adopt *written purchasing guidelines* that would be applicable to foreign as well as domestic suppliers. MITI was to focus its efforts on the food, cosmetics, pharmaceutical, and publishing industries.[60]

Good news it would seem: the agreement offered hope that more progress would soon be made in opening the Japanese market, this time for paper products. But then inevitably, some obvious questions arise. Why did Bush have to raise the issue at all? Why was there a need for special negotiations on this one category of products? Because most of its raw material is imported, with high transport costs for low-value wood pulp, the Japanese paper industry is not, and cannot be competitive. So why didn't the paper-buying companies import sooner, without any need of diplomatic intervention? And what is the meaning of the peculiar promise to encourage the adoption of "written purchasing guidelines"?

Why should it be necessary for government officials to persuade private companies to adopt "written guidelines"? With or without "guidelines," whether written, spoken, or sung, paper-buyers in the food, cosmetics, pharmaceutical, publishing, or other industries should themselves want to buy paper they need at the lowest possible price for any given level of quality. Evidently they have not been doing so, preferring instead to pay more for Japanese-made paper of equal quality, while vaguely telling foreign suppliers that their products were not good enough—and then refusing to specify in writing what quality standards they had failed to meet. Whether this refusal to import is the result of intercompany *keiretsu* links, under-the-table payoffs by domestic producers, or pure import phobia hardly matters. The outcome is that instead of a free market, there is still a web of closed-market relationships that prevents competitive paper exports to Japan.

What would world trade look like if every separate market for every industry in every separate country had to be opened by high-level political interventions and special negotiations to overcome hidden barriers against imports? Did the United States have to negotiate with governments from A to Z, from Austria to Zambia to open *their* paper markets? Did Austria or Zambia have to negotiate with every government in the world to open markets for *their* products, industry by industry? Of course there are tariffs and quotas everywhere, including the United States, and of course there are countries all over the world that must restrict imports because they simply lack hard currency. But no tariffs or any other overt barriers are at issue with Japan, and certainly it is not short of hard currency, its own being the hardest of all.

What is the exact nature of this hidden protectionism? First, it is not the result of government policies that might reflect a popular consensus, but rather of big-business preferences, masked as national customs. Second, it does not serve broad economic, political, social, or cultural purposes, but only narrow industrial interests that are often socially harmful in other ways. In the case of the paper industry, for example, what the intercompany conspiracy has been protecting are not the fine craftsmen who keep alive Japan's wonderful handmade paper tradition but rather paper mills that pollute the water and the air, require much energy from imported oil, and are structurally inefficient to boot.

The same intercompany protectionism is present in other processing industries in which Japan also lacks any comparative advantage, from plywood manufacture (which uses only hardwoods as yet another barrier, causing tropical deforestation), to basic chemicals such as soda ash, to processed foods. Along with the high-technology sectors where similar unofficial import barriers persist (telecommunications, supercomputers, satellites, medical equipment, etc.), protectionism is the cause of the "Japanese difference," the low percentage of manufactured goods in total imports—roughly 50.9% for Japan at the last count as compared to 76.9% even for industrial champion Germany, 78.4% for France, 79.4% for the United Kingdom, and 78.6% for the United States.[61] True, the proportion of manufactured goods has been increasing in Japan's total imports, but much of the increase is accounted for by consumer goods of low technology and low added value (textiles, clothing, cheaper electronics), as well as products manufactured by Japanese corporations in their foreign plants.

The first victims of Japan's import barriers are the millions of ordinary Japanese who have been offered up as sacrifices to foreign trade pressures, the rice farmers and small shopkeepers now declared to be mere "impediments." Even their complete elimination would do little to balance US–Japanese trade, but it is evidently one more tactical maneuver meant to buy time, and destined to raise ill-informed expectations only to disappoint them once again.

But the second victims are undoubtedly the American industries and the American workers that cannot recoup their loss of markets and employment and income to Japanese imports, by exporting in turn to Japan. In 1980, US exports of food, raw materials, and manufactures to Japan amounted to $20.79 billion, as against imports of $32.96 billion, implying that some $12.17 billion of revenues and wages were transferred across the Pacific, mostly in exchange for consumer goods discarded long ago. The resulting import of unemployment was in the high hundreds of thousands at least. In 1989, after the great devaluation of the dollar that should have hugely increased US exports to Japan and drastically reduced imports, the trade imbalance came to $52.55 billion, and the resulting import of unemployment was in the millions; US trade with Western Europe had also been severely in deficit until then, but in 1989, US imports came to $106.04 billion, as against US exports of $100.27 billion, and that deficit would become a surplus in 1990 and thereafter.

Moreover, the content of Japanese imports from the United States is also exceedingly unbalanced. Primary products—that is, food, raw materials, ores and other minerals, fuels, and nonferrous metals—accounted for $19.06 billion of the $44.56 billion of US merchandise exports to Japan in 1989, or 42.8% of the total. Low-technology and generally low-added-value products—that is, semimanufactures, basic chemicals, textiles, clothing, and other consumer goods—came to $12.01 billion, or another 26.9% of total US exports to Japan. Even though the United States remains the world's most advanced industrial country, it is evidently not that for Japan, for only 30.3% of American exports to Japan—including military equipment—were industrial products of higher added value, i.e., machinery and transport equipment, office and telecommunications equipment, automotive products, etc.

By contrast, primary products accounted for only $1.12 billion, or 1.1% of the total of $97.11 billion dollars of all Japanese exports to the United States, low-technology products totaled $16.25 billion or 16.7%, while 82.2% of all Japanese merchandise exports to the United States consisted of higher-added-value industrial products, mostly machinery and transport equipment ($75.93 billion), cars and auto parts ($32.20 billion), and office and telecommunications equipment ($26.08 billion). Those last categories include many products that the United States exports with huge success all over the world—except to Japan. As a matter of fact, the United States would be in surplus in higher-added-value industrial products across the board, if all trade with Japan, both exports and imports, were excluded:[62]

Machinery and transport equipment, billions of dollars, 1989
Worldwide: US exports 165.95; US imports 210.81; Net: − 44.86
Less Japan: US exports 153.62; US imports 134.88; Net: + 18.74

Other nonelectrical machinery
Worldwide: US exports 32.61; US imports 32.37; Net: − 0.24
Less Japan: US exports 30.63; US imports 22.32; Net: + 8.31

Office and telecommunications equipment
Worldwide: US exports 47.38; US imports 63.20; Net: −15.82
Less Japan: US exports 41.95; US imports 37.12: net: +4.83

Electrical machinery and apparatus
Worldwide: US exports 14.72; US imports 18.13; Net: −3.41
Less Japan: US exports 13.72; US imports 13.77; Net: −0.05

Automotive products
Worldwide: US exports 30.85; US imports 78.76; Net: −47.91
Less Japan: US exports 29.95; US imports 46.46; Net: −16.51

Other transport equipment
Worldwide: US exports 30.47; US imports 11.94; Net: +18.53
Less Japan: US exports 28.12; US imports 9.48; Net: +18.64

Total of higher-added-value industrial products
Worldwide: US exports 321.98; US imports 415.21; Net: −93.23
Less Japan: U.S exports 297.99; US imports 264.03; Net:
+15.96

Thus after many years of market-opening negotiations, the United States remains in large part a raw-material supplier to Japan and a market for its industrial goods, while being unable to export its own industrial products in comparable degree. There has been progress to be sure (Japan used to exclude industrial products more fully), but oh so slow that both the promisers and promisees among the trade negotiators on both sides retired long before their fulfillment of the promises.

It is in this setting that the FSX controversy can fairly be said to mark a great historical turning point for the United States itself as well as for Japan, and for US–Japanese relations. At some point, certainly by Act Three if not before, novel economic anxieties had almost entirely displaced the security priorities that had long dominated American foreign policy. In the creative tension between the branches of government, Congress offered economic objections to geopolitical aims as so often before, but this time with far greater effect. Within the executive branch itself, there was a definite reordering of the Cold War hierarchy between the departments of government. It is still the Department of Defense that occupies the several thousand rooms of the Pentagon, and not some American version of MITI, but during the FSX controversy the previously humble Department of Commerce acquired a booming voice quite unheard till then. And in the nation at large, in a far more momentous change, Japan displaced the Soviet Union from its role as the Chief Enemy—the unifying other that guarantees cohesion amidst diversity, and provides the organizing theme of common endeavors.

But the purely geopolitical priorities of the Cold War struggle had long been fossilized into a rigid foreign-policy culture, largely accepted by both political parties, and passed on as sacrosanct doctrine to successive generations of officials. And this culture proved remarkably resistant to the advent of diminished economic circumstances. Even with the US economy heavily indebted and the Soviet Union utterly dissolved, every attempt to impose economic priorities on the conduct of American foreign policy continued to arouse fierce resistance from the professionals of the Cold War—the diplomats, soldiers, sailors, airmen, intelligencers, contract experts, publicists, strategic intellectuals, and even some of the more "foreign-policy-minded" politicians.

Having achieved so much by their sheer persistence in the geopolitical struggle, while so many others faltered along the way, having finally attained their highest aim of demolishing the steamroller of Soviet military power without war, they found it hard to accept the American defeat contained in that great victory, as in all victories. Precisely because the United States has won the geopolitical struggle, its position in the world is much diminished, because its ability to protect a host of allies from Soviet aggression has become worthless. And precisely because the United States had fashioned itself into the world's geopolitical champion, it found itself a mere contender in the economic competition that its own victory has made decisive. As that downfall unfolded, the professionals of the Cold War still could not bring themselves to accept the pettier, even sordid, economic concerns that their own epic success had elevated above the noble endeavors of geopolitics. But then, of course, aristocratic pretensions always outlast their original justification.

Still, only a small minority among more than 123 million Japanese are intent on waging industrial warfare against the United States—that is the prerequisite of the powerful elite of economic bureaucrats and part (not all) of corporate Japan. At least one chief executive of a most successful Japanese corporation—*not* Sony's trendy and politically changeable Akio Morita—has warned that Japan's one-sided trade practices are unfair and most unwise, for they are arousing resentments that will eventually leave Japan friendless, an "orphan among nations."[63] When President Clinton repudiated the futile SII talks in 1993 to demand quick action by the Japanese government to reduce the huge trade imbalance, Japanese officials from Prime Minister Kiichi Miyazawa down loudly protested that they could not possibly interfere with private business decisions to order increased imports. The spectacle of the inventors of "managed trade" professing their horror of managing trade was amusing, but at least some Japanese businessmen were outraged by the insincerity of their own government. They pointedly reminded their American friends that Japanese bureaucrats interfere all the time—to promote industry and exports of course. Americans have long tolerated a pattern typical of colonial relationships in US–Japanese trade. In the process, while unilaterally respecting the principles of free trade, the United States suffered the decline of entire industries and the loss of some millions of well-paid industrial jobs.

CHAPTER 3

MODELS AND MYTHS:
PRUSSIA AND JAPAN

A majority of Americans now declare in opinion polls that Japan is "a greater threat" than the Soviet Union. Many Japanese for their part still define as a national economic goal the overtaking of the United States, in terms that suggest the desire to humble Americans, if only statistically. The French now express fears of German "economic domination," as do other Europeans, while the British are apt to resent the economic success of other countries as if the success of others was the cause of their own travails.

Sentiments such as these can easily cross the line between stimulating rivalry and outright hostility. In international sports competitions, the two may be hard to tell apart, but when it comes to international economic relations the distinction is very precise indeed. Even a fiercely competitive rivalry in any number of sectors remains perfectly compatible with the continuation of whatever trading or financial relations are warranted by advantages on each side. The advent of hostility, by contrast, is marked by the desire to inflict disadvantage, even at the cost of suffering some disadvantage of one's own.[1]

In the past, territory could not be gained without causing another's loss, if only by diminishing the scope of the adversary's own possible future expansion. The geopolitical engagements of the late nineteenth and early twentieth centuries were thus inherently adversarial in the most extreme "zero-sum" sense (with gains and losses appropriately enough adding up to zero). By contrast, the economic success of one country today can positively help the economies of other countries, *if the successful country imports in equal degree over time*. Even if actual circumstances are far removed from the idealized depictions of textbook free-trade theory, at the very least it may be agreed that international economic relations are not inherently adversarial "zero-sum" contests.

Now it is Japan's turn to be also held up as a model. Just as Prussia became the world's model Great Power after its 1870 victory over France, for many people today's model country is undoubtedly Japan, in spite of the downfall of its stock-market-and-real-estate "bubble economy." In the United States, banks touting their savings accounts pointedly remind the public that the Japanese save much more—taking it for granted that the Japanese set the only correct standard for how much should be saved by each and all, as they probably do. Telephone companies lobbying against laws that stop them from selling computer services, stress that there are no such barriers in Japan, again assuming that the public will accept without question the superiority of Japanese practices. When it comes to public education, Americans have been debating whether to copy Japan's nationwide school examination system (itself copied from Prussia), while eager reformers insist that high-school students must learn more algebra and calculus to keep up with the Japanese—as if absent Japan, mathematical ignorance would be quite all right. And of course US corporations have long been trying to imitate Japanese management and production methods across the board, sometimes adopting Japanese slogans translated word by word ("quality circles"). Only Japanese restraint in the salaries of top executives remains uncopied by US corporations.

Europeans are much less likely than Americans to drive a Honda or Toyota to eat at their local *sushi-ya* before rounding off the evening at a *karaoke* singing bar. But in more fundamental ways, the influence of the Japanese model is even stronger. The European Community, as well as several individual member states, clearly favors Japanese-style cooperation between government and business, over the American pattern of adversarial dealings. Japanese style "industrial policy," to strengthen favored sectors with research and development grants, subsidized investments, and some market protection is debated in America but simply accepted in Europe. True enough, in several European countries, notably France and Italy, there is a very long tradition of state intervention in all forms of business, including the state ownership of major enterprises. But with the worldwide collapse of socialism, that tradition of industrial policy would now be in full retreat, if the Japanese example had not arrived to confirm its validity. As it is, even the European Community countries that were once most opposed to state interventions now agree that the development of industry should not be left entirely to the vagaries of free enterprise.

In East Asia, it is Japan's entire economy that is being copied, most faithfully in Korea but also in Taiwan and Singapore, as well as in Indonesia, Malaysia, and Thailand, to some extent. In China the Communist party has chosen to allow the spread of the very different Hong Kong model of totally unguided free enterprise, but only for consumer-good industries, personal services, and commerce. By contrast, heavy industries and public services (e.g., air transport) are being reorganized in the Japanese manner, with government-owned but competitive and profit-seeking corporations in place of the chronically inefficient state establishments of the past. Most recently, even India has repudiated its own brand of socialism, in part to be able to imitate Japan. The new slogan in India is liberalization under free-market rules, but the government's goal is to combine competition among different private enterprises with policy guidance for all—in accordance with the Japanese model.

Now that nationalized industries, telephone companies, airlines, railways, municipal water and sewage services, and even city zoos are being privatized all over Latin America, US-style free enterprise seems to be dominant but it is rather a Japanese-style "development capitalism" that the most ambitious Latin American leaders would want to imitate—if only because it offers the sole alternative to the oppressive attraction of Yankee ways. Only the blatant incapacity of the state bureaucracies to guide economic development in the Japanese manner holds back Latin America's would-be imitators. It is noteworthy that the current Mexican president, Carlos Salinas de Gortari, who obtained his Ph.D. from Harvard, sent his own children to a local Japanese-language school.

To be sure, the imitation of Japan is less than worldwide. For the countries of sub-Saharan Africa, mostly still sliding down into ever-deeper poverty and chaos, it would be an impossible dream: their bureaucracies can only tax, extort, and steal, not develop national economies with sophisticated guidance. In the former Soviet Union, on the other hand, economic survival, not development, is still the only priority for the national republics and emerging ethnic states, while in many Islamic lands a lively appetite for non-Islamic products of all kinds coexists with an ignorant disdain for non-Islamic ideas, especially now that the tide of religious dogma is rising.

Although it was the Prussian army that was most widely imitated in its day, from Chile to Japan itself, as well as throughout Europe and the United States, Prussian schools and universities also found many imitators. Public schools still function on the Prussian model in many countries, strictly following Ministry of Education programs that impose identical course contents, textbooks, and even timetables, as well as identical standards enforced by nationwide teacher certifications, frequent inspections, and identical national exams. Thus rich and poor, sophisticated city-dwellers and children from the most remote villages, receive the same education, whose aim is to achieve a high average standard rather than excellence for a few.

To mask income differences, or perhaps merely for the love of them, identical uniforms were also part of the Prussian model; they have not survived the upsurge of individualism in many countries, but to this day Japanese high-school students still wear the dark blue uniforms and peaked caps of the Prussian *gymnasium*—not merely a uniform, but actually the original one, long since abandoned in Germany itself. As for Prussian high education, it became the basis of modern postgraduate studies everywhere, so that aspiring American scholars still proceed to a Prussian-style Ph.D., after first being awarded their British-style Bachelor and Master of this or that.

For all their differences, the post-1870 Prussian model and today's Japanese model share an important characteristic. In both, a single institution exemplifies the model, undoubtedly forming its very core, and serving as the focal point of imitation. A century ago, the most widely admired and most widely feared of human institutions was the Prussian General Staff. Today it is Japan's Ministry of International Trade and Industry (MITI), the *Tsusho Sangyo-Sho,* that can best claim that dubious distinction.

Endowed with an aura of invincibility ever since the astonishingly quick defeats of both the Hapsburg and French empires, often believed to contain the secrets of victory in its very structure, the Prussian General Staff was the subject of boundless myth, a great deal of popular spy fiction, and much earnest professional study. From exotic Ottoman Turkey to distant Latin America, the officers of many countries came to Berlin to learn its methods, while the greater powers old and new, from the United States to defeated France, faithfully imitated its practices from afar. To this day, military headquarters all over the world unconsciously retain the outlines of the organization of the Prussian General Staff.

Likewise, because it is credited with the decisive role in Japan's spectacular rise to outright wealth in one generation, MITI has also been the subject of much earnest study, and wide imitation.[2] When a new economic superministry was unveiled by the French government in May 1991, Prime Minister Edith Cresson proudly described it as "better than MITI."[3] Even as a subject of popular fiction, MITI can compete with the Prussian General Staff: several novels that depict the doings and undoings of its officials have been best-sellers in Japan, a most revealing indication of how the Japanese themselves have viewed the mainsprings of their economic success. In America and Europe, commerce can provide enough excitement for adventure novels, but their protagonists are invariably fiercely individualistic (and energetically amorous) entrepreneurs, not government bureaucrats.

Just as the 135 officers of the Prussian General Staff[4] received much of the credit for victories in which hundreds of thousands of troops and thousand of field officers also took part, MITI derives its vast prestige from the self-sacrifice, hard work, and skill of the millions of workers, clerks, salesmen, and managers high and low who assured Japan's industrial growth. As its prestige lingers unchallenged abroad, it seems to matter not a bit that in Japan itself MITI has long been overshadowed by the Ministry of Finance, the *Okurasho*. Actually its initials remain a convenient shorthand for what is really meant: Japan's elite economic bureaucrats, creatures indeed far different from the clerks and transient political appointees of the US Department of Commerce.

■ THE TERRITORIALIST DELUSION

Mythic reputations, even if not undeserved, inevitably obscure more complicated realities. Yet they are still most revealing—not of how matters really stand perhaps—but of the prevailing concerns of the age, and its ruling ambitions. For each generation has its necessary myths and best discloses its inner motives by the myths it chooses to believe and circulate. In the case of Prussia and its General Staff, the myth that military power could be used "scientifically" by following its methods was most earnestly believed, because that belief served a new ambition for territorial expansionism, itself abstract and detached from practical rewards.

War and peace had not changed, but the global spread of steam navigation, railways, and the telegraph meant that territory could be *controlled* as never before. Predictably, that induced a wholly new desire in politicians, military leaders, power-fascinated intellectuals, litterateurs, and journalists all over the world to conquer more territory for its own sake, even empty desert, trackless jungle, desolate islands, and barren tundra—almost without exception utterly useless at the time with the technology at hand, even if some contained raw materials of value that would later be discovered and exploited, mostly when the natives had already won their independence. The urge to conquer was hardly new, of course, but with very few exceptions the conquerors of the past had always wanted territory not for itself but for what it contained: mountain ridges and rivers of defensive value, taxable cities and towns, revenue-yielding fertile lands, rich mines, or profitable trading posts. It was the urge to acquire sheer space on the maps that then started to be assiduously consulted and prominently displayed that marked the arrival of the new era.

From 1870 to 1914 especially, the mentality of people everywhere, and therefore the conduct of world affairs, was enormously distorted by this new cult of the map, later intellectually glorified by the pseudo-science of geopolitics, which claimed to explain history as a struggle of nations for vital "spaces."[5] What happened during those years is an object lesson in how powerful mass delusions can be, how they can utterly dominate otherwise able minds, empowering abstract fantasies destructive of substance, including human flesh and blood and the true sources of national wealth, welfare, and happiness.

Russians still under the rule of the czars had little freedom and few rights, but they gloried in their Moscow-centered maps that best depicted the enormous spread of Russian lands from central Europe to the remote shores of the Pacific. British schoolboys were thrilled by their first discovery that so much of the globe was colored in imperial pink; the French of all ages fretted that their empire remained somewhat smaller; and many Germans bitterly resented that their own country occupied only a measly portion of the world map. That Germany contained much of the world's most modern industry, several of its most prosperous cities, and undoubtedly the best universities did not satisfy them. It was "a place in the sun" that those Germans wanted, or actually several places, African colonies even in the most inhospitable savannahs or outright deserts—as long as they would loom large on the map. For that purpose Germany built an oceangoing navy that Britain feared, forcing it into alliance with France, thus setting the stage for two catastrophic wars.

In lesser countries only lesser ambitions could be entertained, but there was the same urge to acquire territory for its own sake, rather than for anything of true value. Italians anxiously searched the map of Africa for any remaining unclaimed spaces they could seize, where they built costly public works denied to impoverished Sicily or starving Calabria. Even little Belgium was overcome by an eagerness to stake out every inch of the vastness of Congo from the few river ports that had until then marked its useful boundaries.[6] The Japanese, so recently forbidden to leave their home islands at all, had started to gaze at maps of Korea, Manchuria, and Taiwan in their longing to create the world's newest empire, while in the very oldest, Hapsburg loyalists disregarded the excess of nationalities that already overburdened the empire in their impatience to acquire Sarajevo and the rest of miserable Bosnia-Herzegovina from the retreating Ottoman empire.

Latin America was also infected. Brazilians sacrificed far more urgent economic priorities to acquire the fullest possible ownership of the vast Amazon basin they had scarcely explored, successfully taking large tracts from Venezuela, Colombia, Ecuador, and Bolivia.[7] Argentinians, already amply provided with the huge endowment of extravagantly fertile land of the Pampas, were nevertheless prepared to devote blood and treasure to secure useless Andean steppe and Patagonian waste against Chileans with the same desires, yet to this day the natural gas of Patagonia cannot be exploited profitably.

Rabble-rousing politicians, sensationalist journalists, bellicose poets, and naive schoolboys were not the only ones who impelled or were carried along by the territorialist frenzy of 1870–1914. The mass delusion of the age did not spare even the professionals—the civil servants and military officers who could actually calculate the true costs of territorial fantasies. Yet the documents that fill official archives show that their views did not significantly differ from the most bootless of popular desires. Thus, for example, the dream of building a trans-African railway "from Cairo to the Cape," under the British flag throughout, was not only a journalistic slogan but also the stuff of serious discussion by otherwise sober civil servants, military officers, and politicians—although even now, a hundred years later on, such a railway could hardly be built to last through a wet season, and still less could it attract enough traffic to pay for its upkeep.

Both in Britain's seasoned Foreign Office and the fledgling American State Department, policies were actually shaped by the apparent truths contained in small-scale maps, to then motivate fears of logistically impossible Russian advances into India, or the hope of fulfilling newly manifest destinies far beyond American shores. As for Imperial Germany, once Bismarck left the scene its rulers became famously eager to risk real lives and real money for colonies that would add some German color to the map—any colonies at all, however costly to acquire, however useless to hold, however impossible to defend. And the French archives are replete with the careful prose of men quite careless of any facts that belied the simplicities of the map. That was the prose that sent soldiers to fight and die in the jungles of Indochina and the sands of the Sahara, before inducing the reckless Fashoda expedition to claim even more useless desert in the most remote Sudan, at the risk of causing a war with Britain a mere ten years before British help would be greatly needed in a desperate war with Germany.

In every vital state, large and small, the same territorialist mentality prevailed,[8] with the same harmony between popular map-gazing and official policy, and with topography, economy, and common sense equally disregarded as worthless conquests were schemed and fanciful "invasion corridors" that no army could possibly transit were fearfully imagined. Thus the professionalization of planning and command, which was meant to replace guesswork with research in the service of a stern practicality in the use of military power, was instead abused for hollow ambitions. Territorialism created a fatal confusion between reality and fantasy—between the very real threat of a surprise offensive against Paris, and the fantasy threat that British power would "control" Africa as a whole, if the Cairo-to-Cape railway were built (hence the Fashoda expedition); between very real opportunities, for example, of establishing a profitable trading zone in Shanghai, and the fantasy opportunities of colonies in the Niger savannahs.

Not every state, but every *vital* state was engulfed by the mass delusion of the age, for it could not infect somnolent Spain, decaying Ottoman Turkey, or disintegrating China. It was only the states that were growing, dynamic, and forward-looking that succumbed to the disease. Now also, as we shall see, it is only the most accomplished and most successful states that can fall prey to the parallel delusion of our own age.

Given this outlook, so naive in retrospect, so compelling at the time, the widespread fascination with the Prussian General Staff was fully justified. No secret formula for guaranteed victory could be discovered in its workings, nor indeed anything that had not been done before in one way or another by the quartermasters, military secretaries, administrators, old war horses, and young aides that sovereigns would assemble in their wartime courts, and whom field commanders would gather to serve them on campaign. Yet there was indeed a novel secret in the relentless systematization of what had previously been done only haphazardly, and only when war was already imminent.

To educate aspiring officers in a permanent war academy instead of relying on the variegated tutoring of young cadets; to then systematically select for the General Staff the graduates best endowed with talents of analysis, planning, and command; and to distribute those privileged few into permanent departments of Intelligence, Operations, Logistics, and Mobilization, whose functions were also methodically defined to avoid overlaps and achieve comprehension, were all fit preparations for the permanent and orderly planning of all possible wars, campaigns, and battles. For the politicians, military chiefs, and assorted enthusiasts who were then searching the map for territory to acquire, or who longed to systematize the boundaries of territories held till then only in their useful parts, the Prussian General Staff was clearly the institution to be emulated.

The geopolitical mentality outlasted the climax of imperial expansion of the 1890s marked by the "scramble of Africa," the American seizure of Spanish colonies, and the beginnings of Japanese colonialism. It propelled the Anglo–French rivalry over the division of the Arab lands of the Ottoman empire in the 1920s, Japan's drive into Manchuria and Italy's invasion of Ethiopia in the 1930s, Hitler's entire foreign policy of conquest from 1938 as Japan's from 1937, and then finally the Cold War into the 1980s, whose ideological dimension provided a warrant for contesting the allegiance of every inhabited land, no matter how remote or utterly unendowed. To be sure, that geopolitical ambitions were delusive did not diminish the urgency of resisting them. Hitler's fantasy of a racial-feudal empire of SS aristocrats and Slavic helots would have become reality had it not been fought to destruction in grim reality. And no matter how disastrous it was for Soviet society itself, the Soviet striving for both military supremacy and the diffusion of Marxist–Leninist regimes anywhere and everywhere would have determined the fate of the world had it not been effectively resisted. The game of nations whatever its form and however futile is always compulsory.

▪ JAPAN: THE MYTH

Today's fascination with Japan's economic achievement closely resembles the fascination of an earlier age with Prussian military success. Beyond the parallel identification of a powerful, sinister but admirable directing institution in the General Staff in one case and MITI in the other, there is a distinct similarity between the widespread imitation of the uniforms, drill, and specific command procedures of the Prussian army, and the often slavish imitation of Japanese management procedures, down to the literal translation of its slogans. Even more broadly, Japanese society as a whole is being earnestly scrutinized for importable models, just as German society once was.

As with Prussia a century ago, the imitation of Japan evokes mixed responses from the imitated. Pride in the accomplishments that stimulate so much attention is irresistible of course. Satisfaction at the sight of foreigners eager to replicate one's own original institutions is equally natural. At the same time, however, many Japanese today, like many Prussians of a century ago, dismiss all attempts at imitation as quite futile, because they hold that the true secret of their success is locked within the nonimportable totality of their culture, supposedly uniquely martial in the one case and uniquely harmonious in the other.[9]

To believe that, as many Japanese seemingly do, one must disregard much recent history, including the violent strikes of the 1920s, the bloody civil-military political struggles of the 1930s, the extraordinary refusal of the Imperial Army and Imperial Navy to cooperate even in war, and the entire record of bitter labor strife that lasted until the 1960s, when the rapid pace of wage increases did indeed induce harmony in labor relations. The uniqueness thesis is thus exactly wrong: it was economic success that yielded Japan's famous harmony, not the other way around.

It was just about a century ago that some Germans began to offer a more absolute racial explanation of their success, to then ridicule the feeble attempts of mongrelized Americans, inferior Asiatics, and decadent Mediterraneans to imitate their military methods. That, too, is an attitude replicated by quite a few Japanese, including former Prime Minister Nakasone. An entire specialized literature (*Nihonjinron*) celebrates the unique virtues of the Japanese race and its perfect homogeneity—a belief held by many Westerners also, though one not shared by anyone who has actually observed a Japanese crowd, in which one may admire a rich variety of skin colors and a wide diversity of facial features.

▪ MITI AND THE SYSTEMATIZATION OF INDUSTRIAL SUCCESS

Needless to say, such claims of cultural or racial exclusivity only evoke hostility and do not deter at all the imitation of specific institutions out of context. Certainly much can be learned from MITI even as most superficially understood, just as much was gained by imitators of the Prussian General Staff who merely introduced standing headquarters manned by professionally educated officers in place of the improvised retinues of field commanders. If all that is learned from MITI's example is that it is worthwhile to have a prestigious and well-staffed government department in charge of promoting exports if exports are needed, that is enough. If all that is learned from MITI's example is that the best-educated talent can usefully assist industry with advice instead of being wholly canceled out in law firms engaged in contesting other law firms, that is also enough. And if all that is learned from MITI is that industry can be helped by the supply of detailed information from all over the world, on each economic sector and each product category for each country, that, too, is also enough.[10]

MITI, to be sure, has not been content to promote, assist, and inform. It had also tried to create and direct industry, at least within the sectors that it chooses to advance under its much-admired and much-deplored "industrial policy." Crudely misrepresented in American right-wing rhetoric as a matter of having (ignorant) bureaucrats "pick winners and losers" in place of the sacrosanct market, equally misrepresented as magically effective by its more innocent foreign admirers, MITI's industrial policy has always in fact been less than dictatorial, and less than infallible. Some Japanese corporations have been obedient to MITI, others have ignored its interventions (including Honda, famously misadvised to remain a motorcycle manufacturer). Some MITI schemes have been costly failures (most notably the $400 million "fifth generation" computer project) and others have simply been in-effectual, but there is no doubt about their overall impact, and overall success.

The most complete example of MITI's industrial policy was its out-right creation of Japan's petrochemical industry from the mid-1950s. Those were the glory days of MITI, when Japan's economic condition still allowed the need, and the opportunity, to substantially create entire industries by employing a wide variety of methods.

First, a MITI investigation established that Japan could, and should, acquire a petrochemical industry in spite of its usual lack of the re-quired raw materials. That was the starting point of Japan's "develop-mental capitalism" in action. By contrast, the standard US belief is that industries will emerge spontaneously in response to market forces; but market forces alone would have perpetuated Japan's dependence on petrochemical imports.

Second, MITI rallied the troops inside the ministry, in the govern-ment as a whole, and in the economy at large by heralding its intention to create a petrochemical industry for Japan in the July 1955 Petro-chemical Industry Nurturing Policy declaration.[11] That would have been a case of (ignorant) bureaucrats picking "a winner," in the lan-guage of US free-market rhetoric, and thus ruled out as reprehensible on principle—even if most useful in practice. When Secretary of Com-merce Robert S. Mosbacher wanted to promote key high-technology industries in 1989–1990, he was stopped cold by the free-market true believers in the White House ("potato chips and computer chips, what's the difference?").

Third, loans on favorable terms were provided by the state-controlled Japan Development Bank to corporate families (*keiretsu*-s) willing to enter the industry. By contrast, the US government has no investment bank; on the contrary, by borrowing money in huge amounts to cover its own deficits it competes for scarce capital with private industry; and only the Small Business Administration provides capital to small and minority-owned companies, in feeble amounts that hardly keep up with inflation: $3.8 billion in 1980, and $4.3 billion in 1990.[12]

Fourth, MITI itself released foreign currency and issued licenses for the importation of foreign equipment and technology (mainly from the United States), because 100% of the required know-how had to be imported. But the industry soon emancipated itself from the need to buy, if not "borrow" foreign technology. Because Japan's Patent Agency

(*Tokkyo Cho*) is one of MITI's well-controlled external bureaus, it is in the habit of holding up the registration of foreign patents sometimes for many years, to allow time for their circumvention by imitative research and development.

Fifth, under Japan's differentiated tax system, MITI gave "strategic" status to the industry, allowing its capital investments to be quickly depreciated, thus reducing taxable income. By contrast, this type of favoritism for preferred industries would violate the US principle of equality before the (tax) law. In the past, investment tax credits were given to all indiscriminately by US tax law; at present they are given to none.

Sixth, state-owned sites suitable for the construction of plants were provided free of charge or at slight cost—a huge favor in land-short Japan. By contrast, land is cheap and abundant in the United States, and this would be the last technique of industrial policy to be adopted, although it was by land grants that railroads and state universities were originally acquired, and state and local authorities still now sometimes offer sites to attract investments.

Seventh, the industry was exempted from having to pay customs duties on its import needs and the otherwise very high taxes on the petroleum products used as raw materials. By contrast, this would again be a case of improper favoritism in US terms.

Eighth, the industry was thoroughly protected from foreign competition by import licensing, outright prohibitions, and tariffs; subsequently, when the Japanese market was officially opened, intercompany collusion continued to keep out whatever imports were unwelcome to big business. By contrast, US free-market principles favor only the consumer interest, never industry.

Ninth, when the different companies in the new industry were already strong and growing rapidly, MITI established a "Petrochemical Cooperation Discussion Group" to help them coordinate investments to avoid overcapacity, and to regulate prices so as to avoid "disruptive" competition. By contrast, the US government does not sponsor cartels; it prosecutes them under the world's strictest and most strongly enforced antitrust legislation.

By employing those same techniques, MITI powerfully assisted the electronics industry in the 1960s, the computer industry in the 1970s, and both the biotechnology and aviation industries in the 1980s and 1990s, while at the same time liberating workers and the capital for them, by orchestrating the shrinking of the textile, shipbuilding, and steel industries.

The benevolent attentions of MITI were also directed at a variety of lesser industries and specific technologies, some very obscure and highly specialized. For example, when amorphous metals were developed in the United States from the 1970s, they mostly remained neglected, but MITI quickly recognized their great potential value in many electrical applications (e.g., high power batteries). But its officials did not want Japan's electrical industries to become dependent on US supplies. They wanted made-in-Japan amorphous metals, or none. They therefore moved to effectively block attempts by the then Allied-Signal corporation to market them in Japan, to remove the temptation for "disloyal" companies that might want to buy them. Next, MITI organized a research and development consortium to circumvent US patents, whose registration in Japan was of course held up—while all the data presented from the US were turned over to the consortium.

True believers in free enterprise and the higher wisdom of the market's invisible hand insist that "industrial policy" must fail, always and everywhere. Other foreign observers, by contrast, see it as a lethal threat to their own industries, unless matched at every turn. The truth is *not* somewhere in between. For the experience of many countries, and not just Japan, shows that industrial policy *works*, whether by creating industries from zero or by accelerating their growth and technical progress. True, the overall results must be consumer-inefficient, for any one Japanese would have been better off with spontaneous production and often just imports all along; but they are producer-efficient for the Japanese people as a whole, by creating a wise range of desirable employment opportunities.

To implement industrial policy, however, bureaucrats cannot just "pick winners and losers." They must also be able to make good on their picks, by helping favored industries in material ways, including both protectionism and hard cash in many cases. Only thus can they turn their predictions into self-fulfilling prophecies. American opponents explain that industrial policy is not only wrong in principle but in any case could never succeed in the United States, because it lacks a MITI staffed by elite officials from the best universities, thoroughly dedicated, and able to become genuine experts in the different industries of interest. The US Department of Commerce has only mediocre time-servers and untrained political appointees, they point out. That is a decidedly odd argument, considering that even little Singapore has been able to establish a highly effective version of MITI, and that the Departments of State and Defense never lacked for talent in the 1950s and 1960s when global security against the Soviet Union was still a burning and uncontroversial concern (pre-Vietnam). Now that geo-economics is the main contention in the central arena of world events, ample talent would naturally be drawn to an American MITI, if one were established in proper form.

A much stronger reservation is overlooked by most skeptics: industrial policy requires effective coordination across the board and the support of financial institutions. In Japan, MITI has been able to provide finance for favored industries through state-controlled or just cooperative banks, in ways that would be hard or impossible to duplicate in the United States. MITI has been able to dictate import and anti-import policies, while in the United States it is mostly Congress that determines tariffs, quotas, and prohibitions (very rare). In Japan, MITI has been able to arrange the cooperation of customs officials to block imports even when they are officially allowed, of the Ministry of Education to supplement its research and development efforts, and of its own patent office, while in the United States, each separate department goes its own way, all following the strict letter of the law. In other words, MITI has been operating in a highly favorable environment that would be lacking in the United States even if an American MITI were to be established.

∎ STATISTICAL DELUSIONS

What are the novel hopes and fears that now conspire to endow MITI with such mythic qualities? In the case of the Prussian General Staff, we saw that it was the territorialist mentality of the age that inspired a vastly exaggerated admiration and the abuse of the General Staff's ruthlessly practical methods for hollow purposes. Today, quite clearly, a different mentality prevails, but it, too, is fascinated by abstractions disconnected from palpable realities.

Instead of map-gazing, we anxiously scrutinize international statistics, to compare the home team's and the foreigners' numbers for labor productivity, rates of growth, life expectancy, and many more such— with all those bare numerals as unrevealing of a myriad of complicated economic realities as small-scale maps ever were of impassable moun-

tains, unredeemable wastelands, and populations that would stubbornly resist civilizing missions. Instead of the urge to systematize and
expand borders till then casually drawn around possessions of real
value, we have the urge to organize economic activity so as to maximize
its desirable statistics—as compared to other countries of course. For
the same adversarial spirit that once impelled the jealous expansion of
meaningless colonial borders is now manifest in the new international
statistical competition.

If you visit Korea, do not complain of the explosively uncontrolled
growth that has transformed Seoul into a gigantic conurbation of 17
million people containing more than one-third of the country's population, all but a few living in identical close-ranked gray cement apart-
ment blocks with huge numbers painted on their sides to tell them
apart, or in worse housing; you will find the Koreans anxiously scru-
tinizing the last set of economic growth figures, to see if they are
keeping their world record. Thailand has long since joined the Chinese
trio of Hong Kong, Singapore, and Taiwan in pursuing rapid economic
growth, and so has China too in part, so that the Koreans are facing stiff
competition. In all these countries too, as in Korea, every urban amenity as well as the air, water, and soil are sacrificed, and with good
reason—only industry and growth can provide rewarding and digni-
fied employment for crowded populations.

But in France there is the same preoccupation with statistical ratings.
In a country where so many live exceptionally well, with the world's
best food for everyday fare, second residences in the countryside for
millions of families (with perhaps a third at one of the ski resorts), it
is precisely the most privileged who speak not of that bounty when
they speak of France but of the statistical comparisons in which French
numbers are already behind the German, and sliding further (in the
immediate aftermath of unification there was another dismal discovery:
with both East German and West German athletes in one team, the
Germans would certainly triumph in the forthcoming Olympic jam-
borees, summer and winter).

The Germans for their part exult in their statistical aggrandizement
as East German numbers are added to their totals—when they are not
anxiously calculating the per capita consequences of reunion. Even if
they live in the same apartments as before, drive the same cars, and
consume as much, their standard-of-living statistics must inevitably fall
once the poorer East Germans are added into the average. As for Italy,

it might as well be renamed *Quinta Potenza,* for so often is the phrase *quinta potenza industriale* (world's fifth industrial power) heard in its public discourse—as if to be the world's fifth industrial power by international statistical comparisons meant anything at all, either for the Italians who live quite badly in the southern belt of poverty and organized crime, or in wealth and pollution in the northern industrial belt, or best of all in the middle regions around Tuscany, where neither poverty nor an excess of industry spoil well-made lives. The British meanwhile groan at their humbling statistical inferiority to Italy, a country that Britishers find especially hard to look up to, even as the Swedes were particularly depressed by Norway's oil-driven statistical rise while it lasted—the sudden enrichment of poor relations is particularly galling.

The Japanese themselves, statistically fixated for much longer than Americans, are varied in this as in all else. But most of them happily celebrate their excellent numbers even while knee-deep in the unwelcome consequences of so much growth, only pausing from celebration to fearfully note that Korean growth numbers are even more impressive than their own. And it was entirely characteristic that when Prime Minister Kiichi Miyazawa declared in 1991 that his government would deemphasize economic growth, to instead promote higher living standards by way of housing, public transport, and so on, he proclaimed his hope that Japan would become the world's "Lifestyle Superpower."[13] Perhaps he did not mean to suggest that Japan would now embark on a new quest for statistical superiority. But it is interesting to note that the Japanese press was suddenly filled with comparisons of Japanese, US, and some European numbers under such headings as "size of average residence," "percentage of homes with central heating," "percentage of homes with flush toilets," "per capita public park space," etc. Because Japan looks either bad or very bad in all those comparisons, most newspapers relieved the gloom by adding life-expectancy and crime figures too, in which Japan looks much better (how many "rapes per 100,000" is 200 square feet of park per person worth?).

It is true, of course, than there are significant realities behind the comparative statistics that are now so obsessively cited in the media, and so widely mourned or celebrated in countless private conversations. For all their inherent errors at the source, for all the multiplied unreliability of comparisons that mingle numbers of different national origins, some comparative statistics can indeed convey useful warnings or stimulating encouragement—at least when they focus on meaningful categories (the Soviet Union's decline was long concealed by excellent production figures for pig iron, cast iron, and wrought iron—in the age of the silicon chip), and when the differences they expose are wide enough to absorb many computational errors, and sustained enough to override seasons, business cycles, and transient circumstances.

It was the same with the maps that were so misleading at the climax of the colonial era. They, too, undoubtedly contained valid information, which could have usefully guided policy if the bare facts of geography were interpreted with care and restraint. While the garish red arrow that showed a further French advance into the Sahara presaged no harm whatsoever for the citizens of Hamburg or Hanover who nevertheless truly resented that illusory gain, any German arrow that curved toward the ports of Belgium was undoubtedly a genuine threat for Britain. Comparative international statistics of economic performance are like the French advance into the Sahara—just possibly another's gain, but rarely one's own loss. Only a few statistics, international but not merely comparative, are like the German advance into Belgium was for the British—another's gain that may cause one's own very grave loss.

As rough-and-ready indicators of the relative evolution of national economies over long periods of time, even gross national product figures that fluctuate with exchange rates are good enough—unless the "base year" is itself grossly misleading (as with the US–Europe and US–Japan 1950 to 1990 comparisons that ignore the peculiarity of 1950 as an early postwar year). But in the American case, it is absurd to moan over GNP growth rates, bad as they are, while ignoring all the blatant evidences of a society internally fragmented to a most unhappy degree. Likewise, the social statistics that are becoming steadily more popular (infant mortality, life expectancy, etc.) are scarcely meaningful because it is not mediocre American averages that count, but rather the enormous variances concealed by those averages.

It is also true that in some specific circumstances, international economic statistics can have an immediate meaning even for individuals. For example, Americans who work in the many industries that are struggling with foreign competitors may reasonably connect the monthly trade-balance figures that are now headlined in the press and broadcast as prime news with the security of their employment.

Equally, Japanese or Italian tourists about to set off on a foreign holiday have every reason to deplore balance-of-payments or relative interest-rate figures that presage some loss of value of their yen or lire.

With these reservations noted, the current obsession with comparative economic statistics directly recalls the mapological follies of a century ago. There is the same disconnection between the tangible realities of life and most of the numbers—a gap as wide as there ever was between actual security and actual wealth, on the one hand, and the coloring of spaces on the map. And yet for all their abstract character, these numbers are today as politically compelling as maps of mere paper once were. Hence there is the same potential for misguided action that would sacrifice real comforts and real cultural satisfactions for purely numerical depictions of success.

CHAPTER 4

WHEN WILL THE UNITED STATES BECOME A THIRD WORLD COUNTRY?

When Buenos Aires was still a leading world metropolis, when the people of Argentina still enjoyed their famous steak-for-every-meal abundance that lasted into the 1950s, they would never have believed that the future of their country would amount to a forty-year slide into poverty. Equally, the people of the United States, still today by far the richest country in the world, have been slow to recognize what has been happening over the last twenty or more years, and what future is in store for them if present trends simply continue. Yet all the relevant numbers confirm the slide and suggest the chilling forecast.

That economic statistics can easily mislead is not in doubt ("there are lies, damn lies, and statistics," goes the jibe), especially when it comes to international comparisons. But everyday life provides the most telling evidences of Third-Worldization, even if no statistics can measure them. Americans living in solidly middle-class city districts, in pleasant suburbs, in untroubled small towns, still have to confront a pervasive and increasingly *accepted* lack of skill in shops, banks, garages, and their own workplaces—for there, too, the more recent products of American high schools daily demonstrate that it is possible to graduate with little reading, scarcely any writing, and no mathematics at all. It is, however, the lack of diligence, the self-will to do each job well and completely, that drives American executives rotated back from Singapore and Zurich into the arms of stress-counselors, and causes Japanese executives posted from Brazil or Malaysia to wonder how far removed America is from those countries' conditions. That is, of course, the other side of the coin of falling real earnings for the rank-and-file employees that even elite Americans must still depend on. The naked plywood and unfinished gypsum board at Kennedy Airport are perfect symbols of the American economy, now replete with disastrous attempts to practice capitalism in the new American style, capitalism without capital.

▪ THE NUMBERS

So when will the United States become a Third World country?

It depends on how we define that unhappy condition. But going by some estimates, the date might be as close as the year 2020. That is hardly much time when it comes to the agonizingly slow timetable of reforms powerful enough to change America's future. More optimistic projections might add another ten or fifteen years. Either way, if present trends simply continue, all but a small minority of Americans will be impoverished soon enough, left to yearn hopelessly for the lost golden age of American prosperity. Of course, statistical comparisons can compound all sorts of counting errors within each country with sometimes grotesque distortions. Certainly nothing at all can be proved by comparing growth rates from, say, 1950 as some have done.[1] At that point, the European and Japanese economies were just beginning to recover from their wartime ruinations, and because it is much easier to rebuild than to achieve fresh progress, American economic performance in the 1950s and 1960s is made to seem downright pathetic, when in fact it was quite respectable. By 1970, however, all reconstruction had long since been completed, eliminating at least that one distortion. Even so, each particular measure misleads in its own way, and none should be taken all that seriously.

For example, all the gross national product figures cited in what follows are indeed gross as measures go: a car accident increases them by the amount of the ambulance, hospital, and bodyshop bills, while a healthy cut in cigarette smoking reduces them as tobacco-company sales and excise taxes go down. Nor can any international comparison be free of all sorts of distortions large and small no matter what criterion is employed, simply because different consumption preferences prevail in different countries: the price of very fresh squid still matters much more for Japanese than Americans, in spite of the spread of *sushi* bars from coast to coast, just as red wine looms much larger in French than in Japanese household budgets. Any yet, after listing all possible objections and all proper reservations, the central fact that all the relevant numbers point the same way is all too conclusive. That is what matters, not the specific numbers with all their gross, or grotesque, distortions. When *all* the statistics point the same way, not over one or two years but over ten and twenty years, their message cannot simply be ignored.

In 1970, the United States was still by far the most productive of countries, with a gross national product of $1,014,750,000,000—1 trillion and 14,750 million dollars—which worked out to $4,950 per man, woman, and child in the total population of some 205 million at that time. In that same year, the equivalent figure for Japan was only $1,950 per person, while for the European Community as a whole it was $2,360 per person. By that *very* rough measure of total output, Americans were therefore still more than twice as productive on average as the Community's Europeans in 1970, and their edge over the Japanese was greater still.[2] But within ten years the pattern of decline had already set in. With a gross national product per person of $12,000 the United States in 1980 was still well ahead of the European Community average at $9,760 and Japan's at $9,870, but its margin of superiority had been cut in half.

At that point, the simplest "straight-line" projection—it requires only a pencil, a ruler, and a bit of graph paper—would have shown that given another ten years, the United States would be overtaken by both Japan and the richer European countries. Professional economists make fun of such crude oversimplifications (they are fond of recalling the pre–motor car predictions that the manure of horse-cabs and wagons would submerge cities), but that is exactly what happened: the 1989 figure for the United States was $21,000, while Japan's gross national product per person had soared to $23,810. Distorted by the entry of three poor countries, Greece, Portugal, and Spain, the European Community average was only $15,980, or 76% of the American level, but Germany at $20,750 was substantially even, while Switzerland, Europe's top performer, was well ahead at $30,270.

Because those numbers clearly show a twenty-year trend of relative decline and not just some brief downturn, it is not utterly foolish to calculate what the future numbers will be if the United States remains on its present path. Already in the year 2000, now just around the corner in the time-scale of significant action to overcome serious national problems, Japan's gross national product per person would be almost twice as large, while the richest European countries would have a 50% edge. In ten more years after that, Japan would be more than three times as productive per person as the United States, while the northern European countries would be almost twice as productive. They are certainly investing enough to achieve that result.[3]

Finally in 2020, when the children of today's middle-aged Americans will themselves be middle-aged, the leading European countries would be more than twice as productive on a person basis, while the gap between Japanese and Americans—at almost 5:1—would be just about the same as the 1980 gap between Americans and Brazilians. At that point, the United States would definitely become a Third World Country—at least by Japanese standards. Certainly, nonelite Americans would no longer be in the same class as *average* Western Europeans.

That particular trend is already established fact. In the 1950s, even American students traveling to Europe on student budgets could stay at the best hotels and eat in the best restaurants. Coming from a far more productive society, they found that the pocket money of summer jobs or minor parental handouts were quite enough to pay for European luxury. Today American students still travel to Europe, but now they complain that the high prices keep them out of all but youth hostels and the cheapest lodgings; in London, Paris, Rome, they congregate at the local McDonald's, and not only because of nostalgia— they can afford no other restaurant or even *trattoria*. As for the luxury hotels that once relied on American tourists, their rooms are now taken by Japanese and Europeans, with only richer Americans still able to pay their rates. If the 2020 projection holds true, most Americans will only be able to travel to Europe as casual labor, just as the poor of Latin America and the Caribbean now come to California and Florida as stoop labor for the harvest and in search of menial jobs.

As of now, tens of thousands of young Americans live in Japan as illegal immigrants at any one time. Many teach English to pay their way, but many others work in bars and nightclubs or as models of various kinds, not all of them for the fashion and advertising industries. American girls serving as bar hostesses and part-time call girls are now so common in Tokyo that their services no longer command a premium (AIDS has put American call boys right out of business). When a country is in economic decline, not only its currency but also its flesh is cheapened.

It is true enough that to project the future by simply extending the past can be very misleading, because unexpected changes can always outweigh continuities. But so far at least, the path seems straight enough—and straight downhill.

It is just as true that international comparisons of national products or any similar statistics can easily be distorted by abrupt exchange-rate fluctuations: one reason why Switzerland reached the astounding per-person figure of $30,270 in 1989 was that the Swiss franc happened to be very high that year. In any case, all fluctuations aside, exchange rates routinely distort comparisons. For one thing they reflect only the international supply and demand for capital, goods, and services—as well as speculative tides and the manipulations of central banks—and not the much greater amount of purely domestic buying and selling.

Currencies can therefore be greatly overvalued or undervalued as compared to their actual purchasing power at home—a distortion familiar to any tourist whose dollar can buy so much more in Mexico than in Switzerland—or in Mexico, too, a week or a month later, if the peso is suddenly uplifted by rising oil prices, eager capital investment, or just exchange-rate speculation.

The US dollar, as it happens, has been deliberately undervalued since the 1985 "Plaza" agreement of the chief industrial countries, in an attempt to increase US exports by making American goods and services cheaper for foreigners, and to discourage imports by making them more expensive for Americans. It is by high-quality exports at high prices and not by price-cutting that a nation's prosperity can be assured—in cheapening the currency, the work of Americans is also cheapened.

That, however, was the textbook solution for the huge deficits of the 1980s—which predictably worked much better in selling to the Europeans than to famously import-resistant Japan or Korea. Thus trade deficits continue, but the results have been to reduce the dollar's exchange rate to the point where much more can be bought at home than in most of Europe or Japan with a dollar's worth of currency.

If that particular distortion is corrected by using a "purchasing-power parity" measure, the United States certainly scores much higher in international comparisons. In 1988, the gross domestic product per person was $19,558 for the United States, $14,161 for West Germany as it then still was, $16,700 for Europe's champion Switzerland, and only $14,288 for Japan[4]—as opposed to the straight exchange rate comparison for that same year, in which Japan's gross *national* product at $20,960 per person already exceeded the $19,820 figure for the US.[5] Those figures are also intuitively much more realistic, certainly for middle-class Americans who compare their spacious houses to the cramped two-room apartments of most residents of Tokyo or Osaka (in rural Japan there are plenty of large houses), and the smaller share that goes for food in their own family budgets, as compared to what Germans or Italians have to pay.

Does that make the gloomy forecasts based on straight exchange rates invalid? Not so. Purchasing-power values at home certainly depict living standards more realistically. But when a country's exchange rate must go down to improve its trade balance, it shows that its overall ability is in decline as compared to its competitors. Thus living standards, too, must eventually slide. After all, even Bangladesh can export by selling cheaply enough. Moreover, it is only comparisons based on straight exchange rates that determine the "who-does-what-to-whom" of the international economy—including the little matter of which side can buy out attractive pieces of other (open-door) economies, and which side can only sell off buildings, golf courses, forest lands, or entire multibillion dollar corporations to pay for its imports. As productive assets are sold, and loans taken to finance the daily intake of imported goods, services, fripperies, and baubles, the enjoyment of even splendid living standards becomes rather ephemeral.

In any case, even if we switch to the purchasing-power measure of gross domestic products, we find that although the United States is still ahead, the trend is just as unfavorable. In 1970, the per-person figures for the United States, West Germany, Italy, and Japan were $4,922, $3,380, $2,848, and $2,765, respectively. In other words, the United States was almost one and half times as productive per person as Germany and 1.8 times as productive as Japan. Because there was so much inflation in the years that followed, all those figures were much higher by 1988, but while the American gross domestic product per person had increased by less than four times ($\times$ 3.97 to be exact), the West German increase was distinctly larger ($\times$ 4.18), the Italian increase was greater still ($\times$ 4.55)—in spite of the notorious undercounting caused by the explosion of Italy's underground economy during those very years—while Japan's figure was more than five times greater ($\times$ 5.16).[6]

In yet another and especially careful comparison, focused more directly on the gross domestic product per *employed* person, West Germany as it then was increased from 61.9% of the American level in 1970 to 79.1% by 1990; France likewise went from 63.9% to 89.7%; Italy ascended from 63.6% to 88.4%; and Japan went from 47.3% to 76.9%.[7] The United States is therefore well ahead, but again its margin is shrinking—and nothing is changing the *direction* of that trend.

It is reassuring to discover that the situation seems much better if we look at the purchasing-power numbers, but the pattern of relative decline is just as evident. That pattern is certainly continuing as this is written, even though the collapse of its stock-exchange-and-real-estate "bubble economy" is pushing Japan into a recession, just as the United States is fitfully recovering from its own. A most careful estimate presented to the Joint Economic Committee of the US Congress in May 1992 projected future growth of the gross national product of the United States at the rate of 2% per year over 1990–1995 as compared to 3.75% for Japan.[8] That may seem low for Japan when compared to the heady 8% and 10% annual growth rates of the 1960s, and the difference, too, may seem small. But it takes thirty-six years to double the total output of a national economy that has a 2% annual growth rate, and only 19.5 years at 3.7%—for any one individual, an additional 16.5-year wait is not trivial. And it is all very well to proclaim with every sign of satisfaction the end of Japan's economic miracle, as some are doing—one would think that the slowdown is some sort of gain for the United States: actually it is likely to increase Japan's already notorious unwillingness to import.

Yet even as the Japanese economy cannot expand at the extraordinary rates of the past, it seems that the United States cannot replicate its own most modest achievements either; the same estimate predicts that its economy will only grow at the rate of 2.3% per year from 1995 to the year 2000—which implies a miserably low 1% growth rate per person, given the projected increase in population over those same years.[9] At that rate, it would take seventy-two years, almost the full span of two working lives, to double the national product per person. If that particular estimate holds out, it will be fair to redefine the national myth as the receding "American mirage," even if the long-standing shift of total national wealth to fewer and fewer Americans were to be stopped by Clinton's tax increases—and of that, there is at present no prospect at all.

While lesser arguments persist, the great debate that started at the end of the 1980s is now over; it can no longer be denied that the United States has been undergoing a most spectacular economic decline as compared to the leading First World countries.

Of course, to show by whatever numbers that other advanced economies are catching up is not the end of the world, and certainly does not begin to prove that the United States is becoming a Third World country. On the contrary, even a pathetically slow growth rate is still growth, all set to make the United States—by far the richest country in the world—even richer as a country. In what follows, therefore, nothing more will be said of gross national product and gross domestic product figures, except to poke fun at attempts to compare them as if they were exact measures.

Unfortunately, the slow-growing American economy also happens to be an increasingly fractured economy, in which the top 1% have been becoming rapidly much richer, the top 20% as a whole are also increasing their share of all income,[10] and the remaining 80% of all Americans have absorbed *all* the slow growth, and more than that—with a large fraction actually impoverished.

The United States therefore remains a First World country and the richest, too, but a distinct majority of all Americans have long been headed "south" in stock-market parlance. For them, Third-Worldization is an ongoing reality manifest in that novel American phenomenon: the son who cannot afford a house like his father's when he matures into employment, nor his vacations and leisure as more hours are worked in the attempt to offset the lower wages. As of now, the average of 1,847 hours per year of American industrial workers greatly exceeds the German, Swedish, French, Italian, and British averages, being exceeded in turn only by the Japanese—who work more hours even though *their* wages keep increasing. The month-long summer vacations of their European counterparts are out of the question for American workers.[11] Many can no longer find industrial employment at all and must instead poach traditional underclass jobs as janitors, warehouse loaders, cleaners, groundsmen, and security guards—the jobs that used to provide a first toehold on the lowest rung of the economic ladder for the black underclass especially. It is hard to rise when pressed down from above.

The underclass, urban or rural, perhaps 6% of the population at most,[12] already lives in full Third World conditions, but without the solace of tropical sunsets or the heartening family stability that can be retained even in extreme poverty within well-rooted traditional cultures. Instead, their often disordered lives are bereft of hope, as many of their children start out on careers of atrocious schooling, unemployment, crime, addiction, imprisonment, and violence. That accounts for some 15 million Americans, who would have been better off morally if not materially if they had been born in Nepal or Thailand. Another 28 million Americans are already listed as poor or near-poor by official reckoning.[13] By world standards, they are not poor at all, but they *are* becoming poorer rapidly enough to be undergoing Third-Worldization toward Brazilian if not Indian levels. And that fate will be shared in turn, if more slowly, by many more Americans if present trends continue. How could it be otherwise when the real hourly pay of eight out of ten Americans in all forms of nongovernment employment is now smaller than it was twenty years ago?

That poverty should mark Third-Worldization is obvious enough. But as any visitors to those countries can readily see, a special kind of wealth is also one of the traits of Third-Worldization. At the end of a dirt road lined with shacks along which barefoot children play, there is a fenced mansion with manicured gardens, illegally dug antiques, private zoos (a Latin American fad), modern art, satellite dish, and all the latest Japanese entertainment machines—although garden, house, and kitchen need no labor-saving appliances given the abundance of gardeners, servants, cooks, and maids. The charming host and hostess, recently back from their latest shopping trip to Paris or Miami, well educated or at least magazine-sophisticated, are happy to entertain at length, often offering to escort the visitor to the local attractions in gratitude for the diversion that can occupy their ample time. Naturally they are nationalistic, if only politely, readily protesting their intense love of country.

But do not ask them why the children along the way are not in school, or why the road is unpaved, as most of the country's roads still are. Usually that special kind of wealth is disconnected from any real work, and your hosts are thus profoundly uninterested in improving public education, for that would require "new" taxes, while they employ only gardeners, servants, cooks, and maids, the less educated and more pliant the better. Paved roads would be convenient, sparing the Mercedes or Range Rover, but are not worth "new" taxes either, because there is no daily commute to the office, and no factory or depot with trucks to send off and receive. Actually there is almost no public investment at all that your hosts are willing to pay for with their taxes. For they actually live on their land on urban rents, stocks and bonds, trusts, and bank deposits safely overseas. Such "rentiers," are very different creatures from the *working* rich, whether professionals or businesspeople, who do need well-educated employees and good roads, among other public services.

At the last count, and by the best estimate, the richest 1% of all American families owned $1.25 trillion of rental real estate, $1.12 trillion of stocks and bonds, $221.9 billion in trusts, and $524.6 billion in bank and other accounts, for a total of some $3.1 trillion, as compared to only $2.5 trillion invested in their own business enterprises. As a group, their "rentier" income was roughly half their total income of $503 billion,[14] and even though they must make do with few servants, to that extent they resemble the Third World rich. Of such wealth, poverty is made.

CONSEQUENCES

America's economic decline, even if it is only relative, cannot remain only economic. The arts, scientific research, and all culture cannot flower and grow in poverty. Only an increasing prosperity can maintain the world lead of American universities, research centers, libraries, museums, theaters, orchestras, ballet companies, and artists of all sorts. It was the ample earnings of Italian traders and bankers that fed the scholars, painters, sculptors, architects, and poets who gave us the Renaissance. When Italy was bypassed by the new flows of ocean trade, its impoverished merchants and bankrupt financiers could no longer commission artists nor keep scholars at work. Many emigrated to embellish Paris, St. Petersburg, and half the towns in Europe, and to adorn the courts of foreign princes. Thus commercial decline was soon followed by the bleak downfall of Italian art and scholarship.

As it is, many American academic and cultural institutions are shrinking rather than growing as their funding diminishes, while some of the most celebrated eagerly solicit foreign donations in pathetic competition with Third World hunger campaigns. In September 1991, Arima Tatsuo, the chief cabinet councilor for external affairs in Japan's prime minister's office, complained of the dozens of begging letters from American universities and research centers that were stacked on his desk. He had been a student in the rich and confident United States of the 1950s, and was now plainly embarrassed by the undignified pleadings of once eminent institutions.

Democracy, too, must become fragile when better hopes are worn away by bitter disappointment, opening the way for the strong, false remedies of demagogues. Once the politics of affluence for all—the politics of the American dream—become too blatantly unrealistic for most Americans, the politics of racist, xenophobic, or class resentment can more honestly gain votes; all they promise are emotional satisfactions that even an impoverished government can readily provide.

To hope is human, but to expect a fair share in an ever-increasing prosperity is distinctly American. If that ambition is relentlessly denied, the political consequences can hardly fail to be catastrophic. After all, Americans have no shared national culture to unite them as the French or Italians have—there are many different cultures in our pluralist society. Nor can Americans rely on ethnic solidarity alone, as the Japanese say they can—we have many different ethnic origins. What Americans have in common are their shared beliefs, above all in equality of opportunity in the pursuit of affluence. It would be too much to expect that democratic governance would long survive the impoverishment of all Americans except for a minority of fortunate inheritors, talented professionals, brilliant or merely lucky businesspeople, 700,000 often rapacious lawyers, and a few cunning financial manipulators.

CHAPTER 5

CAPITALISM WITHOUT CAPITAL

It seems only yesterday that the eternal optimists among us were still pointing to the continued American dominance of the world's entertainment, biotechnology, computer, and aviation industries to assure us that all was well, in spite of the virtual extinction of the US consumer electronics industry, the large retreat of the auto industry, the drastic decline of the steel industry, and the downfall of the machine-tool industry, still very much the very foundation of all industries.

Since then, Columbia Pictures, maker of countless famous films, has been sold to Sony, which had already purchased CBS records in 1987, and went on to buy RCA/Columbia Home Video and also Culver Studios in 1991, for a combined total of $6,195 million. MCA, America's leading "multimedia" corporation, alike huge in movies, television, and music recording, has been sold to Matsushita for $6,125 million; and MGM now belongs to a French bank. Outright sales aside, 12% of Time Warner, which includes HBO, has been sold to Toshiba and C. Itoh for the nice round sum of $1 billion (a commitment to buy Toshiba's rather than US or any other equipment is part of the contract); and a stake in the small but enterprising Carolco Pictures of *Basic Instinct* and *Terminator 2* has been partly sold to Japan's Pioneer Electronic for $75 million. Even hugely successful Disney, long the toast of Wall Street, chose to sell off ownership of the hugely profitable Disneyland in Japan to local investors, in yet another exercise of capitalism without capital in the new American style.

Thus Michael Jackson records may still sell by the million all over the world, American films may continue to dominate the global market, but the profits, the resulting opportunity to accumulate capital, and therefore the ability to make further investments at home or abroad, will go to foreign owners. Those who insist that the sale of MCA, Columbia, etc., does not matter a bit in national terms, because in the aftermath both the money and MCA, Columbia, etc., remain in the United States, miss the point: today's profits are the best source of tomorrow's capital. Because the Japanese are better than Americans at producing cars and many other things, Americans buy cars and many other things from Japanese companies—which further improves their production through the investment of the profits they earn in the US market. Americans are better than the Japanese at producing mass-market entertainment with worldwide appeal, but the Japanese will no longer have to buy MCA, Columbia, Carolco, CBS, and HBO films or CDs from US companies, but only from fully or partly Japanese-owned companies that happen to operate in the US. Thus the profits earned by those films and records in the Japanese market, and in all other markets worldwide, will accrue in full or in part to those Japanese companies, serving to fund their further growth. What had been US exports to Japan will still appear in official statistics as US exports to Japan, but as far as the profit flow is concerned, it will be strictly an intra-Japanese trade.

In theory, as textbook economists would have it, all of the foregoing is irrelevant nonsense. MCA, Columbia, etc., were not stolen but bought, so that a grand total of some $13,394.8 million was sent from Japan to the United States. That, too, is a nice bit of change that could pay for a great deal of productive capital investment, which would in turn generate its own income flows. In the world imagined by *Wall Street Journal* editorialists where all money slides smoothly to its appointed destiny for the greater glory of global economic efficiency, the previous owners of MCA, Columbia, etc., must necessarily invest their $13 billion plus, and being sensible fellows will invest efficiently. After all, if they sold MCA, Columbia, etc., it must have been because they had a better use for the money. Equally, while the Japanese economy will undoubtedly benefit from the profit flows of MCA, Columbia, etc., the US economy as a whole will benefit from profit flows of whatever businesses are started or expanded with the $13 billion plus.

Unfortunately, reality is quite otherwise. First, over the years 1987–

1991, when the Hollywood sell-off was going on, the United States was running huge foreign trade deficits, for a combined total of some $550 billion dollars; over 1987–1990 alone the merchandise trade deficit with Japan came to $199 billion, much of it for consumer goods.[1] In other words, the profits from MCA, Columbia, etc., will still be flowing to Japan for many a long year after the cars, motorcycles, video-cassette recorders, watches, color TVs, cosmetics, toys, etc., bought with the $13 billion plus will have been crushed for recycling, abandoned in attics, or just thrown away to fill waste dumps. More simply, Japan acquired long-lived fruit trees, while the United States acquired only some fresh fruit.

As for the private use that the ex-shareholders made of the money they received for MCA, Columbia, etc., there is no definite information, of course. Some of it may have been invested in other Hollywood ventures, brave new biotechnology start-ups, or even in the established industries that suffer from a shortage of capital. But given the attractions of earning perfectly safe and very high interest from the US Treasury for the ocean of bonds it then sold to cover exploding federal deficits, much of the money was probably used to finance that other sort of day-to-day consumption, which paid for Desert Storm and the inflated Medicare bills of yesteryear, among other things.

An unknown but large part of the money that came from Japan probably had a simpler destination: the buying sprees of the shareholders themselves. Guided by the example of the hostile takeover artists who were the heroes of the day, during those years especially, many a husband was badgered by his impatient wife to acquire the basic necessities of life, if he did not crave them himself: the G-4 or Gulfstream IV jet that can cross the Atlantic was virtually compulsory for membership in the super-rich club (how else can one bring back the new season's gowns from Paris?) and so was the Aspen, Colorado, skiing chalet, the cowless California "ranch," or the French-chateau-style Connecticut estate, the essential signature artworks including at least one French Impressionist, not to speak of minor fripperies and foibles such as Ferraris and Rolls-Royces. Certainly the ex-shareholders of MCA, Columbia, etc., were not so un-American as to conserve their money excessively in a country where saving was out of fashion, and gross domestic investment came to a total of only some $3,000 per person in 1989 (as compared to $7,000 for Japan).[2]

The Hollywood sell-off also has another effect. Unlike most other products, films can convey political messages—sometimes very powerful messages. Thus the Japanese ownership of leading film studios raises the question that hardly arises when a trophy building in Manhattan or a famous golf course is sold. That is a question easily answered: ownership automatically brings with it editorial authority, even if the new owners say not a word to enforce it, indeed especially if they say nothing. Very soon after its purchase of MCA, Matsushita was accused of active interference because the script of a US ballplayer-in-Japan film was abruptly revised to tone down criticisms of Japanese ways (the fans like to shout racist invective, etc.). Matsushita very credibly denied that it had issued orders to that effect. But, of course, the entire debate was impossibly naive or dishonest: silent authority is even more effective than power loudly asserted.

Hollywood producers are well known for their steely devotion to the principles of artistic freedom, but being themselves such sensitive fellows they cannot be expected to ignore the sensitivities of those who pay for their Beverly Hills mansions, Rolls-Royces, and Rodeo Drive shopping sprees. It is not by accident, as the old *Pravda* would have said, that the anti-Japanese mood of the public is not being meretriciously exploited by anti-Japanese films. Nor was it an accident that none of the Japanese-owned studios even placed a bid for the film rights of the 1992 best-seller *Rising Sun* by Michael Crichton. That fiercely anti-Japanese thriller is not likely to be long remembered in the annals of world literature, but it was a Book-of-the-Month-Club main selection, and as such of compulsory interest to all major Hollywood studios. None had stayed away before when a mass-market fiction success was auctioned.[3]

Needless to say, it would be foolish to blame the Japanese for all these harsh economic and political consequences. They merely bought what was freely offered to them. Nor is there any sign of a sinister conspiracy masterminded by the Elders of the Rising Sun from their headquarters dug deep below the imperial palace in Chiyoda-Ku. Except for the perfectly normal joint venture between the manufacturer Toshiba and the C. Itoh trading company, there was no coordination on the Japanese side. On the contrary, Matsushita and Sony compete fiercely both at home and abroad, and their Hollywood purchases were an extension of that competition. And neither Matsushita's famously nationalistic management nor the famously changeable Mr. Akio Morita of Sony (coauthor of an anti-American tract in Japanese, and a tireless booster of the United States in English) descended on Hollywood at the head of commandos sworn to conquer MCA, Columbia, etc., or die. Instead it was a simple matter of capital available for long-term investment, as in "American, lack of."

Every child can tell that American popular entertainment products utterly dominate world markets, except for the odd French film sufficiently exquisite to fill a few art houses, and the occasional CD of British, Swedish, or Israeli pop stars. There should therefore have been American bidders aplenty when word got around that MCA, Columbia, etc. could be bought, all fabulous properties with their ups and downs of course (films can bomb, pop stars can suddenly fade), but all sure to be highly profitable *in the long run,* as leisure time continues to expand and so does the demand for mass entertainment.

That was the rub. Amidst the pervasive shortage of capital in the United States, the result of much shopping and miserably small savings, and of government financed by endless borrowing instead of taxes, there is a more acute shortage of *patient* investment capital. And, of course, all really productive investment must be patient: factories are not built in a day, nor is a new airliner engineered in a year. Supposedly, the key function of Wall Street and its satellites around the country is precisely to convert the rivulets of savings, pension contributions, reinvested dividend and interest earnings, and foreign placings into the river of longer-term investment, by way of stocks, bonds, and direct loans, to pay for builders to build, for factories to turn out new plant and machinery, and for the costs of research and development.

But it is now clear that there is a fatal defect in the present workings of the system: the "investment bankers" at its very core have *no* interest in long-term investments, or long-term anything. They do not earn their money from dividends, interest, or profit-shares in operating businesses, but from fees, transaction by transaction. Each time they arrange a bank loan, underwrite a new issue of shares or bonds, assist in a merger, acquisition, hostile takeover bid, or a corporate defense against the same, they receive a fee. Routinely, these are multimillion dollar fees, and sometimes they are much larger. In the most famous and largest takeover so far, which disposed of RJR Nabisco for some $25 billion, Drexel Burnham Lambert was paid a $227 million fee for arranging a $3.5 billion bridging loan from commercial banks, another $109 million went to Merrill Lynch for arranging a second bridging loan (to cover the gap between the takeover and the disposal of part of

RJR for cash); a grouping of 200 banks that itself loaned $14.5 billion, received $325 million in fees, while Morgan Stanley and Wasserstein Perella were paid $25 million each just for their advice. Finally Drexel Burnham Lambert earned a separate and larger amount for raising more billions in cash for the takeover, by issuing their now infamous high-risk "junk bonds" and selling them to captive financiers (who bought them only because they needed junk bond issues for their own deals), as well as to savings and loans associations and pension funds that had no business in converting money into such dubious paper.[4]

Even if most fees are much smaller, they are still money by the million earned in days or hours and it is money largely paid out to the investment bankers themselves in salary and bonuses. Money that is actually invested productively is asleep and quite useless from their point of view. What they want are transactions—the more transactions the better. Ideally, a public company should first be taken over, preferably in a hostile bid (generating fees from both sides). Then the winner will have to repay some of the high-interest loans that were used to buy the company by selling off its own divisions, departments, or company assets (paying disposal fees). Then the winner should want to issue new shares (paying underwriting fees), to extract quickly the winnings from the stock market, instead of waiting for operating profits (that generate no fees). And then, finally, the company having become public again, its shares should be bought out in another takeover, starting the cycle all over again.

The most obvious result is to divert billions of dollars that could have gone to builders, equipment makers, and research staffs to the personal bank accounts of investment bankers, in part to be reinvested productively, but in large part to be spent on suitably luxurious personal consumption.

But the far more harmful result, as soon as the last crash, and the last lot of scandals, indictments, debacles, and bankruptcies has been safely forgotten, is to infect the entire business world with fast-buck fever. For investment bankers and their tipsters do not wait for deals to arrive at their door. Before F. Ross Johnson, chief executive of RJR Nabisco, put the company "in play," when he launched his failed attempt to head his own leveraged buy-out,[5] he was constantly badgered and tempted by investment bankers hungry for fees.[6] They kept telling him that his Gulfstream jets, multiple corporate residences, celebrity golf tournaments, huge salary, and guaranteed $700,000 annual pension (or $49 million upon dismissal) were a sordid pittance as compared to what he could extract for himself from RJR Nabisco if he got rid of the shareholders. Nor was Ross Johnson an exception—in fact the chiefs of corporations large and small all over the country were frequently distracted from the business of their businesses during Wall Street's last exuberant season, and will be again when the next one starts.

Those who could not be tempted to attempt buy-outs of their own were diverted anyway from the work of development, production, and sales by hostile takeover threats, by the need to prepare defenses ("poison pills"), or by company raiders who accumulated shares for the express purpose of being bought off by directors and management determined to stay in place. Many a US corporation has gone into debt, closed down laboratories and plants, fired workers, and sold off divisions to pay above-market "greenmail" to company raiders. In the wake of the 1989–1991 insider-trading scandals, and during a period of reduced inflation (which nicely erodes debt), Wall Street's fever seems quiescent at this writing. But as long as investment bankers and their hangers-on are paid by the transaction, the quick-deal culture will still fundamentally prevail in American finance, even after the collapse of the superfollies of the junk bond and merger-mania 1980s.

In sum, that is the reason why there were no US buyers with a long-term view ready to outbid Matsushita, Sony, and Pioneer for MCA, Columbia, etc. Wall Street Journal editorialists and other true believers in the perfection of "the market," as they reverently call it, are unmoved, of course. They argue that if "the numbers" had been right, US buyers would have come forward; if they did not, it must have been because MCA, Columbia, etc., were overpriced. Perhaps they were and the Japanese foolishly overpaid, and perhaps what they say is all true, but how many US corporations or investors actually act on the basis of ten-year growth plans, rather than next quarter's financial results? In explaining why his company paid the nontrivial sum of $500 million for 6% of Time Warner, a senior executive of C. Itoh achieved just the right touch of self-contradiction that the Japanese always aim for: "It wasn't just for financial reasons. . . . By joining with Time Warner, we lock in an existing end market, not just a potential one."[7] Matsushita, by the way, apparently has some sort of 250-year plan, and shows every sign of following an actual 25-year plan. The hare runs straight for immediate profit. The tortoise patiently crawls toward market control.

Tacit censorship is not a problem in the biotechnology industry, by now the classic home of the dynamic creativity and bold entrepreneurship that are supposed to offset all other weaknesses of the American economy. But while the names of both buyers and sellers are far more obscure than in the Hollywood pairings, and the deals are much smaller (e.g., Chugai's $100 million purchase of Gen-Probe), the great sell-off is under way just the same. Outright transfers of ownership are rare, because there is so little of physical substance in companies that consist mainly of talent and test tubes in rented space. But several dozen US biotechnology companies have signed "intercompany agreements." Having found that in nine out of ten of those agreements the flow of technology is strictly one way from the United States to Japan in exchange for rather small amounts of hard cash, a 1992 report of the National Academy of Sciences was categorical: "Unless concrete steps are taken by government, industries and universities . . . [to stop such deals] . . . the U.S. biotechnology industry will lose its strong leadership position.[8]

The report might have added a word about the "venture capitalists" who frequently provide the starting funds for new biotechnology companies. Increasingly, they have not been willing to wait until the enzyme, the cell, the vaccine, or similar creature grows to maturity as a developed product of known and tested value. Instead they impatiently pressure their scientific partners to issue early announcements of forthcoming breakthroughs that will, could, or might offer a cure for cancer or the common cold or pimples, so they can launch an initial public offering of shares on Wall Street to make a quick killing by selling their own holdings, or else attract the "Japanese" (or Swiss or Germans or anyone) to buy out the company or a piece of it. It was the revelation that many microorganisms were still elusive, and that many promised cures for this or that ailment were far from ready to be used, that caused the 1991–1992 downfall of the previously booming biotechnology stocks on Wall Street. Increasingly, therefore, scientists disinclined to play the game out of respect for the truth, or in fear of professional ridicule and academic sanctions, have preferred to seek more patient and more responsible money elsewhere—often from US or European pharmaceutical companies, but mainly from famously patient Japan.

In the contemptuous tones that are now becoming habitual in foreign commentaries on the American economy, the Japanese monthly

Business Tokyo opened a lead article on the industry as follows: "The Americans come every day, like monks seeking alms. They are among the world's top scientists in specialties ranging from genetics to cancer research to protein engineering. Some hail from major universities, others from tiny venture-capital firms. All are disciples of a field—biotechnology—that promises future riches. And their pilgrimage to Japan is for money. 'Whether by phone, by fax, or in person, we're swamped by requests for financial support from US biotech scientists,' says Akira Furuya, managing director of industry fermenter Kyowa Hakko Kogyo Co."[9]

The rest of the article provides chapter and verse on the latest Japanese acquisitions—and also the most unreassuring assurance that American dominance of *basic* research is unchallenged. Such fields as genetics and biophysics can yield wonderful discoveries, truly in the service of humanity, but research is also pure cost. The payoff is in the development of usable products, and the big profits are earned only in production—by the "fermenters" that actually produce the stuff. In the biotechnology industry, the pattern is by now well established: Americans still do most of the research and much of the development, but because they cannot find capital at home to build the required facilities, they sell out to Japanese and European companies, receiving millions in license fees for products whose sales can eventually earn billions (year 2000 estimates for biotechnology sales exceed $50 billion, as compared to only $2 billion in 1990).

Unfortunately it is only the millions of fees—and not the billions of sales that will be earned mainly by foreign companies—that can be taxed to pay for basic research as well as all other government expenditures. As it is, the United States spent $5 billion on biotechnology research in 1990, as compared to only $1.7 billion for Japan,[10] but it is the Japanese fermenters that are prospering, in great part by selling products originally developed in the United States, mostly at the taxpayers' expense.

That is just as true when US biotechnology is sold to European buyers, as in the 1991 purchase of 60% of SyStemix by the Swiss pharmaceutical giant Sandoz for $391.8 million.[11] That is far from a trivial amount, but consider the nature of what was bought: SyStemix was a four-year-old company formed by Stanford University researchers and venture capitalists to patent and refine a process for separating blood stem cells from bone marrow—a separation very hard to achieve, potentially very effective in the treatment of cancer, and, if so, of enormous, multibillion, commercial value. Not coincidentally, by the way, Stanford University is one of the very largest recipients of federal grants for exactly this type of research.

Where and how did those brilliant researchers learn how to separate cells? It seems unlikely that the idea came to them only after they had already established SyStemix, given that the company was established specifically to refine and patent the separation technique. Whether or not its technique will help cancer patients, SyStemix has definitely helped the adventurous but impatient original investors, whose $2.67 shares were bought at $70 by Sandoz, a tidy profit by any standards even after a four-year wait.[12] And all concerned have certainly shown great talent in the delicate art of separation; whether or not they can separate the blood stem cells, they have already succeeded in separating private profit from the public expenditure that made it possible, and also in separating the American economy that feeds Stanford University and all its researchers from 60% of the revenues that might eventually be earned.

When it comes to computers and data processing in general, the United States is no longer as dominant as it once was in making big mainframe machines—it could hardly be otherwise, given the strong government support that eventually made Japan's Fujitsu a head-on competitor for IBM all over the world, after long years of tariff protection, easy loans for buyers (denied for imported computers), government purchases of costly new machines whether needed or not, and outright research subsidies. And the United States no longer dominates the low end of the market either—though your average made-in-Taiwan personal computer is likely to have an American-made microprocessor at its core, and perhaps pirated US-made software as well.

These retreats, however, are not tragic. The classic mainframes with their rotating disks and blinking lights, even the once much touted supercomputers, are in rapid decline because it is increasingly possible to perform just as well if not better with networks of smaller and much cheaper machines. As for the run-of-the-mill personal computers, they are so easy to assemble from parts that prices have declined dramatically, profits are very slim, and the industry is imploding. Even the laptop computers that used to be much more profitable than garden-variety PCs are becoming mere commodities sold by the pound; they too are best made in Taiwan, if not more cheaply in Thailand or China.

By contrast, US companies still dominate the most interesting, the most rapidly advancing, and the most profitable parts of the industry, from the hardware of midsize "work-stations," to every variety of software (Microsoft is a continuing phenomenon), to most categories of related machines and ancillaries—the "peripherals" in industry jargon, except for laser printers and optical disk readers, where the usual Japanese giants are dominant. As everyone knows, and even IBM has lately discovered, this is an industry where creativity counts more than size, and the disorderly advance of literally thousands of different US companies, large, small, or tiny, can comfortably outpace the stately progress of big-company Japanese and European competitors.

As in the case of the entertainment industry, however, the result of superior creativity has not been to secure future exports, but rather to attract buyers for part or all of the producing companies themselves, not for their products. There is no listing of all the US hardware, software, and peripheral equipment and tooling companies that have been fully or partly sold to European buyers, but the Japanese purchases alone make an impressive list—especially impressive, indeed, when the very small size of some the deals makes it clear that those buyers at least are not of the type that has more money than sense.

Showing that there is a great deal of fine-tuned scouting going on, or perhaps a full-scale intelligence search, during the single year of 1991, the giant Mitsubishi Corporation (1990 sales: $120 billion) managed to find the tiny Cymer Laser Technologies, paying just $2 million for a stake in its very advanced laser lithography for semiconductors, the core of all computers. Along with three other small investments, Mitsubishi also bought a $750,000 stake in one of Silicon Valley's classic start-ups, Tera Microsystems—the smallest purchase reported at all. Sumitomo Corp., another trading company giant (1990 sales: $133 billion), also has acute vision: after it had already bought the East Asian rights to the unique semiconductor-production technology of Prometrix Corporation of Santa Clara, it accepted the offer of an equity share for $1 million, a truly penny-ante amount, yet not forthcoming from an American investor. Likewise, Nichimen, another trading company (1990 sales: $43 billion), bought a stake for $1.3 million in Navigation Technologies, maker of highly advanced digital mapping systems. Even Toshiba, a company especially proud of its own technology, evidently needed some more, for it bought Vertex Semiconductors outright for $19.4 million, gaining full control of its process for making ASIC chip sets.

There were many more such small sales of part or full ownership in 1991 alone (Paradigm Technology, C-cube Microsystems, Maxoptic, etc.), not counting the deals that were never disclosed to begin with. But a large industry cannot be sold off in such small pieces. Nippon Electronic Corporation bought Honeywell's entire computer division in 1987 for $250 million; Mitsubishi Kasei bought Verbatim, maker of the familiar diskettes, in 1990 for $200 million; TDK bought Silicon Systems, naturally a semiconductor producer, for $200 million in 1989; Hitachi bought National Advanced Systems (which keeps the "national" name) for $199 million also in 1989; Konica bought Royal Business Machines for $93.8 million in 1986; Canon benevolently invested $100 million in the NEXT restart of Apple's pioneer Steve Jobs in 1989; Nissei Electronic bought the printer maker Dataproducts for $80 million in 1990; and so it goes, down to the $70 million purchase of 87% of Therma-Wave Inc., a California semiconductor producer that is a recognized industry "gem," by a joint venture of two Japanese companies that are to buy the remaining 13% by 1995.[13]

Perhaps as the free-market optimists insist, all this too does not matter—the US computer industry is so large that even with sales at $200 million a shot much of it is still left over for the future—to pay for some more imports of cars, watches, etc. Besides, the industry is still growing, though it is revealing that even the smallest start-ups can apparently obtain investment capital more easily from foreign companies than at home (even Tera Microsystems' $750,000). No doubt, all the other governments around the world that would never allow *their* companies to sell off highly advanced technology to foreign competitors for rather small amounts of ready cash are simply being foolish— too blinkered by outdated economic nationalism to understand that we live in an age of global industry and global companies. If so, it surely would not have mattered a bit if Apple Inc. had been sold off to a far-sighted company like Fujitsu right from the start, allowing the entire personal-computer revolution to be made in Japan; or if Microsoft Inc. had been sold early on for, say, $500,000 to Germany's Siemens, sold before it could grow into today's multibillion dollar company that employs several thousand highly skilled Americans to write the software now used all over the world.

Now it is the turn of the aviation industry, which contributed $30.8 billion of net exports to alleviate the US trade imbalance at the last count.[14] For all its success in manufacturing a great part of all the world's airliners from the best-selling 727 and DC-9 series, to the 747 jumbo and much else, it too cannot find enough capital at home. After having launched the 757 and 767, even mighty Boeing decided that it could not afford to engineer and produce its next airliner on its own. Having failed to find partners in the capital-starved US aircraft industry, it turned to a Japanese consortium,[15] which now has a 20% risk-sharing partnership in the future Boeing 777. Widespread myth attributes sinister and secret intentions to the bureaucrats of Japan's MITI, the Ministry of International Trade and Industry, whose over-blown reputation as the planners of Japan's prosperity is now in any case rather outdated. But MITI has been perfectly candid about its goal of creating a world-class aviation industry for Japan, even publishing pamphlets on the subject, and in English!

By timely government purchases of unneeded aircraft to help struggling producers, which would not be possible in the United States,[16] by generous direct grants for civilian research and development, here discouraged by free-market dogma, and above all, by quietly channeling private bank finance on very favorable terms (here an outright impossibility), MITI's goal is steadily being accomplished. Japan had a substantial aircraft industry before the Second World War, which was advanced enough to produce a full range of transports and combat planes—including one of history's great fighters, the Mitsubishi *zero-sen* of astonishing range. After the war and the Occupation, Japan's aviation industry had to start almost from zero (no pun intended), but it has now reached the point where its different companies can produce all three elements: airframes for both helicopters and fixed-wing aircraft, jet engines, and most types of avionics for both civil and military aircraft. As we have seen, Japan's own aviation technology developed far enough to prompt an attempt to engineer an entirely Japanese jet fighter in the FSX project.

It is no secret that MITI and the industry are aiming for greater self-sufficiency in the development of civilian aircraft as well. Nor is it a secret that Japan's "chosen instruments" are precisely the members of the consortium now in partnership with Boeing: Kawasaki Heavy Industries, Fuji Heavy Industries, and the designated design leader, Mitsubishi Heavy Industries.[17] Thus the shortage of capital in the United

States has forced Boeing to introduce its future competitors to the very latest civil aircraft technology, and much else besides: as a risk-sharing partner, the Japanese consortium has access to every phase of the process, from the initial design, to the detailed engineering, to the complexities of international marketing. As in the case of biotechnology and data processing, a leading US industry whose advancement owes much to basic research and specific technologies that US taxpayers have funded in one way or another[18] is selling pieces of itself to foreign buyers, instead of only selling its products.

When a farmer is reduced to selling off acres instead of selling only crops, the ultimate fate of the farm is not in doubt. But, of course, the analogy should be false, because instead of a waning stock of acres, there is the seemingly unending flow of new technology that comes from the constantly celebrated creativity of our pluralist, multiethnic, undisciplined, but very dynamic society. Note, however, the small print that accompanies the dramatic announcement of the very latest example of that famous creativity: as soon as the Korean-born chief developer of *digital* High-Definition TV revealed that the small U.S. company he works for had totally overtaken the Japanese giants and their merely analog HD-TV, the company's owner, General Instrument, let it be known that it would not even try to raise the capital needed to produce and market the new invention, preferring to license production to established TV manufacturers, i.e., the Japanese electronics giants.

In a manner literally pathetic, for pathos is the emotion evoked in the spectators of an inevitable downfall, a company spokesman hopefully speculated that if 20 million HD-TV sets are sold annually, its royalties at $10 per set could amount to as much as $200 million a year. That is a nice bit of change for a small company—but mere change when compared to the $20–$25 *billion* that the actual producers would earn each year—largely no doubt by exports to the United States.[19] But that is by now standard operating procedure given the bootless capitalism without capital rife in the US economy: it was Ampex, a US company, that first developed the video-cassette recorder technology that was licensed for small change to Matsushita, Sony, and the rest of those vigorous exporters. Though their VCR export earnings eventually did come back to the United States, by way of the purchase of CBS Records, Columbia Pictures, and MCA. Obviously this, too, is not a case of wicked foreigners preying on Americans but of Americans unable to keep their technology, because as a nation they would rather wheel and deal than invest money patiently and productively—assuming that it is not simply spent for immediate gratification.

One possible reason to be worried about the foreign acquisition of US corporations and technologies is that "globalization" is something of a one-way street. Forty percent (or 100%) of McDonnell-Douglas's commercial company or even 40% of Boeing could be acquired by Japanese interests at any time, as many a US technology or commercial "gem" has already been bought. But an American buyer would have rather greater chances of being allowed to acquire 40% of Michelangelo's Sistine Chapel than 40% of Mitsubishi Heavy Industries. Far less sensitive acquisitions have been blocked before by Japanese officialdom, usually by quietly telling the shareholders to lay off. They do not always obey (officially there is no such policy) but mostly they do. In any case, virtually all Japanese companies that qualify as "gems" are largely owned by banks and other companies, whose shares they own in turn. In America or much of Europe, even the most complicated holding companies ultimately have private owners, Mr. and Mrs. so-and-so who own some or all of the shares and can sell them. But in Japan the ownership chain goes on right around and back again endlessly. The original and major purpose of interlocked ownership is to keep out *Japanese* outsiders, such as riffraff billionaires who made their money in real estate or worse speculations, and who might seek the dignity of becoming industrialists. Foreign buyers are excluded only incidentally, but very firmly.

To be sure, there is no objection to American purchases of Japanese soft-drink bottling plants or office buildings, and even high-technology sectors officially open to foreign acquisitions (e.g., the computer industry, in any case dominated by Fujitsu, Hitachi, NEC, and Toshiba), but enterprises that are considered technologically important are another matter. Certainly any American attempt to acquire Fujitsu, Hitachi, NEC, Toshiba, or companies like them (Kyocera, FANUC, etc.) would be most effectively resisted; and in any case their interlocked owners would simply refuse to sell. MITI officials especially view the open-door investment policies of the United States with a bemused incredulity that the passage of years cannot diminish.

Some individual Japanese, however, do have an explanation. For example, Mano Teruhiko, the nationally known senior advisor of the highly important Bank of Tokyo, has cautioned Japanese investors that the United States is not actually governed by idiots as it may appear, and that wholesale confiscation is likely in due course.[20] Mr. Mano is a perfectly nice man who is no more anti-American than is justified, to paraphrase the well-known saying, but only thus can an exotic American practice be understood in Japan.

It is plain that the "Japan Inc." myth of a bureaucratic big-business conspiracy to conquer the world economy is nothing but a sinister fantasy, distinctly evocative of anti-Semitic libels. Yet it is also plain that habits of business-government cooperation, quite natural in the Japanese context, are amply sufficient to keep out foreigners from key sectors of the economy.

In theory, even if local companies cannot be bought out, there is nothing to prevent US corporations from establishing brand-new affiliates abroad, as foreign corporations sometimes do in the United States, for example, by building auto assembly plants ("transplants") on greenfield sites, far from unions, aged work forces with high health costs, and urban areas with their large black populations, which most foreign executives simply do not want to deal with. Many US corporations have done just that all over the world, but it is still a thing much easier done in some countries than others. Overall, in most places, it is infinitely easier to buy an existing company, building it up as needed or even substantially rebuilding it, than to start from scratch.

For industrial plants as opposed to, say, insurance offices, the first step is to acquire land, and that can be very difficult in itself: quite a few countries simply prohibit foreigners from buying land at all; in others, very little land is offered for sale at any one time, or willingly sold at any but impossibly high prices. In crowded Japan, for example, highly subsidized rice production and strict controls on rezoning mean that land used for rice cultivation is rarely available for any other purpose, and almost *all* flat land suitable for industrial sites is either already built up or under rice cultivation. For some purposes, that is not much of an obstacle: an existing factory, warehouse, or office building can be acquired. But when a large purpose-built plant is needed, say for auto assembly, the chances of finding suitable real estate in built-up areas is slim. IBM established its very successful IBM–Japan affiliate in 1960 from scratch, real estate and all, and others have done it too, but for most corporations that would follow them the difficulties of acquiring going concerns is a very effective barrier.

It is this lack of reciprocity that justifies concern over the scope of

Japanese direct investment in US manufacturing and research companies—far more consequential acquisitions than the Rockefeller Center or any number of golf courses. At the last count, total European direct investment in the United States was still very much larger, at $262 billion, than Japan's $69.7 billion.[21] But it is not racism that accounts for the widespread anxiety over the latter and not the former, as even well-informed Japanese sincerely believe. Most European investment is in inoffensive real estate, buildings and land, not in the purchase of leading-edge companies; most of them in turn have been acquired by British companies, and Britain has a totally open-door policy that offers complete reciprocity. It is not that Japan's policies are unique—far from it. Korea, for example, is much more restrictive, indeed xenophobic in a way that Japan has not been since the 1930s. The Koreans want American troops to protect them, but they refuse to allow American investors to buy Korean companies so as to take advantage of their extrarapid growth. In fact, until 1992, US citizens could not even legally buy the publicly issued shares of Korean corporations. Likewise, except for recent British governments, which have sacrificed all at the altar of free enterprise (and to let foreign owners cope with the vulgar working class), the major European countries also tend to have industrial policies and economically activist bureaucracies. They, too, will not allow "gems" to be bought by foreign interests.

Deutsche Aerospace is a private company (owned by Daimler-Benz of Mercedes fame) but also Germany's chosen instrument in aviation; the Germans would think it absurd to allow foreigners to buy it. The same is true of Aerospatiale, which in any case is owned by the French state, and it is true also of other French and German companies of like significance. When Italy's celebrated but much troubled Alfa Romeo was offered for sale by the Italian government, foreign bids were not seriously considered, and so it goes. There are even barriers to intra-European acquisitions. When Mr. Carlo de Benedetti (l'Ingegniere) of Olivetti and much else tried to buy Société Générale, Belgium's premier bank, an octopus of an industrial holding company, and the national institution with the possible exception of the monarchy, the Belgian establishment employed every legal and imaginative trick in the book to stop him, and did.

Given the increasing undercapitalization of the US economy, naturally not much could have been invested in Japan or Korea anyway. But of the very unimpressive worldwide total of $158 billion of United

States net direct investment abroad from 1980 to 1989, only a tiny fraction went into both countries, with a mere $1.3 billion in Korea and only $13 billion in Japan.[22] The reason is not only poverty, nor only the notorious myopia of US big business. Even young children know that the economies of both countries have been booming for years, offering blatantly attractive investment opportunities. Incidentally, it was entirely characteristic of its outdated geopolitical fixation that in late 1991 the US government interrupted the planned troop reduction from Korea without even trying to ask for investment (or import) reciprocity.[23] Thus we see our badly underpaid officials emulating aristocratic disdain for mere commerce.

For free-trade plus "globalization" true believers, this entire discussion of foreign investment in the United States, and of the barriers to American investment abroad, misses the point entirely. For them, the supposed problem here raised is actually a solution, absurdly misunderstood. Foreign investment, they ceaselessly point out, "brings jobs," thereby neatly offsetting the consequence of their other article of faith: import-caused unemployment. Equally, American investment abroad would only "export jobs," and if other countries are foolish enough to keep it out (thus "losing jobs" *and* US know-how), the loss of potential earnings for capital[24] is at least compensated by the keeping of jobs within the United States. Both claims are perfectly valid, but to leave it at that ignores the more important implications of foreign investment in the United States and of barriers to US investments abroad.

In the first place, many foreign-owned industries in the United States offer only *some* jobs. When American automobile production, for example, is displaced by the output of foreign-owned factories and assembly plants ("transplants"), the complete employment pyramid of technical designers, development engineers, stylists, corporate managers, and sundry ancillary professionals is decapitated, leaving only the base of assembly-line workers with a few junior-executive positions thrown in. And with the best will in the world, there is little prospect that locally recruited employees will ever be promoted above the plant level, if only because not many Americans are willing to learn Japanese, or even German. Transplants do replace some of the jobs lost to imports (another subject, another chapter), but what jobs? Are they the jobs that we would want for our children?

Certainly, not all the US affiliates owned by foreign corporations are mere assembly plants that employ mostly blue-collar workers. Some, indeed, are research establishments that employ scientists, engineers, and assorted experts. In other cases, only the head-office management and finance roles are missing from the complete employment pyramid. But those too are important—indeed critical—roles: they represent the essence of corporate power. Much more commonly, however, it is transplanted assembly lines and decapitated employment pyramids that prevail, depriving Americans of the opportunity to be employed in the more accomplished, better-paid, and more open-ended roles at the top of the employment pyramid—which is also part of the social pyramid as a whole. A country of foreign-owned assembly plants will become in that degree a blue-collar country, still offering much scope for country-and-western music, less for Bach, providing employment for the high school graduate but not for the university-trained. Proletarization is a step closer to Third-Worldization for American society.

Even if the US affiliates of foreign corporations provide a virtually complete employment pyramid, as very few do, corporate power inevitably remains back at the head office, in Munich or Nuremberg, Nagoya or Tokyo. One decision established an assembly line in the United States. Another might close it in order to move production to Mexico or Thailand, where labor is cheaper. Corporate headquarters decides if the new research center will be established in Los Angeles or in Lyon, France; it decides if the latest in flexible-production technology will receive its first foreign trial in the US transplant, or the one in Malaysia; it decides if American executives will be allowed to rise to the corporate headquarters level, or kept in more junior positions at the US affiliate. *Corporate power matters* in many different ways that are ignored by those who deal only in equations of the investment = jobs variety.

When it comes to the mostly tacit, yet very effective, barriers to US direct investment abroad in plants and research and development houses, one consideration is that US-owned assembly lines and their equivalents would add high-end headquarters roles at home, offsetting the proletarization of American society caused by foreign transplants in the United States. But beyond that, when investment barriers keep out US-owned companies from especially profitable markets, it is not only the would-be investors who are harmed but rather the American economy as a whole. First, the overt or covert protectionism that is the rule when foreign investment is restricted results in high domestic prices and large profits for the local companies, which in turn help them to export successfully to the United States.

Sometimes the relationship is direct. When goods can be sold with high margins at home, they can be underpriced in the United States in order to conquer markets from US competitors. The constant stream of "dumping" cases that goes before the US International Trade Commission attests to that (Japanese minivans were the leading 1992 example, following microchips in 1991). In theory, if and when US production is totally driven out of business, prices could be raised with impunity— but, of course, other foreign competitors persist: "Japan Inc." has most of the US consumer electronics market—TVs, audio equipment, VCRs, telephones, answering machines, small appliances—but there is no such all-Japanese conspiracy, and Matsushita, Victor-JVC, Toshiba, Hitachi, Mitsubishi, Sony, and Sharp continue to fight among themselves, while the European holdout Philips/Grundig fades, and Taiwanese, Korean, Hong Kong, and lately Chinese products slowly move up the quality and price ladder.

The indirect effect of investment barriers and protectionism is more important. Large profits at home allow investments in efficient new plants too costly for American corporations that have no protected high-margin markets of their own, and which therefore cannot accumulate the necessary capital internally. When US affiliates cannot be established to sell high-margin goods and services, there is therefore a double loss, first of the profits that could be earned locally to provide capital at home, and second because those profits and the resulting capital accumulation cannot be denied to local producers, in order to reduce their ability to compete on the US market. It is perfectly true, as the Japanese loudly insist, that many American corporate managers are greedy and hopelessly shortsighted as compared to their Japanese counterparts, and that Wall Street and American shareholders in general demand quick returns on the scant capital they provide. But it is just as true that overt or covert protectionism secured by investment barriers provides a secure home base for the Japanese and Korean companies that are so successful on the US market.

More important still is a new phenomenon. World-class corporations now need to be present as producers as well as sellers in all three of the world's three major economic regions: North America, Europe, and Japan-Korea-Taiwan.[25] They need to be in contact with their local customers to keep up to date on demand trends, to know as early as possible what new configurations and features are desired. At different times, one region leads the others in tastes and demand trends in any given sector; hence the corporation that is present *and* responsive can anticipate the emergence of those same tastes and trends in its other markets worldwide. And world-class corporations need to *produce* within the region, to more rapidly absorb relevant new technologies that "grow" there, and also to supply their customers as responsively as possible. To the extent that US corporations are kept out of Japan and its region, deliberately or otherwise, they are much weakened. In fact they can no longer be considered world-class corporations at all, even if they still seem to be so on the US market.

That is why it is very serious that there is no US-owned and US-managed word processor, integrated circuit, watch, steel, industrial robot, color TV, machine-tool, VCR, automobile, motorcycle, cosmetics, beer, publication, or advertising company that operates in Japan, while Japanese companies in all those sectors not only sell but also produce in the United States. In fact, the US production presence in Japan is largely limited to oil companies, IBM (with 24.2% of the market for large computers and 7% for small ones), and Unisys (10.3% of the large-computer market). Ford is a part-owner of the Mazda automobile company, with 7.8% of the market at the last count, but it does not manage the company, and the transfer of Mazda techniques to Ford plants has been slow.[26]

A final benefit denied to the US economy by investment barriers is more subtle, yet highly important these days. It is true that technologies, i.e., the knowledge of how to make things, are easily reproducible by competent people of appropriate qualification. But some critical processes still depend on unwritten skills (as in gun making, to cite an antique example) or are strongly protected by patents. When small companies have unique abilities in making essential materials and components for larger products, their acquisition can disproportionately strengthen the entire competitive position of the enterprises that make those larger products. Just as European as well as Japanese companies routinely gain access to broadly valuable technologies by acquiring narrowly specialized US companies for rather modest sums,[27] US corporations would like to do the same abroad, and especially in highly skilled Japan.

Even in its reduced condition, General Motors could still easily afford to buy out some of the Japanese companies that are world leaders in the manufacture of certain automobile components and in the development of advanced engine materials. And even though its management is famously shortsighted, General Motors might well desire such acquisitions. But no such acquisitions are possible: even if the Japanese government would allow them, they would be blocked by the informal alliances and cross-shareholdings that characterize Japanese industry. In the meantime, US auto makers must compete against imports and transplants in a US environment in which almost every modern steel mill that makes sheet for cars is wholly or partly Japanese-owned,[28] as are dozens of component manufacturers and two of the large tire makers (Japan's Bridgestone owns Firestone, and Sumitomo Rubber owns Dunlop). As against that, there is only the feeble protectionism that limits the number but not the value of car imports, and allows huge auto-parts imports for transplants that are mere assembly lines.

All this is not to say that Japanese corporate expansionism, or foreign interests in general, are responsible for the woes of the American economy. Decades of unilateral market access, and one-sided "open-door" investment policies have undoubtedly weakened American business, contributing to its decapitalization. But it would be foolish and escapist to blame foreigners for American policies and American delusions. MITI commandos never descended on Washington to impose one-sided access to American markets and American technology, nor can Tokyo or Hyundai be blamed if the US government simply fails to insist on genuine reciprocity, trusting instead in the gentle comfort of interminable negotiations that yield insignificant results.

The negative side effects of foreign investment, and of the barriers to US investment abroad should neither be overlooked nor underestimated. But far from blaming the Japanese or any other foreigners for our troubles, we should recognize that they have actually mitigated the very broadest shortcomings of the American economy, and of American society: the inadequacy of both capital and labor, that is *patient* capital, and *diligent* labor. Indeed, they have provided their substance to augment the former, and their good example to improve the latter. It is by now a hoary cliché that foreign competition in general, and

Japanese competition in particular, has served to reduce managerial sloth and self-indulgence while inducing employees to pay more attention to the quality of their work.

Certainly neither our European competitors nor the Japanese can be blamed for the long list of self-inflicted wounds that are directly causing the Third-Worldization of America.

They had nothing to do with the most original invention of American statecraft since the Constitution: Representation Without Taxation by limitless deficits, so that savings already scant because of private overconsumption are borrowed by the Treasury to pay for the government's own day-to-day spending, instead of being invested productively in new plant and machinery for industry, in commercial research and development, and in the public infrastructure of ports, highways, airports, bridges, schools, and more.

They did not arrange the wholesale deregulation and cultural changes that allowed the morality and urgencies of Las Vegas to infect Wall Street and corporate boardrooms across the land, making heroes out of those who can best sacrifice future growth for quick payoffs.

They did not seize control of our classrooms, to discredit the discipline and absolute standards that are the prerequisites of all education, nor lately to appoint the "multiculturalism" inspectors who equate arithmetic with racism, and annex historiography to group therapy by endorsing fantasies about the true origin of Greek civilization (Egypt = Africa). Nor is it foreigners who prevent us from adopting here too a nationwide school system that would reproduce the same high standards everywhere, thus giving each child an equal chance to learn.

They did not corrupt America's most excellent legal principles into a grotesque legalism that now employs more than 700,000 lawyers (soon to be a million),[29] to complicate every government regulation and every private contract, to pursue every slender opportunity for litigation, and thus impose huge, uncounted costs to avoid, resist, insure against, and pay tort claims propelled by lawyers' contingency fees.

Nor did foreigners devise our spectacularly antisocial "social" programs, by now most nefariously entangled in both racial politics and the crudest racism.[30] There are very few Afro-Swedes, yet because Sweden is very generous to unmarried mothers, they logically enough account for 50.9% of all births, as opposed to 25.7% in the less generous United States, and only 1% in notably ungenerous Japan, where

99% of all children are still compelled to grow up with both fathers and mothers.[31] That, no doubt, is yet another of those exotic Japanese practices devised by the sinister Ministry of International Trade and Industry—certainly nothing enhances a country's competitive position more than a population of stable families that can actually guide their children's education.

CHAPTER 6

THE POOR AND THE

SUPER-RICH

merica's slide toward Third World conditions is even now being prepared by the sheer force of demography: the proportion of poor Americans is increasing, the concentration of wealth in the hands of the richest 1% is also increasing, and the proportion of Americans in between who have enough wealth and income to claim genuine middle-class status is therefore in decline. Thus we approach the typical Third World pattern of a very small rich minority that stands above a vast poor majority with only a thin middle class in between.

The poor whose growing numbers are changing the character of American society are almost invisible. They are not unmarried black welfare mothers with 2.5 children, improvident males chronically un-employed, or inner-city youths heading for prison or an early death by gun, knife, drugs, or AIDS. Instead they are mostly white, they are not on welfare but rather have year-round, full-time jobs, and they are as law-abiding as anyone. Because of the phenomenal extent of crime and recurrent riots, the latest and most famous in South-Central Los Angeles in May 1992, Americans are very aware of the black and Hispanic urban underclass with its familiar cast of characters. But although the urban underclass already lives in full Third World conditions, it is quite incapable of causing the Third-Worldization of America: it accounts for 3% of all Americans at most.[1] By contrast, the *working* poor of all races are far more numerous, and their impact on America's future is bound to be much greater. Yet their very existence is often simply overlooked by social commentators and politicians who focus exclusively on the highly visible "inner-city" poor, as the current euphemism goes.

Talk of the "working poor" was largely a matter of anecdote and conjecture until recently. But official Bureau of the Census statistics now show that the percentage of all full-time, year-round workers (forty hours a week, fifty weeks a year) who did not earn enough to keep a family of four above the official poverty line ($12,195 in 1990 dollars) increased from 12% in 1979 to 18% in 1990—i.e., not much less than one-fifth of all fully employed Americans.[2] Of course, earning less than $12,195 per year only results in that statistical poverty if there really is a family of four to keep, so that of all such workers only 12.9% were actually living below the line in 1990. The 3.9 million low-paid workers (the 2,000 annual hours imply less than $6.10 per hour) who were married women mostly had a working husband, and thus only 5.5% of them were living below the poverty line. On the other hand, many more of the 2.9 million low-paid husbands did not have working wives because 21.4% were below the line. That proportion was only exceeded by the 1,025,000 female householders in full-time work but with no spouse present, 27.8% of whom were not only below the poverty line but were mostly living in true poverty if they had more than one child and had to pay rent.[3]

To be sure, the single, nationwide poverty line is a highly arbitrary concept of poverty, because $12,195 is a much more tolerable income even for a family of four in rural Tennessee or in Pueblo, Colorado, than for a family of one in downtown New York, or for that matter in Palm Beach, Florida, during the fashionable season. For a deer-hunting, bass-fishing, nutria-trapping, and vegetable-gardening man who lives along the rich, clean waters of the Alabama River, $12,195 in cash income might do very nicely to sustain an invigoratingly bucolic lifestyle, even with a wife and two children to support. But the same income results in true poverty in a major metropolis where only slum housing is to be had for whatever rent can come out of that amount.

Nevertheless, even if most were not actually poor, the increasing proportion of low-paid workers already exemplifies Third-Worldization: to work at a seemingly respectable job and yet live in poverty if there is a family to support is the common lot of Brazilian workers and Indian government clerks. In any case, low-paid workers along with the actual poor and the underclass as a whole not only represent but also accelerate the Third-Worldization of America—not because they *are* poor or near-poor, but because of what even $12,195 per year poverty means for the education of children in contemporary America, lacking as it does a powerful system of national education.

Of the 31.5 million Americans living below the official poverty line at the last count, 12 million were under eighteen years old (the government's definition of "children"), with some 4 million in the looser category of the near-poor. In combination, that amounts to just about one in four of the total population of some 64 million under the age of eighteen.[4] Inevitably, they will also account for roughly a quarter of the overall total of 24.3 million Americans in the start-of-life age brackets of eighteen to twenty-four projected for the year 1995, which will supply most of the new entrants in the labor force.[5] When the country's ability to compete in the international economy is being soberly evaluated, that may be the most decisive fact.

Raised by hard-pressed families at best, usually very badly taught in the neglected schools of low-income school districts or in ruined "inner-city" schools, many of the poor children of today are destined to struggle against the current of an economy that offers fewer and fewer job openings for the unqualified. Many high-school graduates are virtually illiterate, more are innumerate. As they become improvident parents at an early age, bringing children into the world at higher rates than the most affluent, poverty perpetuates itself and grows instead of declining, as it did in America's past decades.

The rising proportion of low-paid workers marks a most unhappy reversal of a historic trend that long exemplified the reality of the "American dream" even for the worst-paid employees in the economy. In 1964, nearly a quarter (24.1%) of the country's year-round, full-time workers did not earn enough to keep a family of four above the poverty line (then defined as $3,144). Behind that average there were sharp inequalities, because the rate for males was very much lower at 16.5% than for female workers at 45.2%, a clear reflection of the status of women in the economy at the time. As between the races, inequality was even more acute at a time when the civil rights revolution had just started. Fully 48.4% of all year-round, full-time workers listed as black did not earn enough to keep a family of four above the poverty line; for male workers alone, that proportion was 38%; for females it was 69.6%, a statistic that encompassed a multitude of housemaids and manual workers at the bottom of the employment pyramid.

Ten years of fairly rapid economic growth, "Great Society" social programs, and the civil rights revolution for women as well as for blacks drastically improved the situation. In 1974, only 12% of all year-round, full-time workers did not earn enough to keep a family of four above the poverty line ($4,843 in that year). For males alone, the proportion was much lower at just 7.4%, but even for female workers it was lower at 22.1% than it had been for all workers in 1964. Blacks shared fully in this rapid progress, for in 1974 the proportion who could not keep a family of four above the poverty line had declined drastically from the 48.4% of 1964 to 18.1%, significantly but not disastrously more than the proportion of white workers alone at 11.4%. For black females, the situation improved even more dramatically, with the proportion down to 24.5%, as compared to the 69.6% of 1964.

These statistics depicted a society in which more and more people could afford to pay for the basic needs of housing, food, education, and medical care. But beyond that, overall social behavior was also influenced in desirable ways. Workers who between 1964 and 1974 acquired the ability to keep a family above the poverty line were also more inclined to marry, have children, and act as effective parents in settled households. Between 1960 and 1970, the marriage rate for men over the age of fifteen increased from 2.5% to 3.1%, a change by no means insignificant.[6]

But then this most encouraging progress stopped as the poor were caught in the two-way squeeze between deteriorating public education and the shrinking demand for uneducated workers. By 1980, the official counting of the poor included 13% of all Americans, and since then that percentage has moved up and down with economic cycles (reaching 15.2% in the 1983 recession), but it no longer seems to decline below 13%.[7]

Between 1979 and 1990, the number of all year-round, full-time workers who did not earn enough to keep a family of four above the poverty line actually doubled from 7.8 million to 14.4 million. Among female workers alone, the proportion did not increase very much, evidently because the still favorable "sexual equality" trend was softening the impact of the overall employment trend. Thus in 1990 the proportion was 24.3%, as compared to the 20.4% of 1979, showing that the condition of female workers had already regressed beyond the 1974 mark (at 22.1%) and was heading back toward the 1969 level of 27.6%.

For black workers, the trend has been more disastrous. After the vast progress registered between 1964 and 1974, when the proportion was much more than halved from 48.4% to 18.1%, there was no more progress. In 1984, the figure was up to 21.5% and it remained at roughly that level until the 1990 recession, when it increased sharply to 25.3%. In other words, one in four of all black Americans who did have year-round, full-time work did not earn enough to keep a family of four above the poverty line. For black females alone, the proportion was higher at 28.5%, almost one in three; for black males alone it was somewhat lower at 22.4%. For both, it marked a disheartening downfall for people who were playing the game strictly by the rules—not unemployed, not on public assistance, not in prison, but working full-time, year-round.

True enough, poverty will always be with us, but it is all a matter of percentages—in other First World societies it rarely exceeds 5%. For the vast majority of Americans who are not poor, the devil is in those percentages. In the fast and hard game of international economic competition, the team that must carry more nonplayers on its back while striving for the ball is unlikely to win.

Many of the poor now fail as parents in spite of sound habits and good intentions, because of wretched schools. But in the lower depths of society, our own "inner-city" Third Worlds come complete with an entire generation of children as doomed as the street waifs of Rio de Janeiro. The newborn son of a long-gone teenage father and a fifteen-year-old mother, with a grandmother in her thirties and a great-grandmother in her forties—all of them unmarried, uneducated, and mostly unemployed—has become a rather familiar American type, destined from birth to roam the streets in between fitful episodes of useless schooling, casual labor, crime, addiction, and imprisonment.

That condition is certainly extreme, but it is simply not rare enough to avoid terrible consequences for American society as a whole. The 1990 detailed census revealed that out of 14.3 million Americans aged sixteen to nineteen of all races and all social backgrounds, almost 1 million were neither enrolled in school nor high-school graduates, neither in the armed forces nor in civil employment.[8] A million pensioners can live out quiet lives of serenity or distress that alike have no broad impact on society. But 1 million unemployed and scarcely employable teenagers at the peak of their physical energy, with appetites raw and habits of prudence undeveloped, are quite another matter.

They certainly add far beyond their numbers to the extraordinary prevalence of crime in the contemporary United States, a phenomenon unique for its sheer proportions as compared to all other developed countries, but quite in line with, say, Nigerian conditions. That, incidentally, has curious side effects: American multinationals encounter no special difficulties in sending staff from New York or Los Angeles for postings or visits to their affiliates in cities such as Lagos or Nairobi. Quite used to crime as a constant reality, they get on with their work and frequently enjoy themselves greatly. European and Japanese multinationals, on the other hand, find that a significant proportion of their employees sent to those places are too paralyzed by fear to work effectively, or simply refuse to stay. That, too, is a competitive advantage no doubt, but hardly desirable.

Americans are thoroughly habituated to lives of corrosive insecurity, but European and East Asian visitors are often left speechless when they encounter what Americans take for granted: the unending wails of police sirens in the city night; the near-universality of burglar alarms in private homes; the throbbing and searchlights of helicopters searching for fugitives over our largest cities; and the "gated" communities with their own private police, obsequious to residents, brusque to straying outsiders with the wrong clothes, diction, or color. First World visitors are even more amazed by the casual acceptance of barbarous violence as an everyday norm by the Americans they encounter—their fearful steps as they approach their own cars in dark parking lots; their insistent warnings to avoid this or that entire part of town, their matter-of-fact tales of brutal crimes seen or actually experienced; and their firm advice to surrender wallets and watches quickly and uncomplainingly if asked, even, or especially, if the robbers are mere children.

For all their protestations, Americans are no longer truly shocked by the huge dimensions of our own permanent uprising, even though its 8 million larceny-thefts, 3 million burglaries, 1.6 million motor-vehicle thefts, 1 million life-threatening aggravated assaults, 639,000 robberies, 102,000 rapes, and 23,000 murders at the last count, have recently been increasing at an equally phenomenal rate of 6% to 10% per year, and have long since spread to suburbs and once tranquil small towns. In a futile attempt to overcome the dulled impact of mere numbers, the FBI even publishes an official "crime clock" for dramatic effect, which last recorded one murder every twenty-two minutes, a rape every five minutes, a robbery every forty-nine seconds, an aggravated assault every thirty seconds, a burglary every ten seconds, and so on.[9] Still, Americans hesitate to visit Naples because sometimes cars are stolen, and the State Department in Washington, DC (1990 population: 606,900; FBI index major crimes: 65,389), solemnly issues "travel advisories" warning tourists to stay away from Israel, Northern Thailand, and Colombia, where fewer tourists have been killed, robbed, or beaten over ten years than in any recent Washington, DC, summer season.

There is no counting of the many crimes that simply remain unreported, of the brutal acts of violence that are overlooked because no known deaths or serious injuries ensue, of the humiliating intimidation that is the daily lot of many millions of city-dwellers, especially the elderly, many of whom literally live in fear. But America's permanent *intifadah* has huge proportions even in the very incomplete official statistics.

With its 248 million all-out individualists, diverse and sometimes clashing races, and a long history of violence, America could never be compared to famously law-abiding Japan, cohesive Finland, strict Switzerland, or indeed any First World country at all. Of late, however, it cannot even be compared with itself: between 1980 and 1989 the number of inmates in federal and state prisons more than doubled, from 329,821 to 710,054, and the number has now passed 1 million including jail prisoners and juveniles in detention.[10] And even that number is still increasing rapidly—almost 9 million Americans were arrested for all causes in 1990, as compared to 6.8 million in 1981.[11] It seems that the prisons are absorbing quite a few of the people that the economy can no longer employ.

Fittingly enough, it is the nation's capital that offers the most extreme example of the prevalence of crime in the abandoned slums called "inner cities." In 1992 it was estimated 42% of all black males between the ages of eighteen and thirty-five living in the District of Columbia were in prison, on probation, or on parole awaiting trial.[12] Because there is a large black middle class in Washington, of well-paid government employees and professionals who lead settled lives, that 42% must represent a terrifyingly high proportion of all underclass black youths raised by single parents—or rather birthed by unmarried girls. In 1988, out of just over 1 million American children of all races born out of wedlock in that one year (53.7% of them white), 312,500 had mothers aged fifteen to nineteen (another 9,900 had mothers under fifteen).[13] Inevitably, many will join the 7.5 million children already on the welfare rolls, not many of whom will have a chance to grow up into educated, employable, and law-abiding adults.[14]

Still, it is not the extremes and lower depths that will determine the fate of American society—not even the phenomenal magnitude of crime, which does have all sorts of repercussions on the economy, from very high property insurance rates to the sheer cost of caring for the 710,054 state and federal prisoners at some $21.3 billion per year; not surprisingly, "correction officers and jailers" are in the fastest-growing employment category,[15] along with computer programmers.

Altogether more important, however, is the widespread inability of today's poor and near-poor to do what even the very poor of the urban slums of yesteryear could often do very successfully: raise children who could make their own upward way in society, after first receiving a sound education in public schools. That is still possible in much of Europe, as in Japan, Korea, and Taiwan. Under nationwide educational systems operated by central governments with nary a trace of "community control," free and compulsory education is conducted in schools that function as fortresses and vacuum cleaners in low-income urban areas, and remote rural districts.

They are fortresses because they impose totally uncompromised *national* standards enforced by uniform tests and frequent inspections and propagated by well-educated teachers who are well paid as compared to other locals. No variance is allowed: from one end of the country to the other, the same classes must be taught on the same day and at the same time, to cover the same number of pages in the same prescribed textbooks. And the schools are vacuum cleaners because they extract all children rich and poor from their domestic circumstances: the same books and learning aids are provided to all; strict dress codes or uniforms (if necessary supplied free of charge) deliberately obscure income differences; and parents who do not help with homework are visited at home and pressured to do better, or are supplemented by after-school study periods. By all these means the schools systematically impose their priorities on the children, their families, and their neighborhoods, instead of absorbing local attitudes. Teachers, of course, rely on their authority, compounded as it is by their high social status as well-paid professionals. But discipline, needless to say, is invariably strict.

As against such authoritarian horrors and near-totalitarian uniformity, the United States has local school boards, which often serve as the first venue of aspiring local politicos; local funding, generous or miserly; local administrations, whistle-clean or notoriously corrupt; and highly variable standards. There is but one constant amidst all this diversity: the children who have the least at home and need the most from their schools also receive the worst schooling.

Just as self-perpetuating and expanding poverty is one aspect of the Third-Worldization of America, another is the increasing concentration of wealth in fewer and fewer hands. That, too, is a clear sign of degeneration, indeed in many ways it is a more significant symptom than the increase in poverty. As everyone knows, even Third World countries can contain a great deal of private wealth, but they still remain poor *as* countries because while their rich are often very rich, the vast majority of the population is very poor, and the class in the middle that dominates First World societies is instead quite small. What is less widely recognized is that the concentration of wealth found in Third World countries is not only a result of their underdevelopment, but also one of its causes.

The middle class is small because there are few opportunities for it in a primitive economy, but also because potential opportunities are systematically denied by the rich. Not submerged by a vast middle class as in First World societies, the rich minority can also be politically powerful in Third World countries—not merely disproportionately powerful, as in many societies of all kinds, but almost exclusively powerful. And they have many ways to use their power to become even richer, or at least to protect the privileges that made them as rich as they are.

While the great mass of the population struggles to survive from day to day, hardly in a position to know what is happening in politics, let alone influence its workings, the rich minority alone participates, and therefore dominates. Only the rich can finance political parties if there happens to be a functioning democracy, or else influence the ruling dictatorship by providing jobs for the relatives of the powerful, by marriage alliances, or simply by bribery in one form or another. That is how rich Third World contractors monopolize government contracts, denying start-up opportunities to everyone else; rich importers obtain all the scarce import permits going; rich businesspeople make sure that licensing restrictions keep out would-be competitors; rich landlords stop land-reform laws that would force them to share their acres with the landless poor; and rich entrepreneurs ensure that the long-awaited coastal highway reaches their resort hotel, instead of the hundred modest beach motels of lesser fry.

Usually, of course, the webs of influence function much more finely and altogether more informally to keep the rich rich and a middle class from rising and growing. The ambitious young man who elsewhere might modestly prosper by starting some new, small business, say a fertilizer depot, is quietly warned off because the rich and locally powerful X family already in the fertilizer business desires no competition. Banks will extend no credit, landlords will not rent premises, suppliers will refuse supplies. If the would-be entrepreneur is unusually determined (most give up) and persistent, anything can happen. If the local style of informal power is violent, the business or the entrepreneur himself may be attacked by hooligans, whom the local chief of police will show no interest in pursuing. Where the formalities of law and order are carefully respected, government inspectors never before seen will arrive to find violations, exact fines, or simply close down the business, while studiously ignoring far greater irregularities in the X family's operation. But nothing so active as outright reprisals, let alone special-interest legislation or customized decrees are ever needed in many places and many cases. In Saudi Arabia, for example, no businessman in his right mind would even think of competing head-on with an established business owned by a prince—and there are some 5,000 princes, most of them in business.

When wealth is highly concentrated, as it is in the Third World, the usual result is thus the denial of opportunities for advancement to all who are not already wealthy, ensuring, in turn, that wealth remains highly concentrated in the hands of the very rich.

That is why the rapidly increasing concentration of wealth in the United States is such a sinister omen. During the 1980s, the media was suddenly filled with accounts of the lives of the super-rich and the newly famous. In their extravagance, they recalled the legendary J. P. Morgan—who once explained that if you have to ask how much a yacht costs, you can't afford it. (With that, Morgan of course started a fashion for yachts. Even for sea-hating financiers it became a simple matter of credit-worthiness to have one.) Like Morgan, the new super-rich faithfully followed a set pattern of extravagance. First the palatial apartments and multiple mansions with extravagant grounds, then the art works—not J. P. Morgan's Chinese ceramics, Gobelins, and Old

Masters but rather hyperfashionable contemporary artists popularized by weekly magazines, huge Victorians to cover all those vast walls, and the essential French Impressionists. Unlike Morgan, however, the new super-rich also needed a "trophy" second wife, a fashion designer or ex–air hostess, very tall, ultrathin, and of excellent form if not always significantly literate.

But there was a much more important difference between J. P. Morgan and the new super-rich. In his day, Morgan was prospering hugely but the population at large was also rapidly climbing the ladder of prosperity; his display was therefore an encouragement, a token of still brighter futures to come. The rise of the new super-rich, by contrast, seemed to coincide with diminishing prospects for everyone else.

We now have the numbers that seem to prove the correctness of that impression. Wealth is much harder to estimate than income, partly because artworks, fancy furniture, and, above all, real estate are not truly valued until they are sold, and in any case it is hard to tell who owns what. But according to a rather careful study that remains unrefuted,[16] in 1983 the net worth of the richest 1% of all American families accounted for 31.3% of the nation's total private wealth, already a huge proportion, evidence of a sharp inequality at variance with the general American belief that the United States is largely owned by a broad middle class. But by 1989 the richest 1% of all families had increased their share to 36.2% of the nation's total wealth. That is an inordinate proportion by First World standards, but common in countries of privilege and exploitation such as the Philippines. At $6.14 trillion ($6,140 billion), the combined net worth of the richest 1% was greater than the total net worths of the bottom 89.9% of all American families at $5.2 trillion. Thus the 83.8 million families that were not rich enough to rate within the top 10% owned much less between them—almost a *trillion* less—than the 932,000 families within the magic circle of the top 1%.

Even more striking is the shift in wealth within the top 10% according to the same study. In 1983, the 7.5 million families within that already very affluent group that did not, however, make it into the top 1% had a combined net worth of $3.6 trillion, some $400 billion more than the $3.2 trillion in the hands of the top 840,000 families. But by 1989, the 8.4 million families that fell within the top 90% to 99% of all wealthholders had a combined worth of $5.6 trillion, that is, $530 billion dollars *less* than the total wealth at the top 1%. In other words, the richest American families have been becoming richer even as compared to the affluent minority at the top of the wealth pyramid.

The drift toward the full Third World pattern of income distribution, with a poor majority, a rich minority, and a small class in the middle, can now also be documented. According to a 1992 Bureau of the Census study,[17] the proportion of all American families with "low" incomes ($18,576 and below) increased from 10.9% of all families in 1969 to 14.7% in 1989, i.e., the poor and semipoor are becoming more numerous. The proportion of "high" income families ($74,304) also increased, from 14.7% to 22.1%, but most significant of all, the proportion of American "middle" income families (i.e., between $18,576 and $74,304) *declined* from 71.2% to 63.3%. Thus over two decades, the great American middle class became significantly smaller, even as the middle classes continued to expand in all the advancing countries of the world.

Actually even those numbers understate the slide to extremes of inequality, for it turns out that the super-rich have been gaining ground on the merely very rich. In 1983, just under a quarter (24.1%) of the nation's total private wealth was owned by the richest half percent of all families, 419,968 families in all, with an average net worth of $5.86 million. By 1989, however, the top half percent of 477,361 families owned 29.1% of all private household wealth, and their average net worth had almost doubled to $10.3 million.

Looked at in another way, the results of the same study show that the trend toward deeper inequalities in the distribution of wealth has been progressing very rapidly. In a mere six years, from 1983 to 1989, the share in the nation's total wealth of 99% of all American families declined from 68.7% to 63.8%—by just under 5%. That amazingly rapid rate of relative impoverishment—almost 1% per year—has many causes but in some large degree it must reflect the much-celebrated structural changes in the US economy. One is the "globalization of industry" that seems to chronically consist much more of job-displacing imports rather than job-giving exports, and which impoverishes the many while enriching a few importers and financial operators. Another is the breakdown of the traditional corporation that used to provide both high union wages and lifetime jobs for white-collar employees, mostly to assure a quiet life for its (moderately paid) top executives, with the tranquillity coming at the expense of slow growth and moderate dividends for shareholders.

Business schools had been preaching for decades against such "satisficing" corporations that refused to maximize profits as the textbooks prescribe, and in the 1980s their preachings were heard. Threatened by corporate raiders who had spotted its unexploited value, or actually taken over by them, the old quiet-life corporation was transformed into the "lean and mean" corporation, liberated from its "dead wood" midlevel staff by decisive chief executives, often appointed after leveraged buy-outs financed with high-interest "junk" bonds in need of being rapidly paid off by quick sales of strippable assets and by mass firings to cut costs.

In the process, the fortunes of millions of families were also cut down, when laid-off executives were cast out into unemployment, or lower-paying jobs, or nonjobs as commission salesmen or precariously self-employed "consultants."[18] Their humiliating loss of self-respect, the unsettling shock to their families, even their psychologically induced decline in health and life span define the parameters of those very American tragedies. But unless experienced, the plight of employees ejected from middle-class jobs must seem as nothing when compared to the broader effect of the same structural changes: the decline in working hourly earnings, and the stagnation in underclass incomes.

To some degree, the further shift in the distribution of wealth within the top 1% of all families can also be related to the structural changes in the US economy. The 1980s witnessed a rapid increase in the earnings of top corporate executives, as well as the sudden rise to enormous wealth of the chief architects of those structural changes. Some became household names: T. Boone Pickens, Ron Perelman, and Carl Icahn among the corporate raiders, but above all Henry Kravis and George Roberts, lords of KKR, the premier "leveraged buy-out" house of the 1980s, masters of Duracell, Safeway, and others, but chiefly overlords of RJR Nabisco, the biggest ($25 billion) leveraged buy-out of all time; and of course Michael R. Milken of $500 million per annum fame, at this time earning less in his prison workshop, who invented the mass-produced junk bond as a takeover tool for his employers, Drexel Burnham Lambert, till then merely respectable, after that, all-powerful, and later still, bankrupt. Milken was not alone, not even within his Beverly Hills outpost of Drexel: his closest associate, Peter Ackerman, received

$165 million in the one year 1988—and without even being indicted.[19] To be sure, Milken and Ackerman were only two among dozens of others: every Wall Street firm tried its best to imitate Drexel, and several had their own hugely paid junk-bond and acquisition stars. Yet, as with J. P. Morgan, the wealth of architects, though individually huge, was nationally not that significant because they were few in number.

That is not true, however, of the much more numerous beneficiaries of the structural changes wrought by the architects. They are, of course, much fewer than the millions of victims, but still to be reckoned in the thousands. Wall Street investment bankers are supposed to earn their income by channeling investments, but they are actually paid by the transaction, one fee at a time. The structural changes brought about a huge number of transactions as corporations were made and unmade, loans given (each carries a fee), bonds sold (for a fee), shares issued (for a fee), and bought out again in takeovers (for another fee). Besides, just as millers remain with flour on their hands, money-dealers are left with money; even in 1991, when the takeover fever had temporarily abated, the roughly 1,200 managing directors of Wall Street firms had average earnings of $1.1 million.[20] This being America, law firms naturally have their share in every transaction, to write contracts and immediately sue and countersue; the partners of the most important law firms do not earn less than investment bankers on average, and some earn much more.

And then there are the entrepreneurs, who can be beneficiaries too as long as they do not allow themselves to be distracted from financial maneuverings by the sordid business of actually developing, producing, or marketing goods and services. When Milken was still financing leveraged buy-outs with his Drexel junk bonds, he made himself a billionaire but he made multimillionaires by the hundreds; and so did his competitors in other firms. Mr. Smith would buy up all the issued shares of the Northland Corporation for $250 million, with $45.50 of his own money (telephone charges) and $350 million provided by pension funds and S & Ls in exchange for brand-new "Smith-Northland" junk bonds that promised to pay much higher interest rates (15%, 18%) than boringly reliable "investment-grade" bonds.

At that point, the new Smith-Northland corporation was saddled with huge payments on its high-interest $350 million debt—$350 and not $250 because Mr. Smith must hand over the extra $100 million to the junk-bond issuer for its huge "fees," and also to buy junk bonds issued by earlier ventures. To be sure, Mr. Smith had no need of those bonds, nor of any bonds, because the money it cost to buy them further increased the already huge burden of debt suddenly placed on Smith-Northland Inc. But it is all part of the deal: Mr. Smith must show his gratitude for the bounty he has received by taking off the issuer's hands leftover bundles of junk bonds ("dogs"), too blatantly speculative even for financially intoxicated investors—such as the many S & L chiefs and pension-fund managers of the late 1980s, who converted the life savings of millions of Americans into "financial paper" that was just that.

Mr. Smith must then begin his work—not to develop, produce, and market Smith-Northland goods or services, but to raise cash quickly to reduce the crushing burden of $350 million in high-interest debt. The tax code, very perversely, is most helpful: while the shareholders of the old Northland had to pay taxes on the dividends they received, Smith-Northland can *deduct* the interest it pays on its junk bonds. That in itself is a standing encouragement to leveraged buy-outs, because the taxpayer offers a free bonus when shares are replaced by bonds. Further help from the taxpayer is also substantial: when the paper Smith-Northland buys Northland it is allowed to deduct the cost of the tangible assets it takes over.

But even with all the tax windfalls, Mr. Smith must still sell off what he can as quickly as possible to reduce the debt—that unnecessary warehouse in Hackensack, New Jersey, the original factory building kept by old Mr. Northland for sentimental reasons, but also perhaps the research laboratory that held the promise of Northland's future. That, too, is not sufficient in most cases. Mr. Smith must squeeze enough profit out of Smith-Northland to keep up interest payments on the bonds, *and* pay them down. That usually requires mass firings to reduce costs. Finally, Mr. Smith can emerge as a brand-new million-aire. There were many noisy Mr. Smiths during the 1980s. New ones are still being made, only more quietly.

Not all the beneficiaries of structural change owe their fortunes to the architects. Some still become rich because of the broad policies that result in huge trade deficits. When cars or any other products manu-factured by hundreds of thousands of high-wage union workers, man-aged by tens of thousands of foremen and executives, are instead imported, all the foregoing lose income if not their jobs altogether, but some hundreds of importers and dealers can become very rich.

Still, among the new super-rich there are more top corporate executives than either architects or beneficiaries. In the old-style "satisficing" corporation, the top executives were certainly well paid. But because union workers, white-collar employees, junior executives, and midlevel executives were also well paid and also kept their jobs, the top executives could not be grossly overpaid. That all ended when the new-style "lean and mean" corporations redefined what it meant to be a chief executive. It is no longer enough to be a solid, reliable commander of the troops. Now the chief executive officer and the top managers must all be cost-cutters, red in tooth and claw, eager to fire white-collar workers and less powerful fellow executives, even more eager to beat down union demands or break unions altogether.

Actually not all chief executives are all that ruthless or especially inventive, but a great many have at least discovered how to ensure hugely increased earnings for themselves, as well as lavish fringe benefits. Keeping the board of directors—and especially the "compensation committee"—very happy, with expense-paid invitations to golf tournaments, free holidays at company-owned mansions in premier resorts, and costly souvenirs presented after lavish dinners, had long been mere routine. But to an increasing extent, the responsibility of directors to protect the interests of shareholders is subverted by the simple device of paying them off.

In the case of RJR Nabisco, for example, in the 1987–1988 period—when there was too much lavish overspending by and for the CEO to overlook—one member of the board of directors, William S. Anderson, was paid $80,000 to chair the infrequent meetings of the company's International Advisory Board; another, John Medlin, was more substantially rewarded by the contracting-out of shareholder services (!) to his Wachovia Bank; still another, Juanita Kreps, was given $2 million to endow two chairs at Duke University, one of them named after herself; one Bob Schaeberle was given a six-year contract at $180,000 per year; Andrew G. C. Sage II did better with a $250,000 per-year contract; Charles E. Hugel served as the company's ceremonial ("non-executive") chairman at $150,000 per year; and all directors were paid a $50,000 annual fee and also encouraged to use the company's executive jets anytime to go anywhere, at no charge.[21]

Such abuse is more rule than exception in corporate America. With IBM long in trouble, drifting along on its outdated reputation, the unfortunate shareholders lost 15% of the value of their holdings over

1989–1991. One would imagine that the directors would have reacted swiftly, at the very least to find a new chief executive to belatedly replace the hapless John F. Akers. Instead Akers remained in place until 1993, and the directors graciously allowed him a total of $7,178,000 for his dubious talents over 1989–1991, while the shareholders gained their minus 15%.[22] The mystery is easily resolved: the outside members of IBM's board of directors each receive $55,000 per year to attend the rare meetings, courtesy of Mr. Akers, while ten of them reportedly had insignificant shareholdings in IBM, hardly suffering as a result. Mr. Akers served them very well.

The outside directors who serve on the boards of public companies are supposed to represent the interests of shareholders. But shareholders are remote, mostly silent, and can give no payoffs, while the CEO is always present, and often generous. The method may be crude, but the results are spectacular: US chief executives earn much more than their European or Japanese colleagues, including the heads of bigger and more successful companies.

In 1991, Anthony O'Reilly, chairman, president, and CEO of H. J. Heinz, received $75,085,000, roughly $300,000 per working day, $37,500 per hour. And O'Reilly was merely the highest paid of ten public corporation chief executives who received more than $11 million for that year's work. So many were paid so much that Robert C. Stempel, the hapless chairman and CEO of money-losing General Motors, was missing from the list of the hundred best-paid of 1991, because he received only $1 million. In some corporations, moreover, many non-CEOs also received multimillion dollar amounts, with the 1991 champion being Turi Josefsen, executive vice-president of U.S. Surgical, the highest-paid female executive ever.[23] Even in a much larger count of 8,000 senior corporate managers, most of them necessarily in medium-sized companies, average 1991 earnings were $664,000.[24]

A new record set in 1992 was also an example of the current standards of decency in corporate America. The award of restricted stock worth more than $80 million to Roberto C. Goizueta, chairman and CEO of Coca-Cola, on April 15, 1992 (in addition to his multimillion dollar salary and bonus), is very interesting because of who gave it to Goizueta. Herbert A. Allen is a director of Coca-Cola, i.e., a representative of all the shareholders. Herbert A. Allen is also the chairman of the "compensation committee" that determines how much Goizueta and other top executives are to receive for their services. But Herbert A. Allen is also an investment banker, trading as Allen & Co. And it so happens that Coca-Cola, i.e., Goizueta, has recently paid almost $24 million in fees to Allen & Co.[25]

Moral outrage at other people's money making comes easily, but a serious economic issue is involved. As Japanese executives often point out, when managers at the top earn huge amounts, ordinary employees are liable to think themselves fools if they work really hard for wages that have been made to seem downright trivial. In Japan, for that reason, even the largest and most successful corporations rarely go beyond a 20:1 ratio between the salaries of the lowest-paid and highest-paid employees, not counting (often very generous) fringe benefits. By that standard, O'Reilly of Heinz would have received perhaps $400,000 and as much again in fringe benefits, instead of his $75 million plus.

For many years now, US corporations have been imitating Japanese methods in every aspect of business, from management to production to marketing. But for some reason, US chief executives seem uninterested in imitating Japanese restraint in paying chief executives—or European restraint for that matter. On the contrary, in yet another manifestation of the corrosive increase in inequality, the earnings gap between rank-and-file employees and chief executives continues to widen. In 1980, those included in the *Business Week* large-company list received an average of $624,996, forty-two times more than the average pay of ordinary factory workers. That was already a very high ratio, which would have been socially and politically unacceptable in most First World countries. But eleven years later in 1991, the average earnings of the listed CEOs had increased to $2,466,292, *104 times* as much as ordinary factory workers.[26] Such disproportions are also to be found elsewhere in the world, of course, but only in countries such as the Philippines.

There is worse. In recent years, many a corporation has fired employees by the hundreds "to cut costs," while at the same time paying more than their combined salaries to a handful of top executives. In those circumstances it is impossible to sustain a sense of company loyalty among the remaining employees, who must feel like sheep caged with wolves. It is not clear how managers who themselves earn thousands of dollars per hour can negotiate successfully with unions over a few cents per hour. They do it, of course, some even demanding wage reductions from, say, $10 to $7.50 per hour, while themselves collecting the equivalent of $3,750 per hour—or $37,500 in O'Reilly's case. Such is the state of supply and demand for labor in the degraded state of the US economy, in which capital is scarce and labor therefore cheap.

When chief executives are grossly overpaid, shareholders suffer large uncounted indirect losses, along with the entire US economy, simply because employee morale is depressed. Money can be saved in a thousand invisible ways in workplaces, and it can also be wasted with none the wiser—it is all a matter of caring. Is it likely that the recipients of today's bargained-down wages will strive mightily to save on bolts or paper clips as they hear of the CEO's latest extra million? Work can also be made more efficient in many little ways, by the shop-floor initiatives that US business is supposed to be imitating from Japan. As they lose $2.50 an hour in the latest union "give back," are workers likely to wrack their brains to find ways of further increasing the CEO's bonus?

But, otherwise, shareholders are actually supposed to *benefit* from high CEO earnings—and very directly. Most of them come not from straight salaries but rather from stock options. Because stock options are profitable only if shares go up in value, when CEOs are richly rewarded, in theory shareholders are also supposed to gain through the increased value of their holdings. That is the theory; practice can be very different.

Between 1989 and 1991, for example, Chrysler's world-famous chairman of the board Lee A. Iacocca received a total of $11,965,000, while in the meantime shareholders lost 43 cents on every dollar they had invested—perhaps Iacocca was actually being rewarded for Chrysler's most spectacular success of 1991: the finding of a pool of 3 billion cubic feet of natural gas and 600,000 barrels of oil reserves underneath its Sterling Heights assembly plant in Michigan.[27] Nor was Iacocca the worst offender. J. S. Reed, chairman and CEO of Citicorp, the nation's largest bank, received $4,854,000 over 1989–1991 (with another $3,183,000 for the bank's president, R. S. Braddock) while Citicorp's shares lost 44% of their value—an achievement duplicated by K. H. Olsen, president of Digital (for $2,927,000), and G. Grinstein, chairman and CEO of Burlington Northern (for $4,462,000), who happened to inflict exactly the same disastrous loss on their shareholders.

How CEOs are lavishly rewarded with incentives even when their companies are doing poorly is interesting in itself. It seems that Third World standards of inequality are accompanied by Third World standards of probity. In 1991, Westinghouse Electric had a poor year, in fact it lost roughly $1 billion. Its chairman and CEO, Paul E. Lego, could hardly demand a bonus in the circumstances, but seemingly he was actually punished, for his salary and bonus were drastically reduced by $1.5 million to the miserable pittance of $667,000. At the same time, however, Lego received stock options on 700,000 shares, a huge grant yet seemingly worthless because their exercise price was reported in the company's official proxy statement as $22.28 on average, while the shares were selling for much less. The suffering shareholders could therefore at least have the satisfaction of knowing that Lego was suffering with them, what with his tiny salary and worthless stock options. But if they did think they were enjoying his companionship in misery, they were dead wrong. For some reason, the proxy statement had neglected to explain that Lego had in fact received his 700,000 stock options in two separate lots of 350,000 each, and that the reported $22.28 average price concealed the low $16 price on one of the two lots.[28] It was only the $16 option that Lego exercised, needless to say, thus over 1989–1991, Lego's total compensation came to $5,323,000, while shareholders lost 17% on their investment.

What is most important, however, is that the entire justification for huge salaries, huge bonuses, abundant stock options, and the other rich incentives is quite simply and demonstrably false. All are granted on the theory that multimillion dollar rewards will evoke heroic efforts to improve corporate performance, especially as determined by share prices. But in fact shares mostly go up or down in accordance with economic, financial, and industrial cycles. When the stock market rises and they exercise their options or sell their "restricted" shares, CEOs receive millions without necessarily having done anything to earn even a dime above their already very ample salaries. In 1991, for example, the stock market was booming during the recession, so while unemployment increased above the 7% level, the average earnings of the chief executives of 363 large public corporations increased by 26% over the 1990 level (as opposed to the less-than-inflation 2.6% increase for all private sector employees).[29]

But the decisive evidence that special income incentives for CEOs are simply unnecessary comes from abroad. No Japanese corporation and hardly any European corporations grant stock options, yet their performance is just as good if not better. Evidently large salaries, generous fringe benefits, and above all the status, power, and satisfactions of running large corporations are quite enough to motivate the chief executives—except, we are to believe, in the contemporary United States. Oddly enough, it is still sometimes claimed that American CEOs deserve more because American corporations are bigger.

That of course is an illusion. Du Pont, the leader of the US chemical industry, is smaller than Germany's BASF and three other foreign companies in total sales; GE, though in every way a corporate powerhouse, is outranked by Hitachi; in oil and gas, even gigantic Exxon is exceeded by Royal Dutch Shell; in the key pharmaceutical sector, the largest US company, Johnson & Johnson, is smaller than the Swiss Ciba-Geigy; in tires, the US leader, Goodyear, is outranked by both Japan's Bridgestone and France's Michelin; in textiles, a Turkish company, Haci Omer Sabanci, is one of five foreign companies larger than the US leader Levi Strauss; in industrial and farm equipment, Mitsubishi Heavy Industries and two others are larger than the largest US company, Tenneco's J. I. Case division; Alcoa is outranked by Germany's Preussag and three others in nonferrous metals; and neither the largest US steel company nor the largest US bank is one of the top twelve in their sectors. According to a worldwide survey,[30] only in the aerospace (Boeing), computer (IBM), automotive (GM), food and beverage (Philip Morris), and forest product (International Paper) sectors are the leading US corporations also the world's largest.

Nor is the overpayment of US senior executives limited to the largest of corporations. A 1991 survey compared the total compensation of the chief executives of manufacturing companies with annual sales of at least $250 million, essentially medium-sized companies that is, in seven major industrial countries.[31] United States chief executives averaged $633,000, as against $377,000 for their German colleagues, $365,000 for the Swiss, $338,000 for the French, $336,000 for the Italians, and $308,000 for both the British and the Japanese. Any claims that fringe benefits may be greater elsewhere are unlikely to begin with, and even if sometimes true, that difference is likely to be more than offset by the superior purchasing power of a dollar in the United States compared to a dollar's worth of Swiss francs, German marks, or Japanese yen.

Actually not even dismissals, resignations, or outright bankruptcy prevent the lavish overpayment of US corporate executives. Thomas Plaskett was the chief executive of Pan Am when that once great airline had to file for bankruptcy court protection in January 1991. *After* the filing, Pan Am, i.e., Plaskett, decided to make a severance payment of

$1.5 million to Plaskett, as part of a $14 million package for executives (in Europe, severance payments are for all employees). Creditors objected, and after months of negotiations Mr. Plaskett had to accept a mere $1 million.[32] It is now perfectly normal for fired chief executives to receive—award themselves by prior plan—up to two years' worth of salary *and bonus*. That, incidentally, reveals that a "bonus" is no longer a bonus in corporate America, i.e., a special payment for special success, but merely a second salary mainly designed to make the salary-salary look modest, or almost so. If that is normal, the "golden parachute" plans that reward executives fired after a change of own-·ership are far more generous: typically they are equivalent to three years of salary, and "bonus," of course.

Golden parachutes for top executives were once a rare device, justified by rare circumstances. During the takeover fever of the 1980s, however, they were sometimes prearranged to discourage hostile takeovers ("poison pills"), and sometimes they were simply arranged by senior executives determined to safeguard themselves, even if they could not safeguard—or effectively manage—their companies. In a survey of 975 corporations, more than 35% had such plans for their senior executives in 1987, and that proportion had increased to more than 45% by 1990.[33]

That generosity is not dead in this cruel world is proved by the magnitude of many golden parachutes. As of 1991, the top five executives of Baxter International had inscribed themselves in the book of postdeparture payments in the amount of $56.8 million, an impressive sum for a rather less-than-world-class corporation; in the case of Promus Inc. the amount was $41.4 million, with $17.3 million for Waste Management, $13.9 million for Browning-Ferris, etc., down to a mere $8.5 million for Chubb. Remarkably, even savings and loan associations and banks that were swept away during the financial collapse of 1989–1991 could be most generous, even after they lost every penny for their shareholders and bondholders, and much more for the US Treasury, which had to assume their obligations to depositors. When Charles Zwick was removed from his post as chairman and CEO of the failing Southeast Banking Corporation in January 1990, he nevertheless obtained the promise of thirty monthly severance payments of $41,667 each. When all its banks had already collapsed, Southeast stopped paying the monthly checks. Naturally Mr. Zwick sued his former company, which he had managed into insolvency.

Only gross corporate self-indulgence can explain these facts, a species of corruption that exemplifies the fracturing of American society between successful manipulators on the one hand and the manipulated on the other, be they shareholders or rank-and-file employees.

The architects, the beneficiaries, and the chief executives who have entered the magic circle of the richest 1% of American families number in the thousands—but there are almost 1 million families in that category. What families are they, and who are their breadwinners, if such a word applies? Many no doubt are professionals, highly paid lawyers, investment bankers, top athletes, and entertainers, even especially acquisitive doctors. There are many professionals—but not that many: in 1991, average earnings for the country's 400,000 doctors were only $170,000, certainly not enough to accumulate enough wealth to make it into the top 1%, and even partners of major law firms averaged only $445,000.[34] And then there are the talented or hardworking or simply fortunate individual businesspeople who own their own companies in full or in part—as well as the handful of eccentric mega-entrepreneurs such as Ross Perot, the late Sam Walton of Wal-Mart fame, and Bill Gates of Microsoft stardom.

What they all have in common are two things. First, the architects, beneficiaries, CEOs, best-paid professionals, and entrepreneurs actually work. Second, even in combination, they account for only a minority of the richest 1% of all families, for nowadays the majority of America's very rich and super-rich do not work at all.

■ THE RENTIERS

For the first time in its history, American society now contains a large class of nonworking "rentiers," who live off dividends, bond interest (they hold much of the national debt), and real-estate rentals, rather than the active conduct of a business or profession.[35] When seen on the golf courses and boat docks of the fenced-in and carefully guarded residential enclaves they so greatly favor, from Palm Springs, California, to Hilton Head, South Carolina (where the various developments are actually called "plantations"), rentiers kitted out in their Ralph Lauren clothes superficially resemble businesspeople or professionals on vacation. But their vacation never ends, and their priorities are actually very different.

First, rentiers are exceptionally unwilling to pay taxes, simply be-

cause they have so little use for government services of any sort—
including those that are essential for the *working* rich and super-rich.
The latter may rely entirely on private schools, private medicine, and
private security guards for themselves and their families, but they still
need public education for their employees, not to speak of public
health, public law enforcement, and public infrastructures of all kinds,
beginning with the streets and roads on which they drive to their offices
and factories each day. Equally, their businesses rely on many kinds of
government services, from the information supplied by the US geolog-
ical survey, to the conduct of trade negotiations with foreign countries.
And many of the working rich benefit very directly from government
largesse, from procurement contracts to outright subsidies.

None of this applies to rentiers. In the guarded and fenced golf and
residential enclaves where they prefer to live, rentiers have private
substitutes for almost all public services, from road maintenance and
private schools and hospitals to the private police forces that keep out
the unwanted from their landscaped prospects and manicured lawns.
Even in the deep real-estate slump of 1992, a basic five-bedroom,
five-bathroom house with oceanside pool in the Sea Pines Plantation of
Hilton Head Island—by no means the most affluent of the rentier
enclaves—was listed at $3 million, though there were several offerings
for a mere $2 million. Only the descendants of the slaves who used to
pick the island's cotton, who now live along the causeway in shacks
and mobile homes, rely on public services.

Nor do rentiers benefit from federal services, contracts, or subsidies,
except in the broadest sense—too broad to motivate their political
conduct. There is nothing to prevent individual rentiers from being
exceptionally compassionate, or superpatriotic, or enthusiastically favorable to government activism of every sort, or all of the above. As a
group, however, they are none of the above, and they relentlessly
campaign for lower taxes on unearned income and capital gains, even
at the expense of the public services that the working rich need and
may therefore support.

Because so much of what the government does at all levels is of
questionable value or even counterproductive, the influence of rentiers
on US economic policies is far more weighty.

Unlike all those who still work, from millionaire entrepreneurs to
casual laborers, rentiers are fundamentally uninterested in economic
growth, because growth tends to be inflationary, and their overriding

concern is always to limit inflation, which rapidly erodes the value of their bonds. Hence they are unmoved by the shortage of capital that afflicts the American economy. On the contrary: the less capital there is, the higher are interest rates, and the greater is their income. Having themselves inherited or saved enough, the low rate of savings and the resulting shortage of capital that weighs so heavily on active business-people is the least of their concerns. Equally, they are unaffected by the decline of public education and the resulting deficiencies of the American labor force: they employ no skilled workers, expert clericals, technicians, engineers, or scientists, but only maids, gardeners, and pool attendants—the less educated (and thus less demanding) the better.

Those are not the preferences of any active business or professional class in any modern society, but rather of Third World rentiers, content to live in luxurious villas at the end of unpaved streets lined by the hovels of the illiterate and indigent. Yet those are the specific anti-inflation and antitax preferences that have been so dominant in our political life of late. Nor is that surprising: rentiers, like the rich in general, are obviously well placed to fund political campaigns. More-over, unlike the working rich, they also have plenty of leisure to organize and attend political gatherings, and even to serve as unpaid campaign staff.

Their influence has been duly felt. Certainly if the Republican party would still represent business and industry, its first priority would be economic growth rather than the reduction of taxes and the control of inflation—which entrepreneurs, at any rate, positively welcome up to a point, because it reduces the real cost of borrowing money for their enterprises. It only remains to say that if the Republicans no longer represent working capital, the Democrats for their part hardly represent working labor, as opposed to white-collar and government employees, believers in the very separate rights of all sorts of minorities, environ-mental activists, and others of their ilk, all representing worthy causes, but not the interests of labor.

There is no reason why the much-interested concentration of wealth in the United States should not have the same political consequences as in the Third World societies where wealth is also greatly concentrated. Of course, the techniques that convert wealth into political power to acquire yet more wealth are rather difficult. Few rich Americans would think of forcing their sons or daughters to marry the children, nieces, and nephews of the powerful to safeguard family interests (a commonplace in countries as diverse as Korea and Mexico). Few rich Americans are likely to hire bandidos to deal with impediments to their business affairs, then relying on political influence to escape all prosecution (not unheard of in Brazil). And few rich Americans routinely rely on bribery to obtain permits and licenses denied to everyone else—although the connection between, say, the valuable rezoning of real estate by local politicos, and campaign contributions to the same, is not a million miles removed from bribery. Still, America remains a "country ruled by laws not by men," as the saying goes.

The trouble is that there are so *many* laws, and new ones are made all the time, in an atmosphere pervaded by expensive lobbying. Just as Lagos and Mexico City have their "fixers," people of no particular origin or characteristics but for their magical ability to extract favorable decisions from the government, Washington is the territory of public-relations firms that have no interest in relating to the public, and of law firms that practice no known version of the law, but do have ex-Representatives and ex-Senators in their ranks. What both practice is the influencing of legislation by the US Congress, as well as in smaller degree the influencing of executive-branch decisions. Both have their counterparts in state capitals and even in some county seats and large city governments. In each case, the lobbyists of whatever ilk convey campaign funds, develop political support (typically by organizing fund-raisers), and bestow strictly personal favors, ranging from fishing and golfing holidays to routine dinners and occasional gifts. In each case, they expect favors for their clients that pay for any or all of the above, and their own fees.

In theory, lobbying is supposed to contribute usefully to the "political process" by representing the many diverse interests in America's very diverse society. When regional telephone companies fight it out with the data-processing industry for the right to offer computer services over their wires, theory and practice are one: the money each side spends to lobby cancels out, and what remains is the added information supplied to congressional staffs by the blizzard of "fact sheets," "position papers," and briefings that descends upon them. But when it comes to, say, tax legislation, all the money and all the lobbying are likely to be on one side, leaving the nonlobbying ordinary taxpayer quite unrepresented. At this very time, for example, the Ways and Means Committee of the House of Representatives is considering H.R.

3035, a bill long and complicated as many bills are, which would introduce some highly technical changes in the tax code.

How many ordinary Americans whose own taxes are withheld at source are familiar with the detailed provisions of H.R. 3035? And yet they should be, because if it becomes law, H.R. 3035 would require them to provide several billion dollars to subsidize corporate "buy-outs" by that same amount. As noted, *leveraged* buy-outs (where corporations are bought with borrowed money) are already inadvertently subsidized by all taxpayers, because interest payments on the inevitably heavy debt are deductible from taxes. In addition, all buy-outs are further subsidized because the depreciation of all the tangible assets bought out is also deductible. Say Shark Inc. buys out Bluefish Inc. for $100 million. At present, when Shark's taxes are due, it can also deduct from its income the calculated depreciation of the Bluefish offices, furniture, plants, machinery, trucks, etc.—an annual percentage for the wear and tear on a total of, say, $50 million of assorted items. But Shark, as noted, paid $100 million for Bluefish. The latter, after all, is not just a collection of desks and machine-tools, offices, and sheds but an operating business, which is profitable or potentially profitable also—or mainly—because of "intangible" assets, such as its skilled people and techniques, its designs, trademarks, and patents, and its good reputation in the market, or "goodwill" as they say in business.

The purpose of H.R. 3035 is to allow the intangibles, too, to be depreciated at so much a year, thus increasing the total amount that can be deducted from income before paying corporate taxes in the wake of buy-outs. The beauty of the scheme is that intangibles, being nonphysical, are also infinitely variable in their definition. Goodwill is the standard intangible, but there are many others: established dealer networks, a unique organization, products easily recognized, etc., as well as—more creatively—"nonunion status" and some 150 other categories.

As H.R. 3035 becomes law, the winners will be the investment bankers who specialize in buy-outs, the law firms that work with them, and the corporations that already have buy-outs to work off against taxes (Citicorp, Honeywell, Gillette, Philip Morris, etc.)—representing at most (shareholders included) the interests of the familiar 1% of the richest Americans. The losers will be the remaining 99% of all Americans who would have to supply an immediate $8.5 billion in tax rebates for done deals, and then an estimated $3.6 billion per year to further encourage buy-outs, with all their dubious results.

Furious lobbying and vast political contributions secured much support for the attempt to make H.R. 3035 the law of the land. What finally happened to H.R. 3035 hardly matters: there are so many other laws equally obscure and equally profitable to a privileged few. The procedure may be less colorful than bandido raids to burn down aspiring competitors, agonizingly slow as compared to the swift passing of well-stuffed envelopes, and certainly less romantic than marriages, even if contrived. But then again, Third World magnates must usually be satisfied with much less than $8.5 billion up front, plus $3.5 billion per year.

CHAPTER 7

WHERE HAVE ALL THE HIGH

WAGES GONE?

When Henry Ford doubled the wages of his assembly-line workers in 1914 to a fabulous $5 per day—the *Wall Street Journal,* wrong as usual, called it an "economic crime"—his announcement swept across America and the world, quickly reaching hamlets deep in Swedish forests and lost in Russian steppes, Sicilian villages, and Polish towns. Overcoming disbelief, men repeated to one another the incredible news: a Ford worker could not only house and feed his family, but even buy a *car,* the ultimate luxury, till then reserved for the rich—in Europe, the truly rich, richer than the local landlord, a wealthy merchant at least.

As usual, war threatened in the Balkans, there was hunger in Sicily, and violent upheavals were tearing apart the Russian empire. But what persuaded more than a million European immigrants a year to suffer crowded ships and brave the hazards of a new country and a new language was the simple arithmetic of American life. Henry Ford's workers earned the $360 price of the model T in just twelve weeks, six days a week, ten hours a day. Even the average production worker in America had weekly earnings of $10.92 in 1914, so he could buy a model T with just 33 weeks of his labor.[1] All it took to make theory into reality was a pair of strong sons still at home whose wages went into the family coffers. New immigrants who actually did it sent photographs of themselves at the wheel, their proud family around them, so that skeptical relatives still in the old country would believe the astounding American miracle.

Immigration is again very high, running at a million a year as it was before 1914. But now they come chiefly from Mexico, the rest of Latin America, China, India, and the rest of Asia; less than one in ten come from Europe.[2] There is again war in the Balkans and the Russian empire is again disintegrating, while postcommunism is in a most painful transition across Eastern Europe. But American wages no longer attract Europeans: they can earn more in France or Italy, much more in Germany or Sweden—and also have vacations twice as long and more. Japan is still sometimes thought of as a low-wage country, but there, too, wages are now higher. That is what a shortage of capital does: it makes labor the cheap resource—and American labor is becoming cheaper all the time. After rising year by year and decade after decade, but for the Depression of the 1930s, American wages and nonsupervisory salaries stopped increasing in real dollars during the 1970s.

Nor can this great downfall be dismissed by more *Wall Street Journal* prattle, this time about the inevitable decline of manufacturing—which, by the way, still accounted for 17.7% of all American employees, according to the latest figures.[3] That implies a total of some 20 million blue-collar and white-collar employees, from factory workers to top corporate executives,[4] with roughly twice as many dependents in their keep. The welfare of 40 million Americans should be a weighty enough concern, but it is not only industrial workers who are losing ground. The downward trend in hourly earnings is manifest across the economy, from construction to the retail trades, and it is just as evident for rank-and-file white-collar salaries—including salaries paid in the banking, insurance, and financial services, which are supposed to flourish in a "postindustrial" society. No more telling evidence can be imagined that the entire economic base of American society is eroding.

Inflation masked the decline at first, but during the 1980s outright reductions began. Economists had long explained that real earnings can be invisibly eroded by inflation, but they cannot be baldly reduced because employee resistance would be furious. But from the early 1980s, they were proved wrong. With capital scarce and valuable, labor was becoming relatively more abundant, not worth employing at all unless cheap. With unemployment as the only alternative, there began the season of union "give backs," and stepped-down employment contracts for newly hired employees. That was not enough at a time of ever-higher earnings for top executives, and ever more fierce cost-cutting in corporate America. Amidst mass dismissals of white-collar employees, it became a badge of honor to overcome blue-collar strikes so as to force outright wage reductions.

How the process works was perfectly demonstrated in April 1992 by Caterpillar Inc. of Peoria, Illinois, maker of the big, yellow, earth-moving machines that are a familiar sight on highways and construction sites. After claiming that Japan's Komatsu, its chief competitor in world markets, paid less for its labor, Caterpillar's management refused to accept the United Auto Workers' contract demands, based on a prior settlement with Deere & Co., also a large manufacturer of earth-moving and farm machinery. Because of productivity gains achieved with union cooperation, Deere & Co. had agreed to a substantial raise. In the past, that would have guaranteed a similar raise from Caterpillar.

That was the "pattern bargaining" tradition of American labor that was once *in itself* an engine of industrial progress: with the wage level across an entire industry set by the amounts that the most efficient enterprise could afford to pay, all its competitors were also forced to become equally efficient, or else they were forced right out of business. In the process, some workers would lose their jobs, but that did not seriously disturb American unions: the unemployed would soon find new jobs—with the more efficient enterprises that could afford to pay them better. The latter would need additional workers, because their sales would be expanding as their less proficient competitors were driven out of business by union demands.

During the postwar years when German and Japanese industry was in ruins, throughout the 1950s and into the 1960s while American industry still had little to fear from foreign competition, it was mainly "pattern bargaining" that compelled investment to increase productivity, and slothful management to work more seriously. In the larger scheme of things, by driving mismanaged and undercapitalized enterprises out of business, "pattern bargaining" ensured the vitality of American industry as a whole, much as wolves improve the gene pool of Arctic caribou by killing off weaker animals that might otherwise reproduce. Most European unions, by contrast, resisted unemployment above all. They therefore tended to moderate their wage demands to allow even the least efficient enterprises to survive. European economists greatly admired what American unions were doing—especially their willingness to risk the jobs of some of their members to gain higher wages for the rest. That, they said, was the secret of American industrial efficiency.

184 . THE ENDANGERED AMERICAN DREAM

But even the harsh Darwinism of "pattern bargaining" was totally outmatched by the impact of foreign competition both at home and in foreign markets. When General Motors loses out to foreign-made cars, the American workers forced into unemployment cannot seek jobs with the more efficient enterprise, 12,000 miles away and most unwilling to accept immigrants (and they are not wanted by "transplants" either, which are located in southern and rural areas precisely because they seek young, nonunion labor). The chairman and CEO of Caterpillar, Donald V. Fites, had a very simple answer for the problem in a 1991 interview: to keep their jobs, American workers would have to accept lower wages—and their wages would have to keep going down:

There is a narrowing of the gap between the average American's income and that of the Mexicans. . . . As a human being, I think what is going on is positive. I don't think it is realistic for 250 million Americans to control so much of the world's GNP.[5]

That is the meaning for American labor of the much-celebrated globalization of industry, according to Donald V. Fites. Philosophically, it is an unexceptional position. Leaving aside the question of incentives, which raises so many other issues, the notion that each person should receive an equal share of the world's gross national product is perfectly defensible. It is much less defensible for one particular American person to decide that 13,000 other Americans (Caterpillar's workers in Peoria, Illinois) should reduce their collective share of the global GNP, while he himself continues to claim a totally disproportionate share. Over 1989–1991, Mr. Fites received $2,014,000 for his labors[6]—not in truth all that much by the excess that is the prevailing standard for CEOs, but still equal to the GNP share of 426 average Mexicans or 5,594 Nepalese.[7]

Actually, as we shall see, it is not foreign competition in itself that determines the dismal outcome Mr. Fites welcomes but does not share, but rather the failure to match foreign competition with more capital and more training rather than cheap labor. Had more been saved by Americans and then invested in American industry by the likes of Caterpillar in order to provide American workers with better equipment to work with; had public education and industrial training by the likes of Caterpillar been constantly upgraded to preserve the skill advantage of American workers; the "globalization" of industry could have progressed without forcing down American wages.

That is exactly how Japanese industry has preserved its competitive advantage while at the same time paying steadily higher wages. That, indeed, is how other advanced economies all over the world operate in the face of low-wage competition. Incidentally, if the CEO of Mitsubishi Heavy Industries were to declare that Japanese workers must simply accept it as inevitable that their wages will have to decline to the Korean level, he would quickly be forced to resign—not for a lack of tact but for a lack of competence, i.e., the failure to recognize that expensive workers can be more profitable than cheaper workers, if sufficiently equipped and properly trained.

Given the views of its CEO, it was predictable that Caterpillar would reject "pattern bargaining" based on the settlement reached with Deere & Co. Instead, it offered only a 13% wage increase over three years—probably less than the rate of inflation according to most forecasts, and therefore a continuation of the long-term trend of falling real wages (for a typical Caterpillar worker hired at nineteen and now thirty-eight, hourly wages have increased 157% from $7 to $11; but the cost of living has increased by 203%).[8] The result was a strike that lasted for months but which ended abruptly after Donald V. Fites announced on April 6, 1992, that Caterpillar would fire all its 13,000 striking workers, hiring permanent replacements for them unless they immediately returned to work while a federal mediator conducted further negotiations.

With little prospect of finding comparable jobs in Peoria or anywhere else during a recession, Caterpillar's workers were faced with the bitter choice of betraying their union or risking the welfare of their families—some of which were split between sons who wanted to return to work to pay their mortgages and fathers who could better afford to stay out. After eight days of harsh confrontations between the pickets at the factory gates and some 1,000 workers who returned to work, the union capitulated. The outcome was hardly likely to inspire the cooperative spirit that modern labor–management quality and productivity initiatives require, including Caterpillar's own six-year effort to form "high performance teams." But Fites was unconcerned: "We just want a contract that will enable us to be globally competitive."[9] In other words, instead of providing more capital equipment and better training to increase output per worker, Caterpillar's method is to compete by reducing real wages. Therein lies the path to Third World conditions, in which the shortage of capital makes labor the cheapest of resources.

With none of Caterpillar's overt ruthlessness, Rubbermaid of Wooster, Ohio, has pursued the same method. That extremely successful company, whose sales increased from some $300 million in 1981 to more than $1.6 billion ten years later, and whose profits have increased even more over the same period from $20 million to more than $160 million, has obviously reaped the benefits of steadily increasing productivity. The dividends it pays to its shareholders have risen accordingly, but instead of increasing wages also, Rubbermaid successfully negotiated a wage reduction—and without provoking a strike. After diminishing its employment in Wooster by shifting production to other sites offering cheaper labor, in 1987 Rubbermaid offered to stop the attrition in exchange for a wage freeze and the end of overtime pay for existing workers, and an outright reduction for new hires, who receive $7.71–$11.00 per hour, as compared to $10–$14 for workers hired before 1987. Faced with the threat of more job losses, the Rubber Workers union accepted Rubbermaid's terms.

When a former president of its Local 302 wrote in complaint to the Wooster *Daily Record*, a reader replied: "Have you any idea how many young men would cut off a finger to start a job at $7.71 an hour? Talk to someone who starts at $4.50 and reaches a high of $5.85 after four or five years."[10] Obviously it is the shortage of capital in American economy that makes labor relatively abundant, and therefore cheap, just as a larger supply of capital would have the opposite effect. As Rubbermaid's former chairman, Stanley C. Gault, put it: "Spending the extra income that comes from productivity [increases] on higher wages is theoretically desirable, but not practical."[11]

In other words, if productivity does not improve to reduce production costs, other things being equal the employer cannot afford wage increases. But even if productivity *does* improve, wage increases need not be paid anyway, if employers have no trouble in hiring all the labor they need without them. In an economy in which the overall shortage of capital, as compared to natural population growth plus immigration, makes labor the relatively abundant resource, even impressive productivity gains need not result in higher wages. In economic theory that cannot be so, because employers must benefit from hiring at the margin when productivity increases outpace wage increases, but that is true only if everything else is also in place, including the required supply of capital and markets ready to absorb the extra output. In recent American practice matters have turned out otherwise.

■ PRODUCTIVITY MYTHS

"Productivity" has become a hotly debated subject in America, and properly so. But labor productivity (that is what is usually meant) is very hard to measure with any accuracy, except in routine industrial processes where the number of widgets or the tons or gallons turned out per hour can be readily counted. That is why overall national productivity statistics, which include many services whose output cannot be counted at all, are very unreliable even by the loose standards of all our economic statistics. Sometimes the numbers one sees published are simply meaningless. Moreover, many a solemn editorial on the subject has clearly been written by people who confuse productivity as such (output per hour, etc.) with productivity *growth rates,* the true subject of concern. It is generally believed that the overall productivity of American labor throughout the economy, including all the services, has been growing at a very slow pace by the standards of America's main trading competitors—and certainly as compared to Japan. If true, that is the natural result of too little investment in both people, by way of education and training, and in plant, machinery, and the overall production environment, including public infrastructures such as highways.

But it is interesting to note that in manufacturing, where productivity can best be measured, US labor productivity has been increasing very nicely. Between 1980 and 1988, it grew by 41.6%, substantially the same as Japan's 41.0% (measuring errors are certainly greater than the difference), more than the French increase (21.3%), and *much* more than the German increase at 13%.[12] But starting from its own very high base, US labor productivity in manufacturing has not increased enough over a longer term of years to preserve its edge, over Japan for example: in 1975, it was 92% higher than in Japan on average; in 1988, in spite of the very respectable upturn from 1980, it was 64% higher.[13]

That still meant that US labor productivity was very substantially higher than Japan's across the board, and especially so in certain sectors, e.g., nonelectrical machinery (294%), clothing (294%), processed foods (286%), leather products (238%), lumber and woods (192%), textiles (175%), pulp and paper (152%), *motor vehicles* (137%), and printing and publishing (127%). By contrast, it was only inferior in the chemical industry (78%), iron and steel (88%), and electrical machinery (88%).[14] Moreover, because the benefits of its increased productivity were generally withheld from US labor, overall wage costs (wages over productivity) have been going down, being last recorded in 1990 at 93.4% of the 1985 level, as compared to 108.9% for the United Kingdom, 105.7% for Germany, 102% for France (in 1987), and 97.1% for Japan.[15]

At first glance all those numbers would suggest that the United States must be tremendously competitive, with a great quantity of jobs to be had in export industries. That is certainly the case in regard to Europe, which has been buying American exports in such large amounts that earlier trade deficits have given way to surpluses. But what of Japan, champion exporter of cars, consumer electronics, and much else to the United States? One would imagine that at least in low-technology sectors where less capital is needed, the formidable US labor productivity advantage and the resulting total cost advantage should have resulted in equally formidable US exports, to offset the loss of jobs caused by Japanese imports.

But that is not how things have been allowed to happen. While the American elite believes in free trade, even if one-sided, the Japanese elite believes in protecting incomes, lives, and the dignity of employment, by *controlling* "globalization" instead of allowing it to dictate the fate of their society. Hence it is not surprising that the sectors in which the US labor productivity advantage is greatest also happen to be the sectors in which Japanese import barriers are most effective: processed foods, leather goods, and wood and paper products. Beyond them, cigarettes, aluminum, agricultural products in general, telecommunications equipment, pharmaceuticals, medical equipment, food additives, supercomputers, satellites, high-cube containers, optical fibers, aerospace, auto parts, and soda ash are also included in the official US list of products and services whose export to Japan is blocked or impeded by overt or disguised trade barriers as we have seen.[16] Nor is Japan alone: the other leading exporting countries of Asia, and especially Korea, emulate Japan in this as in so many other ways.

Thus US workers lose jobs to imports in industries in which they are not productive enough, i.e., iron and steel, electrical machinery, etc., or not productive enough to offset capital-investment disadvantages (motor vehicles). But they do not gain offsetting export jobs in industries in which they *are* more productive. And, of course, as noted, their increased productivity of 1980–1988 reduced the wage costs of US manufacturing industries instead of earning them higher wages.

Only in Britain, the country of quaint curiosity shops and famously uncooperative trade unions, did labor productivity increase substantially more than in the United States between 1980 and 1988: the British increase was 55%, as compared to 41% for the United States. Odd things are going on therefore, or perhaps not so odd: under Margaret Thatcher's policies, traditionally overstaffed nationalized industries and public utilities were privatized and then destaffed, many other businesses were closed by bankruptcies, and there was a great deal of successful union-busting. The overall result was that overemployment secured by famously restrictive labor practices was greatly reduced by mass firings (leading to 10% plus unemployment levels). Thus Britain, starting from a very low base, became much more labor-productive as compared to itself.

By such methods, labor productivity can be increased very rapidly in any economy, at any time. If one bright day all US employers were to fire 10% of their work force, for example, their output is bound to decline less than 10%, thereby increasing productivity overnight. Then the procedure might be repeated. But of course that is not the way to secure economic growth for an enterprise or a country.

■ WAGES AND SALARIES IN AN UNDERCAPITALIZED ECONOMY

Against any one anecdote another can be cited, but in this case official statistics show that Caterpillar and Rubbermaid are not only typical but almost generous. These particular numbers, moreover, do not have the flaws of any international comparison. In 1970, the average hourly earnings of nonsupervisors employed in all industries, all forms of commerce, and all services other than agriculture or government amounted to $3.23; by 1980 they had more than doubled to $6.66; and by 1990 they had again increased greatly to $10.02, more than a threefold increase in twenty years, nothing to complain about it would seem. But those amounts take no account of inflation. If we look again at those earnings in constant 1982 dollars to strip away the false increases eaten away by rising prices, the numbers are dramatically different: those average "nonfarm, nongovernment, nonsupervisory" hourly earnings were $8.03 in 1970, $7.78 in 1980, and $7.53 in 1990. And those numbers are not contrived by statistical fiddling with inflation indices as some would claim. For example, the same earnings in 1978 came to $5.69 in 1978 dollars—and everyone old enough to remember working and shopping in those days will intuitively know from experience that $5.69 was worth much more in 1978 than $10.02 in 1990, after many years of inflation, both the 10% plus of 1979–1980, and the slower but steady erosion of the value of money that followed.[17]

Averages conceal many tales of course, from the rising earnings of federal, state, and municipal employees and the pay raises still to be had in fortunate circumstances, to the degradation of $18 per hour industrial workers into $6 per hour warehouse janitors, or even their desperate poaching of minimum-wage jobs that once were the first and crucial stepping-stones of underclass achievement. It is a mixed picture, but the dark colors prevail, for the numbers show irrefutably that there has been more degradation than advancement.

Thus during the last twenty years—half a working lifetime—while real earnings were increasing substantially in much of Europe, and more than doubling in the high-growth countries of Asia headed by Japan, American rank-and-file employees actually earned slightly less, year by year. Only because inflation masked what was happening could the illusion of rising earnings be sustained. Actually real earnings had regressed to the 1965 level by 1990. Will they regress further—perhaps to the 1960 level by 1995, and then perhaps to the 1955 level by the year 2000? It seems distinctly probable.

I am not a "nonfarm, nonsupervisory" employee, and the chances are that whoever reads these words is not one either. So who are the poor unfortunates whose real earnings have been declining since 1965? Are they perhaps some small and peculiar minority? Not so: in November 1990, the last month for which those statistics are complete, they numbered some 74,888,000, or just over 81% of all nonfarm, nongovernment employees. That is more than eight out of ten of all privately employed Americans who are not self-employed, from corporate executives earning hundreds or even thousands of dollars per hour, to those working at the minimum wage.[18] Far from being a minority whose fate cannot affect the base of American society, they *are* the base of American society, the vast majority of the labor force of manufacturing, mining, construction, transport, utility, wholesale and retail trade, finance, insurance, real estate, and all other service enterprises.

It keeps being said that the decline in hourly earnings does not matter because "family living standards" increased anyway during the 1970s and 1980s. That miracle was easily achieved: wives went out to work to help support their families. In the media, the working woman of the 1980s was often presented as the sharp executive determined to get ahead in her power tailleur, the lawyer who stood her ground with the best of them in court, the occasional woman airline pilot, or even the brash sports reporter who fought her way into ballpark locker rooms. For all of them, undoubtedly, work was the fulfillment of ambition, of lives even.

But the vast majority of the married women who went out to work were not pursuing self-fulfillment, but only trying to offset the stagnant or declining earnings of their husbands. Between 1980 and 1990, while the total number of male nonfarm employees in the American economy increased only from 52 million to 57.5 million, i.e., by less than 10%, over the same period the number of female employees increased by 36% from 38 million to 52 million.[19] Of the additional 14 million female employees, a large part were newly working wives: as late as 1970 only some four out of ten married women worked, but by 1990 almost six out of ten did. A few thus had their opportunity to start or resume interesting, satisfying, even glamorous careers. Most accepted whatever work they could find near their homes, often low-paid, manual work, rarely pleasant.

Nor can it be said that "family living standards" were increased when wives went out to work—often against their expectations and personal desires—and still less can that be said when instead of a full-time parent, children were left with the part-time attentions of a working couple. It is much more correct to say that working wives allowed family *expenditures* to rise significantly even as real earnings per hour did not.

In any case, the great remedy of the 1970s to 1980s can hardly help during the next decade and beyond. If the real hourly earnings of American workers continue to decline, the impact on "family living standards" can hardly be offset by further increases in the number of workers per family—not unless there are mass conversions to Islam to allow "nonfarm, nonsupervisory" male workers to have two wives— and then three or four, if their economic slide continues. (Feminists may rightly object that it is women workers who might instead decide to acquire two husbands to maintain the living standards of polyandric three-worker families.) And those economists who keep invoking the "family living standards" argument may propose that child labor be revived instead. Given the condition of many American schools, it is not clear if that Dickensian solution would be all that harmful.

But that is no longer a fit subject for irony. Federal law prohibits the employment of anyone under eighteen in logging, mining, and roofing, and some other dangerous jobs, it prohibits under-sixteens from working during school hours or too many hours altogether on weekends and after school, and it altogether prohibits the employment of children under fourteen, except on farms. Inspired by repeated death-and-mutilation scandals, as well as the advent of compulsory education, these laws were most effective in protecting children from exploitation and injury in the early years of the century, but they were becoming moot by the 1970s. By then, the employment of under-eighteens (still "children" in official definition) was very largely an innocent affair of weekend jobs in companionable fast-food eateries and other teenager hangouts—a source of extra income, useful life experience, a token of financial independence to come. Of late that is no longer true: child labor in the real sense of the phrase has returned as a mass phenomenon in America.

More than 4 million teenagers between fourteen and eighteen are now legally employed in factories and construction sites as well as fast-food eateries, gas stations, shops, and farms, where the sight of youngsters at work is less surprising. No laws are being broken, but for the full-time employees among them, that kind of work is normally an unsatisfactory start to life as compared to finishing high school, because there are very few proper apprentices anymore—the youngsters who not only carried toolboxes, cleaned floors, and did the simplest routine tasks, but were also being taught how to become craftsmen in their turn. In addition to the 4 million in legal employ, however, it is now estimated—or simply guessed—that another 2 million under-eighteens are working illegally, because they are under fourteen, or because they are paid less than the minimum wage, or because they work longer hours than allowed, or because they have to perform prohibited hazardous tasks, or because they are paid in cash to avoid taxes, or several of those things.

Workplace inspections are sporadic and ineffectual—in New York State, for example, fifteen garment-industry inspectors have 4,000 to

6,000 sweatshops to oversee, and their owners are very well practiced in hiding violations. Hence it is only the increasing number of children arriving in emergency rooms with workplace burns, amputations, deep cuts, and electrocutions that suggests the magnitude of the problem.[20] Clearly we have come far down the road from the days when teenage labor meant no more than the odd evening spent at the neighborhood McDonald's, where the greatest hazard was the overeating of buns with too much fatty meat in between, and assorted other soda-pop excesses. The reason for this sad regression is simple enough, aside from the influx of Third World immigrants for whom child labor is an everyday old country norm: many families now badly need the extra income that their children can earn, even if they already have a fully employed adult breadwinner.

Low earnings also affect work behavior, of course. For some, the inability to earn enough to avoid poverty by working forty hours a week, fifty weeks a year is merely an incentive to work more hours. For others, it is instead a reason not to work at all, if they can get money some other way, either from public assistance or from crime. Because long-term public assistance is generally limited to women (with children) for all practical purposes, crime is the major remaining source of income for nonworking males as we shall see.

That is why the fate of low-paid workers since the 1970s is of such vast significance for American society as a whole. It has a direct bearing on social stability and on the prevalence of crime.

■ **THE ROAD TO HERMOSILLO**

As the ineffable Mr. Donald V. Fites of Caterpillar memorably suggested, one brutal reality behind the falling earnings of US workers is that American industry is increasingly competing internationally not with superior technology, nor with more efficient plant and machinery, nor with better education and training, but simply with cheaper labor. Indeed it is with cheap "international" labor that American corporations increasingly compete at home as well, relocating production overseas, or simply across the border in Mexico, with an ease that makes Caterpillar, still in Peoria, Illinois, seem a paragon of patriotism, or provincialism.

In 1987, long before there was any prospect of a US–Mexican Free Trade Area, Ford inaugurated a new assembly line in Hermosillo, Mexico, where by 1992 some 700 cars were being produced each day by some 2,400 employees. Very advanced, highly automated, the plant—inevitably—is described as "Japanese-style." And, true enough, over-turning long prejudice, Hermosillo with its Mexican workers turns out cars not only very cheaply but also with the lowest proportion of defects in need of correction of any American-owned car assembly-plant anywhere in the world, definitely including the United States. In fact, Hermosillo became exhibit "A" when Detroit started to claim that it had caught up with Japanese quality standards.

It one respect, however, Hermosillo is not advanced at all, indeed it is backward in extreme degree, certainly pre-1939, perhaps pre-1914. In 1991 entry-level workers earned $1.50 per hour while experienced welders could earn $1.75 per hour, with as much again in subsidized lunches, health insurance, and other fringe benefits. That is roughly the same as the 1947 hourly earnings of American car workers, *in 1947 dollars* that is, which today would be worth not the Mexican workers' $1.50 or $1.75, but rather $8.80 to $10.35 per hour.[21] In Mexico, of course, Ford's wages are very attractive and it can afford to be very selective in its hiring: only secondary-school graduates, already a priv-ileged group educationally in Mexico, are considered at all among the great number of applicants. Subcontractors that supply Ford with com-ponents pay more normal Mexican wages: $1.16 an hour on average.[22]

There is rich irony in the meaning of Hermosillo for the American economy. It was Ford, in the person of Henry Ford, that invented not only the moving assembly line for cars—a mere adaptation of estab-lished production techniques—but also that altogether greater and far more consequential novelty: the *well-paid* industrial worker who can afford to purchase the car he himself assembles. In Hermosillo, Henry Ford's invention stands disinvented: at $1.50 or $1.75 an hour, the purchase of a Hermosillo-made Ford is a distant dream for assembly-line workers. They are not car-owning householders as Henry Ford's employees became even before 1914, but true proletarians who own essentially nothing except their children. Yet it is with Hermosillo that US assembly lines must already compete, and will have to compete more directly still if all tariffs are abolished by a US–Mexican Free Trade Agreement.

That of course means an ever more direct *wage* competition between American and Mexican labor—if, that is, American workers have no advantage over their Mexican counterparts in the organization, technology level, capital equipment, and skills applied to the job. As against Mexican assembly-line workers at Hermosillo, American workers have none of those advantages. If anything, that plant is better equipped than the average Ford facility in the United States, while assembly-line work simply does not offer that much scope for education and skill advances, if any.

The fatal equation is simple: if organization, plus applied technology, plus capital investment, plus applicable skill levels are the same, the wage rate must be the same too in a directly competitive setting. That convergence would result in catastrophically lower, *pre-1914* wages for American workers, unless a drastic labor shortage in the combined US–Mexican economies were to lift wage rates in both. Of that there is absolutely no prospect, as we shall see.

In addition to Ford at Hermosillo, Chrysler has an assembly line in Toluca that makes cars for export to the United States and another in Mexico City that assembles light trucks for both markets. General Motors produces cars in Ramos Arizpe for both the US and Mexican markets, as well as some twenty-six *maquiladoras* near the border that produce Packard Electric components. Ford itself is building a major engine factory in Chihuahua.[23] "Detroit south" is thus expanding, but if the US–Mexican Free Trade Agreement accelerates the convergence between US and Mexican wages, there will be no need for GM, Chrysler, and Ford to continue exporting American jobs south of the border, because Mexican wage rates will be moving north.

That is a matter of capital and labor, of supply and demand. In Mexico, a tractor driver can claim only one-tenth of the hiring fee of a tractor/driver team, with nine-tenths going to the owner, because capital—the money that can be invested in buying tractors—is so scarce. In the United States, by contrast, the driver can claim a larger share of the hiring fee than the tractor's owner, because capital is less scarce as compared to the supply of labor. If the profuse abundance of Mexican labor and the meager quantities of Mexican capital are both added to American labor and capital within a common economic zone, the total supply of labor will have increased much more than the total supply of capital. With capital now more scarce and therefore more valuable as compared to labor, the earnings of US capital will greatly increase, by way of interest, dividends, and the direct ownership of business enterprises. The earnings of Mexican labor will also increase somewhat, because it will have become less abundant as compared to the totality of (mostly US) capital within the common economic zone—certainly much less abundant than within the Mexican economy, which has so little capital. But the earnings of American labor must greatly decline, because there will be such a vast supply of unemployed and under-employed workers within the common economic zone.

Thus free trade with Mexico is a very good idea for the small proportion of Americans with significant amounts of capital to invest, and a very bad idea indeed for the large majority of Americans with no significant savings. Perhaps our free-trade negotiators should instead be encouraged to make an offer to Switzerland, because it has much more capital than labor, so that a common economic zone would actually help the majority of Americans to earn more. And if that were to encourage a wave of Swiss immigration, Americans would be content enough with their rising wages to tolerate a fair amount of noisy yodeling.

Immigration, or rather illegal immigration specifically from Mexico, is certainly on the mind of many supporters of the agreement. They seem to believe that moving American jobs south of the border will stop or at least very substantially slow the arrival of illegal Mexican immigrants north of the border. Actually that is a vain hope. Since 1970 the number of births in Mexico exceeded 2 million a year, and by 1985 it reached 2.6 million per year.[24] It appears that the almost annual visits of the Pope to preach for more faithful Catholic children and against birth control are achieving a gratifying success, for Mexico's population of 87.9 million in 1990 is expected to increase to 108.5 million by the year 2000. Certainly the number of unemployed and underemployed Mexicans already exceeds 12,749,000—the *total* number of nonsupervisory manufacturing jobs in the United States at the last count.[25] Moreover, there are those 2 million plus new arrivals each year into the labor force that the Pope so greatly welcomes. Hence even the abolition of all manufacturing in the United States and its wholesale transfer to Mexico would hardly make much of a dent in the inflow of illegal Mexican immigrants.

There is, moreover, a most peculiar aspect about this rather muted debate. Television news from time to time features cameo stories about the valiant struggles of the Border Patrol to stop illegal immigrants at the US–Mexican border. At the last count, 832,000 illegal Mexican immigrants were apprehended by the Border Patrol, but it need not have bothered.[26] Its officers wait in ambush at the most popular crossing places, they solemnly arrest a few dozen out of the hundred seen passing unmolested all around, send them back—and fully expect them to try again the very next night, which they do. In reality, it cannot be said that the United States government is seriously or even half-seriously trying to stop illegal immigration from Mexico. As of 1990, a grand total of 3,857 (that is *three thousand eight hundred fifty-seven*) Border Patrol agents were on duty, with some presumably on the Canadian border, in Alaska, etc.

Sophisticated explanations for the impossibility of stopping illegal immigration from Mexico stress the exceptional income disparities on either side of the border, as opposed to, say, the Swiss–German border. Simpler souls merely point to the sheer length of the border, the broken terrain in some of its segments, etc. Both explanations might be worth examining if there were not 3,857 but 38,570 Border Patrol agents on duty, or better still twice or three times that many. Governments all over the world *do* control their borders, even very long borders, by combining fences with or without modern sensors and alarms, with a decent number of guards (Italy, for example, has 53,000 *Guardie di Finanza* to guard its borders plus *Carabinieri* plus police for passport control). For a cost far smaller than that of the schooling and other social services provided to illegal immigrants, the US–Mexican border could be closed very effectively, except to the handful of illegal immigrants who can execute commando-grade clandestine infiltrations.

But preemptive declarations of impotence that disregard perfectly available remedies have become something of an American habit. When gangs were rampaging in Los Angeles in their regular everyday fashion even before the spectacular May 1992 riots, the city authorities reacted by asking for sociological studies of the gangs. Actually it is the city authorities themselves that are sociologically much more interesting and definitely worth studying: with a population of 3.5 million, the city had a grand total of 8,381 police officers (yes, eight thousand three hundred eighty-one), a ratio of 2.3 per 1,000 inhabitants. That would be just about enough for, say, quietly industrious Nagoya in law-abiding Japan. By contrast, the Italian countrywide ratio is 4.2—though even crime-ridden Italy is a paradise of tranquillity as compared to Los Angeles. The Border Patrol, or rather the lack of it on the Mexican border, is exactly the same category: self-inflicted impotence, rationalized as an inherent impossibility.

Certainly the Mexican Free Trade Agreement, as with the "globalization of industry" in general, would further deepen the gap between rich and poor in American society. Sharp income inequalities are not new in America, and in a way they have even propelled its prosperity in the past—poverty being undoubtedly the best incentive to acquire wealth. But if only because formal education is increasingly an absolute requirement for access to a growing proportion of all jobs, those at the bottom of the employment ladder simply cannot escape from their condition, and their desire to do so results in frustration, not in extra efforts to succeed.

For many of the roughly 25 million Americans employed in "goods-producing" industries of all kinds (not just manufacturing) and especially the 17 million in nonsupervisory production jobs,[27] the imminent prospect of a US–Mexican Free Trade Agreement merely compounds an already bitter predicament. As trade barriers are reduced, as the incidence of transport costs in total costs continues to decline (it costs less to airlift a million dollars of VCRs than to ship a million dollars of pig iron), and as the global spread of modern production techniques continues, it is only with constant technological innovation, a rising capital investment, and even higher skill levels that the productivity advantage of American workers could be maintained.

But many sectors of production are just like car assembly lines in offering only a very limited scope for individual skills, others cannot absorb more capital investment even if capital is available, and even technological innovation can be simply irrelevant. For American workers trapped in those sectors whose earnings are stagnant or actually in decline, the future will be like the past, only more so.

As of now, German and other European industrial corporations are establishing "transplant" factories in the United States, not just to have access to the American market, but also to save on wage costs. In the auto industry specifically, in addition to a longer work week, much shorter holidays, and scarcely any severance pay, American workers are already willing to accept 20% less in hourly pay than their German counterparts. As an investment specialist explained in 1992: "Many German companies feel they should have manufacturing in this country. *They want [its] cheaper labor.*"[28] That is something quite new for America, and not at all the stuff of which the American dream was made. Bangladesh may still be very far down the road, but the "Mexicanization" of the American labor force is definitely under way.

■ "GLOBALIZATION": WINNERS AND LOSERS

To be sure, free trade in general, and the US–Mexican Free Trade Agreement in particular, has a very different meaning for Americans employed by the superinnovative Microsoft Corporation in Redmond, Washington, or by one of the other 1,500 or so software houses in the salubrious Northwest, or by any business enterprise of any kind anywhere in the country that is internationally competitive not because its labor is cheap but rather because of technological, organizational, or entrepreneurial advantages in developing, producing, or marketing goods or services. Most familiar in the guise of the "high tech" companies large and small that produce everything from jet aircraft to living cells, these enterprises may also be low tech or nontech (e.g., public relations consultants), but what they all have in common is that they tend to require selected skills, intellectual preparation, or even individual talent from their employees, not just a willingness to work for low wages.

For Americans who can find employment with them, as for the usual roster of traditional professionals from dentists to investment bankers, as well as all the new breeds of experts and consultants in a great variety of verbal and numeric trades, Mexican workers offer no competition at all. Hermosillo with its $1.50-an-hour workers holds no sinister omen for those more fortunate Americans. On the contrary, the more open the world economy, the smaller the obstacles to trade, the greater is the likelihood that they or their companies will be able to find foreign markets or clients—not least in Mexico. Even in the short time since the liberalization of the Mexican economy, some American investment bankers have made their fortune in privatization sales, quite a few lawyers and consultants have earned large fees to help arrange the very investments that transfer American jobs south of the border, and many more have gained from increased exports to Mexico and the rest of Latin America.

For the textbook economists that abound in America, the desirability of the US–Mexican Free Trade Agreement is a simple question of numbers—a matter of comparing the additional Mexican exports to the United States that the agreement will allow, with the expected growth in US exports to Mexico. Because US tariffs on Mexican imports are already very low, they conclude that the main result will be to increase US exports. And because US corporations can already move production to Mexico, they deny that the agreement will change anything—thereby overlooking its psychological impact in encouraging hesitant corporations to shift production south of the border. If forced to examine the impact on employment, they stress that the jobs lost to imports, or because American employers transfer production to Mexico, are of low value because they are low-skill, low-wage jobs, while the additional US exports will tend to be of higher technology, and will thus offer higher-skill, higher-wage jobs. Even if many more Mexican than American jobs are created, they conclude that the agreement will still be beneficial to the United States as well as to Mexico: total earnings will increase in both countries.

Missing from this comparison is any recognition of the *social* impact of the agreement—or rather its very different impact on low-skill and higher-skill Americans.

In theory, there need not be any difference. By moving out of industries where they compete directly with cheap Mexican labor to industries that expand their exports to Mexico, workers could find jobs, and at higher wages. In reality, many less-skilled employees cannot seek out those jobs, perhaps at the other end of the country. Certainly such workers cannot be expected to maneuver smartly in the ebbs and flows of economic tides. Because they lack savings to keep them and their families together, they search for jobs hurriedly, not carefully, and even if they have time, they lack information. Those who are hardest hit by trade-induced or any other structural changes also have the least flexibility to cope with change of any sort. If their real wages are eroded by inflation, they will accept what they can get rather than face unemployment; if they lose their jobs anyway, they will accept lower-paying jobs to be able to remain where they live, rather than lose even their dwellings and the company of relatives and friends by moving away in search of work.

Economists applaud labor mobility and deplore the refusal of laid-off workers to move away or change industries in search of jobs. But when unemployed low-skill workers do move in search of jobs, as many Michigan car workers moved to Texas during the post-1973 car slump and oil boom, their general lack of information about the world and the economy increases the risk of being caught by another turn in the tide—as the Texas newcomers were caught by the oil slump of the 1980s. The "smart money" understood that the oil boom would end by the summer of 1980, when the oil-producing countries started to quarrel over output quotas. But few laid-off Michigan car workers are regular readers of *Platt's Oilgram* or the *Middle East Economic Survey* (subscription: $750 per year). They paid heavily for what they did not know about world oil prices. Even if they could keep their new Texas jobs, as many did not, the homeowners among them usually lost their modest, hard-won, wealth—the equity in their homes that was their miserably small share of the wealth of the "world's richest country."

Having sold their houses in Michigan after prices had collapsed because of the car slump, they bought Texas tract houses and town-houses at oil-boom prices—usually assuming much larger mortgages for smaller dwellings. When Texas real-estate prices collapsed in turn—not to recover until now—the newcomers were left with "negative equity," mortgages often much larger than the value of their homes. That of course is the common predicament: where there is unemployment, real-estate prices are also low; where there are jobs, they are high. Thus when workers move, they tend to lose what house-wealth they have.

Those who are averse to sentimentality can instead rely on a few numbers to define the bitter predicament of America's industrial workers in the age of "globalization." Back in 1909, when those statistics were first collected, production workers in all forms of manufacturing worked an average of six days a week for a total of 51 hours. By 1929, with the general progress of society and the advance of union protection, average weekly hours had gone down to 44.2, often in a five-day work week. During the Great Depression, many workers who did not lose their jobs outright were put on "short hours" to spread the work around, reaching a low point in 1934, when the weekly average fell to 34.6 hours. It was not until the armaments boom of the Second World War that workers could work a full week again, passing the 40-hour mark in 1941 and reaching the maximum war-effort peak of 45.2 hours in 1944 (the total number of production workers including many women had already reached its peak in 1943, exceeding 15 million—three times the Depression's low point of 5.3 million in 1932).[29]

After the Second World War, however, the eight-hour day and five-day work week became firmly established. And once the industrial countries of Europe had recovered from the ruinations of the war, the 40-hour week became universal. During the 1980s, however, just as American labor was entering its time of troubles, the 40-hour standard began to be challenged by European unions, so that in Germany and other richer European countries a 38-hour week is common, a minority of workers is already on a 35-hour week, and a 32-hour *four*-day work week is not unknown, in motor industry production-line work, for example. There has been no such trend in the United States, however: the 40-hour week remains standard, and actual weekly across-the-board average for production workers in all forms of manufacturing was last recorded at 40.8 hours.[30] Overtime, banned by many European work contracts, actually increased in America, from an average of 2.8 hours in 1956 when the statistics were first collected, to 3.9 hours by 1990.[31]

American industrial workers therefore have little to worry about when it comes to the Great Leisure Problem that was once a staple of magazine articles: "What are we all going to do with our time, when machines do all the work?" *On average, they now have only four more hours of leisure than their predecessors of 1929.* The short annual holiday, now little more than *half* the European standard at two to three weeks, is imposed by employers: American corporations refuse to shut down their factories for four or five weeks a year as their European counterparts do, and they also refuse to absorb the costs of rotating labor to allow month-long holidays while plants keep running right through. But workers do have a choice about overtime, and often they are very eager for more work, not less. That reflects once again the dismal reality of declining hourly earnings. In constant 1982 dollars, official Bureau of Labor statistics show that the earnings of industrial workers peaked in 1978 at $9.11 an hour (as opposed to $7.00 twenty years earlier in 1958) and then declined to $8.44 by 1988, declining further to $8.29 in 1989, and $8.05 by the end of 1990.[32]

Overall, the sadly reduced condition of American manufacturing workers by world standards was starkly depicted in a 1991 comparison with other leading industrial countries, Japan, Germany, France, Italy, Britain, and Sweden.[33] As compared to the 40-hour work week in the United States, also standard in Sweden and Italy, German industrial workers had an average work week of 37.6 hours, the British 38.8, and the French 39; only the Japanese worked more hours than the Americans, at 41.5 hours per week. In the actual number of total hours worked per year on average, including all forms of overtime, the United States at 1,847 was once again exceeded only by Japan at 2,139; the Germans worked only 1,499 hours, the Swedes 1,568, the French 1,619, the Italians 1,622, and the British 1,635.

There is even more dramatic evidence of the downfall of what was once the world's most privileged industrial working class. The number of days of paid holidays and vacation is the most basic measure of leisure but it is also more than that: for the many people who work for a living, rather than live for their work, it is also a basic index of happiness. With a miserable 23 days per year on average, American workers are worse off than *all* their counterparts. Even the Japanese have more leisure with their 25 days per year, while the Germans had almost *twice* as much at 42 days a year. That allows for their typical five-week vacations, often taken in camper tours for the whole family that span across Europe, or in Spanish beach resorts, or in sunny campgrounds everywhere. The British, French, and Swedes can also have a full month of vacation with their 31, 35, and 38 days, while the Italians do even better at 40.5 days a year.

This, then, is the bitter outcome of the increasing automation of US industry. Instead of gaining more leisure for production workers, as had been universally expected when robotization began to supplant mere mechanization from the 1970s, it merely threatens the security of their employment. That in turn weakens the bargaining position of unions, if any, and allows employers to deny longer paid vacations among other things. But that result also reflects the overall political weakness of US trade unions under the post-1968 sequence of Republican administrations, interrupted only by the Carter interlude from 1977 to 1981, until Clinton's advent in 1993. In West Germany, as it then was, the same technical trends had a very different result, in a very different political atmosphere, and with far more self-confident and accomplished unions. Taking the initiative from the 1970s, German unions decided that with automation increasing, only a reduction of the annual hours put in by each worker could mitigate the resulting unemployment. German law requires at least three weeks of annual paid vacation, but four is the actual minimum, some 30% of all workers have five weeks, while the roughly 70% who are covered by collective-bargaining agreements have six weeks of paid vacation, the spread being reflected in the actual averages quoted earlier.

But of course wages are the most important of all comparative measures of the relative market price of labor. In a 1990 estimate of average hourly wages in all manufacturing industries, American workers at $10.84 earned significantly less than their West German counterparts at $12.42 or the Swedes at $12.37. Japan was once upon a time a low-wage economy, but the Japanese average was $11.62 (at an exchange rate of 137.96 yen per dollar), some 7% more than the US average. As late as 1970, American manufacturing workers with their average of $3.35 per hour were much better off than their Japanese counterparts, who then earned 336 yen per hour on average; that amounted to only 93 cents at that year's exchange rate of 360 yen to the dollar, and would not have been worth more than $1.30 per hour even at a more realistic 250 yen to the dollar exchange rate.[34] Of course, $11.62 in Japan is probably worth less to most people than $10.84 in the United States because Japanese prices are higher, but once again the trend is most revealing. Between 1970 and 1990, the real decline of American hourly earnings and the sharp Japanese increase brought about a complete reversal: in 1970, Japanese manufacturing employees earned only just over a quarter (or more precisely 27%) as much as their American counterparts. In 1990, they earned 7% more.

Benefits are also important, of course, especially health care, which in Europe and Japan is invariably provided by national schemes that cover all medical costs, and which do not depend on the employer's honesty or ability to pay—bankruptcies do not leave workers stranded without insurance coverage. In a 1991 comparison of the overall total of average hourly pay and benefits, the United States at $15.39 came in higher than Britain at $13.70, but lower than all other countries examined. The Germans had the highest figure in the industrial world at $24.36 per hour—58% more than the United States, followed by Sweden at $22.28, Italy at $19.49, and France at $16.09. In Japan, at $17.83 per hour, the average cost of industrial labor was 15% higher than in the United States—a very significant difference for industrial firms in direct competition with each other, and further indirect evidence than US industrial wages are now lower than those of Japan on average.[35]

Viewed from a business perspective, these last figures would not be a cause of gloom but of satisfaction, a token of the American ability to compete on the world market. But it is not by lower wages and thus lower prices that a country's prosperity can be assured, but rather by the efficient production of high-quality goods, made possible by large investments in plant and machinery and improved technologies. German industrialists naturally complain about high labor costs, but Hans Georg Wehner of the German Trade Union Association made light of their threats to transfer production abroad: "For 20 years industry has whined that costs are too high here. In that time, we have become world-champion exporters, producing high-technology, high-quality goods."[36]

■ THE BOOMING SERVICE SECTOR— AND ITS NONBOOMING WAGES

The significance of these grim numbers stands, in spite of the decline of manufacturing employment in the modern American economy. Services of all kinds—from airline transport to dry-cleaning through computer services, cable TV, banking, and finance—loom much larger in the American economy than they did in 1914, or in 1965. But at the last count, 24.7 million Americans were still employed in "goods-producing" industries as opposed to service activities, and they accounted for 26% of all American nonfarm, nongovernment employees. Of them, 17.3 million were listed as production or nonsupervisory workers—not a triviality to be vapidly dismissed by talk of a "service economy," especially because the average pay of the 86 million employees in all private services was very far from the $1.1 million annual pay and bonus of the average investment banker.[37]

During the 1980s, hopelessly outdated trade union officials and other incurable romantics bitterly complained that foreign (a.k.a. Japanese) imports were robbing American workers of the best-paid industrial jobs, and forcing them into minimum-wage "hamburger-flipping." The lusty defenders of the infallibility of free-market economics in the style of the Reagan years silenced them in a series of Wall Street Journal editorials, which pointed out that many of the added jobs were in fact in the "money-flipping" banking, insurance, and financial services, as well in booming real-estate offices—and therefore presumably creative and highly paid, with opportunities for advancement, and no heavy lifting required.

It now turns out that the Wall Street Journal presumed too much, while the outmatched defenders of the working class surrendered too soon. At the last count, more than 6.8 million Americans were employed in banking, insurance, finance, and real estate, a privileged lot one would assume, yet the average earnings of the 4.9 million nonsupervisory employees among them were only $10.14 per hour at the last count.[38] Within that entire group, the 1.1 million clerks, tellers, and other rank-and-file bank employees earned much less than the entire financial sector's average at $8.19 per hour, while 48,500 of their counterparts in stockbroking and commodity-dealing offices—at the very heart of the economy's "money-flipping pinnacle"—duly earned much more at $13.53 per hour. Still, the overall average of $10.14, as noted, was considerably less than the $10.98 of plain vanilla production workers in manufacturing.[39] In reality, few industrial workers laid off in Detroit or Akron, Ohio, went to work for the neighborhood bank or bought themselves the required red suspenders to look for their fortune on Wall Street. But if they did, they would have found the entire money sector less rewarding than their old job—even if it was certainly free from heavy lifting.

As for less exalted service employees, most are paid much less than their counterparts in manufacturing. In retail trade as a whole, from department stores to street-corner newsstands, the 17.7 million "nonsupervisory" employees earned an average of $6.88 per hour in November 1990. In their case, the slide in real wages was even steeper, for in constant 1982 dollars that remove false inflation increases, average hourly earnings have declined substantially, from a peak of $6.20 in 1978 to $5.04 in 1990.[40] The retail trade is full of part-timers, of course, including teenagers still in school who work only on weekends and holidays, and married women who do not work much more, and sometimes only as a diversion (nonsupervisors worked an average of only 28.4 hours in November 1990). The presence of so many part-timers can be expected to depress earnings and it does. Besides, many retail employees earn commissions on the sales they make, which are not reported to the collectors of labor statistics. Neither part-timers nor commissions are to be found in transportation and public utilities (including railroads, local bus services, mass transit, trucking, courier services, river barges, airlines, telephone companies, etc.). Yet the 4.9 million nonsupervisory employees in that entire sector had average hourly earnings of $13.07 at the last count in November 1990—substantially more, $2.09 more in fact, than their counterparts in manufacturing, but still substantially less than in the 1970s in real money. Their earnings peaked in 1978 at $11.18 per hour in constant 1982 dollars, as opposed to $9.58 at the last count in those same dollars. Again, an intuitive comparison shows that there is no distortion: the $7.57 of 1978 were surely worth more than the $13.07 received after twelve years of sometimes high inflation.[41]

So far, a total of 22.6 million "service" employees have been surveyed—surely not another group that can be counted out as unimportant. Beyond them, among the greatly varied mass of service employees, there are predictable highs in specially favored industries with stellar earnings at the top. For example, at the end of 1990, the government counted 135,400 nonsupervisors (and non–movie stars) among the 165,000 employed in filmmaking in Hollywood and elsewhere in the country. They did very well indeed at $18.87 per hour,[42] better even than the $15.02 of their presumably well-skilled 646,100 counterparts in engineering and architectural services.[43] In fact, the production workers and clericals of the movie industry outearned the $15.29 per hour of the rank-and-file employees of computer and data processing services, whose "nonsupervisors" numbered only 87,700 in 1972, but had reached the impressive total of 637,700 by the end of 1990, having no doubt further increased since then.[44]

The lows are just as predictable. For example, the 1.3 million who work for hotels and motels in nonsupervisory jobs did poorly at $7.14 an hour on average— though quite a few also receive tips no doubt, sometimes in large amounts. But nobody tips the 436,900 line employees of detective, armored car, and security agencies who last earned $6.35 per hour on average—presumably they are mostly security guards and night watchmen rather than today's versions of Philip Marlowe, who charged $125 a day plus expenses even in 1940 black-and-white movies.[45] And so it continues through category after category, from the 0.4 million employees of fire, marine, and casualty insurance companies, to the 1 million plus who work in amusement and recreation services, where there at least tips are to be had to augment average earnings of $8.62 as last recorded.[46] From advertising to zoological garden–keeping many jobs paid better than that, of course. But to no avail: because the average earnings of all nonfarm private employees were less at $10.17 per hour than those of manufacturing workers ($10.98), the brave new service economy can hardly offer a better prospect for the average American, flattered by politicians as "middle class," but in fact usually a mere proletarian with diminishing real earnings and an insignificant net worth.

■ UNDERCLASS ECONOMICS

The economic pressures that have been cheapening the value of American labor have a downward impact as well. To an increasing extent, men and women who are high-school graduates and whose parents were often well-paid industrial workers or had stable employment in the better class of service jobs have been joining laid-off industrial workers in taking away the traditional jobs of the urban underclass, i.e., often the black underclass. In uncounted numbers, they are now to be found working as manual laborers, janitors, restaurant workers, groundskeepers, office cleaners, warehouse loaders, etc. In Washington, DC, as in other cities, waiters and waitresses used to be mostly black, but are now often white high-school graduates, often with some junior college education as well.

To be sure, in many cases it is Latin American and Caribbean immigrants, legal or illegal, who have taken away the traditional underclass jobs. Changes in the immigration law have greatly increased the proportion of Third World immigrants, the ones most likely to compete with American underclass blacks for minimum-wage jobs. Between 1961 and 1970, roughly 48% of all immigrants came from European or other First World countries. In the next decade, between 1971 and 1980, that percentage had fallen drastically to 22.5%. At the last count, in 1989, only 17% of all immigrants came from these countries, i.e., all of Europe, Japan, Canada, Argentina, and Australia.[47] Third World immigrants, moreover, tend to concentrate in metropolitan areas with large black populations. In 1989 alone, for example, the Los Angeles–Long Beach conurbation absorbed 149,827 immigrants from Mexico and 32,693 from El Salvador, among a total of 262,805 new arrivals, mostly from Latin America and the poorest Asian countries. In the New York metropolitan area, by contrast, the largest influx came from the Dominican Republic (15,778), with much of the rest of the total of 116,598 again coming from Third World countries.[48]

And then of course there are the illegal immigrants ("undocumented aliens" is the euphemism preferred by Hispanic-American politicos) in huge but uncounted numbers, most of them, too, from Latin America and the Caribbean. Current estimates for the inflow of illegal immigrants hover around 300,000 per year, mostly accounted for by one-quarter of a million Mexicans; in equally tentative fashion, the total number of illegal immigrants in the country is guessed to be 3 million at very least, with estimates up to 7 million.[49]

It is an article of faith with the celebrants of American prosperity that no immigrant ever takes away the job that an American black might have had, but only does work that native-born Americans of all races simply refuse to do. Perhaps that is true, though it seems unlikely in the extreme. In my Washington, DC, surburb, for example, one used to see blacks working for remodeling contractors and in "yardwork"; now only Latin Americans are in evidence. An unscientific poll of their employers revealed the unsurprising news that they greatly preferred to employ Latin Americans, because they were less demanding and more deferential. But another reason is more surprising, though perhaps it should not be: it appears that the products of the elementary schools of El Salvador, one of the poorest countries of Latin America and ravaged by civil war throughout the 1980s, have some educational skills that Washington, DC's, poorest blacks lack, including a knowledge of basic arithmetic. Perhaps it is true that black job-seekers in Los Angeles–Long Beach would have been no better off in 1989, if they did not have to compete with 262,805 new immigrants, most of them young, most of them willing to work exceptionally hard. But doubts are in order.

The lost jobs of the black underclass were all poorly paid, of course, and scarcely replete with prospects of further advancement. But they did once offer at least a toehold on the lowest rung of the economic ladder. They allowed the black underclass to survive before the advent of welfare programs, and more than that. Historically, they also made it possible for families to progress upward over time—if they were willing to sacrifice for the sake of their children. Many a black middle-class professional now well established in suburban comfort is the child of parents who lived in a slum and lacked formal education, but who did have regular jobs, however poorly paid, all the dignity that comes from self-reliance, and enough of an income to provide at least minimal educational opportunities for their children. Moreover, because it is employment itself that provides the best education for economic sur-vival in American society, some members of the black underclass could begin the climb to better jobs on their own account, if they were both lucky and persevering. As a result of such processes, the poor, as officially defined, account for 30.7% of the black population by the standard measure or 28% by another,[50] which means that two-thirds of all blacks are not poor, while conversely, not all of the officially counted poor belong to the underclass because they have year-round, full-time if poorly paid jobs.

The Appalachian Scotch-Irish underclass romanticized in folk songs that lived on the margins of society and often just beyond the law ("my father he made whisky, my grandfather did too, we ain't paid no whiskey tax since 1892 . . . we just lay there by the juniper while the moon is bright, and watch them jugs afilling in the pale moonlight . . .") still exists, and even not all that far from the glass towers of Birmingham, Alabama, the busy downtown of Knoxville, Tennessee, or even the metropolis of Atlanta, Georgia, as well as in West Virginia, little more than an hour's drive from Washington, DC. Even today, some of its errant members keep the "alkies" busy—the agents of the Bureau of Alcohol, Tobacco and Firearms—who hunt for illegal stills, as well as agents of the Fish and Wildlife Service, forever resisting poaching (now aimed at bears especially, because monied idiots in Asia have high confidence in the curative properties of bear gall bladders). Appalachian-underclass lawbreaking reflects cultural proclivities but is also a source of income.

Of late, the underclass, black, white, and Hispanic, has found a new major illegal source of income in drug dealing. In 1990, the FBI's partial count of arrests for drug-abuse violations, both possession and selling, listed 503,315 whites and 349,965 blacks.[51] In metropolitan areas with large black populations, black drug dealing naturally prevails, and the best study available of one particular city, Washington, DC, indicates the huge proportions of the trade, and its great economic importance. It estimated that in 1987 there were more than 11,000 regular drug dealers and almost 13,000 occasional drug dealers in the District of Columbia, i.e., some 4% of the District's total population, though of course they sold to customers who came from the entire metropolitan area. Moreover, the 24,000 total is *certainly* an underestimate because the investigators were denied access to information on juvenile (i.e., under eighteen) drug dealers.[52] The study further estimated that the net earnings of the 24,000 dealers amounted to $300 million, as compared to the legal income of some $1.2 billion for all black males aged eighteen to thirty-nine living in the District of Columbia. In spite of the high risk of injury or death from violent competitors, and the moderate risks of legal sanctions, drug dealing is thus sufficiently profitable to be a reasonable career option. For the adolescent black male dropouts of Washington, DC, who have very few job opportunities and mostly at minimum wage (or less), drug dealing is the *only* career option of significance, and those who enter the trade are making a rational choice based on correct information.[53]

Squeezed between the descending working class and the flood of illegal immigrants willing to work even below the minimum wage if they have to, the black underclass has been losing its few breadwinners—its own precarious elite, which does share at least some common economic interests with society at large, and which does have a stake in public order. On the other hand, the illegal drug trade both employs and criminalizes the more enterprising and best-informed among the youths who cannot proceed to higher education. In the circumstances, it is not the Los Angeles riots of 1992 that are surprising but rather the semblance of tranquillity in most places most of the time.

CHAPTER 8

FROM LAW TO

LEGALISM

The impoverishment of a net majority of nonelite Americans, the sinister intrusions of criminality in everyday life, and the general degradation of standards now so evident in comparison with either the recent American past or the Euro-Japanese present, are all too obvious to be denied. Some of the *immediate* causes are also quite obvious: chiefly the scarcity of patient investment capital and the general inadequacy of public education that jointly depress the country's economic performance, but there are others, including the simple failure to prevent migration across the Mexican border with an ordinary frontier guard, as is done all over the world. All such explanations, however, themselves require explanation—Why is what could easily be done not done? Why is what was once done very well, e.g., public education, now done so poorly? A search for deeper causes would take us very far, though it might simply be said that all-out individualism in the American style could only be successful as long as there was still enough Calvinist self-discipline to go around.

Is it mere coincidence that the economies of all the individualistic "Anglo-Saxon" countries—of Australia, Britain, Canada, and New Zealand as well the United States—have been sinking steadily by world standards? Australia was once a country of outstanding prosperity that attracted many more immigrants from Europe than it wanted to accept; now that its gross national product per person is rather smaller than the European Community's average,[1] Australia still attracts an excess of immigrants, but mostly from Bangladesh, India, and Pakistan. Britain was once the leading European country in almost every way; today its gross national product per person is still larger than Spain's but definitely smaller than Italy's.[2] Even more than the United States, Canada was once Europe's dream country, American-affluent without the gangsters and slums seen in the backdrop of American movies. Of this there is oblique testimony from the very gates of hell; the warehouse where the belongings of new captives were searched for valuables at the Auschwitz concentration camp was named "Canada" by the starving inmates—it was the only place where crusts of bread, jam, even tinned meat might be found in the confiscated satchels and bags. Now Canada is still a very rich country, but less rich per person than the richest European countries or Japan. New Zealand's relative decline has been more dramatic: as late as 1970 its gross national product per person was larger than Japan's and only slightly lower than the European Community average; at the last count, it had fallen to half the Japanese level and two-thirds the European average.[3]

Countries so different in every way share only one thing in common aside from language: a culture focused on the individual rather than the group, on individual rights rather than collective interests, on individual self-fulfillment rather than group achievement. As long as all this individualism was coupled with a strong Calvinist sense of duty to family and community, Calvinist self-restraint in all things, and the more purely Calvinist drive to accumulate wealth by saving, a wonderfully dynamic balance was preserved. Out of it came the most successful human societies in all history, which combined exceptional personal freedom with social order and political stability, and exceptional individual prosperity with a high sense of responsibility to the community and the nation.

That balance has now broken down. Perhaps the very affluence and security so successfully achieved made further striving and self-denial seem unnecessary. Whatever the reason, the American culture with its laws and its norms has decisively tilted toward an unrestrained individualism that knows no balance. With that, self-fulfillment is pursued even at the expense of immediate family, let alone community. Young children are now quite routinely abandoned by fathers or mothers who divorce, not to escape brutality or bitter hatred, but to pursue a strictly personal hope of greater happiness, or merely to "find themselves": at the last count, during the year 1987, both bride and groom had been married before in 23.5% of all marriages; the median duration of marriages was then seven years; and the number of children left behind by the departing spouse was just over 1 million in that one year.[4]

Likewise, purely individual rights are now commonly asserted, and allowed, at the expense of the widest social interests, as with the right of vagabonds to foul city pavements depriving multitudes of their amenity, of personal-injury claimants to obtain fullest redress even at great cost to millions, and of marginally wronged individuals to wreck large institutions that serve many. For such purposes and more, the typically Anglo-Saxon cult of the law has given way to an inordinate litigiousness that inserts legal hazards into every ordinary transaction of life.

America's legal system was once its greatest glory, for it assured a constant striving to perfect individual rights, while still safeguarding communal needs. That was America's supreme and continuing achievement, greater than that of all past civilizations even if it left no physical monuments for posterity to admire. But the waning of the Calvinist impulse has unkeeled that balance and tarnished that glory, turning the American legal system into the complaisant arena of unrestrained assertions of dubious claims. That perversion of the principle of redress is powerfully advanced by the explosive increase of America's population of lawyers, and their increasingly predatory disposition in an economy that has grown much less than their numbers. Just as even well-fed rats in a cage become cannibals after their number exceeds a certain level, America's lawyers have also changed, driving the law before them to suit their own professional purposes.

Precisely because ranting and railing at lawyers has been a popular diversion for centuries, even the most powerful evidence that the American legal system has of late become perverted is too easily dismissed. Whenever the subject comes up, it is lawyer-legislators, lawyer-judges, and lawyer-legal experts who dominate the public debate. Along with the profession's lobbies that immediately move into action to stop any attempt at legal reform—and the American Trial Lawyers Association is perhaps the most powerful of all lobbies in America—they generally declare in appropriately lawyerly fashion that: (1) there is nothing wrong with the present workings of the American legal system; (2) that if there is anything wrong, the cause is human nature itself, so that no reform is possible.

Both of those things are demonstrably false, but there is no impartial court where the demonstrable can be demonstrated, because lawyers dominate the legislatures of every state and the US Congress. Only in America among all the countries in the world is the legal profession the most important of all professions, numerically, financially, and politically. It would be naive in the extreme to believe that America's lawyers will ever agree to legislate reforms that would hurt their own interests, unless confronted by a veritable political uprising. Of that there is no sign so far. Thus the country meant to be governed by "laws not men" is instead captive to its lawyers. What is less obvious is that the costs of this captivity have increased enormously since the 1960s, greatly weakening America's entire competitive position in the world economy.

Already present in huge numbers (655,191 in 1985, some 700,000 now),[5] the number of lawyers is projected to rise to 860,000 by the year 2000, because of the much increased output of law schools: in 1970, a total of 145 law schools awarded 14,916 LL.B. and J.D. degrees; by 1987, there were 180 law schools and the number of their graduates had more than doubled to 36,172 (over the same period, the total number of engineering M.Sc.'s only increased from 16,443 to 22,693).[6]

In 1960, when the population of the United States was 180.7 million, there were 285,933 lawyers, one for every 632 Americans. As of now, it has been estimated that there are some 307.4 lawyers per 100,000 inhabitants in the United States, as compared to only 12.1 in Japan. But, of course, as American lawyers are forever pointing out, Japan is distant, exotic, and oh so different, what with its foolishly simple civil code and the widespread use of low-cost legal clerks instead of lawyers, who are indeed rare birds in those parts: in the whole of Japan, not more than roughly 700 (*seven hundred*) are allowed to pass the bar exam every year. What of Great Britain? Its legal system after all can hardly be dismissed as bizarre or exotic, being the foundation of our own, and still very similar in every way. And yet the British make do with a mere 102.7 lawyers per 100,000 inhabitants. But Britain, it might be argued, is much less affluent, with its affairs that much less complicated. What of Germany, then, which is more affluent than the United States? It has only 99 lawyers per 100,000 inhabitants.[7]

How do all these US lawyers find work? In every way imaginable is the answer—and too many of them are dysfunctional for American society at large. An excess of bakers does not lead to an excess of baking, because consumer demand for bread and cake dictates how much baking can go on. But the law is also an instrument of power, and lawyers habitually use it in the normal course of their work to force their services on society. In the process, the inordinate number of lawyers badly distorts the workings of the American economy in several different ways.

■ LAWYERS IN THE PUBLIC SERVICE

At the last count, there were more lawyers working as federal, state, and local officials (53,035) than in actual legal capacities in the federal, state, or local judicial bodies (21,677).[8] In government at all levels, federal, state, or local, this great abundance of lawyer–civil servants powerfully advances legalism, the overelaboration of laws, in ways that subvert their intended purpose. In the process, every regulation can be transformed into overregulation.

All modern states regulate all manner of private activities, to protect health and safety, the environment, and the "public interest" as variously defined. Nor are American regulations all that restrictive in the actual physical limits and norms that govern emission levels, land use, industrial safety, etc. For example, European Community rules for animal husbandry are more severe, notably prohibiting hormone injections to increase the weight gain of cattle, which the US Department of Agriculture allows. (Moreover, in both the Netherlands and Sweden, under "animal rights" regulations, chickens may no longer be caged for life, nor cattle kept confined in fattening pens.) In Switzerland, industrial pollution is much more strictly controlled, and—of far greater economic consequence—Japan has much more sweeping energy-conservation regulations.

Yet even when American regulations are not more strict, or are even less strict than in Europe or Japan, the true economic cost to all concerned is often much greater. It is the extremes of legalistic formality now prevailing in the United States that lead to that extraordinary result, because the effort required to *demonstrate* compliance on paper can exceed the substantive, physical effort needed to comply in reality. In other words, the filing of forms, and the assembly and presentation of data can cost more—often much more—than the materials, equipment, and labor needed to actually assure that health, safety, or the environment are duly protected. In this as in many other ways, the excessive presence of lawyers in government complicates its workings so much that those who must deal with government increasingly need lawyers to do so, a neat mutual-employment arrangement. It is entirely characteristic that when the Bush administration set out to fight "over-regulation" in 1991–1992, it did so by proposing *substantive* changes to let trees be cut, wetlands to be built over, etc. The notion that legalistic formalities were the greater problem would hardly have occurred to the official White House "regulation-slayer," the executive director of the Council on Competitiveness; he, too, was a lawyer. Often businesses cannot cope with the required applications, certifications, and impact statements and must therefore pay costly specialist firms that do nothing else but prepare regulatory paperwork.

Moreover, the entire structure of government regulation at every level simply assumes that all private entities are large corporations. In the name of an equality that is purely theoretical, many of the same highly elaborate formalities are inflicted on General Motors, and on machine-shop outfits, home-improvement builders, roofers, and small businesses in general. Armed only with a pencil, the owner-manager-foreman confronts the same forms and formal correspondence that is required of world-class corporations with their own legal departments, sundry law firms on retainer, and vast clerical staffs.

Pervaded as they are by legalistic extremism, the detailed rules issued by government agencies are often absurdly impractical. These are the requirements that a roofer must meet in the attempt to repair a leaking roof:

> First, he must examine the offending roof to find out if asbestos is present: even asphalt roofs may contain asbestos in flashings and cements. Often a sample cut from the roof (perhaps creating another leak) must be sent to an accredited laboratory for analysis. In some states only a certified "abatement" contractor can make the test cut. In any case, the work cannot begin until the laboratory issues its response (for a fee of course, and after a work-stopping delay).
>
> If the roof does contain asbestos, the nearest Regional Office of the Environmental Protection Agency (EPA) must be notified *ten days* before the work can begin (while both leaks continue); and

then at least one person in the work crew must be specially trained in accordance with EPA requirements, with due certification of the same. Once work begins, "air monitoring" must be carried out in compliance with Occupational Safety and Health Agency (OSHA) regulations. During the work, the EPA requires that the asbestos-containing material be kept "adequately wet" in order to "thoroughly penetrate" it—even though roofs are of course made of waterproof materials, specifically intended to resist the penetration of water. Further, EPA rules require that all work be stopped if there are "visible emissions," even if it can be shown that they contain no asbestos fibers. Moreover, the dust generated by any cutting must be vacuumed and transferred to double bags, for disposal in an approved landfill. Finally, the roofer is responsible for prohibiting smoking on the job site, and is subject to fines if any employees smoke nonetheless.

All of these rules would not perhaps be an excess of caution if asbestos-containing materials were in fact significantly harmful in roofing work conducted in the open air. But in hundreds of tests, not even one case of dangerous exposure during roofing work was encountered. Asbestos is only the beginning of the story—and that roof is still leaking:

Assuming that no trace of asbestos is found in the leaking roof allowing work to begin, the roofer is responsible for training his employees in the handling of all other "hazardous materials," including the gasoline that powers the pumps of roofing kettles. OSHA inspectors do *not* independently determine whether, or how, such training has been given, they do not observe training under way, nor do they ask the roofer what training he has given to his crew. Instead they merely ask the employees, and act on that basis. Further, even if the crew is thoroughly familiar by long habit with all materials and containers, "Material Safety Data Sheets" must be kept at the work site, and all containers must be "properly" labeled.

When the roofer transports hot asphalt to the job site, to avoid having to wait two to three hours for the asphalt to heat while he and his crew are idle, further regulations apply:

—the kettle must bear a sticker with the word HOT in capital letters;

—shipping papers must be filled out before the truck that carries the hot kettle can leave the roofer's yard;

—emergency-response procedures must be ready, to cope with the danger that the truck will turn over in an accident;

—the truck must have a hazardous-materials placard in addition to the HOT sticker on the kettle itself;

—the roofer must ensure that the truck driver has been tested for drug abuse, that he has a commercial driver's license, and that he has been properly trained;

—the roofer is responsible for seeing that the driver completes his log sheets for the day;

—if the distance to the job site is over twenty-five miles, the roofer must ensure that the truck driver will stop to see if the load has shifted;

—the roofer is responsible for ensuring that the driver wears his seat belt; if he does not, the roofer will be fined—as in the case of any other violation of any other of the above rules.[9]

Needless to say, all these regulations issued in 1989 have dramatically increased the cost of repairing that garage roof. They have also forced the smallest roofers out of business, simply because they were intimidated by all the elaborate procedures now required of them, and properly fearful that fines and mandatory stop-work orders could drive them into bankruptcy at any time.

It is not known if the new regulations have succeeded in reducing the number of accidents that occur in roofing work, but it seems doubtful: neither the EPA nor OSHA have yet been allowed to complete their blessed work by prohibiting any roofing work above ground level, to preclude the real danger of falling off roofs. On the other hand, the EPA and OSHA do indeed have a very great achievement to their credit: when my roofer apologetically showed me his estimate for a tiny repair of my own leaking roof—very much higher than the cost of his previous visit—I ignored the man's plaintive story of all that the EPA and OSHA had done to him, and braved the heights to do the work myself. The EPA has not succeeded in stopping the asbestos plague among the roofers, simply because it did not exist to begin with. But it has found a sovereign cure for home-owner vertigo.

Of tales of formalistic overregulation and legalistic overenforcement, there is no end. They range from the hapless workshop owner who was hounded by writs and by fines because he was short half a minority employee to meet his minority-employment quota, to the formal compliance (and *not* substantive) rules that have caused thousands of enterprises large and very small to solve their endless regulatory problems by simply closing down. Every industrial zone and former industrial zone has its quota of abandoned factories, processing plants, and workshops. Very few foundries and casting shops are still in business anywhere in the United States, their work now transferred abroad—usually to Mexico or other such countries where regulations are ignored or simply absent. Many of the closed plants should have been closed. Others were closed by owners unwilling to invest reasonable amounts to reduce their excessive pollution. But others still have been lost to the economy simply because their owners could not cope with formalities of compliance more costly than the needed physical remedies.

American society needs regulations that protect the environment, promote work safety, and provide equal opportunity in employment. What American society has actually been given by the legalistic extremism that pervades the workings of government is some substantive regulation (which in some cases falls below the standards of other advanced countries), together with an enormous burden of formal compliance by way of form-filling, certification procedures, and the preparation of impact statements. In the process, many lawyers and clerks are nicely kept employed, along with the new breed of expensive "environmental impact" writers, while more and more beautiful trees are cut down to be pulped into paper for the needed forms. Perhaps the time has come to require EPA and the rest of them to file their own "forest-impact" statements.

▪ PRIVATE LAWYERS AND NONLAWYER LAWYERS

As their numbers grow rapidly in an economy that is only growing slowly, lawyers employ various techniques to keep themselves profitably employed. Collectively, as noted, they lobby with predictable success against measures that would simplify or eliminate costly legal procedures, or reduce litigation. Individually, they can only diversify, overelaborate any procedure that a client will pay for, and litigate, often inducing reluctant clients to file lawsuits by working on a contingency-fee basis.

Diversification has scattered holders of legal degrees as salaried employees throughout American society, but it accounts for only a small minority of all lawyers (83,843 out of 655,191 at the last count in 1985). The largest number (63,622) are employed by business entities, sometimes as in-house counsels, more often as executives who merely happen to have a legal education; some are chief executive officers.

It is often remarked that while European CEOs tend to have a broad classical education if they are not five-year degree engineers, as many Japanese CEOs are, the top executives of large US corporations are often lawyers. Naturally this fits them for survival amidst the legal entanglements of the modern American economy, but it unfits them to cope with the complexities of either modern technology or the vagaries of the international economy. A legal education, after all, is most especially a provincial education of little international value: any physician can attend a victim on a foreign road (unless it be the United States, for fear of a malpractice suit); no engineer can encounter physical laws abroad that differ from those he has learned at home. But an American lawyer in foreign parts is usually bereft of useful knowledge when faced with foreign practices.

Most lawyers, however, do function as lawyers, i.e., they are in private practice (460,206 out of 655,191 in 1985). How do they all survive, and even prosper as many of them do? In Washington, DC, in every state capital, and in cities and county seats too, there are lawyers who do work in law firms but practice lobbying instead of the law. But all of them are not that many of course, lobbyists being only really numerous in Washington, DC. Thus most lawyers in private practice must attend to legal procedures, elaborating them as much as possible. That litigation inflicts large costs on the economy and society at large is by now well known, but the plain overelaboration of legal work that has now become habitual in America is also costly.

Contracts are a basic commercial necessity even to define very simple transactions; but in a country where in US District Courts alone 61,975 contract claims were filed in 1989[10] (and the vast majority of all such claims are filed in state courts), no contract can be simply made. It is not enough to assign "world rights" in a book contract—the publisher's lawyer will initiate a correspondence (exacting a fee for each letter sent) to demand rights "throughout the universe," even if no book-reading aliens have yet been encountered in outer space. Nor is it enough to assign those rights exclusively—the publisher's lawyer will write another letter to demand the wording "solely and exclusively." And so it goes: a standard British book contract runs to two or three pages but the American equivalent is considered quite short at ten.

Commercial contracts very often offer far greater scope for overelaboration than mere book contracts. Foreign business executives negotiating with their American counterparts find it bewildering that instead of concentrating on the money-making substance of the business at hand, the latter often divert discussions to the legal minutiae of the proposed agreement. They are even more bewildered when confronted by the wording of a normal American-style contract, clearly already drafted with a view to possible litigation and containing elaborate provisions for the same. At a time when the parties need confidence in each other to start off the new business relationship, the American side seems all set to start a lawsuit instead. European and Japanese contracts, by contrast, merely state in a line or two what legal jurisdiction applies, unless they provide for commercial arbitration instead, as they often do. But US corporations consider it quite normal to sue and countersue each other in the ordinary course of their business, while in almost all foreign countries an intercompany lawsuit is a rare last resort, which invariably causes an irreparable breach.

Civil litigation is not actually a large part of the total business of private lawyering, but it still generates profitable work for many, and huge incomes for some. On the one hand, clients are nowadays commonly urged to accept a costly excess of legal precautions against any remotely possible litigation. On the other, clients are commonly encouraged to be litigious, and with great success: in US District Courts alone, the number of new cases filed stood at 233,529 at the last count in 1989, while those pending came to 242,433. As one indicator among many that the degeneration of the American legal system is accelerating, in 1980 the total number of new cases was 168,789—already enormous but 30% less than in 1989, and the country's population and its economy grew by less than 10%. Contract actions and copyright, patent, and trademark cases—typical law suits between corporations—increased at a particularly healthy rate, from 52,835 in 1980 to 67,952 in 1989.[11]

Those numbers do not begin to convey how much civil litigation is actually taking place, because very few cases ever reach US District Courts. In state courts, the number of lawsuits are counted in the millions, not mere tens of thousands or hundreds of thousands—and those numbers, too, have been going up at a rapid pace: 14.1 *million* suits were filed in 1984, 15.5 million in 1986, 16.6 million in 1990.[12]

Lawsuits are filed for any number of reasons by individuals and institutions, but corporate America is making its lusty contribution. To cite just one intercompany duel, in December 1990, the Cyrix Corporation, a Texas semiconductor producer, filed an antitrust suit against the industry's leader, Intel. A month later, Intel sued Cyrix for patent infringement. Before that case was heard, Intel filed a second suit against Cyrix, that is, three suits for two companies in just over a year. Such is the insouciance with which US corporations go to law against each other that during the early 1980s, when the Northrop Corporation and McDonnell-Douglas were coproducing the F/A-18 Navy fighter (which of course required them to maintain a most intimate collaboration), they were also filing lawsuits against each other replete with accusations of dishonesty and malfeasance.

It seems that while European and Japanese corporate managers waste their time on research and development, improving production, and refining their marketing, US corporate managers enjoy discussing the quaint intricacies of their latest lawsuits with their own staff lawyers, and the distinguished outside counsel they invariably retain.

Is it simply that Americans are especially litigious? Perhaps. But what is certain is that some peculiarities of US legal practice seem deliberately calculated to powerfully encourage litigation. The most important is undoubtedly the so-called "American rule" whereby losers in civil suits do not have to pay the legal costs of the winners. Thus anyone can sue anyone for almost any reason, and walk away happy to have inflicted anxiety, time-consuming preparations, and perhaps huge legal costs, even if the case is lost. By contrast, the so-called "English rule," which prevails not only in England but almost worldwide, compels the loser in money-seeking civil suits to pay all legal costs inflicted on the other party. That is a most powerful deterrent to frivolous lawsuits, and to deliberate harassment by way of law. Obviously if the "English rule" were adopted, the number of lawsuits would be drastically reduced.

No doubt because they are so patriotic, American lawyers (and lawyer-judges and lawyer-legislators) vehemently defend the "American rule" on the grounds that the "English rule" favors the rich, who can sue more freely because they can better afford the costs of losing. So it does. But given that it is civil money-seeking that is involved, not criminal justice, why should there be a rule that tends to equalize the ability of rich and poor to go to law when there is no trace of such equality in the buying of houses or yachts? What is certain is that American lawyers would suffer a catastrophic loss of income if the worldwide rule were adopted, as it should be. And, of course, the legal entanglements that entrap American society would then diminish drastically.

The second peculiarity of US legal practice is "discovery," i.e., the unlimited right of each side to review the opponent's business records and files before a trial to uncover any relevant evidence. That alone encourages exploratory lawsuits based on the hope that something or other will turn up that will make the case productive. It also inflicts huge costs on defendants. Large corporations are nowadays routinely asked to produce for inspection records going back for decades, or covering such common transactions that many tons of paper are involved. Very often, the sheer clerical costs of retrieving and sorting the records are so large that defendants pay off the claimants in out-of-court settlements, even if utterly convinced that they would win the case.

Some law firms have become quite expert in the record-keeping methods of specific corporations that they target again and again; they therefore pitch their claims just below the clerical cost they have calculated, confident of being paid off even if they have very little to work with in constructing a claim.

Discovery is not unknown outside the United States, but it is invariably most narrowly limited: the claimant has to ask for specific documents by name, date, etc., and cannot invade the archives of defenders for the mere price of filing a lawsuit. Naturally, the American legal profession resolutely defends unlimited discovery—half the members of the American Trial Lawyers Association would lose half their incomes without it.

The third peculiarity of American legal practice is that almost all judges take the view that in an imperfect world, civil litigation alone should achieve perfection—by allowing unlimited time for its accomplishment. Thus successive postponement motions that endlessly delay the actual trial are routinely allowed. As a result, very high legal costs can accumulate before a case ever reaches a court. Dow Chemical, a favorite target, faces some 2,000 product-liability suits a year (plus some 20 from outside the United States, a most revealing disparity).

Because of discovery and years of postponement motions, Dow must spend some $250,000 on average simply to reach the point when the trial can begin. Hence even a completely successful defense becomes a financial defeat: "Even when you win, you lose."[13] Many lawyers file suits, and then prolong themselves in discovery, filing successive delay motions until a defendant settles out of court to be rid of the case (representation must be paid for at each hearing).

The overall effect of all three peculiarities is that US corporations are apt to pay off hungry lawyers and clients even when their claims are very farfetched. At the lowest end of the business, auto insurance companies, for example, will routinely pay $6,000–$10,000 for "whiplash" cases, even when it is proven that the "accident" was a 1 m.p.h. rear-ender at a traffic light, which inflicted no damage at all on car or passengers, and even when no doctor can be found to certify any injury. At the higher end of the spectrum, corporations routinely pay $100,000 amounts on no-merit racial or sexual discrimination cases to avoid bad publicity. That is not more than prudence and economy call for, but it encourages others to try their hand as well.

For many American lawyers, even the system's three powerful encouragements to litigation are not enough. Some potential clients are deterred from going to law by ancient fears of endless, costly entanglements. Some may have read *Bleak House*. Others are unwilling or unable to pay for legal fees up front. But those restraints are no longer much of an obstacle to litigation, because many lawyers are now willing to become their own clients, in effect. Asking nothing from the plaintiff, who may be absent, uninterested, or even mildly uncooperative, lawyers work for "contingency fees" only, i.e., a share of the proceeds if the legal action is successful, usually in the amount of 30% of the winnings. Contingency fee lawyering is ruled out as unethical in England and throughout Europe; in notably unlitigious Japan, a success fee is common but the client must pay a retainer up front that covers basic costs and provides moderate remuneration for the lawyer.[14]

The reason for such risk taking is not mysterious. Even the most accomplished lawyers cannot charge much more than, say, $800 per hour, to earn $1,600,000 per year at most, not counting various expenses. Thus even the most successful lawyers cannot hope to become super-rich in the ordinary course of their profession. But working on a contingency basis, lucky lawyers can gain millions of dollars by winning a single commercial or product-liability case. Some have received tens of millions of dollars, and at least one Texas lawyer made off with more than $500 million. Heroic achievement inspires emulation. Contingency work was once a most unusual practice, despised by respectable lawyers. Now it is very common.

A final peculiarity of current American legal practice is the trial by jury of product-liability and personal-injury cases including medical malpractice suits. Juries are qualified to assess human behavior, including the truthfulness of witnesses. But medical malpractice cases require them to assess medical procedures; other personal-injury cases often require them to evaluate complex dynamic situations; while product-liability cases require them to assess products—all of which call for highly specific expertise of a scientific or technical nature that most jurors lack. That is why in England judges were given the power to dispense with juries in personal-injury cases as far back as 1883; in Canada either party can ask for a nonjury trial on the grounds of complexity; and jury trials for tort cases are simply unknown in Continental Europe.[15]

Trial by jury is a wonderful guarantee of justice in criminal cases. Human beings face the human being who stands alone as the accused in the dock, who himself faces the entire power of the state bearing down on him. Even before the judge reminds them that they must give the accused every benefit of the doubt, that is often already their inclination, as it should be. But in product-liability and personal-injury "tort" cases, trial by jury is almost a guarantee of injustice. There is no hapless, lonely human in the dock. Instead the accused is an abstract entity: a corporation, an institution, an insurance company, all presumed to be rich. Only the party that claims to have been injured is a human being. Perhaps it is a helpless child, a young man crippled in an accident, an old man dying of some unknown cause blamed on a product or a workplace, or perhaps a bereaved family—and now the jury has its opportunity to alleviate tragedy with a gift, even if the accident was his or her own fault, and even if the doctor did nothing wrong and is nice too (after all, malpractice insurance will pay the money).

Who can resist giving a gift to the suffering, a gift that seemingly comes free? To be sure, there must be few members of any American jury who do not understand that by way of insurance or by way of operating costs, when nobody pays, all pay. But abstract economic calculations do not stand a chance before the emotional impact of suffering, especially if the case is tragic, or the lawyer can make it seem so. Who is to tell that the fervent advocate on the verge of tears is actually emoting about a contingency fee?

■ PRODUCT LIABILITY

That victims deserve proportionate compensation for the damage inflicted by negligent design or manufacture, that knowingly inflicting harm by willful negligence deserves the additional penalty of punitive damages, are beyond question. But under the rule of "strict liability" first propounded by the California Supreme Court in January 1963 and since widely embraced, manufacturers are held responsible for the harm that products cause—or even marginally contribute to causing— even if there is no willful negligence involved. Strict liability, moreover, implicates all involved in designing, producing, supplying components for, wholesaling, and retailing the product, allowing juries to accept claims based on even the most farfetched extrapolations of responsibility. Finally, the compensation awarded in product liability cases is almost routinely disproportionate. By now nobody is surprised to hear of the fantastic acts of generosity of which juries are capable:

—A California court awarded a high-school football player $11 million because the helmet manufacturer, Riddell Inc., did not include a warning label about the risks of ramming onto opposing players. Of course it was not actually Riddell that did the brutal ramming that caused the injury, but in order to give their gift to the poor suffering boy, the jury duly determined that his share of negligence was only 7.5%, making Riddell 92.5% responsible for what happened on that football field.[16]

—A toilet-seat manufacturer was ordered to pay $90,000 to the family of a ten-month-old baby who fell through a toilet seat *while unsupervised* and was left brain-damaged by sustained drowning. With a baby involved, a multimillion dollar award would have been certain had there been any hint of real culpability by the manufacturer, hospital, or doctor. As it was, to make their gift to the sorrowful if careless parents, the jury had to rely on the most slender of excuses: the toilet seat lacked a warning label and unspecified "safety devices."[17]

—Johnson & Johnson was ordered to pay "substantial" but unknown damages to the parents of a baby who aspirated baby oil from a bottle that fell out of his mother's purse, when said mother "yelled at him" as she saw him drink from said bottle. Johnson & Johnson was found culpable for the absence of a warning label; that many millions of its baby-oil bottles had long been in circulation without causing harm was an insufficient defense.[18]

—Caterpillar Inc. was ordered to pay $11.7 million including $5.8 in punitive damages to a man severely injured in a collision while operating a front-end loader. As it happens, Caterpillar had provided a safeguard against that very type of accident, a protective frame against rollovers. It was agreed that the safeguard *would* have prevented the accident, but the man's employer had removed the rollover protector to allow the front-loader to be used in confined spaces aboard ships. The accident, however, had taken place in a warehouse that could have accommodated the protector. Nevertheless, the South Texas jury that deliberated on this case was allowed to find that the (unnecessary) removal of the protector was irrelevant. And it found against Caterpillar, rather than the employer who had deliberately removed the rollover protector.[19]

This last twist brings us to the final peculiarity of recent American legal practice: the "deep pocket" doctrine, whereby claims are made against the richest defendant, not the most culpable. In the front-loader case, the employer and the victim together were roughly 99.9999% responsible for the injury—but the employer was evidently not wealthy enough to be worth suing. Caterpillar may only have been 0.0001% responsible—after all it does exist, and it even manufactured the front-end loader. But simply because Caterpillar is a major corporation and thus presumed rich, it was forced to pay 100% of the damages, partly "punitive" to boot.

One need not be a moral philosopher of world repute to recognize that the "deep pocket" doctrine violates the most elementary principle of justice, by distorting the very notion of responsibility, even to the point of turning the most slender degree of responsibility into exclusive guilt. As it happens, the "deep pocket" approach has increasingly been applied in American courts, just as lawyers have increasingly been willing to work on a contingency basis. Of course, only the most malicious would linger over the coincidence.

The toilet-seat case, *Kathy L. Kemp et al.* v. *Universal-Rundle Corporation,* before the District Court of Clark County, Nevada, is worthy of longer note because it exemplifies the workings of excess. The "common facts" alleged by the plaintiffs in their complaint, *as the heart of their argument,* are notable because they are so distant from any responsibility that the manufacturer might have had:

VIII: on or about August 25, 1986, while at home Jennifer [age 7] discovered Ryan [age 10 months] in a toilet with his face under water.

IX: Jennifer immediately summoned her mother, Kathy, who, together with her brother Phillip [age 2], saw Ryan in the toilet.

X: Kathy immediately removed Ryan from the toilet and provided appropriate care for Ryan.

XII: The suffocation of Ryan caused Ryan extreme brain damage, emotional distress, and bodily injuries.

XIII: Ryan currently requires 24-hour convalescent care, can make movements of less than an inch and then only with his extremities.

XIV: Though Ryan is now 2 years and 9 months old, he does not now and will probably never speak.

XV. The manner in which Ryan was injured, his discovery in the toilet and the extent of his injuries proximately caused the following to the Kemp family:
1. The breakup of Kathy and Timothy's [husband] marriage;
2. Nightmares of Phillip;
3. Retardation of Phillip's speech development;
4. Kathy, Timothy, Jennifer, and Phillip perpetually blame themselves despite the lack of rational basis for doing so;
5. Perpetual crying spells by the Kemp family except for Ryan;
6. Loss of income, past and future, and loss of potential income;
7. Medical expenses past and future;
8. Loss of care, comfort, society, consortium support of all family members of each other [sic];
9. Severe emotional distress, past and future;
10. Pain and suffering, past and future; and
11. Other damages provided for by law to be proven at the time of trial.

XVII: Prior to Ryan's suffocation in the toilet, Kathy and Timothy did not know their son could drown in the toilet.

First Claim for Relief, Battery . . . XXV: The *intentional* conduct of the Defendants proximately caused Ryan harmful and offensive contact with the water inside the toilet . . .

Second Claim for Relief, Intentional Infliction of Emotional Distress . . . XXVII: the conduct of the Defendants is extreme and outrageous and proximately caused Plaintiffs' and their ward severe emotional distress and other damages as set forth above.

Third Claim for Relief: Strict Products Liability . . . XXIX: The toilet and its component parts were defective and unreasonably dangerous [apparently because it lacked a warning label and unspecified "safety devices"].

Fourth Claim for Relief, Negligence . . .

Fifth Claim for Relief, Parents' and Guardians' Action for Injury to Minor Child . . .

WHEREFORE, Plaintiffs pray for judgment against the Defendants as follows:

1. Special, general, and punitive damages in an amount in excess of $10,000,000;

2. For costs of suit and reasonable attorney's fees;

3. Interest from the date of Plaintiff's ward's injuries [date of accident] until satisfaction is provided by law; and

4. For such other and further relief as the court deems just . . .

As it happens, these claimants encountered an unusually severe jury that awarded only $90,000. A California court might have awarded the full $10 million plus interest, going by the football-helmet case. What is certain is that no such suit would ever have been started in any other country of the world; if started, not accepted by the court; if judged, lost—with all costs awarded to the defendants. As it is, this is merely one more "failure to warn" precedent that exposes the manufacturers of kitchen knives, forks, nails, screws . . . and indeed every object one can think of to product-liability litigation.

Defenders of current American legal practices invariably depict product-liability suits as brave and most unequal fights against rich and powerful corporations. That is why, they say, contingency fees are justified—without them, many victims could not afford to hire a lawyer at all, and only a few could hire first-class lawyers willing and able to match wits with the premier law firms that serve corporate America, the likes of Wilmer, Cromwell, Cravath & Rich of New York, Los Angeles, Washington, Houston, London, Geneva, and Tokyo, with their 999 lawyers, all possible expert consultants in tow, and many ex-partners in judicial robes.

In reality, however, the product-liability offensive mounted by the American legal profession does not exempt even the smallest manufacturers. In a 1990 survey, the Wood Machinery Manufacturers Association of America (WMMA) found that the average gross sales of its remaining forty-eight members were only $6.1 million, and their average number of employees was only fifty-six. With such numbers, there is no question of hiring Wilmer, Cromwell, Cravath, etc.; the nearest attorney in a one-person office in the nearest town is more like it. Yet in 1990 alone, 95 new product-liability claims were filed against the forty-eight members of the association; 65 cases were settled during that year, and 115 still remained pending.[20] Wood machines have a notable peculiarity. Because trees have been cut into wood for millennia, and log-trimming, plank-cutting, and planing machines date back to the Romans (who used water-powered machines), innovation has been much slower in this industry than in many others. Moreover, metal does not easily wear out against wood. Hence wood-working machines can continue in use for a very long time.

In present legal conditions, however, the virtue of longevity has become a vice with catastrophic consequences, because manufacturers are exposed to accident claims for machines designed long ago, some before the First World War, when far less stringent safety standards prevailed. Moreover, even newer machines are apt to be ill-used over the course of many years, while safety gear, not to speak of warning labels, is apt to be removed. None of these conditions are accepted as a sufficient defense because the law is now commonly interpreted to firmly exclude commonsense logic. Two of the 1990 claims against WMMA members involved machines that had been manufactured (not designed) twenty-eight years before the accident, two were eighteen years old, two were eleven years old, and another two were nine to twelve years old.

When manufacturers are held liable for what their fathers may have built on their grandfathers' design, when machines in daily use totally beyond the manufacturers' supervision can bring about their financial ruin, only the most comprehensive insurance coverage justifies remaining in business at all. But with no safeguards against the wild excesses now common in American law courts, comprehensive coverage is out of the question. Thirty-eight of the WMMA's remaining forty-eight members pay an average of $78,804 per year for product-liability insurance, for a maximum coverage of $3 million on average (much less than many a contingency predator has carried off) with an uncovered deductible of $108,822 per case on average. Ten of the manufacturers have given up on insurance: they are "self-insured," i.e., exposed to bankruptcy at all times. Still more wood machinery manufacturers no longer appear in the roster of the WMMA, having gone out of business altogether: their owners closed down their factories or workshops rather than face the constant risk of a bankrupting legal attack.

Judging by the scant public interest in "tort reform," i.e., the elimination of trial by impressionable juries, the adoption of the "English rule," the imposition of limits on both delaying motions and discovery, it seems that many Americans still believe that product-liability claims are not more than incidental to the normal conduct of business in the United States. Many still assume that legal expenses, the managerial attention that liability suits require, and the spectacular gifts juries like to grant to accident victims can still be absorbed as part of the normal costs of doing business. When businesspeople assert that this or that entire industry is in danger because of product liability, there is a tendency to dismiss their complaints as self-serving and overdone. Yet that is exactly what is happening in more than one sector, and has indeed already happened to the US general aviation industry.

At the industry's peak in 1978, Cessna, Beech, Piper, and lesser manufacturers delivered 17,811 general aviation aircraft, from single-engine trainers to nineteen-seat corporate jets; some 25,000 people were employed in actual production, and up to 60,000 were employed by suppliers of materials, parts, and components for which the industry was an important customer.[21] Cessna and Piper both offered single-engine piston aircraft (the Cessna 150 and Piper Cub) in the $50,000–$60,000 price range.

By then the industry was already faced with a rising ride of injury claims, arising from the spreading acceptance of the California Supreme Court "strict liability" doctrine. In 1976, the general aviation manufacturers and suppliers of power plants, propellers, avionics, and other components paid out a total of some $24 million in settling claims and for direct legal costs. That was already a large amount for an industry whose total billings were below $2 billion. But claims continued to multiply and what had been an irritant became a severe crisis.

From 1985, reinsurance companies began to withdraw coverage for product-liability insurance for US general aviation manufacturers; as a Lloyd's underwriter put it: "We are quite prepared to insure the risks of aviation, but not the risks of the American legal system."[22] By the year 1986, the industry paid $210 million in settlements and legal fees, an enormous sum as compared to its total billings of less that $1.5 billion in that year. Beech alone was reportedly sued 203 times between January 1, 1983, and December 31, 1986. The average amount claimed was $10 million. Each case was investigated, as all air accidents are, by the National Transportation Safety Board. The latter is the official body trained and equipped to assess the causes of accidents and define the corrective action needed. In the Beech survey, the board's investigations found the pilot responsible in 118 cases, and a design or manufacturing defect in zero cases (the rest being due to weather, air traffic control errors, etc.). United States courts, however, entirely ignore the board's findings, preferring to trust to the guesswork of juries confronted by rival experts on each side. The average cost to Beech by way of legal fees, payments, insurance reratings, etc. was $530,000.[23] By 1987, Cessna, Beech, and Piper calculated that their annual costs for product liability (including insurance) ranged from $70,000 to $100,000 per aircraft, i.e., more than the total costs of manufacture for the smallest models.

By 1991, the industry's total deliveries were down to 1,021, Cessna and Beech had stopped manufacturing light aircraft (claims and costs can be the same on a $53,000 trainer or a $5 million executive jet), Piper is in Chapter 11 bankruptcy, and total employment in the industry is now below 10,000. Cessna executives have declared that they would reenter the small-plane business "in 24 hours" if tort reforms were enacted.

In the process, the United States was transformed from a net exporter of general aviation aircraft to a net importer. The industry used to export up to 30% of its products, while imports were rare. By 1981, imports exceeded exports by some $200 million. By 1988, the deficit in this sector had increased to $700 million—and strictly because foreign manufacturers did not have to face the deadly hazards of the US legal system. United States importers were not exempt, of course, but their exposure was limited by the small size of the outstanding fleets, as compared to the 100,000 aircraft built by Cessna, 50,000 by Piper, and 24,000 by Beech that were in service at the last count.[24]

The peculiar vulnerability of the industry is an ironical by-product of Federal Aviation Administration safety rules that ensure that aircraft are sturdy indeed. So many aircraft built thirty and forty years ago are still flying that the *average* age of US general aviation aircraft is now over twenty-four years, and some 25% of the 210,000 airplanes in all are more than thirty-two years old. The result is an enormous exposure to product-liability suits for old aircraft. While the revenue produced by the sale was earned once and long ago, insurance costs to cover liability risk must be paid each year, and the risks of undercoverage and non-coverage last twenty, thirty, even forty years. Characteristically, the American Trial Lawyers Association has had no difficulty in defeating legislation that would put a time limit on liability.

Cessna, once maker of the $53,000 entry-level 150 on which a great many pilots had their first flight, now offers no aircraft cheaper than a $887,400 turbojet. But it must still set aside $25 million each year for product-liability costs on the tens of thousands of its aircraft that are still flying. Piper is at least as exposed as Cessna, but with total sales of $17.6 million in 1991, it was hardly in a position to set aside $25 million to cover itself, and was simply uninsured before becoming bankrupt.[25] As of now, a Canadian company plans to buy Piper out of bankruptcy, to reestablish it north of the border where punitive damages are limited, contingency fee lawyering is rare, and losing plaintiffs can be required to pay the legal costs of defendants.

One particular case, by no means extreme, illustrates the workings of the justice system for this industry. At Mid Valley Air Park, a private airport near Los Lunas, New Mexico, in July 1983 a Piper Supercub trying to take off while towing a glider collided with a van. That van had been deliberately driven onto the runway by the owner of the private airport, because he was in a dispute with the glider-towing service. In 1984, the badly injured pilot reached an out-of-court settlement with the airport owner. But then he and his wife sued Piper demanding $5 million in damages on the claim that the accident had been caused by design defects, including the aircraft's "poor forward visibility" and the lack of a shoulder harness.

The jury awarded $2.5 million to the couple, even though: (1) the pilot *had removed the front seat* to install a large motion-picture camera, which presumably interfered greatly with forward visibility; (2) Piper could show that Supercubs had been safely operated in great numbers for many years; and, (3) Roberta Bruce, a Federal Aviation Administration flight examiner, testified that the pilot "did everything wrong" during the takeoff, violating the FFA's safety regulations. Bruce's testimony, however, was stricken by the judge, E. L. Mechem, who accepted the contention of the plaintiff's lawyer that she was not "an expert qualified to determine the cause of aircraft accidents"—unlike the jury presumably. On the other hand, the judge did allow testimony from the plaintiff's doctor that the twenty-nine-year-old pilot had been left an epileptic, with short-term memory loss, and severe dexterity problems. When the verdict was announced, the couple's lawyer, Don Cathcart, declared "under the circumstances, I think it was fair." A reporter in court described Piper's lawyer as "stunned."[26]

Finally, the general aviation industry exemplifies the impact of the product-liability offensive on innovation. First, in general terms, managerial time and energy are absorbed in such great amounts by the current crop of liability cases that all nonroutine activities are sacrificed, including research and development. Instead of conferring with engineers and designers, managers must confer with lawyers. Second, also in general terms, the huge costs of the liability crisis diminish resources for everything else, including research and development. But beyond that there is more than a vague "chilling effect," but rather a standing disincentive against innovation: the more innovative the design, process, or concept, the more open it is to legal attack. Flying of course involves risks, but the Federal Aviation Authority already supervises and regulates the design, testing, and production of aircraft precisely for that reason. Each aircraft flying has a certified design, but the latter is not accepted as valid defense by US courts. Hence innovation still takes place in the industry, but more and more often only abroad. Between 1950 and 1960, Beech, Cessna, and Piper developed and produced seventeen new models. Between 1960 and 1970, they offered twenty-two new models. Between 1970 and 1980, when sales were reaching their all-time peak creating excellent conditions for innovation, but the product-liability attack was in full force, the three manufacturers introduced fourteen new models. Finally, between 1980 and 1990, they marketed only seven new models.[27]

Many other industries are also affected, though few in equal degree. The overall costs to the US economy are simply not calculable, especially because in delaying or even stopping innovation, the product-liability offensive is weakening the strong suit of American society, the other side of the coin of its lack of civic order and discipline.[28] Yet no loud protests are heard, and business associations regularly fail to gather the wide support they would need to overcome the lawyers' blockades in state legislatures and the US Congress.

Perhaps, however, some popular reactions might be forthcoming when Americans realize that the parallel medical-malpractice offensive has begun to seriously affect medical innovation as well. The United States spends more money than the rest of the world on medical and medically related research, and continues to be the chief source of *theoretical* medical advances, in laboratories, and in experimental programs. Yet nowadays, the patient who needs some of the latest drugs, procedures, or surgical interventions is often better off abroad. In some fields, such as urology, standard American procedures are regarded as downright old-fashioned by foreign specialists. In a French, German, Israeli, or Japanese hospital, the patient may not have a personal color television over the bed, and there might be no bedside telephone. But, on the other hand, there is no overshadowing threat of predatory legal claims to prevent doctors from doing what is best for their patients, just as they do not have to submit them to the pains, indignities, and cost of a whole slew of unnecessary tests to safeguard themselves against possible law suits. For in medicine, too, as in so many other things, the Calvinist exhaustion has tipped the balance toward the unrestrained claims of individuals against the interests of the many.

CHAPTER 9

THE SAVINGS GAP

Calvinist self-restraint is not exactly the type of commodity that businesslike people can measure and weigh. But its excessive dilution in the life of America has at least one highly measurable effect: an exceptionally low rate of savings, caused by inordinate consumption. The higher the total income, the easier it should be to save, other things being equal. The United States still has the highest national income per person, and yet its savings rates are lower than those of all its major economic competitors: between 1980 and 1990, American private savings amounted to 16.1% of the annual gross domestic product on average, as compared to 29.9% for Japan, 23.8% for Canada, 22.6% for Italy, 20.8% for West Germany, and 18.8% for France. Only in the United Kingdom did private citizens save less from their much lower average income, at 15.4%.[1]

As usual, all those numbers are not nearly as exact as decimal points might suggest, being made up by adding personal savings, undistributed corporate profits, plus or minus inventory changes, and the sum total of depreciation allowances less actual depreciation. But even if the numbers contain errors as great as 2% either way, the national differences would still remain, and they would still be greatly consequential over time, as anyone who has ever considered the arithmetic of a retirement plan well knows.

The immediate reason for the failure to save is simple in the extreme when it comes to individuals: Americans save very little because they consume so much, buying objects large and small with rare abandon ("shop till you drop," in teenage parlance) and using costly services too in great amounts. According to World Bank estimates, in 1989 US private (= personal) consumption per person amounted to $12,760 as compared to $11,800 for Japan and $8,830 for the European Community average (all in constant 1987 dollars).[2] Americans, of course, had more to spend on average, because of their sharply higher after-tax incomes (especially after the 1986 tax cut), but it is interesting to compare gross national income per person with private consumption per person.

National income, to be sure, is not merely national but highly notional in all the usual ways,[3] and certainly very distant from the actual average of personal incomes after tax. Still, as a very rough rendition of rough proportions and not more than that, the comparison (in 1989; per person; 1987 dollars) is most revealing: the statistical American consumed $12,760 as compared to a national income of $19,620, or 65%; his Japanese counterpart consumed $11,800 as compared to a national income of $21,350, or 55%; and his European Community counterpart consumed $8,830, as compared to a national income of $14,840, or 59%.[4]

That 65% would not be half bad if the remaining 35% were not mostly consumed as well—by the US government. Of course, if they collect more tax revenues than they spend, governments too can save. Thus between 1980 and 1990, the Japanese government saved a further 5.6% of the country's gross domestic product, Germany and the United Kingdom both saved 1.9%, and France saved 1.4%. The US government, by contrast, was on a binge of its own, financed by borrowing on a huge scale, so that it saved: − 2.5%. (Canada exceeded that at − 3.5%, and Italy in turn exceeded Canada at − 6.4%.)

Hence between 1980 and 1990, the *net* saving rate for the United States, both public and private, amounted to a pathetic 13.6%, as opposed to Japan's 31.9%, Germany's 22.7%, Italy's 21.7%, Canada's 20.3%, France's 20.2%, and the United Kingdom's 17.3%.[5] Those, too, are figures more approximate than they seem, but at least the proportions are valid, and it is far from surprising that the US government should be making a bad situation worse. The same self-indulgence that prevents Americans from safeguarding their own individual futures by saving is naturally reflected in the country's politics. Americans once laughed off politicians who promised to provide them with more pub-

THE SAVINGS GAP   ▪   241

lic services while cutting taxes at the same time. But for years they voted for them in great numbers. It is the opposite that would have been surprising, namely, the prudent upkeep of national finances at a time when personal finances are reckless.

Comparing US consumption per person in 1970 at $8,650 and in 1989 at $12,760 (both in 1987 dollars), we see that average Americans awarded themselves a 47.5% increase in personal spending between 1970 and 1989—including a large dose of imports, from specialty steels to Nintendo games. By contrast, the gross national income per person increased much less during those same years, from $14,140 to $19,620 (also in 1987 dollars), i.e., by only 38.7%.[6] That is why the crops of the wastrel farmer are so meager that he must sell his acres to foreigners: he has been eating the seed corn he should have planted.

It is especially revealing to compare the overall US rate of saving, both public and private, with those of the wide range of countries surveyed by the World Bank.[7] According to those figures, in 1989 the US rate of saving was just 14.1% as compared to Japan at 34.9% and the European Community average at 22.7%. It is worth listing the countries whose people saved *less* than the United States:

—In Europe: only Greece, then ravaged by inflation, which induced most people to spend whatever money they had before it would waste away. By contrast all listed European countries (including poor Malta and Portugal) saved a greater proportion, usually much more.

—In the Middle East: only Egypt and Jordan, the former exceedingly poor, the latter then in the grip of an exceptional crisis.

—In Latin America: only Bolivia, Haiti, Honduras, and Panama, each either extremely poor even by Latin American standards or in acute crisis or both. By contrast, Venezuela reached 26.6%, Brazil 25.6%, and Colombia 23.8%, just ahead of Chile's 23.7%.

—In East Asia and the Pacific: only Papua, New Guinea, whose population still includes many hunter-gatherers culturally distant from any concept of saving (jungle pigs cannot be stored, and tree-rot worms are best eaten fresh), and which is also very poor. By contrast, as could be expected, Korea is the regional champion at 37.3% and even Fiji came out ahead of the United States at 15.1%.

242 ■ THE ENDANGERED AMERICAN DREAM

Only in Africa below the Sahara are there many countries with an even lower national rate of saving than the United States, but of course those are mostly very poor countries where the bare necessities of life consume whatever income most people have.

■ A NATION IN DEBT

Instead of saving, Americans much prefer to borrow. Indian peasants turn to the moneylender to feed their families through a bad harvest, mortgages are a necessity for many home buyers all over the world, and most cars are sold on the installment plan in every country. But Americans go into debt largely for a better house, a flashier car, and for the most frivolous reasons, even to buy porcelain baubles advertised on television. There is no counterpart to this peculiar readiness to go into debt, anywhere in the world or in history. Americans who become acquainted with European ways are often amazed to discover that the dividing line between the social classes is marked by the red line of debt: the working class lives in rental housing and borrows only in small amounts to buy cars; the salaried lower middle class must struggle to pay off mortgages on its apartments or small houses; but the real middle class of business executives and lesser professionals has no debt at all, and neither do the classes above it, unless they are improvident landed inheritors much given to gambling at Monte Carlo or St. Vincent.

In the United States, by contrast, a heavy burden of debt is quite normal at all income levels because Americans quite routinely want to buy and consume everything in sight, or rather right up to the limits of their ability to pay interest charges and obligatory repayments of principal. It is odd indeed that a nation so enormously concerned with political freedom, and founded for it, is so careless of the loss of economic freedom that debt inflicts on families and individuals. The rare birds who refuse to borrow, buying only what they can pay for in cash, are regarded as quaint eccentrics by most Americans. That attitude reflects not only the low value attached to self-restraint and the peculiar disregard for personal economic freedom but also the honest inability of many—perhaps most—Americans to calculate the true interest costs of their borrowings.

To be sure, more than a cultural propensity and mathematical ignorance is involved, because the tax laws used to allow Americans to deduct all interest payments from their incomes before paying federal income tax—a most powerful incentive to borrow and spend. They also used to allow the subtraction of all sales taxes for those who itemized their deductions. Even now, interest on own-home mortgage loans remains fully deductible. No other country in the world allows such a deduction, except to low-income taxpayers in some cases. In the United States, by contrast, even well-off people routinely have mortgages on their own houses, simply because they want to have houses even larger, more luxurious, and better placed than those they could afford to buy in cash. The continuing dilution of Calvinist self-restraint is manifest in this regard as well, because Americans have been borrowing more and more, increasing their debts at a much faster rate than overall economic growth.

At the national level, the results have been spectacular. Between 1970 and 1989, total residential mortgage debt increased from $358 billion to $2,691 billion, i.e., seven and a half times. The gross national product, by contrast, increased from $1,015 billion to $5,200 billion, i.e, just over five times.[8] Likewise consumer debt (installment loans for automobiles, etc.) increased from $131.6 billion in 1970 to $778 billion in 1989, i.e., six times, again more than the increase in the size of the economy as a whole. Finally, aside from $50.8 billion in home-equity and other debts, by 1989 Americans also borrowed $206.7 billion on their credit cards, that too having greatly increased from the $80.2 billion of 1980, i.e., two and a half times, while over the same period the gross national product did not quite double.[9]

Credit-card and home-equity debts are last resorts of desperation for some, and the apotheosis of frivolous consumption for others. Home-equity lenders trying to entice householders to accept their high-interest offerings routinely suggest in their advertising how the money might be spent, from home "remodeling" and college fees to trips down the Amazon or around the world. One Washington, DC, "finance company" (for that is how moneylenders style themselves nowadays) preferred to name the luxury imported automobiles that could be bought with the money it was prepared to lend. Thus a rather melancholy transaction, the endangerment of what is often a family's only real wealth, and the roof over their heads, is presented as a discovery of idle assets, which it is foolish to leave fallow.

Overall, adding mortgages, installment debt, bank loans, and assorted credits, the total liabilities of all American households, i.e.,

244 ■ THE ENDANGERED AMERICAN DREAM

families in most cases, increased quite phenomenally, from $493 billion in 1970 to $3,561 billion 1989, that is, more than *seven* times, as compared to the fivefold growth in the total economy, all in current, much-inflated, dollars. Of course, American families and single-person "households" also have financial assets (real estate aside), including the creditor end of some household liabilities, as well as US government and corporate bonds, equities, money-market accounts, life insurance holdings, and more. Naturally these assets greatly exceed liabilities, and have also grown phenomenally in plain dollars because of inflation: from $2,488 in 1970 to $13,770 in 1989—but that is still only a 550% increase, as compared to the 740% increase in household debt.[10]

Large though it is, the growth in the private household debts of 248 million Americans is unimpressive as compared to the increase in government debt. In 1970, the federal debt (or "national debt" in popular parlance) amounted to $301 billion in all; by 1980 it increased 2.46 times to $743 billion, but, on the other hand, the gross national product—the size of the overall economy—increased even faster, 2.69 times, from $1,015 billion to $2,732 billion. During the years that followed, however, the Reagan and Bush administrations practiced "deficit finance" on a huge scale—that being the final repudiation of Calvinist prudence even by the political party once associated with "sound" money and balanced budgets. The result was that while the size of the American economy did not quite double when measured in inflated dollars, the federal debt increased more than four times, to pass the $3 trillion level by 1990.[11] That is not the end of government debt, of course, because states, cities, and counties also sell bonds to raise money and borrow in other ways; their combined debts increased from $150 billion in 1970 to $598 billion in 1989.

Over and above that, there was the great increase in corporate debt, propelled by the "leveraged buy-outs" that bought up the shares previously issued and replaced them with debt—i.e., bonds, usually high-interest "junk" bonds (which proved not be very binding at all). Debt implied a loss of control. In 1991, for example, the McDonnell-Douglas corporation decided to separate its commercial division, maker of the familiar DC-9 and DC-10 airliners, into a separate company so that 40% of it could be sold off to a foreign buyer without arousing Pentagon objections. With no signs of any US investment capital available, the Taiwan Aerospace Corp. seemed the best prospect (though Mitsui & Co. of Japan was also interested). For its 40%, "MacDac," as the industry calls it, was hoping to get $2 billion. Of that, only half a billion was meant for fresh investment—very much less than the cost of engineering a single new airliner nowadays. The remaining $1.5 billion was needed to reduce the company's crushing burden of debt, then in the amount of $2.6 billion and with a high-interest "Baa3" rating, only slightly better than the junk bonds issued by the most troubled Atlantic City gambling casinos.[12]

That places McDonnell-Douglas in a very crowded field. For it is not only the public finance of the United States that is already in Third World conditions, with the federal government, many state governments, and most large municipalities hugely in debt, but also private finance, with a multitude of banks and insurance companies as well as the notorious S & Ls badly "undercapitalized," as the euphemism goes, if not actually bankrupt—another 400 savings and loans were expected to fail in 1992 alone.[13] And many industrial and commercial enterprises of seemingly solid standing are just as afflicted with the disease; they, too, are surviving on bankers' doles ("unscheduled refinancing"), just like the much more colorful real-estate tycoons who once bought everything in sight with money recklessly borrowed and recklessly lent. And every day another great name among our major corporations falls below even that minimal standard, with bankruptcies that leave pension funds short, medical benefits cut off, and customers as well as suppliers abruptly stranded, often with large invoices unpaid. Because many of them are in turn badly undercapitalized, they, too, can easily be dragged down into bankruptcy, spawning still further insolvencies.

In 1970, nonfinancial corporations, i.e, regular corporations as opposed to banks or S & Ls, had an outstanding debt of $353 billion; by 1989 that had increased to $2,096 billion, again much more than the growth of the economy. Of course, "financial corporations" also went to the credit market—borrowing to lend is their business after all—and in some cases the growth in their debt was rapid too, though none could match the truly spectacular increase in mortgage-pool debt, from just $5 billion in 1970 to $876 billion. That exceeded even the growth in the debt of S & Ls, from $11 billion in 1970 to $145 billion in 1989, much of it acquired to finance real estate usually at least overbuilt and sometimes downright bizarre, such as the Phoenician Resort hotel near Phoenix, Arizona, whose very name revealed a used-car dealer's sensibility when it comes to word associations. With its Mogul-style walls of white marble and Babylonian hanging-garden swimming pools, the entire hotel is indeed a used-car dealer's dream of luxury, but very expensive it was to build all the same.

The Phoenician Resort will forever be famous as one of the achievements of Charles Keating, Jr., of Lincoln Savings and Loan fame, whose $2.5 billion collapse in April 1989 finally brought on the climax of the entire S & L crisis (incidentally, all the 1990 bank robberies in America netted only $75 million, a mere 3% of what was lost by Keating's hapless bondholders, including 23,000 mostly middle-class purchasers of his American Continental Corporation bonds, now worthless). In spite of having provided the entire country with such a convenient symbol of its excesses, Keating has received no gratitude: already convicted on seventeen counts of security fraud in a state court, on December 12, 1991, he was the target of a federal grand jury indictment on seventy-seven counts of racketeering, conspiracy, bank fraud, securities fraud, misapplication of funds, and interstate transportation of stolen property, thus facing sentences of up to 525 years plus $265 million in forfeited assets and $17 million in fines.[14] In the meantime, there are no indictments against the federal and state officials, the local bankers, and businesspersons who saw it all happening before their eyes and did nothing to raise the alarm. Outraged good taste if nothing else should have stopped the Phoenician Resort as soon as the first white-marble wall went up.

The reckless accumulation of debt here recorded in all the transitions from 1970 to 1989 begins to cast an odd light on the very recent American past, which in retrospect appears as a time of dour sobriety and the utmost restraint in the full Calvinist style. So it was. The total size of the "credit market," i.e., the totality of loans outstanding (with some degree of duplication), was estimated at a mere $1,597 billion in 1970; by 1989 it had reached $12,393 billion, an increase of 7.7 times, as against the fivefold increase in the size of the economy.[15]

How exactly is a $12 trillion plus debt paid off in an economy that did not grow and cannot grow in proportion? The answer is that it isn't—paid off, that is. As far as the federal debt is concerned, it is *possible* that the United States will acquire a neo-Calvinist government that will raise enough taxes to actually pay its way year by year, as Clinton is far from doing, and thus stop adding to the debt. If so, the gentle erosion of 4% inflation per year will do the rest, i.e., reduce the debt to the point where interest payments will no longer account for a crippling 25% plus proportion of the total federal budget. But it is altogether more *probable* that the national debt will sooner or later be "monetized": a suitable period of very high inflation has the effect of diminishing its size as compared to current tax receipts. For political leaders fearful of provoking the wrath of taxpayers that is the easy way out. Until that happens, however, the crushing burden of a gross excess *private* debt will continue to result in the transformation of junk bonds into mere paper, without the scrap value of true junk, and it will continue to result in bankruptcies large and small.

The falling real-estate markets of the late 1980s and early 1990s have destroyed the net worth of many millions of anonymous home owners, driving them into bankruptcy along with once famous and now notorious real-estate tycoons. But corporate bankruptcies are much more damaging to the national economy, leading as they do to mass firings, the depletion of pension funds, if not worse, and the repudiation of health benefits to retired employees. Few Americans have day-to-day dealings with steel companies or airfreight reinsurers, but consider what has been happening to the most familiar among all corporate names, the department-store retailers:

—Macy's, with 247 stores, was first saddled with a junk-bond debt of $3.5 billion by a leveraged buy-out carried out by its own management, and then with a further $1.1 billion when its owner-managers purchased the I. Magnin and the Bullock chains; it went into Chapter 11 bankruptcy on January 27, 1992.

—Federated Department Stores, with 140 outlets, including the Bloomingdale's, Abraham & Strauss, and Lazarus chains. That debt was created when the Campeau Corporation of Canada bought Federated in 1988 for $6.6 billion; it went into Chapter 11 bankruptcy on January 11, 1990.

—Allied Stores, with 82 outlets, including the Bon Marché and Stern's chains. It, too, was a Campeau junk-bond acquisition, when bought in 1986 for $3.4 billion; it went into Chapter 11 bankruptcy on January 11, 1990.

—Carter Hawley Hale stores, with 88 outlets including the Emporium and Broadway chains in California, with a $1.3 billion debt produced by a 1987 equity swap; it went into Chapter 11 bankruptcy in February 1991.

—Revco D.S., with 1,141 drugstores in ten states and a $1.25

billion leveraged buy-out debt; it went into Chapter 11 bankruptcy in July 1988.
—Ames Department Stores, with 371 discount outlets and $788
million debt acquired in 1988; it went into Chapter 11 bankruptcy in April 1990.
—Hills Department Stores, with 154 outlets in twelve states and
a $637 billion leveraged buy-out debt acquired in 1985; it went
into Chapter 11 bankruptcy in February 1991.[16]

Retailers, to be sure, are a flighty lot as compared to the premier
industrial corporations such as General Electric. But a close scrutiny of
their books would reveal that a great many American corporations
including many a famous name in industry are closer in condition to
Macy's et al. than to General Electric. After all, even the sum total of the
retailers' debts listed here does not begin to add up to the $2,096
billion carried by US "nonfinancial" corporations.

■ THE INVESTMENT GAP

The American refusal to save, and the readiness to borrow and spend
for frivolous purposes, is not only a symptom of the dread ACDS
(Acquired Calvinist Deficiency Syndrome) disease, but also results in
the pervasive shortage of *capital*, the chief source of advancement for
any society, ancient or modern.

Capital, to be sure, can also be borrowed from abroad, and the
borrowing that went on through the 1980s was quite enough to transform the United States from the world's leading creditor into the world's
leading debtor. As late as 1982, net US holdings, claims, and investments abroad, both public and private, amounted to $136.7 billion.
But by the end of 1989, the net US position was *minus* $663.7 billion
by rather misleading historic accounting (e.g., a US investment of 1953
is still valued at its 1953 cost),[17] or roughly minus $280 billion ac-
cording to current market-value accounting. Even that amount, however, is more than the combined debts of notoriously indebted
Argentina, Brazil, Indonesia, Mexico, and Venezuela—all of them countries developing quite rapidly, for which foreign borrowing is perfectly
appropriate, and the entry of foreign investment a clear sign of the
world's confidence.

Still, the US economy is so large as compared to the world economy that it cannot possibly borrow in amounts large enough to offset its own lack of savings. Between 1980 and 1990, for example, total net borrowing came to just under 2% of the gross domestic product on average, as opposed to 13.6% for net domestic savings, pathetically small as they were. Moreover, as some seem to forget, foreign loans must be repaid one day, interest must be paid on them each day, and foreign investments must be repaid forever in the profits that flow back overseas.

There are many lesser complications, but the overall situation is quite simple. All research and development, all renewal of plant, machinery, and public or private infrastructures, all new creations of the same, can only come into existence if there are accumulated savings— i.e., capital—that can be invested to pay for them. Overall, they determine the competitive position of the United States in the global market, for invested capital is the difference between the Japanese car worker who controls several assembly-line robots and the Indian artisan with hand tools, the difference between a modern office fully equipped electronically and one with only a few battered typewriters. Both can exist in the world economy, but only the highly capitalized can prosper, and nowadays highly capitalized corporations can drive the competition right out of business. In the case of the United States of recent years, the flow of new net savings has been feeble because of overconsumption, while the flow into actual investment has been even smaller, because so much money has been drawn off to provide loans to individuals and the government, federal, state, and local. Some of that individual and government borrowing has flowed back into investment instead of paying for day-to-day consumption, but not much, as we shall see.

That need not have weakened the competitive position of the United States in the world market, had others also gone on a consumption binge with their rising prosperity, thereby failing to invest. But it was not so. During the entire period 1869–1938, Americans actually invested in all different ways ("gross fixed capital formation") the equivalent of 19% of the gross national product, a greater proportion than Japan, Germany, or Italy. But while others have taken the opportunity of rising incomes to save and invest much more, in the 20%–30% range, Americans have reacted in the opposite way, taking the oppor-

tunity to consume more. It is this failure to reinvest the fruits of past
prosperity to assure its continuation that now threatens the future of
the United States.

Thus there is a direct connection between the moral values prevailing in a nation's society and current culture—actual operative values,
that is, not the self-glorifying "values" of political rhetoric—and its
economic destiny. For there is no substitute for savings to accumulate
capital, but for the feeble and costly contribution of foreign investors,
and no substitute for capital if there is to be investment for the future.

Once upon a time, long before any college program listed economics
among its subjects, and two centuries before "junk bonds" and "T-bill
futures" made a mockery of its meaning, Americans knew all about the
meaning of capital. When the first pioneers set out from their first
landfalls to cut trees, remove boulders, and plant seeds in newly cleared
fields, they were investing capital accumulated by prior savings. More
sacks of grain and more barrels of salt beef had been produced in
Britain than were immediately consumed, and those food savings provided nourishment for the voyage, and then for life in America until the
first successful harvest, just as the ship itself had been built with prior
savings. Their "working capital" turned out to be just sufficient to feed
the Pilgrims until they could reap their first crops of corn, pumpkins,
and sweet potatoes, and gather the cranberries, and hunt the wild
turkeys that completed their Thanksgiving dinner, and ours. It was
almost certainly starvation and its diseases that claimed the Lost Colony
of Roanoke, which ran out of saved-up food before the first successful
harvest, and it might have claimed the Pilgrims too if they had not been
frugal enough. Nothing has changed: in today's American economy
many new ventures fail because they lack the working capital to await
the moment of reward.

Next there is the capital invested in the hope of developing new
products or new processes. The Pilgrims needed little of this "research
and development capital" at first, because they brought over the ancient farming skills of Europe, while the native Indians showed them
how to grow the native crops. But the new land had new needs, while
the freedom of unbounded ambition soon started the stream of American inventions. Whatever the differences between mechanical reapers,
ice cream, and carbon-fiber composites, their trials and errors all had
to be paid for in advance, and so did the waiting until production
would begin and sales could start. Already important before, healthy

amounts of development capital are now essential for sheer survival in many industries.

Except for a diminishing number of traditional products valued precisely for their unchanging nature, from apple cider to milk of magnesia, foreign or domestic competition brutally forces the pace of innovation nowadays. Even if the old seems good enough, it can be entirely driven from the market by the new, to go the way of eight-track tape recorders or car radio-telephones. In all innovative industries, there is no standing still, only falling behind if advances are not fast enough. And to rest on the laurels of past success is twice wrong, because it is precisely past success that attracts competition.

Everyone in American industry knows these things, but merely to know is not enough. The Ford Motor Company, the world's second-largest industrial corporation, succeeded on a grand scale by investing some $3 billion over five years to develop its new Taurus/Sable midsize models that were first offered for sale on December 26, 1985. With their radically aerodynamic shape, dashboard and controls of Germanic austerity, and solidly advanced engineering in a fully updated front-wheel drive layout, the new cars were in fact, and looked, quite different from all other offerings on the market, won several design awards, and attracted a flood of eager buyers. They were fit competitors for even the best imports and more than that: they were trendsetters that other car makers around the world *had* to imitate.

Almost any manufacturer can boost total sale numbers at almost any time by making minimum-profit "fleet" sales to rental companies, the largest corporate buyers, and the government; likewise sales can be expanded by discounts on prices or loan interest rates, again sacrificing profit. But when buyers in huge numbers actually want a specific car because it offers unique design advantages, the undiscounted sales that result can change the entire financial position of the manufacturer, even when it is the world's second-largest industrial company. That is what happened to Ford after it introduced the Taurus/Sable. Such were the profits of the new cars, that in 1986 Ford was more profitable than much larger General Motors for the first time since 1926, when Henry Ford's model T was still on sale. As for the company's share of the US car market, it increased phenomenally from 14% in 1985 to 38% by late 1991. Ford had actually achieved what advertising slogans routinely (and falsely) promise: it had redefined the automobile.

At that point, Ford was exceedingly well placed to emulate its market-conquering Japanese rivals. By reinvesting a good part of its exceptional Taurus/Sable profits in a drastically expanded engineering effort, it could have combined whatever "dream car" concepts of the day were practical into economically producible road models. In that way, as soon as the competition would begin to match the Taurus/Sable innovations, Ford's entirely new cars could be unveiled to win a still-larger share of the market, by offering really important advances (there is no shortage of them still awaiting their day even now, from head-up displays to ceramic engines that need no cooling). In the global car market, saturated as it is by ordinary quite-good cars of all sizes and prices, genuine design leadership that results in radical innovation at moderate prices is all-important. It not only ensures large sales and extra profits, because true qualitative distinction allows sellers some exemption from head-to-head price competition, but it also brings with it all the advantages of the "initiative" in war: competitors are forced to guess where the leader is going, with a heavy penalty for guessing wrong—a penalty that was duly paid by the boxy cars left behind by the taste-shaping Taurus.

Toyota or Nissan would certainly have reinvested their Taurus/Sable profits to be able to reap the advantages of design leadership. Actually that is exactly what both companies did do, using the profits of their 1980s mass-production cars to create the new Lexus and Infiniti models, which have deprived BMW and Mercedes of their near-monopoly of the world's sporty-luxury car market. But Ford had better ideas.

What Ford did with its Taurus/Sable profits exemplifies the cultural disease that ravages American industry. First, its management deliberately decided to hold down capital investment in factories, assembly plants, and also new-car engineering development to roughly 5% of sales revenues,[18] much less than Toyota's proportion, for example. Second, it used some of the accumulated profits not paid out in dividends and the usual enormous management salaries, to diversify, partly by buying into the "financial services" sector at the boom-time premium prices of the later 1980s. First Nationwide Financial Corporation, acquired in 1985 as Ford's chosen instrument, had been the first of the savings and loans to take advantage of deregulation to expand across state lines to buy other S & Ls. So far, First Nationwide has cost Ford some $1.5 billion, for which it has also acquired some $1.2 billion in bad real-estate loans. By late 1991, some of the company's debt issues were derated to junk-bond status, and after severe losses, Ford could only hope that modest 10%–12% returns might be earned in several years.[19]

The ostensible reason for this use of some of the company's capital, including the accumulated Taurus/Sable profits, was the result of a typical business school calculation: Ford wanted the steady profits of "financial services" to offset the ups and downs of the car market. Because there is an entire financial industry already in place to handle the extra cash of industrial corporations, the actual reason for Ford's entry into the sector was almost certainly the magnetic attraction of the great Wall Street casino and S & L boom, before the 1987 market crash and the downfall of junk bonds.

But the urge to diversify away from its own industry was manifestly broad: Ford also seized the opportunity of joining the great defense-industry feast of the Reagan years, by investing in its subsidiary Ford Aerospace at great cost. As it happens, Ford again missed the boat, because defense purchasing peaked in 1985. Ford Aerospace was finally sold in October 1990 after suffering severe losses.

Having overpaid for acquisitions outside its own industry that had already become a disappointing burden, in 1989 Ford did finally make an automotive investment—not to improve its own plant or engineering—but to acquire Britain's Jaguar for $2.6 billion. It is not clear how anyone at Ford could have imagined that Britain's quaint antiques on wheels could compete against the highly advanced Lexus and Infiniti, and Germany's BMW and Mercedes. What Ford received for its $2.6 billion is a badly outdated factory, a cadre of designers still living in the 1930s, and Jaguar's famously retrograde engineers, who could not even cope with basic electricity until the late 1980s. But nonindustrial considerations may also have had an influence in persuading Ford managers to spend $2.6 billion for a car company in decline, living off a fading snob appeal. Instead of consorting at great length with mere engineers to advance in-house research and development, perhaps Ford's managers preferred to fly off to make quick deals in London as well as points nearer home (in 1986 Ford tried and failed to spend more billions on the worthy but money-losing Alfa Romeo, but the Italian government chose to sell it to Fiat instead).

With the money that was dissipated from 1985, Ford's own engineers could have developed a radically new Taurus/Sable successor by 1988/89, when the rest of the world's car industry was still trying to catch up with the original. As it was, between 1985 and 1991 they were given only $100 million a year to mildly update the Taurus/Sable, so that when the revised version finally appeared in 1992—after *six years*, an eternity for the trade—it hardly marked a dramatic advance with its minor and mostly cosmetic changes. At that time, Ford did announce its intention of producing a totally redesigned Taurus/Sable by 1995. The consequences were entirely predictable.

Instead of having to chase a rapidly advancing target, Honda was given all the time in the world to redesign its compact Accord into a midsize sedan competitive with the Taurus/Sable, Toyota did the same with its own Camry compact, and all others in the competition followed suit. American buyers can now find Taurus/Sable copies in the showrooms of every marque, US or foreign. Ford did succeed on the greatest scale in the sports/utility market with its Explorer model, which is the undisputed design leader, but again it failed to invest research and development funds to produce an entry for the rapidly expanding minivan market—although such an entry did finally appear in 1992, the joint Ford–Nissan Villager, designed and engineered by Nissan, and based entirely on the mechanical parts of the Nissan Maxima.

All this goes to show that it is truly a warp in the country's business culture, and not merely a shortage of capital, that induces the managers of US industry to surrender the advantages of technological leadership by shortchanging research and development. True, because R & D capital must be especially patient, it is also especially hard to find in an economy that demands rapid payoffs. But that is precisely why Ford's example is so significant: the company had all the money it could possibly need for product development from its own profits, without having to depend on the Wall Street casino of the 1980s, when junk bonds and acrobatic leveraged buy-outs were all the rage. True again, shareholders might protest if a company in some declining industry were to invest its capital internally, instead of finding more profitable uses for it in other industries. But that was not the case with Ford, for just as the Taurus/Sable was hugely profitable, with the Explorer not far behind, other radically innovative motor vehicles could also have earned vast profits.

▪ A GREAT RESEARCH NATION?

A great many US business enterprises have performed much worse than Ford as developers of new products, notably including America's and the world's largest industrial corporation, General Motors. By contrast, some entire sectors, such as the computer hardware and software industries, are dominated by companies whose very existence and progress derive from their research and development achievements.

Nationwide, however, the condition of research and development cannot but reflect the fundamental shortage of patient investment capital in the US economy, aggravated by the leveraged buy-outs and share buy-backs that have saddled so many US corporations with excessive debts in need of being paid off. One solution has been to cut research and development budgets, and close down entire research establishments. "All of you are a variable [i.e., reducible] overhead expense," a Wall Street advisor of passing fame told corporate research chiefs at a 1990 meeting of the Industrial Research Institute; "Let me repeat," a reporter further quoted him, noting that he was wagging his finger at the audience, "you are all a variable overhead expense."[20] That is how worthless manipulators lord it over the chief source of the nation's future prosperity—and indeed they do, according to the figures.

In 1992, total research and development expenditures, both governmental and private, were expected to amount to just $157 billion, only 2.6% of the gross domestic product. Of that total, the federal government was to provide some 44% ($69.8 billion) primarily for military projects ($41.5 billion), with the rest of the money coming mostly from private industry (roughly half of the total) but also from universities, foundations, and state governments. That $157 billion of 1992 is only 1% more than in 1991 after allowing for inflation, but still a welcome increase after the outright decline in R & D investment that took place in 1990 and 1991. Actually, those expenditures were rising at a good clip until the mid-1980s, having increased from just over $80 billion in 1975 to almost $120 billion by 1984 (in constant 1987 dollars), i.e., a 50% increase in ten years; but over the next seven years, from 1985 to 1992, the increase came to only 8% in total (from $120 billion to $130 billion in constant 1987 dollars).[21]

Needless to say, US investment per person in R & D is now much smaller than Japan's—in fact on a straight exchange-rate basis, Japan outspent the United States by $854 to $622, a gap of $232 per person in 1991.[22] That difference is potentially very significant, of course, because in many industries nowadays the better-developed, more advanced product can completely drive the competition from the market. On the other hand, when it comes to research especially but also development in some degree, there is a forest of treacherous uncertainties between spending money and actually obtaining economically worthwhile results.

First of all, research and development are especially vulnerable to waste and mismanagement, simply because there is no measurable output day to day; a great deal of fooling around is normal even in the best of research laboratories, but in some it accounts for a remarkable proportion of all activities.

Second, research especially but also development in some degree are especially vulnerable to plain errors of direction, with hard work and talent wasted simply because the chosen path turned out to be a blind alley. No factory is likely to keep turning out widgets for years on end while none can be sold on the market, but any one research project can continue for years with no results at the end of them. Even complete R & D programs that involve many separate projects, such as Japan's $400 million Fifth Generation computer program, can fail. While it certainly had valuable spin-offs through the establishment of a structure of working laboratories that did not exist before, and the training of a whole cadre of scientists and technicians who are now mostly working on private-company projects that may be less ambitious, more realistic, and perhaps better managed, the program failed to achieve its goal of developing "artificial intelligence" hardware or software.

In theory, there is a sharp distinction between research, whose goal is to achieve intellectual breakthroughs, and development, which is a matter of designing, engineering, and testing. The point of the distinction is that while in research success must be the product of imagination, creativity, even genius, in development, on the other hand, progress is supposed to be assured by the sheer volume of resources applied to the task. In practice, the distinction is often blurred because both require money for laboratories, instruments, and materials—and also imagination and creativity. Hence American society, with all its cultural variety and freewheeling individualism, is not only undisciplined and lacking in the Calvinist virtues as noted, but also exceedingly well peopled to pursue research and development, much more so than Japan's or any other society in the world.

The staffs of the better US laboratories and research centers are even more varied than the American population at large, attracting as they do enthusiasts, devotees, and merely ambitious scientists and engineers from all over the world. At the National Institutes of Health in Bethesda, Maryland, for example, as in other premier research centers in different parts of the country, the foreign-born actually outnumber the natives. The interactions of both, the great variety of cultural perspectives they all bring to the problems at hand, lie behind many of the recent breakthroughs in different fields.

On the other hand, the United States has also suffered from a very great handicap when it comes to research and development—the huge proportion of all money and talent that has been devoted to military purposes. Even before the defense build-up of the early and mid-1980s, roughly one-third of all R & D expenditures in the United States, public and private, were devoted to military efforts. During the peak years of the build-up, practically all the growth in federal funding was related to defense, so that the proportion increased still further. As a result, by the late 1980s, military programs absorbed the efforts of roughly *one-third* of all scientists and engineers in the United States, and accounted for roughly *half* of all university research in computer science and electrical and electronic engineering.[23] At its peak in 1987, defense-related R & D accounted for 69% of all federal funding, and it was expected to remain at 59% even in 1992. Out of the US total, both public and private, of $157 billion, the military portion was still very high, at 26% at least (in addition to the Department of Defense, some of the work funded by the Department of Energy is also military, because that department is responsible for the development and testing of nuclear weapons).

Military research and development is not useless, of course. American airpower certainly benefited hugely from its achievement in the 1991 Gulf War, and far, far more important, the United States relied on innovation above all to keep the Soviet Union off-balance during the Cold War, offsetting the psychological and political impact of Soviet numerical advantages with a constant stream of military innovations. The argument can even be made that it was the Strategic Defense Initiative of the Reagan administration that finally induced Soviet military leaders to demand the reforms that Gorbachev started, but could not finally control. In the post–Cold War era, however, when the new international competition is industrial rather than military, the United States has little to show in the way of marketable products and services for the lifetime efforts of one-third of its scientists and engineers.

There has always been much talk of spin-offs from military research and development, but there was always more talk than substance in the matter. That is only in part due to the most obvious reason, i.e., that only a few weapons can be sold abroad, and none can be sold at home. If it were only that, it would not be so bad—because military R & D also embraces computers and data processing software, transport aircraft and helicopters, telecommunications, even trucks and a great many other "dual use" goods and services also found on the civilian market and freely exportable. The real reasons for the low economic value of military research and development are quite different.

The truth is that most of it was never intended to achieve breakthroughs in the first place, but only to produce new versions of weapons and systems firmly kept within their established configurations. During the 1980s, the US Navy never asked its many scientists and engineers how airpower could best be provided for the unknown conditions of the third millennium (ship-launched missiles?); it was only interested in bigger/better aircraft carriers of traditional 1945 design with a few more gadgets. The US Air Force, likewise, did not unleash its vast R & D establishment to invent radically new forms of (unmanned?) airpower. Instead, it asked for new fighters, bombers, and transports that its crews could fly, and which would fit right into its existing structure of squadrons, wings, and commands.

Hence there was very little R and a great deal of rather unimaginative D in military projects by order, nullifying the talents absorbed by them. It is as if the goal of Sony's product-development efforts of the 1980s had been to improve classic 33 and 45 plastic records, instead of the laser-read compact disk. Actually a sizable proportion of all military R & D was only meant to improve weapons and other equipment *already in service*, for example, to upgrade the Phantom F-4A/B fighter into the F-4E, the M-1 tank into the M-1A, and so on.

There were always exceptions, of course. Boeing would not have been able to engineer the first successful jet airliner, the 707, as early and as cheaply as it did, had it not already developed the KC-135 tanker aircraft and the B-52 jet bomber before that, at the taxpayers' expense (it is unfortunate that the bombers that followed, the supersonic B-70, the B-1, and the Stealth B-2 were of no use in that regard). Likewise, the air-defense research and development work of the early 1960s virtually created the US software industry (for the SAGE system), and there are others such, including the Strategic Defense Initiative as a whole. Because it was not trying to come up with a marginally improved battle tank, fighter, or destroyer, but rather to explore truly new configurations and techniques, SDI has already generated valuable spin-offs of commercial value.

Moreover, even when military R & D is devoted to nonweapon items much used in civilian life as well, such as desk-top computers for example, the exceedingly demanding military specifications (heat/cold tolerance, ruggedness, immunity to interception, etc.) result in designs absurdly expensive for civilian markets. There is a coda to that story, now that defense spending is rapidly decreasing and many scientists and engineers working till now on military projects are seeking work in civilian product-development: their long-established habits that favor the best solution regardless of cost are not easily changed, and much diminish the economic value of their talents.

Finally, there is perhaps the most surprising feature of military R & D: its glacial pace. Partly because it is governed by the annual budget cycles, and partly because the military customer does not quietly wait for the product to arrive in a package, but intervenes at will to ask for this or that change in performance with all the ensuing delays, military R & D projects tend to be so slow that their spin-offs are often overtaken by events.

For all these reasons and more (e.g., security rules that keep innovations under wraps), the economic value of military R & D has been small indeed.

That casts an interesting light on the accumulated R & D funding of the United States and Japan. On a straight exchange-rate basis, Japan spent a total of $427 billion in the five years 1987–1991; the United States, on the other hand, spent $717 billion, i.e., rather less than twice as much. To be sure, these are cost numbers, not results numbers, and, moreover, purchasing-power comparisons would alter the figures in various ways. But although there is some military R & D even in Japan, if one-third is baldly removed from the US side to allow for military R & D, the United States with its much larger economy would have spent only some 11% more than Japan.

Private industry performs some 70% of all R & D, both funded by the government and by itself, but of course when it comes to developing goods and services for the market, it is company-funded efforts that are most productive. Overall, private-industry R & D has not been exempt from either the scarcity of capital in the economy or the short-term mentality associated with it. The same basic life choice that leads many Americans to consume in the present rather than save for the future also stands against the inherently long-term business of conducting research and development. After almost doubling between 1975 and 1985 in real terms, the growth of private-industry funding for R & D slowed decisively, and in 1990 it was only slightly higher than in 1985. Most recently, there has been a declining tendency. A 1992 survey of the 217 largest R & D spenders among all US companies showed that their 1991 expenditures had increased by just 3.5% over 1990, i.e., less than the 4% rate of inflation; and it was the same in 1990.[24]

The roster of industries most active in funding their own research and development is predictable.[25] As of 1989, the industrial chemicals sector spent the equivalent of 4.3% of its net sales on R & D (or 4.4%, adding the scant federal funding it received) as opposed to only 0.5% for the food and tobacco industry, or the 0.4% of the textile and apparel industry. Close to the pinnacle are the pharmaceutical giants that dominate the drugs and medicine industry, at 9.3%, i.e., almost $1 for every $10 of revenue, not counting federal funding. Even that was exceeded by the computer and office equipment industry at 13.4%. On the other hand, the very important but also badly undercapitalized and fragmented machine-tool industry ("other machinery, except electrical" to the statisticians) spent only 3%. Other industries over 5% include communication equipment at 5.4%, the electronic components industry (including semipure R & D outfits such as Intel) at a surprisingly low 8.3%, and the entire professional and scientific instruments sector at 7.2%.

Where Ford, General Motors, and Chrysler really stand when it comes to spending money on the development of new models, in spite of all their claims, is finally revealed by the percentage of revenues that the "motor vehicles and motor-vehicle equipment industry" spent on R & D, a mere 3.8%. That being still the largest of all American industries, the repercussions are naturally felt by the entire economy. The production of motor vehicles (including trucks) in the United States actually peaked in 1978 at 12.8 million; after that it fluctuated around the 11 million level, although in 1990 it declined to 9.9 million, including the output of Japanese-owned "transplants."

Thus during the same years when the world's total production (including the then Soviet Union) increased by roughly 2 million, US production fell by roughly the same amount. Had the US auto industry, i.e., the managers of General Motors, Ford, and Chrysler, invested not

3.8% but, say, 5% on R & D (just about Toyota's proportion) and concentrated on actual engineering development instead of face-lifts and cosmetics, there is no reason why the United States could not have produced cars and trucks good enough for 14 million sales in 1990, exporting them by the million, or at least exporting high-value components to US-owned "transplants" in Europe and Japan. That in itself would have transformed the situation and prospects of the manufacturing base of the entire US economy.

But perhaps one should not be too harsh on the managers of General Motors, Ford, and Chrysler, mediocre as they mostly are (half of GM's top managers are graduates of GM's managerial institute—and they do not welcome Harvard, Yale, or Johns Hopkins graduates in their midst). After all, why should they be blamed for failing to invest for the future, when the nation as a whole is not investing enough even for the present, either in its public infrastructures from highways to waste disposal, or in private plant and equipment, from factories to telecommunications.

■ TO INVEST OR NOT TO INVEST

The creation of the America of today from the wilderness is a story told in many ways, but from the first barn raised until the last computer installed it is also a story of fixed capital investment—the savings immobilized and thus made productive in factories and their equipment, in processing and utility plants, in agricultural improvements and machinery, in commercial and administrative facilities of every sort, in residential housing, and, just as important, in all the surrounding public infrastructures. Equally the present, diminished condition of the American economy has other causes too, but the lack of enough "fixed" investment is undoubtedly the most important.

As far as public works are concerned, i.e., highways, airports, mass transit, water resources and supply, sewerage, and solid-waste disposal, total expenditures, federal, state, county, and city, increased from $96.5 billion in 1980 to $107.9 billion in 1987 (both in constant 1982 dollars), i.e., by $11.4 billion, or less than 12%.[26] That $107.9 billion was not *net* investment to provide new facilities, but rather the sum total spent on public works, much of which, of course, went for repairs. Because of the growth in population and general activity, the burdens placed on all those infrastructures have increased much more than the amounts spent to improve them. As a result, from sewage systems to interstate highways, many US infrastructures are now deficient in quality or quantity or both. For example, total spending on highways and streets, federal, state, and local, increased from $41.6 to $48.2 billion (in constant dollars) over those eight years, or by a full 15.8%. But annual vehicle-miles of travel increased by 48.5% on interstates, and 32.6% on all types of federally aided roads, with the greatest increase of all (60.4%) in urban interstates, as anyone struggling in the rush-hour traffic of New York, Los Angeles, Chicago, or dozens of lesser cities well knows.[27]

Road congestion *increases* what statisticians call the gross national product. The extra fuel burned in stop-and-go traffic, the additional repairs needed for fender-benders and abused engines, and the further heart attacks and hospital admissions of the exasperated all add to total billings throughout the economy—but they hardly do much for the true standard of living of the unfortunate souls who must endure traffic jams, twice daily in many cases. But road congestion, along with all other infrastructure deficiencies, also diminishes the useful bits of the gross national product, i.e., the quantity and quality of the goods and services actually produced. One hesitates to calculate how many work hours are lost in stalled traffic alone. For some years now, there has been mounting concern over the underinvestment that is here and there glaringly obvious in overburdened airports and crumbling bridges.[28] A 1990 survey by the Wednesday Group, a Republican body within the US House of Representatives, compared the monies actually spent on various infrastructures in 1985–1986 with estimates of what *should* have been spent each year according to different authorities (all in 1982 dollars):[29]

Highways and bridges: amount actually spent $23.4 billion. Congressional Budget Office analysis: $27.2 billion (i.e., + $3.8 billion); Joint Economic Committee of Congress study: $40 billion (+ $16.6 billion); National Council on Public Works Improvement: $46.8 billion (+ $23.4 billion); Association of General Contractors: $62.8 billion (+ $39.4 billion).

Mass transit, airports, ports, locks/waterways: actual $8 billion. Congressional Budget Office analysis: $11.1 billion (+ $3.1 billion; Joint Economic Committee of Congress study: $9.9 billion (+ $1.9 billion); National Council on Public Works Improvement: $16 billion (+ $8 billion); Association of General Contractors: $17.5 billion (+ $9.5 billion).

Drinking water and wastewater treatment: actual $10.2 billion. Congressional Budget Office analysis: $14.3 billion (+ $4.1 billion); Joint Economic Committee of Congress study: $14.4 billion (+ $4.2 billion); National Council on Public Works Improvement: $20.4 billion (+ $10.2 billion); Association of General Contractors: $32.3 billion (+ $22.1 billion).

One may be allowed to be a tiny bit skeptical about the estimates of the Association of General Contractors, whose members have more than a passing interest in how much is spent on repairing and building highways and bridges. Equally, suspicious souls might wonder at the estimates of the National Council on Public Works Improvement, which by a truly unusual coincidence happen to be in each case the arithmetically exact double of what was actually spent. As for the Joint Economic Committee, it is vulnerable to the accusation that its members have a natural propensity to favor "pork," short for "pork-barrel," i.e., public spending of political value to the members of Congress who can claim credit for it. But the Congressional Budget Office is another matter entirely, one of the most serious establishments in Washington, DC, staffed by rather competent experts of every sort. Moreover, their numbers are the result of "cost/benefit" studies, whose aim is to discover how much additional expenditure would actually bring tangible benefits in proportion, rather than a simple case of defining abstract standards that such and such amount of money could achieve. Thus the overall shortfall of $11 billion (in 1982 dollars) that they estimated for that one year is a figure to ponder soberly, the next time a rusty canal lock fails to open for one's barge—or, more commonly, when suffering in an overcrowded subway or airport, not to speak of an urban interstate that has taken its full 60.4% increase in traffic between 1980 and 1988, with more since then.

Public infrastructures are doubly important, both for the true standard of living of Americans (as opposed to, say, the purchase of the baubles advertised on television for only $9.99 down), and because they form an important part of the overall productive environment. But what goes on inside that environment greatly depends on private investment in business activities of all kinds, from factories to utilities and offices. It has been argued throughout that the United States has been suffering from the economic version of a vitamin-deficiency disease, i.e., a shortage of invested capital, and that claim can be documented. The shortage in question is, of course, *relative*, for the amounts invested would have been magnificent for Bangladesh, while they are inadequate to assure the continued prosperity of 248 million plus Americans, almost all of whom are already amply prosperous by Bangladesh standards, but many of whom are becoming distinctly less prosperous by the standards of other leading First World countries.

For a first approximation, one can compare private, domestic (i.e., in the United States, by anyone) investment with the gross national product. In 1980, the GNP came to $2.7 trillion while *net* private, domestic investment was less than 5% of that at only $133.1 billion. That most unimpressive figure is admittedly the result of wholesale additions, for it includes private housing and inventory increases, and also rather dicey subtractions, including the wear and tear on equipment that business enterprises claim as depreciation for tax purposes—amounts they are hardly likely to underestimate.[30] Still, because these distortions at least remain the same over time, it is worth comparing the 1985 numbers, when the gross national product had risen to 4 trillion inflated dollars, and net private investment was $205.9 billion (again just below 5%), with 1989, when the proportion declined further to a miserable 4.1% at $216.8 billion, as compared to a gross national product of $5.2 trillion.

A somewhat less crude comparison, which begins to approach the substance of private *productive* investments in plant and machinery, utilities, offices, etc., by excluding private housing (but also inventories and dicey depreciation subtractions), shows rather different proportions: in 1980, that measure of domestic investment (gross, fixed, nonresidential) came to $322.8 billion, or 11.8% of the GNP; in 1985, it was slightly less at 11%; and in 1989, it was much less at 9.8%.

Finally, one may examine the "plant and equipment" investment expenditures (versus *net* investment) of US business enterprises of all kinds, from manufacturing to utilities and banks. In constant 1982 dollars, those totals increased from $327 billion in 1970 ($322.6 billion in 1980, a recession year) to $467.8 billion in 1989. Manufacturing industries accounted for less than half of those totals: $124.5 billion in 1970 ($133 billion in 1980), and $182 billion in 1989, when all investment in manufacturing came to 38% of the total.[31] Throughout those years, public utilities (electricity, gas, etc.) accounted for much more investment than any one manufacturing industry, at $45.5 billion in 1970, $43.7 billion in 1980 (!), and $43.6 billion in 1989—in 1970 they were still building nuclear power stations, whose lifetime costs are mostly in the up-front investment.

Not surprisingly, the largest investors in proportion to their overall size were the machinery industries, both electrical (which includes computers) and nonelectrical, which includes machine tools of all types. Their investment expenditures in combination increased from $22.2 billion in 1970 to $24.3 billion in 1980 and $36.8 billion in 1989 (all still in 1982 constant dollars.) By contrast, the motor vehicle industry (i.e., General Motors, Ford, and Chrysler except for their nonauto subsidiaries) invested at a pathetic rate: $10.75 billion in 1970, $10.5 billion in 1980, and $11.7 billion in 1989, and even that was a sharp increase over the $10.2 billion of 1988.

Over 1990–1991 it was believed that there was something of an upsurge in industrial investment. But after some statistical confusions and index errors were cleared up,[32] the revised official estimates of the US Department of Commerce showed that real growth in manufacturing investment has slowed quite sharply in recent years, from 3.9% per year over 1973–1979, to only 2% per year over 1979–1989. So much for the advantages of "lean and mean" corporations, and all the rest of the wild claims made for the restructurings of the 1980s.

Had the chief economic competitors of the United States invested even less, the low and falling proportion of the GNP left over from consumption and free to be invested would not have mattered so much. Less would still be less, of course, but in internationally competitive industries nowadays, less can mean zero—as products built in outdated facilities are completely driven out of the market.

A comparison of the gross domestic investment (both public and private) of the United States and that of its chief economic competitors is as usual gross in various ways in addition to the formal sense of making no allowance for depreciation. Nevertheless, it strongly suggests the chief reason for what has been happening to the US economy, and to the less fortunate employees in it. Already in 1970, Japanese investment per person was $3,770 as compared to $2,460 for the European Community and only $1,900 for the United States, all in 1987 dollars. In 1989, the numbers stood at $7,000, $3,190, and $3,000, respectively.[33] The European Community average was by then depressed by the admission of Greece, Portugal, and Spain, all of them poor countries. But there is no such excuse for the enormous gap between Japan and the United States, especially—and most damagingly—for private capital investment in plant and equipment (in businesses across the board, not just in manufacturing).[34]

On a straight exchange-rate basis, in 1991 total Japanese investment came to $661 billion, actually more than the US total at $550 billion, even though the US economy is still for the time being some 60% larger. On a per person basis—the crucial measure from many points of view—the gap was more dramatic still: $5,320 to $2,177, a difference, which if real, can only mean one thing over time—the drastic impoverishment of Americans as compared to Japan. Some consider those numbers misleading, however, because they are a straight exchange-rate comparison. If Japanese investment is recalculated on a "dollar purchasing-power parity" basis, the United States invested more with its $550 billion than Japan at $464 billion. On a per-person basis, however, even that was not sufficient to close the gap, because the Japanese figure comes to $3,735 as compared to $2,177 for the United States.

That implies a somewhat slower relative impoverishment—but even such slight comfort may be excessive, because it is not at all clear that the purchasing-power criterion is the valid one. True, consumer goods are much more expensive in Japan, but plant and equipment are not, indeed they are often cheaper. Hence the fact that Japan outinvested the United States by $440 billion over the years 1988–1991 (all in 1985 dollars) can be accepted at its full value, and in its full sinister meaning.

To be sure, some of the $3.5 trillion invested by Japanese corporations in plant, equipment, and also product-development from 1986 to 1991 was funded very easily and very cheaply by creaming off the great stock market boom that came to an end in 1992. With all concerned quite persuaded that share prices could only go up, Japanese corporations could raise billions by selling convertible bonds that paid only 1% interest, because they included the right to buy shares at preset prices, which were expected to be soon reached and passed. Now that there is no chance that the target share prices will be reached for years to come, Japanese corporations can hardly hope to turn over those bonds, and must instead raise 7%–8% money to redeem them as they become due. Toyota and others are already doing just that, and raising more money for investment, too, but it is still a safe bet that Japanese corporate investments will stop rising and may well fall.

Nevertheless, the new Japanese products and new production efficiencies already in place because of that $3.5 trillion of investment will make life very difficult throughout the 1990s for the American industries that must compete head-on with their Japanese counterparts in world markets—including the US home market. Already at this writing, with Japan in recession and its purchases of US goods therefore falling, the US–Japan trade deficit is widening again.

Had previous generations of Americans invested so little, the United States would not now be in danger of Third-Worldization, simply because it would already be a Third World country, both in its private economy and in its public sector, both in production and in the amenities that make it worthwhile. As it is, the accumulated result of the investment gap can only be the erosion of the entire economic base of American society, whose clearest symptom is the absolute reduction in real earnings of a great many Americans, including a growing number of white-collar employees.

Only a profound cultural change could overcome the predicament by finding a substitute for the spent power of Calvinism. Unlike Britain or New Zealand, the United States has a fully proven capacity to recast its culture when called for, not least because Americans are far more ready to learn from the immigrants that reach their shores. Perhaps, as many already believe, this time around it will be the Confucian instincts of Chinese, Japanese, and Korean immigrants that will refuel the engine of American progress.

CHAPTER 10

WHAT IS TO BE DONE?

Just as there is nothing simple about the enormous diversities of the United States, there are no simple solutions for its problems. And no father of two teenagers is likely to fall into the delusion that 248 million Americans will be more obedient than the two of them in following all sorts of detailed instructions. Finally, even the solitary author tempted to offer advice must recall the first classic law of medicine: above all, do no harm.

A sense of perspective is the first necessity. Having until now relied on abstract statistics, to escape the influence of mere impressions too often unrepresentative, it is interesting simply to look at the summertime street scene just outside the building where these lines are being written. It is excessively symbolic that alongside the "postindustrial" office buildings and luxury hotels of Connecticut Avenue and K Street NW—the central downtown intersection of Washington, DC, the nation's capital and arguably the world's—one may see on any working day: (1) a white, blonde mother-with-baby sitting on the pavement to beg in full Calcutta style; (2) the stands of licensed vendors of cheap clothing and African "airport art" that narrow the path left to the passing lunchtime crowds, just as in Istanbul until its recent street regulations were imposed; (3) several occasionally insistent panhandlers, some very colorfully dressed; and (4) a knot of unkempt vagrants who actually live in the Farragut North Metro entrance, which they occasionally befoul in full view of passersby, unless feebly interrupted by hapless transit police officers under court orders to let the "public" (i.e., the vagrants) use public facilities "freely."

At this point, it is essential to do a bit of counting of who else is encompassed by a summertime glance down that wide boulevard-style segment of K Street. In addition to the begging mother-with-baby, ten to fifteen street vendors, five to seven panhandlers, and less than ten vagrants, there are perhaps three hundred rather well-dressed office workers of both sexes enjoying a lunchtime stroll, at least two dozen US and foreign tourists, several hurrying figures who seem to be law- yers (they carry hefty briefcases), and a pair of corporate types just then descending from a limousine. In other words, it is important to retain a sense of perspective, for the distressed and the distressing are actually quite few. But all the wage figures reviewed so far cannot be forgotten either, as one looks on evidences of prosperity: the average hourly pay of Washington, DC's, nongovernment office workers, as of rank-and- file blue-collar and white-collar employees all over the country, has never quite caught up with the post-1978 surge of inflation, so that it is now no higher in real dollars than it was at the end of the 1960s. There is, moreover, a lively demand in Washington, DC, for $5 per hour temporary jobs, not least by new college graduates unable to secure better employment.

Fifteen minutes' walk up Connecticut Avenue and just two blocks to the right is Adams Morgan, described as a "wonderfully varied multi- ethnic" district in Washington tourist brochures, which tout its exotic Ethiopian, Nepalese, and Azeri restaurants. But as soon as night falls, Adams Morgan becomes a busy open-air drug market, where some of Washington's roughly 25,000 full-time and part-time drug dealers earn their nightly living. Middle-class customers who would not risk ven- turing into the dark and deserted streets of the real, inner-city centers of the Washington drug trade, where not a night passes without the sound of gunfire, can buy their cocaine at full retail prices but quite safely from the dealers politely waiting right next to the well-lit res- taurants of Adams Morgan. Not far beyond it, there is the semislum that goes by the most inappropriate name of Mount Pleasant. Of late it has been the scene of recurring miniriots featuring Central American illegal immigrants as the glass-breaking initiators, and black youths as the opportunistic looters. Under its strategy of "calculated restraint," the Washington, DC, police observe the proceedings from a block away, but lets the rioters break shop windows and the looters loot while carefully refraining from arresting anyone. That, its chief declared, would be excessively provocative. Any notion of rounding up "undocumented aliens" (the ruling euphemism), to hand them over to the Immigration and Naturalization Service for deportation, is simply out of the question: "Hispanic" politicians, too, have their measure of power in Washington, DC's, otherwise black-dominated politics.

Another ten minutes' walk up Connecticut Avenue past the Adams Morgan turnoff, the solidly white and prosperous North-West begins immediately past the bridge that spans the deep canyon of Rock Creek, with the leafy streets and porched colonials of yet more prosperous Chevy Chase some two miles further up. Stretching well beyond the District of Columbia boundaries, Connecticut Avenue bisects the Maryland suburbs that extend onward and outward for mile after mile. As in suburbs everywhere, ample houses are not that uncommon (the area by the Potomac is known worldwide for its extravagant mansions), and a more modest prosperity is very widely present. But again the numbers are not to be denied. Unless they are within the top 1%, or at least the top 10% in wealth and income, all who live in North-West Washington, DC, in Chevy Chase, in the Maryland suburbs, and in places like them right across America, for somewhat richer or somewhat poorer, are still enclosed in the income statistics that show them slipping year by year, as compared to their equivalents in the leading countries of the world.

It is from that broader viewpoint that the following few suggestions are offered, for it is not the poverty of the already poor, but the relative impoverishment of its nonpoor that is now afflicting the United States.

■ PUBLIC EDUCATION

The one American problem that drives even compulsive optimists into despair is the notorious inadequacy of public education in both elementary and secondary schools. Nothing is more important for the nation's future, yet nothing is less responsive to nationwide solutions. All the speeches, solemn promises, and even laws that emanate from the president of the United States and the US Congress as well as from the governors and legislatures of each state, have but a feeble impact on the country's 15,376 independent, self-governing school districts.[1] It is not the president, the Congress, or even state authorities, but rather the elected board members and career bureaucrats of those 15,376 independent school districts who actually supervise the education of some 41 million children in more than 82,000 elementary and high schools.[2] Anything resembling a "national education policy" is therefore *constitutionally* impossible. Instead, within the loose limits of state policies, if any, the local politicians and bureaucrats of each district steer their own course between clashing educational theories and passing fads (remember the "new math"?), ever-more divisive ethnic and racial politics, jobs-for-the-boys patronage politics, and, of course, union politics.

That a place on the local school board is often the first target of ambitious politicians already aiming for higher office has a profoundly distorting impact in itself. All politicians must court their electorates—and of course schoolchildren do not vote at all and their parents may be outvoted by nonparents, often more interested in stringent economies or ethnic/racial agendas than in education. Moreover, that school districts are also an important source of employment, especially in inner cities and less fortunate rural areas, has a further corrupting impact. Few nonteaching employees, from janitors and administrators to "ethnic resource persons," would allow better pay for better teachers to provide better education. But a larger number of "support staff" can better repay the favor received at election time. Thus in poor West Virginia, where jobs are scarce, school districts manage to employ so many bus drivers, janitors, and clerks that only 48.2% of their operating expenditures were last spent on "instruction," i.e. (one hopes), actual teaching—and the 51.8% that went for other purposes does *not* include whatever was spent on construction, remodeling, etc.[3] Such are the hidden costs of the much-celebrated American system of local educational "independence"—and they are very large costs, both in money wasted or misspent and in politically compromised standards, in the hiring of teachers, in course contents, and even in grading practices.

Needless to say, there are enormous disparities between the average quality of the education provided by different school districts. To be sure, there is much more to education than the spending of money—one really inspired teacher may do more for an entire school than a large budget increase. But money, too, is important, at least to the extent that it is actually spent on valid teaching. Hence the most blatant reason for the gross disparity between the overall standards of different school districts is that the amounts spent each year on each student vary hugely. These are not 10% or 20% differences as between, say, France and Germany, but rather 100% or 200% differences, as between, say, France and Argentina. For example, the Mississippi average for both elementary and secondary education was $3,096 per student at the last count, and the figure for President Clinton's Arkansas was $3,486; by contrast, nine states exceeded $6,000, and five of them exceeded $7,000.[4]

The less obvious reason for the wide variations in the amounts of money spent for actual teaching is that some school districts waste or willfully misdirect a much greater part of their money than others. In some school districts, there is outright and quite routine corruption in awarding and pricing school construction projects, maintenance contracts, and the purchase of supplies. In others, corruption is practiced more discreetly, often by paying large sums to well-connected "consultants," who produce only unreadable reports and useless studies but who have ways of paying back their benefactors.

As far as personnel is concerned, the hiring of friends and political supporters, if only in nonteaching jobs, is not uncommon in some school districts. In many more, the hiring of favored ethnic minorities as teachers and principals as well as janitors and clerks is a declared policy on the basis of the (totally unproven) theory that pupils learn better if they have same-race "role models"—though it is not clear why back-room administrators are also needed as "role models."[5] It seems to have been forgotten that when the big-city school districts of America were still famously effective in educating new immigrants and the children of the poor, their teaching was not performed by new immigrants or the poor, but rather by solidly middle-class "Anglo" teachers whose language and manners truly were educationally useful models for their pupils. In any case, given current hiring practices, it is only by sheer coincidence that the racially preferred are also the most effective teachers—although that accounts for only a fraction of the great gap between putting money in, and getting education out. Thus it is very appropriate indeed that Washington, DC, with its highly politicized school board manages to spend more per pupil than any state of the Union ($8,904) while its test scores are among the most dismal.

When the differences between adjacent school districts are extreme, there is the equivalent of illegal immigration, sometimes followed by exposure and the equivalent of deportation. In 1992 alone, the Sewanhaka Central High School District of Nassau County expelled 227 students, after private detectives and security guards had successfully tracked them to their homes in unmarked cars, to then discover that they were not Sewanhaka residents, but rather infiltrators from New York City.[6]

Not so long ago, the New York City school system was the envy of the world as the magnificent transformer of masses of poor immigrants into productive citizens, and as the employer of many highly dedicated teachers who nurtured world-class talents in their classrooms. Today it has become equally famous for deliberately compromised teaching and grading standards, politically deformed curricula, extravagant costs for such things as janitorial services, a great deal of straightforward corruption, and schools where apathy is the norm, threatening attitudes copied from the movies are so frequent that they remain quite unpunished, and outright violence so common an occurrence that teachers and less violent children live out their school days in fear.

Naturally, even the modestly affluent have long since abandoned what passes for public education in New York City. But not all teenagers whose parents cannot afford private education accept their tragic entrapment in degraded and dangerous high schools. They have been fleeing in such numbers that the nearby New Jersey and Long Island school districts now routinely employ detectives to unmask them and expel them. Some suburban school districts pay $100 bounties to informers (including fellow-students?) who expose New York City infiltrators, guilty of seeking a decent education at the expense of local taxpayers.[7]

Amidst chaotic diversity, the one constant across the country is that whenever the average proficiency of American schoolchildren of any age is compared to that of Western European and East Asian children of the same age, in whatever subjects are comparable at all, such as mathematics, science, or geography, US scores are always close to the bottom.[8] Of that Americans are now amply informed, thanks to a long series of perfectly futile reports of the "nation-in-peril" variety, issued by special presidential and national commissions replete with eminent names.

In the meantime, amidst much public dissatisfaction and parental anguish, the 15,376 independent school districts continue to add "support staff" in great numbers—indeed, they will outnumber teachers if present trends continue. At the last count, 2.3 million teachers were employed by all US public school systems, *but they had almost 4.4 million employees on their payrolls*, including district and school administrators, assorted clericals, janitors, etc.[9]

In European and Japanese schools, announcements are posted on bulletin boards. In American schools there are clerical staffs who compose, reproduce, and distribute leaflets on matters small and smaller, which clutter pupil lockers at great annual cost. In European or Japanese schools, teachers send handwritten notes to parents, naturally limiting themselves to significant matters that actually require parental attention. In American schools, correspondence is routinely mailed home in such quantities that much of it remains unread by all but the most conscientious parents, and it, too, is very costly. European and Japanese schools teach standard curricula for each grade and each subject that are issued by the central educational authorities. In almost every separate American school district, by contrast, "curriculum development"—much of it totally repetitive—is the business of full-time staffers and also provides juicy opportunities to hire costly outside consultants. In European and Japanese schools, classrooms, corridors, toilets, and grounds are kept neat and clean by the pupils themselves, working under the supervision of their teachers (that is considered educational, as well as economical); usually only a lone janitor is employed to look after the plumbing, the heating, fuse boxes, etc. In American schools, by contrast, all cleaning and maintenance is performed by full-time employees and outside contractors, again at great cost. Finally, European and Japanese schools are run by teachers, one of whom is a headteacher, who in turn might or might not have a secretary. American schools are run by an entire hierarchy of administrators, many of them ex-teachers happy to be rid of teaching—a frustrating business nowadays. The overall result is that only just over 60 cents of each dollar spent to operate public schools actually goes for what school districts list as "instruction"—which still includes some administrative items, while the total does *not* include investment costs for construction, remodeling, and equipment purchases.[10]

The constant calls of the well-meaning to spend more on public "education" miss the point. A huge one-year increase of, say, 25% is simply unimaginable, yet even more than that could be found for actual teaching by cutting out all sorts of dubious overhead expenditures.

Big-city school districts are notoriously the most wasteful in using their money, but that hardly affects the quality of the education they provide. Outright waste and corruption are outrageous but almost irrelevant, because the money that honesty and efficiency could save would only be of educational value if it could be spent on better teaching—and there is little chance of that anyway. Aside from union opposition to higher certification standards and teacher-competence tests, and school board opposition to hiring by qualifications alone, the prevalence of violence has a powerfully corrosive effect on both teaching and learning. Certainly it keeps away many of the best potential teachers from urban classrooms. Fear is a deeply shameful emotion for many, not easily admitted especially when full-grown adults are confronting youngsters, sometimes mere children. Yet fully 11% of all urban teachers surveyed nationwide were willing to state that they could not maintain order in their classroom because they feared "student reprisals," while 14% blamed the "lack of, or inadequate security personnel."[11]

Those are huge, inordinate proportions, especially because it is likely that many teachers refused to admit both the cause and the effect, i.e., their inability to keep order in their own classrooms. Certainly, every available source of evidence tells us of intimidated teachers and fearful children, even well away from "inner cities." Episodes of shootings, knifings, and rapes in the very worst schools actually conceal a much more widespread evil yet more sinister in its everyday normality. Even in schools with no shootings or knifings or rapes from one school year to the next, children still cannot concentrate on learning because they are terrorized by bullies of both sexes that nobody tries to control because of racial inhibitions, district rules, court orders, or simply fear. They dread visits to toilets where in-school truants hang out to smoke, and suffer the deeply humiliating consequences; they fear the corridors where provocations may be invented against them by larger boys and girls who threaten to beat them up—with complete impunity; they cannot look forward to their playground free time because out there the teachers do not even have to pretend that they do not see what is going on. Since the introduction of busing, such are the conditions at Westland Junior High School, set amidst the mansions and ambassadorial residences of the most affluent of all Washington, DC, suburbs in Montgomery County, which has one of the highest per capita incomes of all counties in the United States.

The tacit calculation is simple and actually quite rational: bused-in disadvantaged children, for most of whom learning is more difficult, deliberately sabotage the learning of the more affluent neighborhood children, by exploiting their physical superiority, their street-learned fighting skills, and their greater readiness to risk such feeble punishments as are still imposed. It is, in a way, a successful social equalization tactic—or it would be, if there were no private schools. As it is, busing has merely led to the one-for-one growth of private education, which of course widens the social gap even more (though not necessarily the racial gap: black parents of means are just as eager to resort to private education). In inner-city schools, notoriously, the situation is much worse. There, talented children are not only distracted from learning by the constant and sometimes murderous violence all around them; many deliberately fail, to avoid sneering—and threatening—accusations that they are "acting white."

To be sure, strict discipline would allow busing to be very successful in Montgomery County's Westland Junior High, and in similar schools all over the country, where the less privileged would have the opportunity to receive an elite education in an auspicious setting. Likewise, strict discipline would allow the talented to emerge and succeed even in inner-city schools. But that is mere fantasy. Strict discipline, or any discipline to speak of, no longer exists in American public education, for it is neither authorized by school boards nor sanctioned by the courts, which have outlawed all effective punishments and favored lawsuits against expulsions and suspensions. In the circumstances, it is only natural that so many graduate from so many high schools throughout the country without the ability to write usefully, to read at normal speeds, or to calculate at all.

In spite of such brutal problems, the racial politics rampant in US education dictate that schools with a proven inability to teach even the most basic rudiments of one culture are now under orders to impart a "multicultural" or even an "Afro-centric" education—with totally predictable results. In the San Diego Unified School District, for example, course contents and teacher hirings are meant to provide "culturally sensitive" instruction for:

HISPANICS—helpfully defined by the San Diego Unified School District as: "a person having origins in any of the *original peoples* of Mexico, Puerto Rico, Cuba, Central or South America, Spain or other Spanish culture or origin, regardless of race." (emphasis added)

WHITE—"a person having origin in any of the original peoples of Europe, *North Africa* or the Middle East." (emphasis added)

AFRICAN AMERICAN—"a person having origins in any of the black racial groups of Africa."

AMERICAN INDIAN OR ALASKAN NATIVE—"a person having origins in any of the original peoples of North America, and who maintains cultural identification through tribal affiliation or community recognition."

PORTUGUESE—"a person having origins in any of the original peoples of Portugal."

FILIPINO—"a person having origins in any of the original peoples of the Philippines."

ASIAN INDIAN—"a person having origins in any of the original peoples of India."

CAMBODIAN—"a person having origins in any of the original peoples of Cambodia."

CHINESE—"a person having origins in any of the original peoples of one of the following countries: Mainland China, Taiwan, Hong Kong."

GUAMANIAN—"a person having origins in any of the original peoples of Guam."

HAWAIIAN—"a person having origins in any of the original peoples of Hawaii."

HMONG—"a person having origins in any of the original peoples of Laos or Cambodia and are of the Hmong culture or origin."

JAPANESE—"a person having origins in any of the original peoples of Japan."

KOREAN—"a person having origins in any of the original peoples of Korea."

LAOTIAN (NOT HMONG)—"a person having origins in any of the original peoples of Laos."

OTHER ASIAN—"a person having origins in any of the original peoples of one of the following: Burma, Malaya, Thailand, Indonesia, Sri Lanka, Mien, Singapore, Bangladesh, Bhutan, Nepal, Pakistan, or any other country not listed." (emphasis added)

OTHER PACIFIC ISLANDER—"other than the above—a person having origins in any of the original peoples of the Pacific islands other than Hawaii, Guam, Samoa (American Samoa or Western Samoa). Including such as Polynesia, Fiji Islands, Marshall Islands, Melanesia, Palau, Tonga, Truk, Yap, or Tahiti."

SAMOAN—"a person having origins in any of the original peoples of American Samoa or Western Samoa."

VIETNAMESE—"a person having origins in any of the original peoples of Vietnam."

A number of small facts, and one very broad and large conclusion, emerge from this official document of the San Diego Unified School District.[12]

The first small fact is that the district's bureaucrats, or possibly its consulting "ethnic resource persons," have attempted to create their own ethnic/racial map of the world ("original peoples of . . ."), only to fill it with absurd contradictions. As Hitler's SS discovered, life becomes maddeningly complicated for racists determined to classify every single human very exactly, when in reality notions such as "race" or even "culture" are mere abstractions of no fixed meaning. It was all very well back in Germany where it was enough to establish if a person had two Jewish parents and therefore destined to be killed, one Jewish parent and merely persecuted, one Jewish grandparent and therefore excluded from state employment and the armed forces, or one Jewish great-grandparent and so excluded only by the SS itself. But once they ventured into the Soviet Union with its dozens of nationalities, SS killers and SS recruiters alike were faced with insoluble dilemmas. In the Baltic states, they encountered Livs, Kasubians, and Sorbs of ancient Slavic history, yet they could not be classified as Slav subhumans because these same people were fully accepted as pure Germans in East Prussia, the very heart of Germandom. Among the much more numerous Lithuanians, Latvians, and Estonians, many had clearly "non-Aryan" features, but they were also enthusiastic allies both very anti-Russian and anti-Jewish (they were recruited). And what about the often blond, often blue-eyed Circassians of the Caucasus, too blatantly Aryan-looking not to be accepted as . . . Caucasian, yet evidently non-European in culture and dress, and Muslims to boot? (they were recruited, but Hitler complained about it); or the Tats, both Jewish by religion and at the same time claimed as "Aryan" Turks by influential Turkey (they were persecuted but not killed); or the Karaites of Lithuania and the Crimea, the most authentic of all Jews who know only the Hebrew Old Testament, yet non-Jewish in every other way (they were left alone). And then there were the Poles, all of them despicable subhumans by Hitler's declaration and fit only for slave labor—except that hundreds of thousands of them successfully claimed full German nationality and even German old-age pensions as ancient expatriates (Volksdeutsche).

Matters are not simpler for the racists and amateur ethnologists of the San Diego Unified School District. They certainly take their classifications very seriously; in fact their "Employee Identification Card" is as unconditional as any SS order ever was—the underlining is in the original:

"No employee should categorize him/her self in more than one race/ ethnic group and should use only the above listed categories."

Yet the compulsory categories are absurd. A negroid Algerian, Egyptian, or Tunisian whose skin may well be darker than that of most American blacks is forced into the unprivileged white category, but a white Portuguese is Portuguese, and *not* merely white. Evidently the claimants of Portuguese origins, numerous in a navy and fishing town (by internal migration from New England navy and fishing towns), have enough influence in the racial politics of the San Diego Unified School District to escape from the one pariah group that receives no preferences in teacher hiring, and for whom there are no special instruction programs, i.e., the despised whites. That people of Portuguese descent are thus (preferentially) isolated from all others of European as well as Arab, Berber, Kurd, Israeli, and Iranian origin (all of them "white") is quite sufficient in itself to expose the brazen political manipulation of the San Diego categories. But there is much more in the same vein. When it comes to blacks, for example, the criterion is very strictly racial ("a person having origins in any of the black *racial* groups of Africa") regardless of the place of birth or culture of the applicant, or of any traceable ancestors. In flat contradiction to that, however, race is explicitly ruled out as a criterion when it comes to the "Hispanic" category ("a person having origins in any of the original peoples of Mexico . . . Spain or other Spanish culture or origin, *regardless of race*").

Thus a Guatemalan Mayan who has no Spanish ancestors at all and who may speak little or no Spanish (they are not rare in California) is made into a Hispanic—along with lily-white individuals born in Spain. As a former imperial power that once attracted ambitious soldiers, diplomats, and officials from all over Europe, Spain still has many Pedro Schwartzes, Manuela O'Higginses, and (princely) Diego Pignatellis in its aristocracy especially—and any of them may claim and receive the affirmative-action privileges of Hispanics if they reach San Diego, whereas they would be dumped into the white category if they came as Dieter Schwartz, Mary O'Higgins, or Mario Pignatelli from Hamburg, Dublin, or Naples, or for that matter from New York or San Diego itself. This is not a minor matter: there are few Spanish aristocrats in California, but there are hundreds of thousands of Latin Americans of elite background (including tens of thousands of Argentinian doctors, lawyers, architects, etc.) and the San Diego rules allow them to claim the affirmative-action benefits of Hispanic status.

Nor are whites—whatever that may be—the only group that suffers from the ignorant racism of the San Diego Unified School District. The many Chinese from Vietnam, who came to the United States after harrowing experiences as refugees (many of the "boat people" were in fact Sino-Vietnamese), who normally speak only Vietnamese, are not allowed into the well-privileged Vietnamese category (limited to the "original peoples" of Vietnam). Instead they are forced into the Chinese category, by now much too abundant in California to receive any valuable privileges except over whites—in fact, the excessively hard-working and overtalented Chinese are now being squeezed out in University of California admissions by African Americans, Native Americans, and a whole host of others who do actually receive affirmative-action preferment. Equally, all born in India or descendants of the same including Muslim Urdu-speakers from, say, Agra belong to a privileged Asian Indian category of their very own, but an identically Muslim Urdu-speaker born of Agra parents who were unwise enough to flee to Pakistan after the 1947 partition, as many millions of Muslims did, is now forever entrapped in San Diego's ragbag Other Asian category, where he or she has to fight it out for hiring preferences and any other privileges with increasingly abundant Thais and a dozen other nationalities, including the wholly unheard of "Miens," who may indeed have been invented by a bored bureaucrat or a clever job-seeker. Incidentally, while the Chinese of Vietnam suffer as noted, the Chinese of Singapore are rather better off in that same Other Asian category, which is outranked by the real aristocracy of Hmongs, Cambodians, or African Americans (very abundant yet still very privileged), but which nevertheless outranks the low-grade Chinese category. And why, by the way, are the Thais denied their own category while the Cambodians and Lao each have their own? And so it goes.

These distinctions are absurd, but far from trivial in their effect. For many would-be teachers they spell the difference between a secure job and unemployment, just as for students they determine whether they can secure admission to a good university or not. With San Diego's huge US Navy base and the area's defense contractors both reducing employment in these post–Cold War days, teaching jobs are in great demand in the San Diego area. That would, of course, allow the district to be very selective in hiring, indeed it could build up a cadre of elite teachers, perhaps with graduate degrees as well as tested pedagogic skills. But of course the district has not raised hiring standards at all, because that would interfere with its affirmative-action aims. Hence applicants are not weeded out by mere qualifications, and it is the ethnic/racial rankings that are really decisive. That being so, it is obviously important to unmask the inevitable attempts at ethnic/racial cheating.

True enough, few applicants could guarantee a job for themselves by falsely claiming to be a Hmong—an especially privileged category, uniquely reserved for a smallish tribal group rather than a race or nationality. The arrival of the Hmong to American shores is simply too recent for plausible claims of mixed descent. But white-looking Americans are now actively seeking recognition as Native Americans (a.k.a. American Indian), which requires only "cultural identification through tribal affiliation or community recognition" under the San Diego rules. That is not so difficult an obstacle as it may seem: an affiliation certificate can be had for hard cash from some tribal offices. Other Americans who also seem very white indeed now claim African ancestry— possibly real in some small part, possibly long concealed by parents and grandparents and only now rediscovered as a veritable family treasure in modern-day San Diego. Sephardic Jews anciently from Spain try to claim Hispanic status merely because they are fully entitled to it under the rules as stated (". . . or other Spanish culture or origin, regardless of race"), and numerous line-crossers of every hue claim to belong to the favored Hawaiian category.

With scarce teaching jobs, special programs, and lucrative consulting fees up for grabs, the San Diego Unified School District should therefore immediately establish its own ethnic/racial classification office, duly empowered to conduct physical examinations and equipped with skin-color and morphological charts as well as the invaluable skull-measurement racial indices compiled by the SS scientists of the Strassburg Racial Studies Institute. Those gentlemen really had the proper methods to enforce the San Diego rules. Unfortunately, the institute was wrecked and looted after the arrival of Patton's Third Army in 1944, but to the great good fortune of the San Diego Unified School District, its expertise migrated to South Africa, because the Apartheid laws required the establishment of Racial Classification Boards, to decide who was white, black, "coloured," Cape Malay, Natal Indian, etc.

Because residency permits, school admissions, places on trains and buses, the right to stay in a hotel or eat in a restaurant, and even emergency hospital service as well as almost every skilled job were all strictly allocated by race, the Classification Boards worked very conscientiously indeed to decide who was who, eventually to classify many very dark-skinned Afrikaaners as "whites," and many very light-skinned but curly-haired subjects as "coloured." Their sophistication in racial matters was such that they managed to prove that Chinese residents were nonwhite, while visiting Japanese businessmen were white and therefore allowable in hotels and even swimming pools. It is very fortunate for the San Diego Unified School District that with the abolition of Apartheid in South Africa, its racial experts are now unemployed and would no doubt eagerly accept invitations to pursue their trade in San Diego.

For all the progress that may have been made in specifically Guamanian, Samoan, or "Laotian (*not Hmong*)" cultural studies within the San Diego Unified School District, English syntax is seemingly beyond the ability of its officials (e.g., "a person having origins in any of the original peoples of Laos or Cambodia and *are* of the Hmong culture or origin"). One does not expect bureaucratic language to be stylish, but the exceptionally tortured language of the document is no mere stylistic defect. Its awkward contortions reflect the profound intellectual dishonesty of shifting between fundamentally different criteria (race, culture, and "affiliation") to force individuals into artificial categories of relative disadvantage. By such means a Jamaican of solidly middle-class parentage receives preference over an Algerian born in the misery of the Casbah, or the scion of wealthy Latin American landlords is favored over the white offspring of Appalachian poverty.

When it comes to pupils themselves, the damage is done by the very nature of "multicultural" education. There is no doubt that education in *any* culture, however exotic or primitive, can be highly instructive—anyone acquainted with the Inuit of the North or the Masai of East Africa can testify that much can be learned from them alone, even though there are neither Inuit nor Masai literary texts. And of course the classics of other exotic cultures have been popular with Western readers for centuries. So why is "multicultural" education as now practiced in US public education so strongly countereducational?

First, because schools already incapable of teaching adequately the basics of reading, writing, arithmetic, civics, and good conduct now divert the attention of their pupils to all sorts of peripheral subjects.

Second, because teachers who may or may not have a grasp of American and European history and culture are now under orders to teach Mesoamerican, Indian, Chinese, Japanese, and black-African history and culture as well. Inevitably the subject matter exceeds the limits of their knowledge—and inevitably they are caught in the act by some bright pupil or other, so that the credibility of all else they teach is fatally undermined. That is now an everyday occurrence in classrooms all over the country—my own son was mistaught "Japan" by a teacher who claimed that Buddhism was the country's oldest religion—she had never heard of Shinto.

Third, because the additional subjects are taught so superficially that little or no actual *learning* ensues. Traditional "Euro-centric" education was certainly narrow as its critics claim by excluding vast realms of human experience. But when the *reading* of, say, Melville is replaced by a fast excursion through the mispronounced titles of exotic classics, or when an *explanation* of the French Revolution is replaced by a sixty-minute ramble through the totality of Indian history, more becomes less. Without a minimum of detail and depth, neither knowledge nor understanding can be gained. For the same reason, any adequate "multicultural" training of school teachers is an impossibility—unless they happen to be multilingual, world-class scholars to begin with.

Finally, what often makes multicultural education specifically countereducational is that the subject-matter itself is deeply corrupted by "feel-good" social aims. One cannot begin to imagine what goes on under that heading in the San Diego Unified School District, as it provides "culturally sensitive" instruction to pupils who most probably wish to be simply American, but who have "Hispanic," "African American," "Guamanian," or even "Other Asian" identities thrust upon them. But in schools all over the country it is now routine to glide over the blood-soaked paralysis of Aztec culture and Mayan decadence in recounting the evils of the Spanish conquest, to present ancient Egypt as the true source of Greek thought, to depict primitive peoples not as powerless to change their environment but as proto-environmentalists "at one with nature," and generally to celebrate uncritically the phenomenal advances of every civilization except one, in contrast to European backwardness, cruelty, and greed.

Where multiculturalism is rejected as the soft option in favor of "Afro-centrism," even greater crimes of miseducation are perpetrated against defenseless children. The racist fantasy that Negroes could be "kept in their place" by being kept in a state of ignorance is actually now being accomplished at the taxpayers' expense, ironically enough by "black nationalist" educational bureaucrats, teachers, and propagandists. For example, as of the 1992 school year, nearly all of Atlanta's 109 elementary and secondary schools, and more than 80% of their teachers, have been following Afro-centric curricula, as in many other metropolitan school districts.

What that means in substance is exemplified by the teaching of "mathematics." At the Dobbs Elementary School in southeast Atlanta, Brenda Brown, who, one presumes, does not know Swahili, sets problems in English for her third grade class but demands that children use a Swahili language chart to present their solutions. Thus instead of $1 + 3 = 4$ the children write: *moja + tatu = ane*. That is not mathematics but arithmetic, and first-grade arithmetic to boot, gratuitously complicated by being translated into an East African language that was not even the language of the West Africans that slavery brought to America. In an eighth grade class at Bunche Middle School in southwest Atlanta, Carolyn Huff—who is probably not a qualified Egyptologist conversant with hieroglyphics—nevertheless cites "Egypt" to teach fractions with 1 as the numerator, so that ⅝ becomes ⅛ + ½; while in algebra the unknown variable is not the "European" x but *aha*, following an "Egyptian practice dating to 4500 B.C."[13] We are very far from the harmless inclusion of African folk-tales in first grade readings, or the useful addition of Chinua Achebe's novels in high school English Lit. Real confusion is being inflicted on children often already handicapped by poverty, disorder, and ignorance at home (Atlanta's black elite, which sanctions if it did not positively demand the new teaching, of course sends almost all its own children to private schools).

Algebra is itself an Arabic word, and that alone should have made the subject non-European enough (Afro-centrists have been known to claim more with less). But an Arabic source is not in fact good enough, because Arabs are "whites" according to the prevailing new racialism. By contrast, it is the fundamental claim of the Afro-centrists that the ancient Egyptians were the true inventors of all that European racists attributed to the ancient Greeks, and—above all—that they were *racially* "black African," i.e., negroid. Socrates, held to have been an Egyptian immigrant, is specifically identified as an "African" along with other notable figures—on the basis of dubious photographs of sculptures or medallions dating from late antiquity or later still. Qualified classicists and Egyptologists never concerned themselves with such irrelevant matters (except for a few disreputable German academics under the Third Reich) but when pressed they must note that Greek cities recognized only municipal origins, not race, while anyone can see that in Egyptian art figures with negroid features are invariably depicted as slaves or servants. Themselves classified as whites, modern Egyptians of course have no say in the matter.

The equation Ancient Greece = Egypt = Negro Africa may be dismissed as absurd worldwide, but it is now the officially prescribed truth in many American public schools. The theory is that historical falsehood must be taught as a form of group therapy, to boost the collective self-images of black children so they will want to learn *something*. That itself can be considered a racist evasion by inadequate schools and incompetent teachers. But it does complicate matters greatly that often the perpetrators of the deception are themselves ignorant enough to believe the nonsense they teach.

When it comes to racially sensitive subjects, it is not only Atlanta's public schools that now miseducate by deliberate policy but schools all over the country, including expensive private schools, and even many colleges of higher education. Although much other subject matter is affected (from cultural anthropology to genetics to criminology to Mesoamerican history), "Africa" courses especially tend to be sheer romance, in which all is art (Benin), science (the "university" of Timbactu), architecture (Zimbabwe), and peaceful prosperity, until European colonialists and slavers arrive—but everything finally ends well, after decolonialization brings the joys of independence. Of the subsequent miseries, massacres, and relentless decline nothing is said, as the courses end with ritual condemnations of South African Apartheid. Can self-images be enhanced by lies? The answer may well be yes—but only in the short term, until the deception is exposed. Should schools and universities deliberately teach systematic falsehood? The answer must be a definite no.

It would, of course, be absurd to limit education to subjects of economic value—that would be a prescription for a skilled barbarism that would soon enough give way to plain barbarism. Yet because it is usually poorer children who are victimized, the distinct economic uselessness of much of what goes on under the heading of multicultural or Afro-centric education is also an issue. One cannot compete in world

markets with a sound knowledge of Hmong hunting chants, or *moja +
tatu = ane* arithmetic, let alone a solid education in Afro-centric history—an Athens customer might even resent being told that Socrates
was an African, as now taught in many schools pending the emergence
of Hispanic school board factions strong enough to have him reclassi-
fied as a Spaniard (after all, there were Greek colonists in Spain long
before Socrates lived . . .).

REMEDIES

Bearing in mind all the other dysfunctions of American public education, from systematic overadministration to outright corruption, from
rampant indiscipline to the prevalence of ignorant teachers, the broad
and important conclusion one must reach is that the acute shortcomings of many of the 15,376 school districts of the United States can only
be remedied by a drastic two-way reduction in their powers.

On the one hand, experiments in shifting control from school districts to individual school boards have often been quite successful and
should be further extended. Their effect is to increase parental influence—and parents are more to be trusted than local politicos or career
bureaucrats when it comes to the education of their own children. But
that plunge into a still greater diversity and yet more uneven results
should be powerfully balanced by specific federal interventions to raise
standards nationwide.

With orders, prohibitions, or any other sticks either futile or uncon-
stitutional or both, all must be achieved by carrots alone, i.e., federal
money or federal recognition for *proven results*, not just good intentions. School districts already receive federal and state grants for all
sorts of purposes, or merely as a form of revenue-sharing. But the
recommendations that follow are different in their nationwide purpose
and scale.

One excellent carrot would be to award extra federal pay to teachers
who pass uniform, nationwide, written qualification exams, set at different levels (e.g., elementary, junior high, and high school) but always
to notably demanding standards. Thus teachers who pass the exam
("Federal Award" teachers) would receive two paychecks, one from the
school district that employs them, and one from the federal government. At the very beginning, that would create only a small corps of
elite teachers, very probably arousing union opposition and the resent-

ment of colleagues without achieving much to raise nationwide teaching standards. But the extra pay and natural competitive instincts should quickly widen the ranks of Federal Award teachers, raising competence levels throughout US public education—not least by attracting well-qualified newcomers to the profession. That, of course, is the key to everything. Better teaching cannot be had without better teachers. Better teachers will not be forthcoming unless the entire prestige of the profession is raised decisively. And that in turn cannot be done without making teaching an enviable, well-paid job. But to pay more without demanding more competence would merely turn poorly paid mediocre teachers into well-paid mediocre teachers—hence the necessity of stiff qualification exams, themselves a source of prestige for those who pass.

It is true of course that no written *knowledge* exam (the only kind that can be graded objectively, as this must be) can assess teachers' ability to teach, still less their personal talent in persuading pupils to learn. But such exams could at least determine if the teachers know the facts and techniques they are supposed to teach. At present many parents are simply unaware of the crass ignorance inflicted on their children. Some parents are quite apathetic, but even the highly interested minority now has no effective way of evaluating teacher competence. Under this scheme, by contrast, parents could readily count the number of "Feds" on the payroll. With that, school boards and district bureaucrats would soon enough come under pressure to attract a decent proportion of Federal Award teachers, thereby being forced not only to hire by merit but also to provide a decent working environment—by imposing better discipline, for example. In other words, the personal incentive of extra federal pay for individual teachers would not only enhance their individual quality but also create schoolwide and districtwide incentives to improve the quality of education across the board.

To be sure, almost all states require that public school teachers pass the "National Teacher Examination" or their own tests to obtain their initial certification. That, however, guarantees very little—the NTE is a pathetically easy test. And some better-off school districts already award extra pay to select "star" teachers—but that merely adds to the uneven hodgepodge of US public education, doing nothing for the least favored schools, districts, and states. Only a nationwide initiative to enhance the teaching profession can do the trick—and of course it is precisely in the poorest states and the poorest school districts that the extra federal pay for highly qualified teachers would have the greatest impact.

Another effective carrot would be aimed at pupils rather than teachers. Offering prestige instead of money, official federal diplomas for tested educational achievement would be a tempting challenge to students while setting nationwide standards for schools. In Europe and Japan, there are state baccalaureate exams for school-leavers, not only highly prestigious but also essential for university admission—and for access to many jobs that do not require a university education. Their social significance is exemplified by the fact that only recruits with baccalaureates can enter as officer-candidates in European countries where military service is still compulsory. Because they are so important, because they cover a full range of subjects, and because both lengthy essays and orals must be graded, baccalaureate examinations are very elaborately organized. In the attempt to prevent cheating and achieve a maximum of objectivity, they are supervised and evaluated by state-appointed commissions made of selected teachers, who receive extra pay and travel allowances—they are normally brought in from other parts of the country to protect against bribery and favoritism.

In many ways the system is admirable, but it should not be copied in the United States. Aside from the very considerable cost and complication, establishing a federal baccalaureate exam would do nothing for the academically less gifted. Yet it is the inadequacy of their education that is most costly to the country, both because of a plain lack of basic skills in the work force, and also for social reasons—given the nexus between poor education, unemployment, disorderly behavior, and crime. Certainly, a prestige incentive limited to the most successful school-leavers could hardly do much to improve the entire atmosphere of US public education for younger children as well.

Federal achievement diplomas in specific subjects set at various grade levels would be more useful and also much more economical—especially if they are limited, as they should be, to the most important and most easily graded basics. Obvious choices might be arithmetic and geometry for eighth graders, calculus for eleventh graders, English language and literature at two or three different grade levels, commercially useful languages (e.g., French, German, Mandarin, Russian) for twelfth graders, and perhaps civics. Even a narrow range of subjects would suffice to set standards for schools and provide a clear measure of their effectiveness for parents and school boards.

Given the urgent need to revive vocational training in the United States, federal diplomas should also be awarded for demonstrated skills of value in the labor force, insofar as they can be tested economically. As it is, written, pictorial, and computer-administered exams already exist in many fields (e.g., electrical installation, computer operation, diesel repair, word-processing, etc.), and more of them could be developed.

In the name of an empty theory of equality, US public high schools have virtually eliminated any real vocational education.[14] What still goes under that name mostly consists of outdated "wood-shop" sessions, home economics ("for girls"), superficial chitchat introductions to business, and trade and industry classes that teach no actual skills. It is as if *not* learning Shakespeare were more valuable educationally than to actually learn practical skills of economic value. Yet serious vocational training would greatly assist nonscholars to find skilled jobs once they leave school, it would give them their own sphere of achievement until then, and it should therefore reduce dropout rates. For there is no doubt that the first reason that children abandon school is their frustration with courses that are useless for the academically less gifted, and are instead merely humiliating.

The theory that academic education is best for all pupils has been tested for long enough, and it continues to fail catastrophically. The result is that American Ph.D.'s and American professionals are doing very well on the global scene, thank you very much, but less educated Americans cannot compete in skills and work discipline with their counterparts in the most advanced countries. For educational bureaucrats, however, the equality theory is very convenient, for it warrants even the most dismal academic standards in the name of "inclusion."

To be sure, schools and school districts can neither fund nor manage serious vocational training. Everything therefore depends on negotiating combined school-and-apprenticeship programs with suitable local employers large and small, from utilities and auto-repair shops to banks, from hospitals and industrial companies to hotels (for skilled cookery, foreign-language reception, basic hotel management, bookkeeping). Although work-study experiments have usually been successful, their wider application is blocked by fears that pupils would be treated as nothing more than free unskilled labor, exploited (which is all right) but not seriously trained in the process. Such fears are of course manipulated by the ideological and bureaucratic opponents of vocational training.

It is in that setting that federal diplomas for tested skills of economic value would play an essential role. By setting universal achievement standards for hugely variegated work-study schemes, they would provide the vital ingredient of quality control, thus reassuring parents and pupils while providing firm operating guidelines for school districts, all other educational authorities involved, and the cooperating employers. Local work-study programs could be, and should be, structured around the federal achievement diploma or diplomas to be earned.

Less than a quarter of all American high-school pupils proceed with their education until they complete a four-year college, even though more than half attend some sort of postsecondary school (usually junior college). If work-study schemes in high schools were properly organized, with their results given federal recognition in turn recognized by employers, vocational training could become the *predominant form of secondary education for older teenagers*, attracting some of the college-bound, for whom it would be one subject among several, many of those destined for junior college only, for whom it would be more important, and the vast majority of those who now drop out or do not enter any sort of postsecondary school, for whom it should be the major activity, alongside some residual classroom instruction. For all of them, the discipline of a working setting would be a valuable complement to the actual skills learned—there is now a sad deficiency of both.

It is not often realized that establishing serious vocational training in the nation's high schools would also help to raise academic standards. While rescuing many students from futile academic nonlearning and curbing dropout rates, it would also allow—and stimulate—school authorities to pitch their academic courses to the higher standards of the remaining students. For this reason as well, making vocational training the predominant form of secondary education for older teenagers would be a powerful remedy for America's broader social and economic problems.

■ TAXATION

The general upgrading of public education, and the particular enhancement of vocational training, would address America's labor problem, i.e., the lack of skill and discipline in the labor force. But there is an equal need to address America's capital problem, the shortage of saved-up income available for investment.

In the new geo-economic era, capital for public and private investment is as important as firepower ever was in the geopolitical era. And it is above all the scarcity of homemade and home-saved capital that is now weakening America as we have seen.

That is why the physical plant of American public life, from airports to highway tunnels, has been deteriorating, or at least not keeping up with a growing population. And that is why private enterprise does not provide well-paid employment to a growing number of working Americans, who must instead compete with their foreign counterparts by selling their labor cheap. To be sure, the availability of capital does not automatically lead to investment—but a scarcity of capital does unfailingly restrict investment. While capital investment does not in itself force private enterprise to pay higher wages, in an economy where capital becomes relatively more abundant than labor, wages do assuredly increase.

Because it is the lowest-paid workers that suffer most from the capital shortage, it is a cruel deception to offer them the spurious benefits of "fair" taxes, if those very same taxes happen to worsen the capital shortage. There is no doubt, for example, that *consumption* taxes, i.e., sales, excise, and value-added taxes are the most unfair, because the billionaire and the pauper must pay exactly the same amount. But consumption taxes also have another effect: they naturally discourage consumption, arithmetically increasing savings. To be sure, the poorest will continue to spend all their income, merely getting less for it, while paying more in taxes. If that were all there was to it, consumption taxes would merely be regressive. But those with larger incomes are also discouraged from spending by higher consumption taxes, other things being again equal—and that is how savings, capital, investment, and wages can all increase in turn.

Even though America has its Nobel Prize economists who have not noticed the parallel, it is infinitely enlightening to compare the very low US savings rate at 12% with another very low proportion: the 14% of all US tax revenues, federal, state, and local, that come from sales and excise taxes, i.e., taxes on consumption. In most European countries and Canada, at least a quarter and as much as one-third of all revenues come from consumption taxes. This suggests that low consumption taxes = a low rate of savings because spending is most attractive when things are irresistibly cheap. And because a low savings rate = low wages (ultimately, tendentially), it follows that the most "unfair" taxes are the best taxes for the worst-paid *working* Americans, other things being equal. That US politicians have continuously proclaimed the opposite, Reagan-Bush Republicans on the claim that all taxes are bad, and Clinton Democrats on the claim that only steeply progressive income taxes are good, is most unfortunate but does not change the truth: unfair consumption taxes are best for those who most need fairness in society—if they also happen to work (the nonworking poor would merely pay more taxes, which could of course be offset by more grants).

American taxes as a whole are not high by world standards, but they are certainly very peculiar. On the one hand, the very low 14% of all tax revenues raised by federal, state, and local indirect taxes should mean that that much more tax must be raised by personal income taxes, thus discouraging earnings and work. But that has not been the case for three separate reasons, one rather good, one rather bad, and one very bad indeed.

First, the good reason is that earnings and work have not been discouraged simply because federal income tax rates have not been that high at the margin, even for the highest-paid earners: the maximum was 33% under Reagan-Bush, and remains below 40% under Clinton. Only where state and local income taxes are also high does the total act as a disincentive. On the other hand, income taxes, federal, state, and local, are still the greatest involuntary compulsions in The Land of the Free, and as such are resisted more strongly in national and local politics than higher sales taxes would be.

The rather bad reason is that personal income taxes are supplemented by corporate income taxes. No more demagogic cry is heard in the land than the call to make "rich corporations pay their taxes." That means, of course, less money for their owners and shareholders. For owners the effect is only to reduce their personal income, which is still subject to personal income taxes, dollar for dollar; for shareholders the effect is to reduce the net attractions of shareholding, thus discouraging investment in the US economy. To be sure, corporations routinely serve as parking lots for earnings that would otherwise be subject to personal income taxes. While salary and wage earners have no such relief, owners of corporations can use the corporations to defer their taxes. That is very unfair. It is also, however, a form of saving as worthy as any other. Thus much would be gained by abolishing corporate income taxes altogether. The resulting "unfairness" would be twice compensated, first by stopping altogether the present tax deductibility of fancy cars, "business entertainment" beach condos, flowers and fruit, golfing holidays, meals, and even massages; if there were no corporate taxes and therefore no corporate tax deductions, much of that conspicuous, unnecessary, or downright grotesque consumption would come to a most welcome end. Second, the transformation of any and every corporation into a little tax-free Monte Carlo of its own would increase the propensity to save and invest in the same—reproducing exactly what happens in Monte Carlo, which swims gloriously in the money that flees from high French taxes and erratic Italian taxes. Of course, any and all favors and material benefits received *by individuals* from corporations must be fully taxable, as much as any money income received by them. Without that, corporations would not merely serve for the virtuous tax avoidance that increases savings, but also for the sinful tax evasion that increases consumption (your corporation buys a Rolls-Royce for you or a vicuña coat or a house). Indeed, to keep things honest and simple, it might be sensible to charge a very large personal income supertax on the imputed value of any *nonmoney* benefits received from corporations.

The *very* bad reason why the amount that must be raised by personal income taxes is not so large after all is that the latter are supplemented not only by corporate income taxes but also by the worst of all possible taxes: the social security tax. The social security tax, of course, is nothing but a payroll tax, reducible by reducing the *number* of employees on the payroll. It duly achieves that result, causing unemployment. The fact that it is also regressive (Mr. Gates of Microsoft and multibillion dollar fame pays no more than most of his employees) merely adds insult to injury. In theory, social security payments are not taxes at all but "contributions" to the social security fund. But there is no such fund in reality: social security payments are not invested in any productive enterprise that might yield a future income stream, but merely go to the US Treasury as "loans" that only future taxpayers can repay. Hence nothing would be lost if the fiction were abandoned, to acknowledge finally that social security benefits are nothing more than government handouts, paid for by today's taxpayers and not by the putative contributions their beneficiaries made long ago. And with that, the justification for regressive and employment-dissuading social security taxes would immediately collapse.

Federal sales or value-added taxes on goods and services large enough to make up for the abolition of both corporate and social security taxes might bring to a timely end the carnival of consumption for affluent, post-Calvinist Americans. To be sure, such taxes would also restrict the buying power of the poor, perhaps in ways that might require offsetting welfare grants. In any case, in addition to allowing the abolition of rather bad corporate taxes and very bad social security taxes, federal sales or value-added taxes would directly attack the central problem of the US economy: overconsumption, which arithmetically results in undersaving, which almost arithmetically results in underinvestment, which absolutely results in the undercapitalization of research and development, public infrastructures, and private plant and equipment.

True, the *short-term* effect of a sudden one-time drop in consumption caused by new federal sales or value-added taxes might be to discourage business investment, even if capital does become more abundant and interest rates do fall. But businesses able to foresee the eventual rise in productivity, incomes, *and* consumption that would follow from the recapitalization of the entire US economy *would* invest (and of course recapitalized industries would be better equipped to compete in world markets). By contrast, if the present pattern of overconsumption, undersaving, and underinvestment simply continues, the ultimate destination of the United States can only be among the undercapitalized and indebted countries of the Third World.

Sales taxes are simple, but their single point-of-final-sale simplicity can also become a source of distortions. A 5% federal retail sales tax on all goods and services might work quite well, but a 25% tax (a much more likely level) would quickly cause a reversion to barter worthy of the coinless Dark Ages. Thus taxes might be avoided, inflicting certain public harm for dubious private good, because of the inefficiencies of a barter system (you receive 144 eggs all at once; I am owed six months' worth of car washes . . .). A multipoint value-added tax would not have this crippling disadvantage. By now Europeans have had decades of experience with value-added tax. All payments for goods or services include value-added tax set at fixed rates, which are notionally at least meant to reflect the "value" added by the labor of the firm's employees, its invested capital, and its management. Thus a fixed percentage of that "added value" is paid over in tax. The simple arithmetic of a VAT could therefore replace both the payroll social security tax, and the elaborate calculations of corporate income tax in the US style—while displacing the lawyers that are forever litigating its complex results. With a VAT, mere bookkeepers can do the work that now employs accountants and tax lawyers. The resulting savings would be significant in themselves.

Americans love to debate the fairness of the taxes they pay. They should also perhaps contemplate the unfairness of the taxes they do not pay, i.e., the accumulation of public debt. In 1992, the federal deficit alone came to roughly $400 billion. And because public *investment* was quite small, that meant that Americans consumed hundreds of billions of dollars of public goods and services (health care, old age pensions, defense, etc.) in excess of whatever their taxes actually paid for.

A future US government in the full Third World style might repudiate all US Treasury bonds, notes, and bills, and thus the accumulated public debt. Unless that happens, however, today's nontaxes that cause the deficit will merely be imposed with all the added interest on future taxpayers, i.e., our children and grandchildren. That would not be so bad if they could repeat the trick—but there is no chance of that: US public debt was once very low and is now very high at 66% or so of the gross national product. This debt cannot simply continue to accumulate, because interest payments accumulate also—and to pay the interest with more borrowing would discourage buyers of US Treasury paper, thus raising interest rates and causing the need for yet more borrowing to pay the added interest . . . thus further discouraging buyers of US Treasury paper . . . .

'Tis true that there is much ruination in a great country, but that is no fit reason to persist with ruinous methods of public finance. A tax reform worthy of its name would gradually replace both social security and corporate income taxes with federal sales taxes, or better, with a value-added tax. It might also finally abolish all tax deductions and tax credits meant to encourage this or that, because the actual effects are so often unintended and far from positive (e.g., the empty office buildings left behind by past tax incentives, which in turn aggravated the S & L and banking crises). But the pleasurable vision of a *simple* income tax is merely very desirable. What is essential are taxes that dissuade consumption and encourage savings and investment. Calvin would have understood perfectly.

▪ INDUSTRIAL POLICY

Capital and labor, even more abundant capital and better-skilled labor, are not enough to ensure that the American economy will once again offer not merely jobs, but many well-paid industrial jobs. Of course it is not steel mills or assembly lines that are wanting, but industry in the modern sense, with managerial, design, research, technical, and marketing employees, as well as a few maintenance workers and many robots on the factory floor—if there is a factory at all, as opposed to a software lounge, or a hardware craftsroom. Actually the software "house" that is truly someone's house is the logical successor of the machine-tool shop in the alley—classic, product-making industry, in modern guise. By now there should be no need to examine the British predicament, or to recall the Dutch downfall, to determine that there is no substitute for the *making of things* in any economy larger than San Marino's. The experience of the United States itself during the deindustrialization decade of the 1980s should be quite sufficient.

Capital and labor, even more abundant capital and better-skilled labor, are not sufficient to ensure the prosperous growth of industry in these geo-economic times. Especially for the most highly technical industries, the granting or withholding of government favors (a timely purchase, a needed electromagnetic frequency, or just a development grant) can make all the difference in determining the eventual commercial fate of products or techniques. That is the sphere of industrial policy, vigorously pursued from Germany to Japan, long ignored or vehemently criticized by what used to be called the Anglo-Saxon world, but of late more likely to be imitated.

Its American proponents argue that government could and should assist the growth of new industries—especially when their foreign competitors are themselves helped by their own governments for all the usual geo-economic reasons. Opponents insist that any government interference with the free workings of "market forces" is bound to be wasteful at least and counterproductive at worst.

If forced to argue on one leg, the case for industrial policy can be reduced to one word: Japan, i.e., the undoubted success of the Japanese

298 • THE ENDANGERED AMERICAN DREAM

bureaucracy in guiding and supporting the growth of Japanese industry. As we have seen, its methods have included government funding of research and development, to help provide *private* companies entering favored new industries with innovative products and production techniques; the supply of long-term capital at low interest via government-controlled banks, to allow new entrants to start off with efficient large-scale plants from the outset, instead of having to build up their capacity slowly with retained profits alone; tax concessions strictly reserved for favored sectors; and the official or under-the-table restriction of imports, to assure high profit margins for domestic producers, thus enabling them in turn to both invest and also subsidize their exports (hence the frequency of "dumping" charges against Japanese producers: high profits at home allow foreign sales below cost to gain market share).

Further measures aimed at helping particular industries have included government purchasing—regardless of the price or performance advantage of foreign products (critical to the growth of Japan's mainframe computer industry); the manipulation of import restrictions to force foreign companies to hand over technology to their Japanese competitors, in exchange for access to the lucrative Japanese market (much used to nurture the petrochemical industry during the 1960s), and the behind-the-scenes organization of "voluntary" mergers, to consolidate industries that bureaucrats considered too fragmented to compete effectively on world markets. But such consolidation is *not* meant to reach the point of monopoly. In fact it is a basic principle of Japan's industrial policy that precisely because they are collectively protected, the different enterprises within each industry must remain fiercely competitive with each other, lest they become sluggish and self-indulgent. Moreover, any and all government assistance given to private companies presumes that the benefits will be used for investment in their further growth, not for high executive salaries or shareholder dividends.

From the first iron foundries and textile mills sponsored by the government at the start of Japan's modernization in the 1870s, to the outright creation of the computer industry out of nothing in the 1960s, to the present encouragement of software, nano-technology, and advanced ceramic materials, Japan's entire development has owed much to its highly original industrial policy. For just as war did not begin with nineteenth-century Prussia, but *systematic* war mobilization and war planning certainly did, so also the government support of industry did not begin with Japan (it was already old hat in eighteenth-century France), but the *systematic* promotion of new industries—and the equally systematic phasing out of decaying industries—is very much a Japanese invention. American proponents of industrial policy see no reason why the United States should not systematically copy Japan's winning formula, by now widely imitated in both Asia and Europe.

The case against industrial policy can also be summarized in one word: government, i.e., the inability of government officials to outperform the free market in shaping the development of industry—and their propensity to do very much worse than that, because of waste, fraud, mismanagement, and political intrusions.

Generally, i.e., globally, the objection is undoubtedly valid. The state bureaucracies of most countries of the world are certainly not to be trusted with anything as delicate as industrial policy. Even in their most routine functions, from the issue of obligatory documents to the operation of schools, hospitals, prisons, or the armed forces, plain incompetence and outright corruption are almost worldwide norms; only in government purchasing are the highest bidders (who can best include comfortable margins for bribes) routinely successful. It follows that virtually any form of industrial policy is bound to be turned into a further way of exploiting hapless consumers or looting the public treasury or both.

Thus state funding for industrial investment is apt to go to sham enterprises, better supplied with inflated plant and equipment invoices than with actual plant or actual equipment (as in the case of Italy's *Cassa del Mezzogiorno*, whose grants have littered the southern countryside with empty factory buildings, built by companies whose peak earnings came just before they opened for business, when they collected on the phony invoices they had sent in). Likewise, import restrictions meant to increase the profits, and therefore the capital, and therefore the investments of export industries, merely spawn facade industries made up of one-screwdriver assemblers and relabeling outfits, or at best inefficient producers of nonexportable, low-quality goods (as in most Latin American countries until the recent wave of trade liberalization, and most notoriously in Peru, before President Fujimori's abolition of most import restrictions).

The US federal bureaucracy, however, is not supposed to be routinely corrupt, nor even grotesquely inefficient. Accordingly, the opponents of an industrial policy for the United States emphasize its vulnerability to ordinary, everyday, political pressures in the distinctive American style: "pork-barreling," whereby members of Congress push through legislation to secure federal contracts or even subsidies to industries strongly present in their own constituencies; "log-rolling," whereby members of Congress support each other's pork-barreling ventures; and plain vote-seeking by the president and his executive branch, through favors specifically aimed at vote-rich industries, regions, or even specific plants. Thus during his 1992 election campaign, President Bush reversed his own previous policy and authorized the sale of General Dynamics F-16 fighters to Taiwan, specifically to gain votes in Fort Worth, Texas, where the F-16s are assembled.

From the viewpoint of industrial policy, all such politics-as-usual has a most unfortunate bias. What industries can best lobby Congress and the executive branch? And which industries already have many employees who become voters at election time? By definition, they cannot be new industries at best just getting started, but rather older, better-established industries much more likely to have glorious pasts than promising futures. As the opponents of industrial policy see it, government investment funds meant for promising start-up sectors are likely to end up supporting industries already in decline, too weak to compete on world markets but still strong politically. Likewise, import restrictions meant to assure the capital enrichment of industries poised to become champion exporters would instead be imposed for the benefit of declining industries, and the same would be true of all other industrial-policy measures, such as stimulative government purchasing. All would be captured politically to fatten the fattest cows, while doing little to help lean new industries that lack the money, connections, or votes to obtain political favors.

These are weighty objections, but the opponents of industrial policy are not content with such merely pragmatic arguments. They insist that it must fail even in the hands of government officials both perfectly honest and miraculously apolitical, as well as highly efficient in every way. Their argument begins by noting that especially in our times of accelerated change, the most important new products emerge in quite unpredictable ways. That is why IBM was caught utterly unprepared by the personal computer revolution, GM missed the boat on the sudden expansion of both minivan and sport/utility market shares, and America's electronics industry as a whole completely misunderstood both the VCR and the FAX machine as low-volume $20,000 items, of interest only to small numbers of highly specialized users, thus surrendering two huge markets without a fight.

To criticize IBM, GM, and the rest for being complacent, sluggish, and shortsighted misses the point: product forecasting would only be possible if the evolution of technology could be forecast; and that in turn would only be possible if the progress of science and its applications could be forecast. But there is no way to predict future scientific discoveries, or the applications. Hence not even the best analysis of present information can anticipate the configuration of future products, or the future evolution of production technologies. Both are only uncovered by trial and error in the marketplace, through the varied strivings of many different enterprises. Most are destined to fail while a handful succeed triumphantly, as Xerox, Apple, and Microsoft each did in turn, and as smaller start-ups have done within more narrowly specialized sectors, in the biotechnology industry, for example. It all brings to mind the most profligate and cruel workings of nature: the successful fertilization of a human egg by just one lucky spermatozoa out of thousands, the successful growth of just one adult frog from a myriad of tadpoles.

It follows that no group of government officials is likely to do any better than IBM or GM in picking future winners and losers—yet that is the essential starting point of any industrial policy. As opponents of industrial policy see it, if the United States had already established an activist bureaucracy in the 1960s to help fund the growth of promising new industries, it would have wasted a lot of money on production plants for nylon shirts, mechanical mimeograph machines, eight-track tape players, and analog calculators.

Compelling though it may seem, the theoretical argument against industrial policy—i.e., the impossibility of reliable technological forecasting—immediately evokes a practical counterargument, i.e., Japan's evident success. If its bureaucrats have been able to do the theoretically impossible, so should ours. Nor does the highly successful growth of Japan's industry seem to derive from any visible process of natural selection. The great flood of Japanese products that have claimed primacy on world markets has come almost entirely from a few, very familiar full-grown frogs (Hitachi, Toshiba, Canon, Matsushita, Sony, etc.) and not from lucky-tadpole new enterprises.

In response, the American opponents of industrial policy challenge the evidence. They argue that the champion economic samurais of Japan's *Tsusho Sangyo-Sho*, the Ministry of International Trade and Industry (MITI), have in fact failed again and again—except in successfully claiming much of the credit for the achievements of Japan's private enterprise. They hold that Japan's phenomenal industrial success was actually due to hard work, a sound system of public education, the abundance of capital supplied by very high savings rates, and the strength that Japanese corporations derive from the exceptional loyalty of their employees—all the results of deep-seated cultural propensities, not bureaucratic wisdom. By way of evidence, its critics cite the list of MITI's greatest errors: its failure to forecast—or support—the growth of Japan's automobile industry; its overinvestment in steel during the 1960s and in aluminum during the 1970s; the failure of its expensive Fifth Generation computing program; and the encouragement of huge investments in memory-chip production, supposedly allowing US industry (Intel, Motorola) to regain lost ground in the neglected microprocessor sector, which turned out to be much more profitable. As for the virtual absence of start-up tadpoles from the Japanese scene, the explanation of the free marketeers is that natural selection, and the uncovering of developmental paths through trial and error, takes place all the same—but *within* the large Japanese corporate families. They function, in effect, as conglomerations of many different enterprises, some of which fail and wither, while others succeed and grow.

If one accepts these arguments, one can only conclude that the United States and all other competitors of Japan should be grateful for MITI's existence—and of course one must wonder how much more Japan could have achieved industrially had it never existed. In the circumstances, it is decidedly odd that Japanese big business, for all its notoriously excessive influence over Japanese politics, has never even tried to lobby for the abolition of MITI.

Actually, there is no need to rely on Japanese experience alone in evaluating the evidence for and against. Aside from the complex European record of government-business cooperation, replete with both great successes and great failures, America's own experience is highly significant—for the absence of an American MITI has only prevented a *systematic* industrial policy, not all sorts of partial interventions. Of these, perhaps the most revealing has been the very "Japanese" semiconductor policy pursued by the very same Reagan administration that issued long perorations on the evils of industrial policy in general; on the futility of industry-specific policies in particular; and on the especial foolishness of trying to assist the semiconductor industry, which in principle, i.e., in textbook economic theory, is no more worthy of help than any other industry ("computer chips, potato chips . . . what's the difference?"), and is certainly more unstable than most.

While loudly celebrating the superiority of unassisted free enterprise, the Reagan administration: (1) forced the Japanese government to force Japanese business to increase its purchases of US-made semiconductors; the market-share target of 20% finally achieved in 1993 was much more than US suppliers could have gotten on their own, and quite enough to take away the usual home-market advantage of Japanese producers; (2) relaxed the application of antitrust laws, to allow US semiconductor producers to cooperate in the same way that Japanese competitors cooperate, i.e., against *foreign* competitors (e.g., by jointly funding some research or jointly buying out innovative but poor technology companies, to prevent them from falling into the "wrong hands"); (3) cofunded with industry the typically Japanese-style Sematech research and development consortium; and (4) signaled a supportive intent by those actions, which in turn encouraged private investment.

Perhaps free-enterprise true believers will one day prove that it was all mere coincidence, but before this experiment in industrial policy started, US semiconductor producers were steadily losing market shares—which they have since regained. In 1981, they had 48.9% of the global market, as compared to 37.4% for Japanese producers; by 1986, that global market had almost doubled to $30 billion in total sales, but a classic reversal had taken place: US producers only had 39.2% as compared to 47.3% for their Japanese competitors. Six years later in 1992, after six years of unacknowledged but vigorous industrial policy for the sector, US producers had 43.8% of the market as compared to 43.1% for the Japanese—and that was a market whose total size had again doubled to some $60 billion.[15] Even though "US producers" are merely US companies that may actually be producing some of their chips in Spain, the UK, even Japan, their $25 billion market share certainly translates to a great many jobs that might have been lost, and to sales opportunities for US suppliers of related materials, business services, and highly sophisticated production equipment—few of which would have had much of a chance of selling those same things to Japanese semiconductor producers.

Nor is this the only American experiment with Japanese-style industrial policy—among others, there is the US Advanced Battery Consortium, notable mainly for being a 100% pure copy of the standard Japanese government-industry model, and most recently, the "flat-panel" consortium for computer display screens. That is an especially remarkable venture because even without an American MITI, or indeed any visible coordinating body at all, the almost complete Japanese dominance of this very important subindustry is now being challenged by a typically Japanese-style combined action. First, a huge 62.7% tariff was imposed on imported Japanese displays, after the supposedly above-the-fray US International Trade Commission found evidence of dumping. Next the Pentagon's Defense Research Projects Agency (DARPA) took the initiative of sponsoring a development consortium of US companies large and small to fund production experiments and pilot plants. Finally, the word has clearly passed around the industry that the manufacture of flat-panel displays in the United States is a Good Thing—and both Texas Instruments and Motorola duly responded with major investments (though IBM has preferred a joint venture with Toshiba—with manufacture in Japan, of course). Also notable is the overtness of it all. When DARPA first funded the Sematech consortium in the early 1980s, at a time when the Soviet Union was the only great antagonist, and Japan was still not less than a close ally, its only declared purpose was strategic (almost all modern weapons contain microchips) and nary a word was said of any "geo-economic" aims. But that was then. Lance Glasser, the DARPA official in charge, indulged in no such pretense in presenting the new consortium: "This is the next step in a long climb back to prominence for the US in flat-panel displays."[16] Glory is indeed being domesticated.

Given all this, it can quite reasonably be argued that the creation of an American MITI is already overdue. If the United States is to have an industrial policy, why run it sideways from the Pentagon? And why should it be confined to products that have military uses? If it is accepted that new industries cannot grow without tariff protection from the dumping that would strangle them at birth, why leave their protection to an erratically judicial US International Trade Commission? And with US taxpayers already paying billions of dollars for biotechnology and other research, why should its industrial value not be extracted for the benefit of the US economy and US taxpayers?

As it is, the United States has no equivalent of MITI, but it does have both a large Department of Commerce and a mini-ministry of foreign trade in the Office of the US Trade Representative, as well as the International Trade Commission and various bits and pieces of other departments (Defense, Energy, Treasury), which would also belong in an American imitation of MITI.

Actually there is every reason *not* to unify these different bureaucracies. Commerce has long been famous for its low-grade civil servants (try calling up to obtain a simple statistic), while it is an elementary piece of Washington wisdom that any fusion of different offices—let alone different departments—invariably results in massive confusion, which is prolonged beyond all reason.

The best alternative to a conglomeration of departments that would yield only a monstrous parody of MITI would be to create a small industrial policy office directly under the president's authority; Clinton's National Economic Council could be just that. If kept small enough, it could be staffed with an elite cadre of career officials (like the Securities and Exchange Commission) yet it could still be powerful enough to coordinate all other relevant departments. To be sure, not even the strongest presidential declarations can empower a small bureaucracy to control several larger ones. But if in addition to a fine charter the new office would also have *budget control* over the relevant activities of the relevant departments, that miracle could be accomplished quite reliably. Bureaucracies become wonderfully cooperative when their own operating budgets depend on it. By contrast, without the power of the purse nothing whatever can be achieved—and there is certainly no need to set up one more talking shop in Washington, DC.

Arguably, scientific research may well benefit from the freedom left by a chaotic lack of coordination, but even that is only true from a purely scientific point of view—as may be seen from the scant economic returns obtained by the taxpayer from the large US government expenditures on every kind of basic research. In any case, the present lack of industrial-policy coordination is pure loss: government agencies act every day in many different ways that have all sorts of effects on American industry, through the regulations they issue, the equipment and services they purchase, the funds they allocate, the research activities they conduct, and the foreign-trade measures they apply. Economic theory has no use for any sort of American MITI. Economic practice has long required one. Just as the strongest argument for a systematic and comprehensive US industrial policy is that we already have a hit-or-miss version of the same, the strongest argument for a controlling institution is that a full-scale MITI copy *or* a small elite office *or* even a messy conglomerate of departments would all be more effective than the present disorderly confusion.

Many other suggestions press forward demanding a hearing, from a serious attempt to control migration through the Mexican border, to the reinstitution of loitering laws to reclaim urban public spaces for the law-abiding. But first, patients must obey the second law of medicine, by acknowledging that they are sick and in need of a stronger cure than the evanescent hopes that are born with each new presidency.

CHAPTER 11

THE GEO-ECONOMIC
ARMS RACE

In geo-economics, as in war, offensive weapons dominate. Of these, research and development force-fed with government support and taxpayers' money is the most important. Just as in war the artillery conquers by firepower territory that the infantry can then occupy, R & D can conquer the industrial territory of the future by achieving a decisive technological superiority. Japan's new Real World computing program is only one of the many such efforts now under way in the central arena of geo-economics. The European Community and the United States both sponsor their own microelectronics and computing programs, as well as many other projects.

In 1990, for example, the US Advanced Battery Consortium was started to develop a more efficient power source for electric cars than the old lead-acid battery, which is too heavy for the scant power it yields. With $130 million from the US Department of Energy and another $130 million jointly provided by General Motors, Ford, and Chrysler, the consortium's purpose is to fund research and engineering projects that the much-worshipped free market will not fund on its own. In 1992, it claimed to have found a promising candidate in the revolutionary "ovonic" battery now being developed by Stanford R. Ovshinsky and his Energy Conversion Devices Inc. with $18.5 million from the consortium.[1] The brotherly collaboration of all three US automobile companies, which are supposed to be forever competing with one another, means only one thing: this is not merely a business undertaking, but an American geo-economic offensive against the Japanese automobile industry, ironically but fittingly carried out by a typically Japanese-style government plus industry consortium.

The artillery of state-encouraged research and development is crucial, but the infantry of production may also need assistance. Airbus Industrie thus receives operating subsidies, and so do many other favored private companies or entire industries. Usually there is no need to embarrass all concerned by overt payments, with suitcases stuffed with banknotes or more prosaic bank transfers: government purchasing on generous terms achieves the same effect much more discreetly. Japan, for example, had no computer industry to speak of in 1960 when the Ministry of International Trade and Industry launched a five-year program for the *national* production of computers.[2] The first steps were, of course, the imposition of stiff tariffs, which made profitable exports to Japan virtually impossible, and the funding of computer research by government laboratories, universities, and industry. IBM had already established a factory in Japan, but its computers were not considered "national" enough: only the customers of its Japanese competitors, mainly Fujitsu, could receive credit on favorable terms from the government-sponsored Japan Electronic Computer Corporation. That, in effect, was an operating subsidy for Fujitsu and the rest.

Next, MITI offered to allow IBM's competitors, General Electric, RCA, Xerox, and others, to sell their computers on the Japanese market, but only if they agreed to form joint ventures with Japanese companies and agreed to share their technology with them. When IBM introduced its revolutionary System 360 in 1964, instantly making the joint-venture Japanese computers obsolete, MITI's response was the Super High Performance Electronic Computer Program, which pooled the resources of government and industry laboratories to catch up. But in the meantime, the government helped the weak local industry more directly, by purchasing its products although they were both outdated and more costly than IBM's (even long after this, in September 1975, when Japan's market had officially been fully opened, local products accounted for 93% of the computers in government offices, 88% of those in local public bodies, and 90% in universities).[3] In the early 1970s, there was another upheaval that once again upset MITI's plan. The Japanese companies that were sharing the technology of General Electric, RCA, and Xerox were left bereft when all three abandoned the field after IBM unveiled its innovative System 370, which also once again left Japan's industry leader, Fujitsu, far behind.

The response was yet another injection of cash for research and development, and MITI also forced Japan's six companies to combine into three for greater strength. It also counterattacked more directly, by arranging a Fujitsu–Hitachi partnership that purchased its technology from the new US Amdahl company, headed by the noted ex-IBM designer of that name. Amdahl unveiled the secrets of IBM's computer architecture for the Japanese partnership for an undisclosed amount, but certainly much too little for such premier industrial crown jewels.[4] And so it went, year after year, with state support by one means or another (including Japan's ten-year Fifth Generation computer research program that cost Japanese taxpayers at least $400 million)—except that over time, IBM has become ever weaker, and Fujitsu ever stronger. Throughout, while MITI's research programs generally failed, being each time overtaken by fresh American innovations that emerged quite unexpectedly ("work-stations," parallel computing, fault-tolerant programs, etc.), Fujitsu and the rest of Japan's industry has been very effectively helped by systematic favoritism in government purchasing.

The final offensive weapon is "predatory finance." If the artillery of research and development cannot conquer markets by sheer technological superiority; if operating subsidies given by one means or another are not enough; export sales can be achieved even against very strong competitors by offering loans at below-market interest rates. The United States has its Export-Import "Exim" bank that provides loan guarantees and credit on good terms to finance exports, and so do all major trading countries through their own equivalents. Thus foreigners can routinely expect to pay lower interest rates for their credit purchases than local borrowers, whose taxes pay for the very concessions that foreigners receive. That already amounts to hunting for exports with low-interest ammunition, but the accusation of predatory finance is reserved for cases where interest rates are suddenly reduced in the course of a fought-over sale. Naturally, the chief trading states have promised to each other that they will do no such thing. Naturally, they frequently break that promise.

In traditional world politics, the goals are to secure and extend the physical control of territory, and to gain diplomatic influence over foreign governments. The corresponding geo-economic goal is *not* the highest possible standard of living for a country's population but rather the conquest or protection of desirable roles in the world economy. Who will develop the next generation of jet airliners, computers, bio-technology products, advanced materials, financial services, and all other high-value output in industries large and small? Will the designers, technologists, managers, and financiers be Americans, Europeans, or East Asians? The winners will have those highly rewarding and controlling roles, while the losers will have only the assembly lines—if their home markets are large enough, or if fully assembled imports are kept out by trade barriers. We have already seen that when "transplants" replace domestic production, the local employment of manual and semiskilled labor may continue, but finance and all higher management is transferred back to the country of origin.

Geo-economics is therefore a very appropriate projection on the world scene of typically meritocratic and professional ambitions, just as war and diplomacy reflected typically aristocratic ambitions, offering lots of desirable roles for military officers and diplomats who were aristocrats, or acted as if they were aristocrats, or at least relished aristocratic satisfactions. The meritocracy of technologists and managers is not much more modest. They do not desire bemedaled uniforms or the diplomat's ceremonies, but they do want to be *in command* on the world scene, as the makers of technology, not mere producers under license; as the developers of products, not mere assemblers; as industrialists, not mere importers.

Except for those who still insist on seeing only business in what is now going on—strange business, with no balance sheets or normal profit motives in sight—it is obvious enough that geo-economics is spreading, and becoming the dominant phenomenon in the central arena of world affairs. But not all states are equally inclined or equally capable of participating in the new struggle. Quite a few already have economically activist policies and bureaucracies, or are seeking to acquire them (Japan is their model). If they can advance rapidly in skills and education, they may succeed at the new game even if their total economy is small: modern technology offers ever more diverse avenues for industry, including some specialized enough not to require production on any huge scale. Thus small but well-educated countries can be much more successful in geo-economics, as in plain business, than they could ever be in world politics where size always counts, and may alone be decisive.

Be they large or small, most Third World states, however, are cursed with bureaucracies too ineffective to engage in geo-economic activities. In quite a few, and almost everywhere in black Africa, any government funding for any purpose simply becomes another opportunity for wholesale thievery, while every regulation is corruptly circumvented (e.g., raw logs are still exported, by bribing customs officials to write them down as planks). Within the European Community, members were originally variously inclined, from always state-minded France to mostly free-market Britain—but as a group they now seem set to collectively pursue geo-economic goals.

As for the United States, it tends to engage in much geo-economic practice while loudly rejecting its principles. American political leaders have a way of vehemently proclaiming their eternal faith in "the market" while as they simultaneously preside over their own geo-economic interventions, *and* loudly warn off foreign governments from doing the same. Listening to their speeches, one might think that many American political leaders are genuinely unaware of the fact that the two largest US export industries are agriculture and aerospace, both subject to much state intervention and both the recipients of much generous assistance. And yet the grip of free-trade ideology on the American mind still has a powerful effect. When something is branded as improper and yet is still done, it is only done in a furtive and sporadic manner. By closing the door to geo-economic policies openly admitted and openly discussed, free-trade ideology leaves the field clear for the best-organized and best-funded lobbies to extract favors for themselves from the flux of day-to-day politics.

To be sure, even if there are no ideological inhibitions, in no democratic country can the state and its policies be immune to powerful lobbies. In one way or another, they will usually find it easy to present their own private goals in effective geo-economic camouflage. They can persuade politicians to erect trade barriers and profitably differentiate taxes and regulations so as to impose disadvantages on foreign competitors, but also on the citizenry at large; and all state-provided benefits, services, and infrastructures can also be shaped and reshaped in the same way to serve narrow interests. Likewise, when state funds are provided for technological development or production investments, it is not only foreign competitors who suffer but also the fellow-citizens who must pay for it all. Of course they *must* suffer as taxpayers and consumers from any geo-economic action whatsoever, but everything depends on how widely the resulting benefits to them as producers are finally distributed. Does the geo-economic action that at first helps only a few eventually enrich the entire economy and many lives, or does it simply enrich a few privileged citizens at the expense of all the rest?

In Peru, for example, former President García launched an industrial development program during the 1980s that, as usual, imposed prohibitive tariffs on many imported goods. At first, there were many signs of apparent success. Toyota and Nissan both established assembly plants in Peru because, for all practical purposes, they could no longer sell completed automobiles. Factories for the production of everything from pens and pencils to sports clothing and farm equipment were started behind the high wall of tariff protection. Peru seemed to be industrializing, and quite rapidly. But within a few years the experiment had collapsed in dismal failure, with the country and the vast majority of its people left much poorer than before. In constant 1987 dollars, Peru's national income per capita was much lower in 1990 at $940 than it had been in 1980 (at $1,350) or even in 1970 (at $1,270).[5]

What happened was only to be expected in Third World conditions. With less than a huge market anyway, and with all the apparent industrialization in the hands of the country's rich elite interlinked by marriage and by class feeling, there was no real competition between the new Peruvian industrial companies. Instead of bidding down each other's prices and improving on each other's quality as Japanese companies had done behind their own high wall of tariff protection, each of the new Peruvian companies exploited its local monopoly to pass off shoddy goods at whatever prices the import-starved market would bear. Also, it was easy for merchants and the new industrialists to corrupt politicians and the badly underpaid bureaucrats.

With bribes and political connections, imports were brought in duty free, for resale at very high prices. More important, sham industries were set up that merely repackaged imports of finished goods (brought in duty free as "components"), then adding a large profit markup. Car assembly plants, for example, were just that, hardly manufacturing anything as they merely reassembled containers of knocked-down cars. Thus a few Peruvians were poorly employed in mostly unskilled jobs, a few already rich Peruvians became much richer, and the country's standard of living declined greatly as Peruvian consumers were forced to pay heavy tribute for local products that were always costly, often inferior, and often not really local at all. When President Fujimori took office in 1990, his first move was to drastically reduce tariffs, to rid the country of its costly pseudoindustry.

Just as there is no successful warfare without effective armed forces, there can be no successful geo-economic action without effective and honest economic bureaucrats. But even in countries where bureaucrats are honest and efficient, especially in advanced countries, their central role in any geo-economic action is bound to distort it, for consciously or otherwise they will manipulate what is done for their own purposes. Perfectly honest, well-meaning bureaucrats who happen to serve in economic ministries or departments of commerce and industry can be expected to pursue the normal ambition of bureaucrats—to serve the state well, and to gain recognition and power in the process—by furthering their own favored geo-economic schemes of industrial defense or industrial conquest. Equally honest bureaucrats who happen to be in foreign-affairs ministries may pursue their own equally normal ambitions by furthering schemes of tariff reduction and international economic cooperation. But in the states that are in the central arena of world affairs, where war and classic diplomacy have so greatly declined in importance, the bureaucratic balance is now tilted.

For European and Japanese bureaucrats especially, but increasingly for American bureaucrats as well, geo-economics offers the only possible substitute for the military and diplomatic roles of the past. Only by invoking geo-economic imperatives can they claim authority over mere businesspeople and the citizenry at large. Obviously the urge is much more powerful in countries such as France and Japan that have proud bureaucratic elites, highly educated, carefully selected, and greatly respected—and thus especially unwilling to surrender their privileged position of power by allowing unfettered free enterprise to have its way.

In the major European countries, social attitudes and social pretensions are also a factor. Foreign Office diplomats issued from Oxford or Cambridge; their French counterparts who so regularly have an aristocratic *de* to link their double-barreled names; the highly cultured gentlemen who occupy the *Farnesina*, Italy's Ministry of Foreign Affairs; and their colleagues elsewhere in Europe do not have much in common with their fellow-citizens in trade. Of commerce and industry they mostly know little, and care less. Businesspeople of the ordinary sort they scarcely encounter and would hardly wish to meet. If they have studied economics, they may remember the theories in the textbooks, so far removed from the realities of the marketplace, and those theories merely prove that unfettered free trade is best even if practiced unilaterally, so that diplomatic interventions are anyhow best avoided. In spite of many attempts by ministers and commissions to direct their attention to commercial questions as well, it is only most reluctantly that they comply, while steadfastly refusing to act as export salesmen—it was precisely to escape all such sordid concerns that they embraced the diplomatic career in the first place.

For all that, bureaucratic survival interests are already now leading to mass conversions. Those who were ambitious enough to seek career advancement in the great institutions of the state will not want to devote their lives to such petty war and petty diplomacy as will continue in backward regions of the world even in a fully achieved geo-economic era. Well before that point is reached, most First World bureaucrats and their bureaucracies will eagerly embrace geo-economics. For without it, mere commerce would reign on the main stage of international life, under the undisputed control of business-people and corporations. With geo-economics, by contrast, the authority of state bureaucrats can be asserted anew, not in the name of strategy and security this time, but rather to protect "vital economic interests" by geo-economic defenses, geo-economic offensives, geo-economic diplomacy, and geo-economic intelligence.[6]

Actually much more than that is happening in the central arena of world affairs: as bureaucracies writ large, states as a whole are impelled by the urge to preserve their importance in society to acquire the geo-economic substitute for their decaying security role. Thus countries are likely to be pushed further along the geo-economic path than the balance of costs and benefits would warrant.

The overall effect of bureaucratic impulses to find new geo-economic roles, and of geo-economic manipulations by interest groups, will vary greatly from country to country and from case to case. But, fundamentally, states will tend to act geo-economically simply because of what they are: territorially defined entities designed precisely to outdo each other on the world scene. In spite of all the other functions that modern states have acquired as providers of individual benefits, assorted services, and varied infrastructures, their reason for being still derives from their historical function as providers of security from external foes (as well as outlaws within). In the past, these were enemies in arms who had to be fought, today they are competitors in the marketplace with whom free competition is for some reason or other a losing game. The winners in each sector of industry naturally always favor free trade. The losers may accept defeat and leave the field. But geo-economics offers the alternative of a state-supported second round, and every instinct of the state and its bureaucracies is to go for it, thereby being able to remain on center stage, almost as in war.

Not that many of the 180-odd independent states now in existence have fought a foreign war in living memory, and yet the governing structures of almost all states are still heavily marked by warlike purposes. Very few states have had to fight wars in order to exist, but it would seem that all states exist to fight—or at least they are still structured as if war itself were their most important function. In how many countries does the Minister for Telecommunications, or Energy, or Foreign Trade outrank the Defense Minister? Only in one actually—and fittingly enough that country is Japan, where Defense (*Boecho*) is a *cho* (translated as "agency"), a unit inferior to a *sho*, or "ministry," as in *Gaimusho*, the Ministry of Foreign Affairs. And the *Boecho*'s head is a "director-general," equivalent to a lesser "minister of state" in the British style, as opposed to a full cabinet minister, unless he has that status in a personal capacity.[7]

In the train of history, the last wagons, the poorest countries with the most inefficient and most corrupt state bureaucracies, cannot *yet* wage wars, because their armies are incapable of operating much beyond their frontiers, being only fit to rob and oppress their own citizens at home (some of the West African units sent to Liberia as peacekeepers in the civil war of 1991 turned into looting bands). For the same reason, those states cannot yet act geo-economically either, or indeed do anything at all to their own economies that is better than doing nothing at all. For them, the free market and free enterprise are indeed the only salvation.

The wagons in the middle, countries with partly developed economies and state bureaucracies of like quality, some poorer such as India and Pakistan, and some richer such as Turkey or Iraq, are all capable of war against each other, and indeed they are usually much too absorbed in territorial conflicts to seriously pursue geo-economic policies. Often their governments do try to develop industry, but except in the case of military industries, their efforts are usually weak and inconsistent. And those that are free of warlike entanglements, such as Brazil for example, attempt geo-economic action at their peril, for neither their economies nor their bureaucracies are up to the challenge of doing better than free enterprise would do, quite unassisted. Often they do much worse.

The wagons at the head of history's train, the United States, the countries of Europe, Japan, and others like them, are all materially capable of waging war effectively but their social atmosphere has become allergic to war. Certainly their populations and governing elites are now convinced that they cannot usefully fight one another with fire and arms, virtually for any reason. Yet their states are still organized for warlike rivalry, and so they seem set to pursue its same purposes by geo-economic means.

■ PRIVATE ENTERPRISE IN A GEO-ECONOMIC WORLD

Even the most geo-economically active states have to coexist with private enterprise large and small, from individual craftsmen to the largest of multinational corporations. While states occupy virtually the totality of the world's "political space" (except for Antarctica and terrorism), they occupy only a fraction of the total economic space. And that fraction is actually diminishing very rapidly with the collapse of communism and the worldwide trend to transfer state-owned industries and services into private hands.

In France and Italy, the state still owns even automobile and ice-cream manufacturers that compete with private enterprises, as well as entire industries (steel, aluminum), and privatization was not even discussed until the 1980s. In France, state ownership is a secular tradition and often quite efficient too; in Italy, some state-owned companies are very efficient and most are not, but all have provided managerial jobs by the hundreds for loyal followers and financial supporters of the major political parties. None was excluded, even if outside the governing coalition, not even the Communist party, in opposition ever since 1946 (the state radio and television RAI was split into RAI-1, RAI-2, and RAI-3 specifically to share out the jobs as well as the media access among Christian-Democrats, Socialists, and Communists). Now that Italy too has embraced privatization and is cleaning up its politics, France is an increasingly isolated exception on the world scene, along with the likes of Cuba and North Korea.

All over the world, not only in the former Communist countries but in dozens of others from Argentina to Sudan, governments are now selling off everything from airlines to zinc smelters, finding foreign or local buyers or simply handing out ownership coupons to their citizens, following Czechoslovakia's lead.

Everywhere it has been discovered, or rediscovered, that only the eye of the private owner, anxious for profits and most unhappy with losses, can prevent the abuses that come with public ownership, from the hiring of nonworking or fitfully working political followers by the hundreds and by the thousands, to the use of company treasuries for party purposes or plain thievery, to mere lethargy in the absence of competition, or even a complete lack of any actual work (when private companies were abruptly nationalized in Zaire in 1971, in many cases the officials appointed to manage them simply sold off their equipment, materials, finished goods, furniture, and even the windows and doors— with their frames).

Actually, however, the worldwide trend has engulfed many countries where no gross abuses were ever recorded, and even enterprises that were very efficient, simply because of the now fashionable belief that private ownership *must* be more efficient. Most recently, even utilities—electricity, telephones, mass transit, water, and sewage—are being privatized, even though as monopoly public services they might seem quite appropriate for public ownership.

Thus in seemingly contradictory fashion, the spread of geo-economics on the world scene, and the resulting increase in state interventions, now coincide with a rapid decline in public ownership. But actually there is no contradiction at all: not only in Japan, model-country of the new geo-economic era, but world-wide, bureaucrats can guide entirely private enterprise much better than they can manage state-owned outfits. Indeed it is the creative tension between fiercely competitive private corporations and activist economic bureaucrats that best explains Japan's economic success.

Of the different forms of coexistence between geo-economically active states and private enterprise, there is no end. It can be entirely passive, as in the relationship (or lack of it) between the state and the myriad small, localized businesses—restaurants, cafes, dry-cleaners, retailers. Neither wants anything from the other—except for the taxes the state demands and small businesses would rather not pay. Aside from that, there is little communication and no coordination at all.

At the opposite extreme, weighty private businesses in need of help routinely seek to manipulate bureaucrats, politicians, and even public opinion. In the past, they might have pressed their case for tariff protection to avoid market loss and thus unemployment, or asked for more direct help to avoid bankruptcy, as Chrysler did when seeking loan guarantees from the US government. Now, especially if they are in one of the leading industries, aerospace, telecommunications, data processing, biotechnology, amorphous materials, ceramics, etc., private companies can invoke geo-economic arguments to ask for help even when they are not in trouble, but rather to do even better, with state research grants, coinvestments, or credit finance. Or, going the other way, bureaucrats and politicians can try to manipulate (large) private companies to achieve their own geo-economic purposes, or even select a specific company to become the country's "chosen instrument" in a given industry.

Even more common, no doubt, are the cases of reciprocal manipulation, as in the dealings of the largest international oil companies—American, British, French, Italian—with their respective state authorities and government agencies. Senior oil company executives and the government's senior foreign policy officials, oil company representatives overseas and the government's diplomats in place, oil company country experts and the government's intelligence offices, often collaborate so closely that they might as well be interchangeable, and sometimes they are—oil companies are often generous employers for ex-officials.

In the past, unfriendly dealings between governments and *foreign* private enterprise usually featured underdeveloped countries and foreign multinationals. Many were expelled, nationalized, or fined (sometimes only to be readmitted and compensated) in the wake of every imaginable accusation, from the standard claims of tax avoidance and the exploitation of natural resources for little money, to the mistreatment of local employees, the sale of contaminated products, and, of course, interference in domestic politics. Often the accusations were at least partly justified.

But now it is increasingly the governments of the most advanced countries that are coming into conflict with foreign business enterprises. Geo-economically active states striving to develop their country's industry in a given sector obviously oppose foreign private companies that are the chosen instruments of their rivals, and also plain private companies that simply have the misfortune of standing in their way. Thus the US government must confront Airbus Industrie to protect the US airliner industry, while IBM has been under attack from the Japanese government for more than thirty years, simply because Japan's MITI has been trying to conquer the mainframe-computer sector for that long (ironically, it may be on the verge of winning, just as mainframes are displaced by smaller machines).

Certainly an era of intense geo-economic rivalry must become an era of unprecedented risks for private enterprise, at least for businesses in high-technology industrial sectors. As they invest millions of their own funds in the hopes of achieving a major breakthrough in developing some new product, they can find themselves suddenly overtaken by another country's "national technology program," which might come up with the better mousetrap first, by using billions of the taxpayers' money. To be sure, state-sponsored research and development programs can fail, as Japan's Fifth Generation computing project failed—after ten years and some $400 million spent, it did not come up with a single marketable product. Yet even those most confident of the inherent superiority of 100% private brains in the service of 100% private enterprise must now hesitate before investing in a better car battery, for example, for they will find themselves in competition with the US Advanced Battery Consortium, which already has $130 million in public money and might get another $130 million, or $1.3 billion for that matter.

Private companies may also find themselves competing with foreign companies determined to beat them by systematic underpricing, with the resulting losses covered by their sponsoring state authorities. That is already the fate of Boeing and McDonnell-Douglas, but also of many other purely private companies in high-technology sectors, from air-traffic control radars, where purely private companies such as Raytheon must confront several "chosen instruments" (e.g., Germany's Telefunken) that can call on government funds, to all sorts of obscure industrial nooks and crannies. When public funding is concealed, as it often is, a victim-company may even enter a market quite unaware of its fatal disadvantage.

■ A WORLD OF RIVAL TRADING BLOCS?

Most people still seem to take it for granted that the global market can only become more open in the future, with ever-fewer barriers to trade. The possibility that commercial quarrels between Americans and Europeans, the United States and Japan, and the European Community and Japan might instead lead to the emergence of rival trading blocs, each with barriers against the others' exports, still seems outlandish. After all, except for farm products, the European Community is jointly more open to external trade than its individual members ever were; and of course as a practical matter, it is much easier for outsiders to sell in the Community-wide market than it would be if they were still separate national markets. That is just as true of the US–Canadian common market now, and of a possible North American common market that would include Mexico as well. Finally, there is no "yen zone" except in journalistic imaginings. If rival European Community and North American trading blocs do emerge, Japan would be strictly on its own, for neither Korea nor Taiwan, let alone China, would ever accept its economic tutelage, and throughout Southeast Asia, only Malaysia and possibly Thailand might consider any form of exclusive association with Japan. Thus, so far, one cannot even speak of trading blocs, still less of rival trading blocs.

Above all, the semiopen global market of today (except for farm exports) seems so *natural*. Yet it did not come into existence naturally, or even because the theory of free trade persuaded all concerned on its intellectual merits alone. It is very much a man-made object, in fact a US-made object, the result of more than forty years of American diplomacy, American pressure, and the American willingness to open the US market first and the most.

Starting on January 1, 1948, when the original General Agreement on Tariffs and Trade came into effect, all sorts of trade barriers were reduced or eliminated step by step, sometimes item by item, in a long series of negotiations. It was GATT that generalized the "most favored nation" principle, under which any barrier-reducing bargain between any pair of its members automatically applies to all. And the GATT "Kennedy Round" negotiated from 1964 to 1967 was especially important: today's international economy owes much to its unprecedented tariff reductions.

The United States and most other countries had sound economic reasons for wanting the expansion of trade that GATT promised, and has continued to deliver. But it was no coincidence that the original GATT treaty was successfully sponsored by the United States at the very outset of the Cold War (no country under Soviet influence joined), and that the Kennedy Round was concluded as the Cold War was approaching its climax. For the strongest motive for trade liberalization—stronger than the economic advantages against which there were always disadvantages to be reckoned—was always political and strategic. GATT was clearly meant to be the commercial counterpart of the pan-Western alliance against the Soviet Union.

This history would have suggested that if the Soviet threat ever disappeared, GATT and the further progress of trade liberalization would be endangered. And that is exactly what has happened. After the collapse of Soviet power, instead of the almost routine advances of the past, the negotiation of the latest GATT "Uruguay Round" was difficult indeed, with the outcome still an uncertain cliff-hanger at this writing, after eight years of talks.

In the meantime, there has been a proliferation of unilateral trade measures that go against the spirit of GATT and sometimes violate its rules: the nontariff barriers of many countries have been increasing in recent years, instead of being gradually eliminated as in the past. When the US Congress originally inserted the "301" provision in the Trade Act of 1974, its drafters were careful to ensure that both its wording and intent would clearly be consistent with GATT rules.[8] Under "301," the president is given broad authority to act against foreign import barriers. First the US Trade Representative is empowered to investigate suspect foreign trade practices to detect unfairness; if found, they are to be formally defined as such. At that point, the president must alert the foreign country in question that specified retaliatory measures will be enforced by such and such a date, unless the barriers are removed. No public announcements or threats were called for—all could be handled by quiet diplomacy. When, however, the US Congress legislated "Super 301" in 1988, its patience had clearly been exhausted. The US Trade Representative is no longer merely authorized to act, but is formally required to act. That office must publish for the public use an annual list of improper trade barriers, of course identifying the countries responsible for each; it must identify "priority" barriers and priority countries; and it must set firm deadlines for remedies, with retaliation mandatory if the barriers are not removed. ("Special 301" is the equivalent for copyrights and other intellectual property rights.) Thus the president can no longer act discreetly but must instead issue overt threats, which can no longer be quietly withdrawn at his discretion.

That, of course, was the very purpose of "Super 301," the prevailing view in Congress being that the original "301" was not being implemented energetically enough.

The worsening atmosphere should not surprise. More and more, the international economy is being pervaded by the calculations and the fears that come from that fraction of it that is already "geo-economic," rather than simply economic. In the past, the doings of a handful of warlike countries affected many other countries, and indeed militarized world politics as a whole. Today, likewise, the emerging geo-economic struggle for high-technology industrial supremacy among Americans, Europeans, and Japanese is rapidly eroding their old alliance solidarity, and the ill-feelings now released between them are beginning to affect all other trading countries of any importance. They fear, understandably, that they will be caught in the crossfire. As for farm-support programs and the subsidized export of agricultural surpluses—issues having nothing to do with high technology, which are politically intractable—progress seems to have stopped altogether.

The Airbus Industrie/Boeing and McDonnell-Douglas struggle is already acquiring the character of a full-bore commercial war, in which the gains of one side really do require losses on the other. That alone shows the falsity of the oft-cited distinction between war as a "zero-sum" encounter, and commercial relations in which both sides should gain and usually do. Obviously, most commercial dealings are not zero-sum, to use the jargon, but some are. War is indeed different from commerce (in other ways as well)[9] but evidently it is not different enough. In particular, an action-reaction cycle of trade restrictions that evoke retaliation in kind has a most uncomfortable resemblance to the sort of crisis escalation that can lead to outright war of the shooting kind. And if a commercial conflict does break out between any major trading powers, the classic mechanisms of world politics would no doubt be translated into economic terms to extend its reach: one can visualize how the European Community's ambassador to Egypt would patiently explain that Egyptian exports to the community would inevitably suffer, if it were to purchase a Japanese powerstation, as "rumored in the press"; and then his Japanese colleague would arrive to demand the contract, politely threatening retaliation, while the Americans would try to persuade the Egyptians that their only way out is to award the contract to an American company. And if states join to form larger economic blocs, as is now happening in North America with the

US–Canada and prospective US–Canada–Mexico free-trade zone, and as happened long ago with the European Community, the adversarial logic is driven outward but still persists, and on a much larger scale. Alliances are formed against a common enemy, even if only "geo-economic" rather than strategic. If no enemy is already manifest, one will undoubtedly be found.

What should reliably deter a trade war is the cost to all concerned, and eventually to the entire world economy. If it were truly a matter of costs and benefits, then no trade war could possibly start, for it could not be profitable to any side in the long run, or even the short. But when there is no strategic confrontation at the center of world affairs that can absorb the adversarial feelings of the nations, those ill-feelings may be diverted into the nations' economic relations. If that happens, all bets are off. When hostile sentiments are unleashed, there is no more prudent cost-accounting, just the desire to hurt and punish—even if the punisher is thereby also punished.

Many still confidently believe that the economies of the major trading states are simply too "interdependent" to allow geo-economic wars. Now that automobiles are often fabricated in one country with engines from another and dashboard electronics from a third, now that both the chemical and electronics industries rely so heavily on the ceaseless international exchange of countless intermediate goods to make their finished products, and now that both public and private borrowers so often require loans from abroad, it is perfectly true that adversarial economic maneuvers—and the retaliation they would evoke—could easily have disastrous effects on employment and output, as well as on the financial stability of states and firms. Alas, the interdependence that grew so easily in the late Cold War era, when economic cooperation within each camp was the natural adjunct of strategic confrontation between them, guarantees nothing at all.

No two economies were more interdependent at the time than the French and German in August 1914, or the German and Soviet in June 1941. In both instances, each side imported large quantities of essentials from the other, and in both cases there was indeed much economic disruption, yet they went to war uncaring of those and far, far greater losses. If humans acted in accordance with sober calculations of their economic interests, the history of the species would not be such a long record of crimes and follies. Hence it is wildly optimistic to believe that a commercial war between rival trading blocs cannot break out merely because it would impoverish all concerned. War itself did that quite effectively and also killed and destroyed, yet was common enough and still is.

Actually the very emergence of geo-economics shows how weak is the inhibition of economic self-interest. For of course *any* geo-economic activity must be costly as compared to plain, free-trade economics. But that is true only in strictly economic terms, and those terms may simply be irrelevant: the bureaucrats, politicians, and industrialists who favor geo-economic activities do not do so in the hope of profits, and will not stop doing so for fear of suffering losses. Airbus Industrie could continue to lose money for another twenty years without seriously displeasing the governments that support it, for it *has* created an airliner industry—and that was its task all along, not to earn profits. Likewise, it is no use pointing out that all economic activity is inherently transnational, so that it can only be deformed by attempts to force it back into the national boundaries of geo-economics. For that is exactly what is happening, with "local content" regulations, inquisitions to uncover imported components, etc.

Moreover, just because geo-economics must be inefficient from a global viewpoint, it does not mean that it cannot be efficient for any one country or trading bloc. War, too, has always been a losing game: all states would have been better off if none had played it. Yet so long as war and diplomacy dominated world affairs, participation was compulsory to avoid subjection, occupation, defeat, even annihilation. If an industrial country follows strict free-market policies to protect only the interests of its citizens as consumers, while other industrial countries promote the interests of their citizens as producers, the manufacture of all that is deemed important ("high tech," "strategic," etc.) will eventually be carried out by those other countries, except perhaps for some assembly-line work.

The decline of the "free world" strategic solidarity that once suppressed all commercial quarrels is inevitable. But the advent of a geo-economic conflict between rival North American, East Asian, and European trading blocs is *not* inevitable. True, the emotional pressures that could start an action-reaction cycle are already building up. The resentments aroused on each side by severe trade imbalances, by peremptory market-opening demands, and by particularly intrusive foreign investments of the Rockefeller Center type, do not cause only momentary outbursts of criticism. Each episode leaves a durable residue of hostility, sharpening unfriendly feelings against whichever country is at the other side of such transactions. Thus cold-blooded calculations of profit and loss need not suffice to avert the outbreak of unrestrained geo-economic rivalries.

Yet we also know that arms races can be stopped, and that antagonistic emotions can be diverted—against the common human enemy of ecological disruption perhaps. But for that to happen, some sort of super-GATT would now be needed to achieve a consensus on a plan for "general and comprehensive economic disarmament." For the step-by-step approach to trade liberalization followed for decades can no longer keep pace with the proliferation of commercial quarrels over subjects old and new. It has certainly failed to prevent passage in the US Congress of the "Super 301" trade retaliation measures, or the sweeping import bans that Korea and Taiwan have imposed on Japanese consumer goods. In any case, the seemingly more conservative step-by-step approach is actually full of risk, for it could be overtaken at any time by the outbreak of a geo-economic "arms race." As far as the United States is concerned, for example, Fujitsu's very direct attack on IBM has provoked no particular reaction, no doubt because of IBM's diminished status. But one may wonder what reactions a similar Japanese threat to Boeing might evoke.

Certainly a general and comprehensive economic disarmament plan would be a drastic remedy indeed, for it would prohibit *all* subsidies, direct and indirect, *all* forms of state-supported technology development or export promotion, and *all* barriers to imports of goods and of financial, insurance, and professional services. Considering the difficulties recently experienced in the GATT negotiations over a much narrower set of questions, success seems improbable.

Yet the choice that remains for the United States is between the successful negotiation of a sweeping geo-economic disarmament, and the waging of the geo-economic struggle in full force. The looming presence of expansionist international corporations, activist bureaucracies, and economically ambitious governments—none of which is to be found on Main Street, USA, or in economics textbooks—requires that the choice be made and acted upon. Not to choose is to lose.

NOTES

CHAPTER 1

1. 477,381 families; 1989 data. Arthur B. Kennickell (of the Federal Reserve) and R. Louise Woodbum (of the IRS), "Estimation of Household Net Worth Using Model-Based and Design-Based Weights: Evidence from the 1989 Survey of Consumer Finances." Unpublished paper, April 1992, Tables 2, 3.

2. US Bureau of the Census, "Workers with Low Earnings, 1964–1990," Series P-60, Number 178 (Washington, DC, 1992), pp. 3, 4.

3. See Chapter 4.

4. 1,090,900 in 1989. US Bureau of the Census, *Statistical Abstract of the United States: 1991* (Washington, DC, 1991), Table 7, p. 10 (hereinafter *SA*).

5. E.g., Robert B. Reich, *The Work of Nations: Preparing Ourselves for 21st Century Capitalism* (New York: Knopf, 1991).

6. 1988. Keizai Koho Center, *Japan 1992: An International Comparison* (Tokyo: KKC, December 1991), Table 8-7, p. 70.

7. Office of the US Trade Representative, *The 1989 National Trade Estimate Report on Foreign Trade Barriers* (Washington, DC, 1990).

8. "Apple? Japan Can't Say No," *Business Week*, June 29, 1992, p. 32.

9. The classic example of David Ricardo (1772–1823) in paraphrase.

10. The Dutch Fokker company of ancient fame makes only small airliners.

11. Including interest charges. Gelman Research Associates for the US Department of Commerce (1990).

12. Stewart Toy and Michael O'Neal, "Zoom! Airbus Comes on Strong," *Business Week*, April 22, 1991, p. 49.

13. Ibid., p. 50.

14. John Newhouse, *The Sporty Game* (New York: Knopf, 1982), p. 56.

15. J. B. L. Pierce (Treasurer), *Forbes*, September 25, 1978.

16. "Eastern Sticks to Its Gamble," *Business Week*, January 11, 1982, p. 106.

17. Rami G. Khouri, "Jordan Set to Order 12 Airbuses," *Financial Times*, March 6, 1986, p. 46.

18. Howard Banks, "Talking Tough," *Forbes*, July 23, 1990, p. 44.

19. Richard O'Lone, "Profits Elusive for Airframe Firms Despite Record Orders," *Aviation Week and Space Technology*, May 28, 1990, pp. 48–50.

20. "Family Matters," *Flight International*, May 1991.

21. In fact borders have now been extended more than ever before, to include 200-mile "economic zones" into sea-areas, while fiscal borders even go beyond them, as each state seeks to tax multinational corporations and multinational incomes at the expense of all other states.

22. I.e., the logic of conflict in the grammar of commerce; "From Geopolitics to Geo-Economics," *The National Interest*, Summer 1990.

CHAPTER 2

1. In office from November 9, 1964, to July 7, 1972.

2. John K. Emerson, *Arms, Yen, Power: The Japanese Dilemma* (Tokyo: Charles E. Tuttle, 1972), p. 375.

3. Chalmers Johnson, *MITI and the Japanese Miracle: The Growth of Industrial Policy, 1925–1975* (Stanford, Calif.: Stanford University Press, 1982), p. 285.

4. Emerson, *Arms, Yen, Power*, p. 367.

5. Keizai Koho Center, *Japan 1992: An International Comparison*, Table 4-9, p. 37.

6. Under the Voluntary Restraint Agreement (VRA), the Japan Automobile Manufacturers' Association (JAMA) pledged to limit car exports to the United States to 1.68 million units per year from 1981 to 1984; the limit was increased to 1.85 million in 1985, and again to 2.3 million in 1986. Although the VRA was formally declared unnecessary by President Reagan in 1985, the JAMA unilaterally prolonged it through 1991. With the rising output of "transplants," the VRA ceiling became irrelevant after 1987 as outright exports actually declined. MITI's 1992 decision to "advise" JAMA to lower the VRA to 1.65 million thus amounted to only a 5% actual reduction.

7. Edward J. Lincoln, *Japan's Unequal Trade* (Washington, DC: The Brookings Institution, 1990), p. 15.

8. Ibid., p. 9.

9. Government spending minus tax revenues plus investment minus private savings equals the trade deficit (or inflationary excess demand). Robert Z. Lawrence and Robert Litan, *The Protectionist Prescription: Errors in Diagnosis and Cure*, Brookings Papers on Economic Activity 1 (1987), pp. 297–98.

10. Keizai Koho Center, *Japan 1992: An International Comparison*, Table 4-9, p. 37.

11. See, e.g., US Department of the Treasury, US MOSS Negotiating Team, "Report on Telecommunications . . . Discussions" (Washington, DC, August 1986).

12. Paul Blustein, "At Tokyo Fair, U.S. Booth Sparks Rift on Rice," *Washington Post*, March 16, 1991, pp. A1, A14.

13. Karel van Wolferen, *The Enigma of Japanese Power: People and Politics in a Stateless Nation* (New York: Knopf, 1989) has been much criticized but not refuted.

14. Known as the "ruling party" because it has been in power since 1955. The Liberal Democratic Party is not at all liberal in the current US meaning but is certainly democratic, being indeed a loose coalition of competing factions, each with its own chief and its own treasury.

15. The controversy did not hurt Tsutsui's career: he was promoted to director of the Technical Research Development Institute of the Defense Agency in 1990.

16. Or rather the small aviation segments of the very diversified Fuji Heavy Industries, Kawasaki Heavy Industries, and Mitsubishi Heavy Industries.

17. Exclusively for Japan's Self-Defense Forces, because of a self-imposed prohibition on weapon exports.

18. In 1950 there were 1.46 million service personnel on active duty, the lowest number recorded between 1945 and the present day; the defense budget of 14.3 billion was to be multiplied during the next fiscal year, to $45.2 billion.

19. Though initially much allied military production was paid for, or at least subsidized, by US Military Assistance Program grants and loans.

20. In contrast to the immediate post-1945 period, when currency convertibility and the restoration of world trade were most vigorously pursued.

21. From the early 1960s, the US government did begin to ask the richer European allies to contribute more to their own defense; but it was only at congressional insistence that such "burden sharing" requests were pressed, and then not very hard.

22. See the detailed studies reported in Lincoln, *Japan's Unequal Trade*, pp. 39–60.

23. *Joi* "expel foreigners"; Johnson, *MITI and the Japanese Miracle,* p. 80, citing Kakuma Takashi. A senior MITI official would use the term *keto* ("hairy Chinese") to describe Japan's competitors (ibid., p. 81).

24. *Jane's Defence Weekly*, June 3, 1989, p. 1039. The US percentage has exceeded 2% ever since the post–Korean War rearmament.

25. Caspar W. Weinberger, then US secretary of defense, was informed ac-

cordingly when visiting Japan on June 28, 1987. Caspar W. Weinberger, *Fighting for Peace: Seven Critical Years in the Pentagon* (New York: Warner Books, 1990), p. 244.

26. See, e.g., the doyen of Pentagon Japan specialists, James E. Auer, "Japan Spends Well on Defense," *The World and I*, January 1989, pp. 116–20.

27. Keizai Koho Center, *Japan 1990, An International Comparison* (October 31, 1989), Table 4-9, p. 38.

28. Weinberger, *Fighting for Peace*, p. 241.

29. The notion of a monolithic "Japan Inc." is undoubtedly one of the great malevolent myths of our times. Not only do Japanese companies compete fiercely among themselves, but bitter rivalries also divide Japanese officialdom, even on foreign soil. Early-morning shuttle flights from New York to Washington are often filled with commuting MITI officials: the *Gaimusho* continues to prohibit the opening of a MITI Washington office for fear that it would compete with its own diplomats.

30. *The New Republic*, January 22, 1990.

31. Short for *Tokyo-no-dai-gakku*, i.e., "Tokyo of, great school [= university]."

32. Its JETRO (Japan Export Trade Organization) offices allow MITI to compete with Japanese diplomats all over the world; the yet more powerful Ministry of Finance has its own attachés in major countries, so that Japan is blessed with three different and largely noncommunicating reporting chains from overseas.

33. Yasuhiro Nakasone's exceptionally long government was formed on November 27, 1982, and lasted until November 1987.

34. Weinberger, *Fighting for Peace*, pp. 243–44.

35. Clyde H. Farnsworth, "Japan Promises to Ease Trade Tensions," *New York Times*, March 4, 1990, p. 22.

36. Prime minister from November 6, 1987, to June 3, 1989.

37. His successor, Sousuke Uno, also engulfed in the scandal, only lasted as prime minister for two months, being followed on August 9, 1989, by Toshiki Kaifu.

38. Stuart Auerbach, "US-Japan Collaboration on Jet Draws Fire. The Issue: What Role Should Economics Have in Defense Policy?" *Washington Post*, March 15, 1989, p. D1.

39. Carol A. Shifrin, *Aviation Week and Space Technology*, May 8, 1989, p. 16.

40. Andrew Rosenthal, "Action on New Jet to Await a Review," *New York Times*, February 16, 1990, p. A10.

41. Stuart Auerbach and David Hoffman, " 'Ball Is Entirely in Japan's Court' on FSX Jet Deal, U.S. Says," *Washington Post*, March 30, 1989, p. A24.

42. A. E. Cullison, "Japan Defense Minister Slams US on FSX Deal," *Journal of Commerce*, April 3, 1989.

43. See, e.g., John H. Makin, "For Both Sides, FSX Deal Shouldn't Fly," *Los Angeles Times*, March 30, 1989, section 2, p. 7.

44. *The Economist*, February 25, 1989.

45. Kakuei Tanaka, the former businessman and former prime minister (July 7, 1972–December 9, 1974) by then in terminal disgrace, ostensibly because of the Lockheed scandal and its judicial aftermath, actually because the very power of his exceptionally well financed faction was intolerable to the establishment, to which he had never truly belonged.

46. His five predecessors had the standard LDP two-year tenure.

47. John D. Morrocco, "Revised FS-X Pact Eases Trade, Technology Concerns," *Aviation Week and Space Technology*, May 8, 1989.

48. *Congressional Record*, Senate, May 16, 1990, S 5340.

49. Ibid., S 4341.

50. Ibid., S 5342.

51. In spite of endless attempts to avoid them, "cost-plus" contracts remain the norm, and the "plus" is the preordained profit.

52. Of late it is rather civilian transports that have been militarized (e.g., the KC-10), but the world-conquering Boeing 707 was derived from its military predecessor, the KC-135 tanker, while virtually all helicopters now on sale began life as military aircraft.

53. See Tables 8-6, 8-7, and 8-8, pp. 70–71, in Keizai Koho Center, *Japan 1991: An International Comparison* (Tokyo: 1991).

54. In 1990, the assets of the Mitsubishi Bank were $392.2 billion, and those of Mitsubishi Trust and Banking were $226.3 billion. In the same year, the two largest US banks, Citicorp and BankAmerica, had $217 billion and $110.7 billion in assets, respectively. Ibid., Table 3-17, p. 29.

55. *Jane's Defence Weekly*, June 3, 1989, p. 1039.

56. Jacob M. Schlesinger, "US-Japan FSX Venture Bogging Down as Firms Bicker over Technology Rights," *Wall Street Journal*, October 5, 1989; Jacob M. Schlesinger, "General Dynamics, Mitsubishi in Flap over Technology," *Wall Street Journal*, November 2, 1989, section B, p. 9.

57. Jacob M. Schlesinger, "FSX Development to Begin Soon as Contractors Finish Basic Pacts," *Wall Street Journal*, February 21, 1990, section A, p. 70.

58. E.g., *Asahi*'s Kiyofuku Chuma and Profs. Kenichi Ito of Ayoama-Gakuin and Seizaburo Sato of Todai.

59. *New York Times*, January 21, 1992, pp. D1, D5.

60. *New York Times*, "Japan to Open Its Market to Foreign Paper Products," April 6, 1992.

61. OECD, *Statistics of Foreign Trade 1990*, SITC categories 5, 6, 7, 8, 9 (Paris: OECD, 1991).

62. All data (exports FOB, imports CIF) from GATT *International Trade 1989–1990* (Geneva: GATT, November 1990), Vol II, Appendix Table A6.

63. Ryuzaburo Kaku (Chairman of Canon Inc.), "Perestroika in Japan," *Washington Quarterly*, Vol. 15, No. 3, Summer 1992, pp. 5–14.

CHAPTER 3

1. Readers might conduct their own experiment, by asking themselves and others whether they would prefer GNP growth rates of, say, 4% for the United States and 10% for Japan, or 2% for both. Professor Bernard Reich of Harvard's Kennedy School of Government, who has been asking such questions of different groups, reports that only economists prefer higher US growth rates regardless of the Japanese rate of growth.

2. The standard work is Chalmers Johnson's brilliant study, *MITI and the Japanese Miracle: The Growth of Industrial Policy, 1925–1975* (Stanford, Calif.: Stanford University Press, 1982).

3. *Washington Post*, May 17, 1991, p. 22.

4. In 1871. Walter Goerlitz, *History of the German General Staff* (New York: Praeger, 1953), p. 96.

5. Conceived by the Swede Rudolf Kjellen, popularized by the British geographer Halford Mackinder, and further developed by the German (non-Nazi) Karl Haushofer, who coined the term *Lebensraum* (living space of nations) adopted by Hitler.

6. That task had been assumed by King Leopold's scandalous "Congo Free State" until the Belgian government's takeover in 1908.

7. From Venezuela in 1859 and 1905, from Colombia in 1907, from Ecuador in 1904, and from Bolivia in 1867 and 1903; Brazil also acquired territory from Paraguay in 1872, Argentina in 1895, and Uruguay in 1851.

8. Among the anti-imperialist exceptions, Gladstone is perhaps the most famous, he that seemed the impractical idealist while he lived, and who may now be recognized as the most skillful accountant of the true costs and ephemeral benefits of empire.

9. See, e.g., Katsuhiro Utada, "Globalism and Symbiosis," in *Japan Update*, December 1991, Number 3. Utada is widely regarded as an (eminent) inter-

nationalist in Japan, yet he lucubrates at length on the "uniqueness of the Japanese way of thinking."

10. MITI's worldwide intelligence is supplied by JETRO, the Japan Export Trade Organization, which has offices in all major economic centers.

11. Johnson, *MITI and the Japanese Miracle*, p. 236, the basis of this account.

12. *SA*, Table 885, p. 538.

13. T. R. Reid, "Premier Vows to Make Japan 'Lifestyle Superpower,' " *Washington Post*, November 9, 1991, p. 3.

CHAPTER 4

1. Paul Kennedy, in *The Rise and Fall of the Great Powers* (New York: Random House, 1987).

2. The World Bank, *World Tables 1991* (Baltimore: Johns Hopkins Press, 1991), Table 1, pp. 4–5 (hereinafter *WT*). Year-end population estimate. The official April 1 estimate was 203,302,031. *SA*, Table 1, p. 7.

3. See Chapter 5.

4. *SA*, Table 1450, p. 843. The GDP (all factor costs plus indirect taxes minus subsidies) excludes the net factor income from abroad, which is included in the GNP.

5. *WT*, Table 1, p. 5.

6. *SA*, Table 1450, p. 843.

7. US Department of Labor, Bureau of Labor Statistics, Office of Productivity and Technology, July 1991, "Comparative Real Gross Domestic Product, Real GDP per Capita, and Real GDP per Employed Person, Fourteen Countries 1950–1990," p. 6.

8. DRI/McGraw-Hill estimates, cited in Hobart Rowen, "Japan Takes the Lead," *Washington Post*, May 14, 1992.

9. *SA*, Table 16, p. 15.

10. Between 1980 and 1990, the highest fifth in household income increased its *after-tax* share from 40.6% to 43.2% of total income; "Household Income Statistics Before and After Taxes: 1980 to 1990." Special data sheet compiled by the IRS for the author, 1992.

11. OECD and German Institute for Economics data cited in *New York Times*, May 26, 1992, p. D3. See Chapter 4.

12. Baldly assessed as the lower half of the 12.8% of all persons living below the poverty line; 1989 data. *SA*, Table 745, p. 462.

13. Actually 27.7 million in 1989. *SA*, Table 745, p. 462. "Below 125 percent of poverty level" minus underclass.

14. Data from Kennickell and Woodbum, "Estimation of Household Net Worth," Tables 2, 3; passive earnings estimated at 8% per year on $3.1 billion.

CHAPTER 5

1. Keizai Koho Center, *Japan 1991: An International Comparison* (hereinafter KK), Table 5–1, p. 46, and Table 4–9, p. 37.

2. *WT*, p. 17.

3. Verbal communication to the author.

4. Bryan Burrough and John Helyar, *Barbarians at the Gate: The Fall of RJR Nabisco* (New York: Harper Perennial, 1992), p. 508.

5. In which, in effect, a corporation is bought with its own wealth: the shares are bought up with money from short-term bridging loans and high-interest bonds, which usually must then be quickly repaid and redeemed (to reduce the crushing burden of debt) by selling off the company's own disposable assets and divisions, as well as ruthless cost-cutting and, frequently, mass firings. LBOs are virtually unknown in Japan and rarely practiced in Europe.

6. Burrough and Helyar, *Barbarians at the Gate*, p. 99ff.

7. *Business Tokyo*, June 1992, p. 20

8. Cited in *Business Week*, May 25, 1992.

9. *Business Tokyo*, September 1991, p. 18.

10. Ibid.

11. Milt Freudenheim, "Sandoz Busy 60% Stake in SyStemix," *New York Times*, December 17, 1991, p. D1.

12. Stan Hinden, "Orioles Owner Gets a Hit," *Washington Post*, December 17, 1991, p. C1.

13. *Business Tokyo*, June 1992, pp. 20–21, 26–33.

14. 1991. *Aviation Week and Space Technology*, March 30, 1992.

15. The "Japan Aircraft Development Corporation," which already coproduced the Boeing 767.

16. One legacy of former Defense Secretary Caspar W. Weinberger is the Pentagon's relentlessly adversarial contracting procedures, enforced by the several more battalions of auditors and bookkeepers that he raised, who now resist the more cooperative policies introduced by his successors.

17. Each company manufactured combat aircraft that became famous after

Pearl Harbor. The inappropriate "Heavy" in their names is a lingering 1930s euphemism for military. But nowadays the logic of conflict is expressed in the grammar of commerce.

18. In addition to the aeronautical engineering departments of universities and research centers that receive government grants, NASA itself conducts much aeronautical research alongside its better-known space activities.

19. "A Milestone in High-Definition TV," *New York Times*, December 3, 1991, pp. D1, D6.

20. Personal communication to the author, September 12, 1992.

21. 1989 provisional figures. *SA*, Table 1390, p. 794.

22. Or $373,436 million to be exact in 1989. *SA*, Table 1395, p. 797.

23. There is nothing outdated about fears of North Korean nuclear ambitions— but why should the US government not be concerned about US economic interests as well?

24. Forced into suboptimal investments at home or in more open economies.

25. The theme of Kenichi Ohmae, *Triad Power: The Coming Shape of Global Competition* (New York: Free Press, 1985).

26. 1990 market shares throughout. *KK* (1991), Table 3-7, p. 24.

27. E.g., Tateho's 1987 purchase of ACM, maker of silicon carbide whisker wire, for $35 million; Mitsui Mining's 1989 purchase of Magnox, a maker of magnetic recording material, for $35 million; Takemoto's 1988 purchase of Goulston, maker of fiber lubricants, for $37 million; Mitsubishi Rayon's 1990 purchase of Newport, maker of carbon-fiber materials, for $37.8 million; NGK's 1986 purchase of Cabot, a beryllium manufacturer, for $45 million.

28. Inland Steel's Tek and Kote are 40% and 50% owned by Nippon Steel; National Steel is 70% owned by NKK; Armco Steel is 50% owned by Kawasaki Steel; LTV's EG and II EG are 40% and 50% owned by Sumitomo Steel; and even US Steel's USS-K and Pro-TEC are 50% owned by Kobe Steel. There seems to be a cruel irony in these nomenclatures: Inland, National, US.

29. *Business Week*, April 13, 1992, p. 61. The *SA* estimates 582,000 in 1988, with a projected 712,000 to 860,000 by the year 2000. Table 653, p. 398.

30. At least partly disentangled by the studies presented in Christopher Jencks, ed., *Rethinking Social Policy: Race, Poverty and the Underclass* (Cambridge, Mass.: Harvard University Press, 1991).

31. 1988 figures. *SA*, Table 1440, p. 838.

CHAPTER 6

1. The 1989 total of blacks under the poverty line was 9.3 million; the underclass (households without regular and lawful breadwinners) is much smaller. *SA*, Table 745, p. 462.

2. US Bureau of the Census, "Workers with Low Earnings, 1964–1990," Series P-60, Number 178 (Washington, DC, 1992), pp. 3, 4.

3. Ibid., p. 7.

4. 1989. *SA*, Table 745 p. 462; defined by incomes below $12,675 per year for a family of four; and Table 746; "near-poor" defined by incomes below 125% of the poverty line; total under-eighteen population: 64,082,000; Table 12, p. 12.

5. SA, Table 18, p. 16.

6. SA, Table 128, p. 86.

7. SA, Table 745, p. 462.

8. 956,264; long-form data extract. *Washington Post*, May 29, 1992, p. A18.

9. 1990 figures, rounded. US Department of Justice, Federal Bureau of Investigation, *Uniform Crime Reports, 1990* (Washington, DC, 1991), p. 8ff.

10. On December 31, 1989. *SA*, Table 338, p. 195; jails: Table 333; juveniles: Table 332, p. 192.

11. 8,965,099, including 1,165,284 for drunk driving. US Department of Justice, Federal Bureau of Investigation, *Uniform Crime Reports, 1990* (Washington, DC, 1991), p. 178.

12. Cited in *The New Republic*, May 25, 1992, p. 7.

13. Actually 1,005,300. *SA*, Table 92, p.67.

14. Child recipients of Aid to Families with Dependent Children monies, actually 7,571,000 in 1989. *SA*, Table 612, p. 372.

15. From 186,000 in 1988 to 276,000 (high estimate) in the year 2000. *SA*, Table 653, p. 398.

16. Kennickell and Woodbum, "Estimation of Household Net Worth," Tables 2, 3.

17. Cited in the *Washington Post*, February 20, 1992, p. A3.

18. The mean for the 11.8% of all households receiving nonfarm self-employment income was $20,218 in 1990, as opposed to $37,271 for the 77.4% of all households receiving wage and salary income. Long-form data extract. *Washington Post*, May 29, 1992, p. A18.

19. Though he may contribute $80 million to the global settlement of Drexel litigation, still leaving him with some $500 million. *Business Week*, June 8, 1992, p. 93.

20. Ibid., p. 86.

21. Burrough and Helyar, *Barbarians at the Gate*, p. 97.

22. *Business Week*, May 4, 1992, p. 156.

23. Ibid., p. 143.

24. *Business Week*, June 8, 1992.

25. *Business Week*, May 4, 1992, p. 146.

26. Ibid., p. 143.

27. *New York Times*, December 7, 1991, p. 39.

28. *Business Week*, May 4, 1992, p. 147.

29. Standard & Poor's Compustat Service and Bureau of Labor Statistics data cited in *Washington Post*, April 25, 1992, pp. C1, C6.

30. Lawrence G. Franko, "Global Corporate Competition II," *Business Horizons*, November–December 1991, pp. 16–17.

31. By Towers Perrin Inc., cited in *Washington Post*, October 20, 1991, p. H1.

32. Data come from *Wall Street Journal*, November 11, 1992, pp. B1, B3.

33. *Executive Compensation Reports* newsletter, cited in *Wall Street Journal*, November 11, 1991, p. B1.

34. Data compilation. *Business Week*, June 8, 1992, p. 86.

35. By the estimate in Kennickell and Woodbum, "Estimation of Household Net Worth," Tables 2, 3, the richest 1% of all American families owned $1.25 trillion of rental real estate, $1.12 trillion of stocks and bonds, $221.9 billion in trusts, and $524.6 billion in bank and other accounts, for a total of some $3.1 trillion; at a very modest 8% return per year, their "rentier" income would have been $248 billion, 49% of the total income of the richest 1%.

CHAPTER 7

1. US Department of Labor, Bureau of Labor Statistics, *Employment, Hours and Earnings, United States, 1909–90*, Bulletin 2370 (Washington, DC, March 1991), Vol. I., p. 63 (hereinafter *Employment*).

2. 82,900 out of 1,090,900 in 1989. *SA*, Table 7, p. 10.

3. Long-form data extract. *Washington Post*, May 29, 1992, p. A18.

4. But *Employment*, Vol. I, p. 61, listed 18,827,000 at the last count in November 1990.

5. *New York Times*, November 19, 1992, p. 10.

6. *Business Week*, May 4, 1992, p. 153.

7. World Data, pp. 2, 4; GNP per capita × 2.

8. *New York Times*, November 19, 1992, p. 10.

9. *Business Week*, April 27, 1992, p. 35.

10. *New York Times*, April 19, 1992, p. 18.

11. Ibid., p. 1.

12. KK (1991), Table 8-7, p. 69.

13. Ibid., p. 70.

14. Ibid.

15. Ibid., Table 8-6, p. 69.

16. Office of the US Trade Representative, *The 1989 National Trade Estimate Report on Foreign Trade Barriers* (Washington, DC, 1990).

17. *Employment*, Vol. I, pp. 3–4.

18. Total nonfarm employees in November 1990: 111,099,000; total *private* nonfarm employees: 92,385,000. *Employment*, Vol. I, pp. 1, 2.

19. Ibid., p. 1.

20. Gina Kolata, "More Children Are Employed, Often Perilously," *New York Times*, June 21, 1992, pp. 1, 22.

21. Bureau of Labor Consumer Price Index for All Urban Consumers (CPI-U) 1947–1990: 1947 $0.22.3 = 1990 $1.30.7; therefore 1.50 over 22 × 130.

22. *Washington Post*, May 18, 1992, pp. A1, A16.

23. *Business Week*, March 16, 1992, p. 101.

24. Instituto Nacional de Estadística, *Agenda Statistica 1990* (Aguascalientes, Mexico, 1991), p. 52.

25. *Employment*, Vol. I, p. 61.

26. 1989 data. *SA*, Table 313, p. 185.

27. *Employment*, Vol. I, p. 6.

28. *Business Week*, May 25, 1992, p. 42.

29. *Employment*, Vol. I, pp. 60–61.

30. Ibid., p. 62.

31. Ibid., pp. 61–62.

32. Manufacturing; production-worker hourly earnings in 1982 dollars. Ibid., p. 63.

33. OECD and German Institute for Economics data cited in *New York Times*, May 26, 1992, p. D3.

34. KK (1991), Table 8-1, p. 66.

35. OECD and German Institute for Economics data cited in *New York Times*, May 26, 1992, p. D3.

36. Ibid.

37. 86,362,000 in November 1990. *Employment*, Vol. II, p. 688.

38. Ibid., pp. 816–17.

39. Ibid., Vol. I, p. 63.

40. Ibid., Vol. II, pp. 765, 766.

41. Ibid., p. 692.

42. Ibid., p. 856.

43. Ibid., p. 870.

44. Ibid., pp. 849, 850.

45. Ibid., hotels: pp. 838, 839; detectives: pp. 850–51.

46. Ibid., p. 857.

47. *SA*, Table 7, p. 10.

48. *SA*, Table 8, p. 10.

49. Lawrence E. Harrison, "America and Its Immigrants," *The National Interest*, No. 28, Summer 1992, p. 37.

50. CPI-U, and CPI-U-XI. *SA*, Table 745, p. 462, and Table 756, p. 467.

51. As reported by 10,110 police agencies, whose jurisdiction included 192,939,000 people. US Department of Justice, Federal Bureau of Investigation, *Uniform Crime Reports 1990* (Washington, DC, 1991), p. 192.

52. Peter Reuter et al., *Money from Crime: A Study of the Economics of Drug-Dealing in Washington, DC*, RAND Report R-3894-RF (Santa Monica, Calif.: Rand, 1990), p. 92.

53. Ibid., p. 85.

CHAPTER 8

1. $12,330 versus $14,220 in 1988. *WT*, pp. 5, 97.

2. $12,850 versus $13,350, not counting Italy's notoriously large underground economy. WI, pp. 333, 601.

3. In 1988, at $10,180 versus $20,960 and $14,220. WI, pp. 425, 5.

4. *SA*, Table 129, p. 87; Table 133, p. 88.

5. *SA*, Table 320, p. 188.

6. *SA*, Table 653, p. 398. And Tables 284, 285, pp. 167, 168.

7. *SA*, Table 2, p. 7 (total population); Table 319, p. 188 (lawyers); and *Business Week*, April 13, 1992, p. 61 (estimated current ratios).

8. In 1985. *SA*, Table 319, p. 188.

9. Richard Rosenow, "So You Want to Get Your Roof Fixed . . ." *Wall Street Journal*, February 4, 1992, section B, p. 14.

10. *SA*, Table 324, p. 190.

11. Ibid.

12. *Business Week*, April 13, 1992, p. 61.

13. Ibid., p. 62.

14. Gary T. Schwartz, "Product Liability and Medical Malpractice in Comparative Context," in *The Liability Maze: The Impact of Liability Law on Safety and Innovation*, Peter W. Huber, and Robert E. Litan, eds., (Washington, DC: The Brookings Institution, 1991), pp. 67–68.

15. Ibid., p. 648.

16. Jaramillo v. Riddell Inc., Cal. Sup. Ct. San Bernadino County, Docket No. OCV31309, data supplied by Victor E. Schwartz, author of *Schwartz on Torts*.

17. Kemp v. Beneke, Docket No. A267563, Dept. No. XV, Docket U (Clark County, Nevada District Court, 1990).

18. Smith v. Johnson & Johnson Baby Products, 59 Wash. App. 287, 797, P.2d 527. 1990.

19. Shears v. Caterpillar, Texas District Court, Cameron County, 138 Judicial District, No. 90-02-840yB, 1991.

20. Survey data in WMMA letter of May 7, 1992.

21. Timothy K. Smith, "Upward Mobility," *Wall Street Journal*, December 11, 1991, p. 1ff. Jean Reid Norman, "Small-Plane Industry Looks for a Lift," *USA Today*, January 20, 1992, p. 6B. Plus personal communication, Mr. Edward Stimpson of the General Aviation Manufacturers Association, June 5, 1992.

22. Robert Martin, "General Aviation Manufacturing: An Industry Under Siege," in *The Liability Maze*, Huber and Litan, eds., p. 484.

23. Ibid., pp. 485–86.

24. Ibid., p. 480.

25. John H. Cushman, "Makers of Small Planes Wait for Brighter Skies," *New York Times*, January 18, 1992, pp. 37, 41.

26. Arley Sanchez, "Jury Awards Injured Pilot $2.5 Million," *Albuquerque Journal*, May 10, 1986.

27. Martin, "General Aviation Manufacturing," pp. 491–92.

28. *The Liability Maze* contains several attempts to define the impact on various industries.

CHAPTER 9

1. Actually as a percentage of GNP/GDP. Department of Commerce data collated and construed by David D. Hale, "Why the 1990's Could Be the Second Great Age of Global Capitalism Since the 19th Century," October 1991, Kemper Financial Services. Unpublished.

2. *WT*, Table 3, p. 12.

3. The sum of employee compensation, proprietors' business income, rental income, corporate profits, and interest earnings less interest payments.

4. *WT*, Table 2, p. 6.

5. Hale, "Why the 1990's."

6. *WT*, Table 3, pp. 12–13; and Table 2, pp. 8–9.

7. Gross domestic savings as a percentage of gross domestic product. *WT*, Table 14, pp. 54–57.

8. Mortgage debt: *SA*, Table 822, p. 507; GNP: *SA*, Table 701, p. 433.

9. Consumer credit: *SA*, Table 830, p. 510; home-equity loans: *SA*, Table 829, p. 509; credit cards: *SA*, Table 832, p. 510.

10. Households, personal trusts, and nonprofit organizations: *SA*, Table 798, p. 407.

11. GNP: *SA*, Table 701, p. 433; debt: Table 800, p. 498.

12. Anthony L. Velocci, "McDonnell Turns to Taiwan to Boost Douglas' Future," *Aviation Week and Space Technology*, November 25, 1992, pp. 30–33. And Paul Proctor, "Taiwan Backs Maximum 40% Investment in McDonnell-Douglas Transport Div," Ibid., May 4, 1992, p. 25.

13. FDIC estimate. *Washington Post*, December 8, 1991, p. 1.

14. *Washington Post*, December 13, 1991, pp. D1, D3.

15. Including $52 billion in foreign debt in 1970, and $259 billion in 1989. *SA*, Table 800, p. 498.

16. *New York Times*, January 28, 1992, p. D1 (table).

17. *SA*, Table 1388, p. 793.

18. James B. Treece, "New Taurus, New Sable, Old Blueprint," *Business Week*, September 9, 1991, p. 43.

19. "What Could Be Worse than the Car Business? Don't Ask," *Business Week*, October 21, 1991, p. 132.

20. William J. Broad, "Ridden with Debt, US Companies Cut Funds for Research," *New York Times*, June 30, 1992.

21. National Science Foundation, *SRS Data Brief* 1992, No. 3, April 24, 1992, NSF 93-308.

22. Statement of Dr. Kenneth Courtis of Deutsche Bank (Tokyo office) before the Joint Economic Committee of the US Congress, May 8, 1992, p. 22.

23. J. S. Gansler, *Affording Defense* (Cambridge, Mass: MIT Press, 1989), p. 90ff. and letter communication, October 25, 1991.

24. National Science Foundation, *SRS Data Brief* 1992, No. 2, March 20, 1992, NSF 92-306.

25. Data come from National Science Foundation, *Research & Development in Industry: 1989*, NSF-92-307, pp. 75–78.

26. *SA*, Table 468, p. 281.

27. US Department of Transportation, Federal Highway Administration, FHWA-PL-90-024, p. 7.

28. Paul Chaote and Susan Walters, *America in Ruins* (Durham, N.C.: Duke University Press, 1983).

29. The House Wednesday Group, US Congress, *Highway Policy at the Crossroads*, April 20, 1990.

30. GNP: *SA*, Table 699, p. 432; private investment: *SA*, Table 898, p. 544.

31. US Department of Commerce, Industry Branch, Bureau of the Census. Data supplied by request in digital form.

32. *New York Times*, April 24, 1992, p. D1 (table).

33. 1989 figures. *WT*, Table 4, p. 16.

34. Data come from testimony of Kenneth Courtis before the Joint Economic Committee of the US Congress, May 8, 1992 (charts).

CHAPTER 10

1. Including supervisory union components. There are in addition 1,321 regional education service agencies, 183 state-operated agencies, and 102 federally operated agencies. US Department of Education. National Center for Education Statistics, *Digest of Education Statistics 1990*, p. 97.

2. Ibid., children: p. 11; schools: p. 96.

3. Ibid., Table 153, p. 154. 1986–1987 figures.

4. Ibid., 1991 edition; Table 157, p. 160; 1989–1990 numbers, but the proportions are unlikely to have changed.

5. As an indirect way of reaching the same goal, many urban districts impose a residency requirement, shutting out suburban job applicants.

6. Jonathan Rabinovitz, "In Suburbs, a Stealthy War Against Infiltrating Students," *New York Times*, November 6, 1992, p. 1.

7. Ibid.

8. *Digest of Education Statistics*, p. 377; expenditures: p. 379.

9. Ibid., Fall 1988, Table 77, p. 90. 2,316,428 teachers, 4,366,978 total.

10. Ibid., Table 153, p. 154. 1986–1987 figures.

11. Ibid., 1986–1987 figures. Table 137, p. 135.

12. San Diego Unified School District. Employee Identification Card. Current, 1992.

13. Kenneth J. Cooper, "Broadening Horizons: Afro-centrism Takes Root in Atlanta Schools," *Washington Post*, November 27, 1992, pp. 1, A33.

14. Even between 1982 and 1987, the proportion of "vocational" units earned by all high-school graduates (public and private) declined from 18.7% to 15.8% of all units, and that includes "nonoccupational" vocational education, vocational general introduction (i.e., chitchat) as well as agriculture, business, marketing, health, occupational home economics, trade and industry, *and* technical courses. *Digest of Education Statistics*, Table 126, p. 128.

15. Totals and US shares exclude IBM self-production; VLSI research data (estimated for 1992) cited by T. R. Reid, "US Again Leads in Computer Chips," *Washington Post*, November 20, 1992, p. A42.

16. "Flat Panels: Can the US Get Back into the Picture?" *Business Week*, November 30, 1992, p. 36.

CHAPTER 11

1. Boyce Rensberger, "New Battery Required for Autos of the Future," *Washington Post*, May 25, 1992, p. A3.

2. Kenneth Flamm, *Targeting the Computer: Government Support and International Competition* (Washington, DC: The Brookings Institution, 1987).

3. Ibid., p. 144.

4. Ibid., pp. 131–34.

344 ■ THE ENDANGERED AMERICAN DREAM

5. *WT*, Table 2, p. 9.

6. By the summer of 1990, both the Central Intelligence Agency and the National Security Agency were conducting in-house studies of their potential role as suppliers of commercial intelligence. Nothing is more natural than the attempt of bureaucrats to find new justifications to keep their bureaucracies well funded, but of course official intelligence on business decisions, price negotiations, etc. is only of value if there is an official user that can benefit from it, an activist MITI-type body.

7. The Foreign Ministry does enjoy a status higher than MITI's and second only to that of the Ministry of Finance, but Japan's diplomacy has generally followed the leadership of the United States, while its national policy has relentlessly concentrated on economic (i.e., MITI's or *Okurasho's*) goals.

8. Section 301 of the Trade Act of 1974 (codified as amended in 19 U.S.C. SS 2411-2416) was compatible with GATT's Articles XXII and XXIII.

9. The logic of conflict is, loosely speaking, "zero-sum" because the gain of one side is *in itself* a loss for the other, and vice versa. That is so in war, in warlike diplomacy, and in oligopolistic competition, but not in many-sided ("perfect") competition, wherein any two sides can both gain (or lose) concurrently. The logic of conflict is also paradoxical (i.e., governed by apparent contradictions and the coincidence of opposites) because all actions unfold in the presence of an adversary (or several) that try to defeat whatever is being done. That is why the worst of approach roads for an attack may be the best, if it confers the advantage of surprise (making the bad road paradoxically good and the good road paradoxically bad). Or, dynamically—in the coincidence of opposites—why victorious armies that advance too far, advance to their own defeat by overextension, just as weapons that are too effective are the most likely to be made ineffectual by the enemy countermeasures that their very effectiveness evokes. In all dynamic manifestations of the logic of conflict there is such a culminating point, beyond which action evolves into its opposite. And the same logic operates at every level of strategy: e.g., the Soviet Union's accumulation of military strength eventually resulted in its military impotence, once enough states were frightened into forming a blocking coalition against Moscow. In the linear logic of everyday life (and economic competition), by contrast, good is good and bad is bad, and success can facilitate further success without any necessary culminating point. For a systematic comparison, see my *Strategy: The Logic of War and Peace* (Cambridge, Mass.: Harvard University Press, 1987).

INDEX

Petrochemical Industry Nurturing Policy declaration, 108
Pharmaceutical industry, 136, 260
Philip Morris (co.), 173, 179
Philippines, 38, 163, 170, 278
 See also Filipino
Philips Grundig (European co.), 148
Phoenician Resort, 245–46
Pickens, T. Boone, 165
Pierson, Jean, 32–33
Pilgrims, 250
Pioneer Electronic, 129, 135
Piper (aircraft co.), 234
 Cub, 233
 Supercubs, 235–36
Plant and equipment, capital investment in, 266
Plaskett, Thomas, 173–74
Platt's Oilgram, 201
"Plaza" agreement, 121
Plywood industry, 38
Poles, 181, 279
Polynesia, 278
Population, 216
"Pork-barreling," 300
Ports, 262–63
Portugal, 119, 241, 266, 278
 wine industry in, 23, 24
Postponement motions, in lawsuits, 225–26
Poverty, 198
 and blacks, 155–57
 and children, 155, 159–61
 in inner cities, 18–19, 153–54
 and Third-Worldization, 124–26, 161
 and working poor, 153–54
 See also Underclass
Pravda, 132
Preussag (German co.), 173
Prisons, 159, 160
Private domestic investment, vs. gross national product, 264
Private education, 277, 285
Private enterprise, and geo-economics, 316–19
Private-industry R&D, 259–61
Production vs. consumption, 33
Productivity, 186, 198
 See also Labor productivity

Product liability cases, 225, 227, 228–37
Professional and scientific instruments sector, 260
Proletarization, of Americans, 147
Prometrix Corp., 139
Promus Inc., 174
Protectionism, in Japan, 25, 26–27, 49–50, 91–92, 148, 312
Prussia, 298
 education in, 98, 100
 General Staff, 100–101, 105, 106, 107, 111
 gymnasium in, 100
 as model, 98, 100
 See also East Prussia
Public assistance, 193
Public debt, and gross national product, 296
 See also Federal debt
Public education, 151, 160–61, 271–91
 academic vs. vocational, 290–91
 and "multicultural" education, 277–87
 remedies for, 287–91
 and school districts, 271–75
 See also Teachers
Public ownership. See State ownership
Public service, lawyers in, 217–21
Public utilities, 265
Public works, 261–63
Puerto Rico, 277
Purchasing power, 122–23

Quark (co.), 22

Racial Classification Boards, in South Africa, 282–83
Racism
 and "Afro-centric" education, 285–87
 of San Diego Unified School District, 277–84
Raytheon (co.), 319
RCA, 308–9
RCA/Columbia Home Video, 129
R&D. See Research and development
Reagan, Ronald, 76, 80, 81, 83, 293
 years of, 205, 253

Tanaka faction (Japan), 82
Tariffs, 36, 41, 50, 91, 312
See also GATT; Trade barriers
Tats, 279
Tatsuo, Arima, 127
Taxation, 109, 242–43, 291–97
Tazawa, Kichiro, 80
TDK (co.), 140
Teachers, 160, 272–76, 288–89
and "multicultural" education,
283–87
Technology, 310, 319
forecasting, 301
sharing of, US with Japan, 75–76
transfer from US to Japan, 85–88
Teenagers, 157–58, 192
Telecommunications equipment indus-
try, 94
Telecommunications industry, 38
Telefunken (German co.), 319
Telephone companies, 98
See also Cellular telephones
Television. See High-Definition TV
Tenneco's J. I. Case division, 173
Tera Microsystems, 139, 140
Territorialism, 101–6
Texas Instruments, 304
Textile industry, 260
in Britain, 23–24
in Japan, 46, 47–48
Thailand, 38, 57, 99, 112, 125, 139,
147, 278, 320
See also Northern Thailand
Thatcher, Margaret, 189
Therma-Wave Inc., 140
Third World, 17, 127, 180, 186,
312
bureaucracies in, 311
decay in, 16
income distribution in, 164
immigrants from, 193, 208
poverty in, 18–19
standards in, 171–72
wealth in, 126, 161–62, 177
Third-Worldization, of US, 16–19,
117, 118, 120, 124–26, 147,
151, 153–57, 161–64, 245, 267,
295, 296
Thurmond, Strom, 47
Time Warner (co.), 129, 135

Tobacco industry. See Food and to-
bacco industry
Tokyo, 15
"Tokyo Round," 51
Tomen (Japanese co.), 51
Tonga, 278
Tora, Mr. (fictional character), 85
Tort reform, 227, 233, 234
Toshiba, 22, 37, 65, 72, 76, 83, 129,
132, 139–40, 143, 148, 301, 304
Tower, John G., 77
Toyota, 45, 98, 261, 266, 312
Camry, 254
Lexus, 252, 253
Trade Act of 1974
"301" provision, 321, 322
"Special 301," 321
"Super 301," 321, 322, 325
Trade barriers, erected by Japanese,
21, 36–38, 50–52, 72, 188
Trade deficit, 67
with European Community, 54
and Japan, 49, 53, 90, 92–93, 131,
267
Trade Representative. See US Trade
Representative
Trading blocs, rival, 319–25
"Transplants," 310
German in US, 146, 198
Japanese in US, 20, 146, 260
US, 144, 261
Transport equipment industry, 93, 94
Truk, 278
Tsusho Sangyo-Sho, 100, 302
Turkey, 173, 279, 315
See also Ottoman Turkey
Tuscany (Italy), 113

UK. See United Kingdom
UN. See United Nations
Underclass, 207
Appalachian, 209–10, 283
and blacks, 125, 153, 159, 208–11
Underinvestment, 295
Undersaving, 295
Unemployment, 92–93, 157, 182–84
in Britain, 189
Unions, 183, 185, 203
Unisys (co.), 149
United Airlines, 32

United Auto Workers, 183
United Kingdom (UK), 303
   manufactured goods in imports for,
      92
   savings (government) vs. gross do-
      mestic product in, 240
   savings (private) vs. gross domestic
      product in, 239
   savings rate (net) in, 240
   wage costs (overall) in, 188
   See also Britain; England
United Nations (UN), 18
   "peacekeeping" missions, 70
   Security Council, 46, 89
United States
   advancement in, 18
   aerospace industry in, 311
   agriculture in, 311, 322
   aircraft/airliner/aviation industry in,
      27–34, 79, 141–42, 233–36,
      244–45, 308, 319, 324
   airports in, 16, 262–63
   anti-Japanese sentiments in, 40–41,
      45–46, 60, 95, 97, 132
   arms-control talks with Soviet
      Union, 49
   automobile/car industry in, 150,
      194–95, 198, 200–201, 251–54,
      260–61, 265, 307–8, 323
   bankruptcies in, 245, 247–48, 318
   biotechnology industry in, 136–38,
      301
   births from unmarried mothers in,
      151, 159
   central problem of economy in, 295
   CEOs in, vs. Europe and Japan,
      169–70
   chemical industry in, 32, 260, 323
   Chief Enemy of, 40–41, 45–46, 47,
      60, 95, 97, 132
   children in, 155, 159–61, 192–93,
      214–15, 274, 276–77, 285–86
   competitive position of, 249
   computer industry in, 22, 138–40,
      260, 308–9, 319
   conflict with Japan intensifies,
      59–64
   from creditor to debtor, 248
   crime in, 158–60, 193
   drug dealing in, 210–11, 270

   economic decline of, 117–18, 124,
      126–27
   economy, size of, 249
   exports of, 21, 49, 51, 54, 67, 72,
      92, 93–94, 188, 311
   foreign investments in, 249
   free enterprise of, 99
   free-trade ideology of, 23–26, 49–
      50, 52, 311, 320
   and FSX project, 64–88, 94–95,
      141
   Great Depression in, 201
   gross national product vs. Japan,
      114
   growth rate of, 123
   highways and bridges in, 262
   as idea-based society, 45
   immigration to, 20, 181–82, 193,
      196–97, 208, 213, 267, 270
   imports of, 37, 47–48, 50, 54, 92,
      93–94
   infrastructure in, 261–63
   investment abroad of, 145–50
   and investment barriers erected by
      Japanese, 147–50
   investment in Japan, 145–46
   investment per person in, 265–66
   Japanese ownership of companies
      in, 129–32, 135–37, 139–50
   labor productivity in, 21, 85,
      187–89
   land in, 109
   lawyers in, 151, 166, 215–37
   lobbyists in, 178, 180, 215, 222,
      311
   manufacturing industries in, 21, 92,
      201–4, 206, 264–65
   merchandise trade with Japan, 54,
      93
   middle class in, 153, 161–65, 207
   and MOU, with Japan, 76–78, 80,
      82–84, 86, 88
   open market in, 22
   Ph.D. in, 100
   public education in, 151, 160–61,
      271–91
   public works in, 261–63
   rearmament of, 66
   and "respect deficit" with Japan,
      88–89

ABOUT THE AUTHOR

Director of Geo-economics at the Center for Strategic and International Studies of Washington, D.C., and an International Associate of the Institute of Fiscal and Monetary Policy of Japan's Ministry of Finance, Edward N. Luttwak has long been an advisor to United States and European industrial corporations. He has served as consultant to the National Security Council, the White House Chief of Staff, the State Department, and the Department of Defense. Repeatedly called to testify before the United States Congress, he first presented his Geo-economics ideas in the pre-Gulf War *Hearings* of the U.S. Senate which were televised world-wide. His books have also appeared in Arabic, Chinese, Danish, Dutch, Finnish, French, German, Greek, Hebrew, Italian, Japanese, Korean, Norwegian, Spanish, and Swedish editions.

DATE DUE